MUSEUMS AND SOURCE COMMUNITIES

The growth of collaboration between museums and source communities – the people from whom collections originate – is one of the most important developments in modern museum practice.

This volume combines some of the most influential published research in this emerging field with newly commissioned essays on the issues, challenges and lessons involved.

Focusing on museums in North America, the Pacific and the United Kingdom, the book highlights three areas which demonstrate the new developments most clearly:

- **The museum as field site or 'contact zone'** – a place that source community members enter for purposes of consultation and collaboration.
- **Visual repatriation** – the use of photography to return images of ancestors, historical knowledge and material heritage to source communities.
- **Exhibitions** – case studies reveal the implications of cross-cultural and collaborative research for museums, and how such projects have challenged established attitudes and practices.

As the first overview of this significant area, this collection will be essential reading for museum staff working with source communities, for community members involved with museum programmes, and for students and academics in museum studies and social anthropology.

Laura Peers is Curator for the Americas Collections, Pitt Rivers Museum, Lecturer in the School of Anthropology, and Fellow, Linacre College, at the University of Oxford. She has published on First Nations cultural histories.

Alison K. Brown is Research Manager (Human History) for Glasgow Museums and was formerly a researcher at the Pitt Rivers Museum and Junior Research Fellow at Wolfson College, University of Oxford. She has worked with First Nations communities in western Canada, and has published on collecting histories and contemporary museum practice.

i 25/03/04

MUSEUMS AND SOURCE COMMUNITIES

A Routledge Reader

Edited by
Laura Peers and Alison K. Brown

Routledge
Taylor & Francis Group

LONDON AND NEW YORK

First published 2003
by Routledge
11 New Fetter Lane, London EC4P 4EE

Simultaneously published in the USA and Canada
by Routledge
29 West 35th Street, New York, NY 10001

Routledge is an imprint of the Taylor & Francis Group

Typeset in Sabon and Frutiger by
Keystroke, Jacaranda Lodge, Wolverhampton
Printed and bound in Great Britain by
MPG Books Ltd, Bodmin

British Library Cataloguing in Publication Data
A catalogue record for this book is available from the British Library

Library of Congress Cataloging in Publication Data
Museums and source communities : a Routledge reader /
edited by Laura Peers and Alison K. Brown
p. cm.
Includes bibliographical references and index.
1. Ethnographical museums and collections—Social aspects.
2. Museums – Acquisitions – Social aspects. I. Peers, Laura L. (Laura Lynn), 1963–
II. Brown, Alison K. (Alison Kay), 1971–

GN35.M88 2003
305.8'0074—dc21
2002037123

ISBN 0–415–28051–6 (hbk)
ISBN 0–415–28052–4 (pbk)

CONTENTS

CONTENTS

FIGURES

CONTRIBUTORS

Rascha Moatty Nasr Aeish is a part-time researcher for the Community Archaeology Project at Quseir and administrator for the Quseir Heritage Preservation Society.

Michael M. Ames is Emeritus Professor of Anthropology, University of British Columbia, Vancouver, Canada, was Director of the University of British Columbia Museum of Anthropology from 1974 to 1997, and Acting Director 2002–3. He received his PhD from Harvard University and has conducted research in South Asia, Canada and Australia. In 1998 he received the Order of Canada.

Joshua A. Bell is a doctoral candidate in material anthropology and museum ethnography at Oxford University and has recently completed 19 months of fieldwork in the Purari Delta of Papua New Guinea. His interests include the anthropology of visual-material culture, museums and colonial cultures of collecting, the interface of history and anthropology, and the politics of representation in contemporary indigenous art.

Judith Binney is Professor of History at the University of Auckland, New Zealand. Her books include *Mihaia* (with Gillian Chaplin and Craig Wallace); *Ngā Mōrehu* (with Gillian Chaplin); and *Redemption Songs: A Life of the Maori Leader Te Kooti Arikirangi Te Turuki*. She has been chairperson of the Australian Sesquicentennial Awards in Oral History since 1990. In 1997 she was awarded CNZM for services to historical research in New Zealand, and in 1998 was made Fellow of the Royal Society of New Zealand.

Lissant Bolton is Curator of the Pacific and Australian collections at the British Museum. She has worked collaboratively with the Vanuatu Cultural Centre since 1989, as an advisor to the Women's Culture Project. Her research focuses on both indigenous and introduced textiles, and on women's knowledge and practice. Her book, *Unfolding the Moon: Enacting Women's Kastom in Vanuatu*, was published in 2003.

Alison K. Brown is Research Manager (Human History) at Glasgow Museums and was formerly a researcher at the Pitt Rivers Museum and Junior Research Fellow at Wolfson College, University of Oxford. She has been involved in museum-based projects with several First Nations in western Canada and, with Laura Peers, is currently working on a photographic history project with the Kainai Nation of southern Alberta.

Gillian Chaplin has spent most of her working life in and around museums engaged principally in the public programmes arena. She has brought to this work a passion for the photographic image and a consciousness derived from being born into apartheid South

Africa and growing up in New Zealand. She lives in Australia and is currently working as a consultant to museums of many types in the United States and Japan.

Gerald T. Conaty is Senior Curator of Ethnology at the Glenbow Museum, Calgary, Canada, Adjunct Professor at the Saskatchewan Indian Federated College and Assistant Adjunct Professor, Department of Archaeology, University of Calgary. Exhibits he has worked on include *Nitsitapiisinni: Our Way of Life, The Fur Trade in Western Canada, Warriors: A Global Journey through Five Centuries*, and *Powerful Images: Portrayals of Native Americans*. He has written over 30 articles and books.

Andrew Conner is a graduate from the University of Southampton and specialises in children's education.

Elizabeth Edwards is Head of Photographs Collections at the Pitt Rivers Museum, Lecturer in Visual Anthropology, ISCA, Oxford University, specialising in critical history and theory of still photography, and Visiting Research Fellow at the London Institute. Her current research addresses the dissemination and collecting of 'ethnographic' photographs in nineteenth-century science. She is co-editing *Photographs Objects Histories* which considers photographs as material culture and has recently published *Raw Histories: Photographs, Anthropology and Museums*.

Lamya Nasr el Nemr is a full-time researcher for the Community Archaeology Project at Quseir and member of the Quseir Heritage Preservation Society.

Ann Fienup-Riordan is a cultural anthropologist and has published many books on Yup'ik history and oral tradition, including *Eskimo Essays: Yup'ik Lives and How We See Them, The Living Tradition of Yup'ik Masks, Boundaries and Passages*, and *Hunting Tradition in a Changing World*. She has lived in Alaska for 25 years, and received both the 2002 Governor's Award for Distinguished Humanist Educator and the 2001 Alaska Federation of Natives' President's Award for her work with Alaska Natives.

Darren Glazier is a doctoral student in the Department of Archaeology at the University of Southampton where he is writing his dissertation on the socio-politics of archaeology in Quseir, Egypt.

Anita Herle is Curator of Anthropology at the University of Cambridge Museum of Archaeology and Anthropology. A focus of her teaching and research is the relationship between museums, collectors, and members of source communities. Since 1995 she has been involved in several collaborative exhibition projects with Torres Strait Islanders in Cambridge and Australia.

Deanna Paniataaq Kingston is half-King Island Inupiaq Eskimo and an Assistant Professor of Anthropology at Oregon State University, United States of America. She conducts research with the King Island Native Community and teaches about Native North Americans, natural resources, and oral traditions. Her primary interests are in folklore, songs, dances, oral traditions, ethnohistory, and visual anthropology.

Stephanie Moser is a Senior Lecturer in the Department of Archaeology at the University of Southampton where she specialises in archaeological representation and museum interpretation. She is currently completing a book on the history and role of museum display in the construction of knowledge.

Mohammed Saleh Mousa is a part-time researcher for the Community Archaeology Project at Quseir.

Trudy Nicks is Senior Curator of Anthropology at the Royal Ontario Museum, Toronto and an Associate Professor (part-time) of Anthropology at McMaster University. She was co-chair of the Task Force on Museums and First Peoples (1992) and has worked on a number of collaborative museum exhibition projects, including *Mohawk Ideals, Victorian Values: Oronhyatakha M.D.* and *Across Borders: Beadwork in Iroquoian Life*. She is currently developing exhibitions for the ROM expansion project, due to open in 2005.

Eithne Nightingale is Head of Access, Social Inclusion and Community Development at the Victoria & Albert Museum where she manages the South Asian and Chinese programmes, and has developed work with adult learners, black British African Caribbean communities, refugees, older learners and travellers. She is also a photographer, has carried out research on education in Bangladesh and has advised on the development of community education in Kwa Zulu-Natal, South Africa.

Laura Peers is Curator for the Americas Collection, Pitt Rivers Museum, Lecturer in the School of Anthropology, and Fellow of Linacre College at the University of Oxford. She is a historian and anthropologist, and has worked with First Nations peoples on their cultural histories.

James E. Phillips is a doctoral student in the Department of Archaeology at the University of Southampton. His dissertation considers the role of nineteenth-century periodicals in archaeology.

Ruth B. Phillips holds a Canada Research Chair in Modern Culture at Carleton University in Ottawa and was Director of the University of British Columbia Museum of Anthropology from 1997–2003. She is an art historian specialising in Native North American art and critical museology. Her most recent books include *Trading Identities: The Souvenir in Native North American Art from the Northeast, 1700–1900* and *Native North American Art* with Janet Catherine Berlo.

Susan Richardson is a doctoral candidate in the Department of Archaeology at the University of Southampton. Her dissertation addresses the representation of skeletal remains in British museums.

Nancy B. Rosoff is the Andrew W. Mellon Curator and Chair of the Arts of the Americas at the Brooklyn Museum of Art, New York City. She was curator at the National Museum of the American Indian, Smithsonian Institution for twelve years where she worked extensively with Native people from North, Central and South America on a number of collaborative projects such as collections documentation, exhibitions and public programmes.

Michael Seymour is a doctoral student in the Department of Archaeology at University College London and is writing his dissertation on the socio-politics of archaeology of the Near East.

Anthony Shelton is Professor and Co-ordinator of the Research Group in Material, Visual and Performative Cultures at the University of Coimbra, Portugal. He was formerly Head of Collections at the Horniman Museum, London. His most recent publications are the edited volumes, *Collectors: Expressions of Self and Other* (2001), and *Collectors: Individuals and Institutions* (2001).

John E. Stanton is Director of the Berndt Museum of Anthropology, University of Western Australia. He has worked in the Kimberley, Western Desert and South-West regions of Western Australia, promoting contemporary Aboriginal arts through travelling exhibitions and publications, including *Painting the Country* (1989) and *Aboriginal Artists of the South-West* (2000). He is currently involved in a photographic repatriation project with Western Australian and Top End communities.

Deborah Swallow is Keeper of the Asian Department and Director of Collections at the Victoria & Albert Museum where she has led the development of programmes and displays aiming to draw the South Asian community into the Museum: the Nehru Gallery of Indian Art and the exhibitions, *The Peaceful Liberators: Jain Art from India*; *Colours of the Indus: Costume and Textiles of Pakistan*; and the *Arts of the Sikh Kingdoms*.

Paul Tapsell is a Maori descendant of the Arawa and Tainui tribes of Aotearoa New Zealand. Former Curator of Rotorua Museum, Oxford doctoral scholar and post-doctoral fellow at Australian National University, he is now Director Maori of Auckland War Memorial Museum and Senior Lecturer, Museums and Cultural Heritage Programme at University of Auckland.

ACKNOWLEDGEMENTS

We would like to thank the volume contributors, both those who wrote new essays and those who permitted us to reprint their work. Many people helped to make the illustrations possible, and we thank them for their cheerful support. The staff at Routledge have been supportive of this project from its inception, and we thank them for turning our ideas into reality. Our colleagues at the Pitt Rivers Museum and the Institute of Social and Cultural Anthropology, Oxford have been helpful in practical as well as intellectual ways, and we especially thank Norman Weller for his assistance, and Haas Ezzet and Denis Lawlor who tackled a number of electronic gremlins. Finally, this volume as well as we ourselves have benefited from a group of people who have helped to shape our thinking, and in addition to those who are represented in this volume we would especially like to thank Mary Bani, Beth Carter, Drew Davey, Tom Hill, Irene Kerr, Katherine Pettipas, Lorne Carrier, and Margaret Hanna.

We gratefully acknowledge permission to reprint the following articles:

Ames, Michael M. (1999) 'How to decorate a house: the re-negotiation of cultural representations at the University of British Columbia Museum of Anthropology', *Museum Anthropology* 22 (3): 41–51.

Binney, Judith and Gillian Chaplin (1991) 'Taking the photographs home: the recovery of a Maori history', *Visual Anthropology* 4: 341–442.

Bolton, Lissant (2001) 'The object in view: Aborigines, Melanesians, and museums', in Alan Rumsey and James Weiner (eds), *Emplaced Myth: Space, Narrative, and Knowledge in Aboriginal Australia and Papua New Guinea*. Honolulu: University of Hawai'i Press.

Fienup-Riordan, Ann (1998) 'Yup'ik elders in museums: fieldwork turned on its head' *Arctic Anthropology* 35 (2): 49–58.

Rosoff, Nancy B. (1998) 'Integrating Native views into museum procedures: hope and practice at the National Museum of the American Indian', *Museum Anthropology* 22 (1): 33–42.

Shelton, Anthony A. (2000) 'Curating *African Worlds*', *Journal of Museum Ethnography* 12: 5–20.

Permissions to publish or reprint illustrations were kindly granted by: the Alexander Turnbull Library, National Library of New Zealand, Te Puna Mātauranga o Aotearoa; the Auckland War Memorial Museum; Joshua Bell; Peter Bolz; Gillian Chapman; Jane Northcroft Grant; Anita Herle; Stephanie Moser; the National Museum of the American Indian; *The New Yorker*; John B. Turner; the Western Australian Museum; the Victoria & Albert Museum.

INTRODUCTION

Laura Peers and Alison K. Brown

This book brings together work on one of the most important developments in the history of museums, a dramatic change in the nature of relationships between museums and their source communities, the communities from which museum collections originate. During the great age of museum collecting which began in the mid-nineteenth century, this was a one-way relationship: objects and information about them went from peoples all over the world into museums, which then consolidated knowledge as the basis of curatorial and institutional authority. Often this relationship was predicated on another set of relationships, between museums as institutions within imperial powers and source communities in colonised regions. Within this context, ethnographic collections, in particular, were built up on the premise that the peoples whose material heritage was being collected were dying out, and that the remnants of their cultures should be preserved for the benefit of future generations (Cole 1985; Griffiths 1996; Schildkrout and Keim 1998; Krech and Hail 1999; O'Hanlon and Welsch 2000). That those future generations might be the descendants of those with whom early collectors interacted was undoubtedly inconceivable at the time collections were assembled: museum collections were thought to be 'for' dominant-society audiences, whether of specialist researchers or the general public.

In recent years, however, the nature of these relationships has shifted to become a much more two-way process, with information about historic artefacts now being returned to source communities, and with community members working with museums to record their perspectives on the continuing meanings of those artefacts. Museums have begun to see source communities as an important audience for exhibitions, and to consider how museum representations are perceived by and affect source community members. In some parts of the world this shift has occurred in the context of changing relations of power, so that source community members have come to be defined as authorities on their own cultures and material heritage. These changes have been given impetus by new forms of research and relationships which involve the sharing of knowledge and power to meet the needs of both parties. This new approach to research, which also informs curation and display, involves museums and community members working towards building a relationship of trust, often in cases where none has existed before and where there may be a significant legacy of distrust as a result of the dynamics of earlier anthropological and museum research projects. The desire and processes used to build such trust and to share power are the most important manifestations of a new curatorial praxis which incorporates source community needs and perspectives. Using case studies as well as essays exploring the issues and lessons of this type of research, this book provides the first overview of work in this emerging field.

The term 'source communities' (sometimes referred to as 'originating communities') refers both to these groups in the past when artefacts were collected, as well as to their descendants today. These terms have most often been used to refer to indigenous peoples in the Americas and the Pacific, but apply to every cultural group from whom museums have collected: local people, diaspora and immigrant communities, religious groups, settlers, and indigenous peoples, whether those are First Nations, Aboriginal, Maori, or Scottish. Most importantly, the concept recognises that artefacts play an important role in the identities of source community members, that source communities have legitimate moral and cultural stakes or forms of ownership in museum collections, and that they may have special claims, needs, or rights of access to material heritage held by museums. In this new relationship, museums become stewards of artefacts on behalf of source communities. They are no longer the sole voices of authority in displaying and interpreting those objects, but acknowledge a moral and ethical (and sometimes political) obligation to involve source communities in decisions affecting their material heritage.

In the initial stages of realising that their relationships with and representations of source communities were no longer adequate, museums began to consult with members of those communities, and are still doing so. However, consultation is often structured to provide outside support for the maintenance of institutional practices, and source community members are wary of contributing to museum-led consultation exercises which do not lead to change within museums or benefits to their people. Indeed, as Michael Ames has observed, while 'partnering' and 'collaboration' are terms commonly used in museums, they describe arrangements that most frequently reflect the perspective of the museum (Ames this vol.; see also Ames 1991). Similarly, James Clifford has remarked that unless museums do more than consult, they will continue to be 'perceived as merely paternalistic by people whose contact history with [them] has been one of exclusion and condescension' (Clifford 1997b: 208). While consultation with source communities is fundamental to the new ways of working that we describe, it is of a kind that goes beyond simply asking for knowledge and advice, but not otherwise altering the traditional relations of power between museums and source communities. It asks for partnership rather than superficial involvement.

At the core of these new perspectives is a commitment to an evolving relationship between a museum and a source community in which both parties are held to be equal and which involves the sharing of skills, knowledge and power to produce something of value to both parties. This is very different from the traditional curatorial approach in which museum staff, on the basis of professional knowledge and authority, control exhibition content, storage facilities, and other museological functions. It involves learning from source community representatives what they consider appropriate to communicate or to display, or about traditional care practices, and implementing those desires and suggestions. Aspects of what in the social sciences has come to be known as co-management or collaborative or community-based research are part of this new way of working between museums and source communities (Notzke 1996; Ryan and Robinson 1990; Warry 1990), which includes the concept of heritage 'stakeholders', so that projects are sometimes determined by community members themselves and facilitated by a team of museum staff and community people in a negotiated process.

This process, and the intent and ownership of its products, may be formally codified, and the partnership element acknowledged at the outset of a project by the negotiation of a Memorandum of Understanding, or other document, by the appropriate representatives of the source community and the museum (see Ames this vol.). However, relationships between museums and communities vary widely by degree of involvement and commitment, by goals and focus, and by longevity: we explore these differences through a range of case studies.

These shifts represent a radical re-envisioning of the nature of museums, and while obviously challenging, have been of tremendous benefit to all parties. Bringing source community members into museums turns these ordinarily dominant-society institutions into arenas for cross-cultural debate and learning, and can lead to extraordinary exchanges of knowledge as well as opportunities for people from all walks of life to begin to understand the views of someone from another cultural group.

DEVELOPMENT AND DIVERSITY

The development and form of these new relationships have depended in part on the nature of the source community, on the political relationship between the source community and museums (and the need to resolve conflict between them), and on the geographical proximity of museums to these communities. The greatest changes have emerged in relationships between museums and local source communities, whether these are indigenous populations (in, for example, North America and the Pacific), or local, settler, or immigrant groups (such as the social history initiatives in the United Kingdom and elsewhere). There have, however, also been significant attempts to forge new bridges between museums and overseas source communities. The essays in this volume span most of this range of relationships, leaving out only social history projects which have emerged as a genre in their own right. We have chosen to focus on relations between museums and indigenous groups, and with diaspora communities, to highlight the particular dynamics these relations involve.

Projects between Maori and New Zealand museums, Aborigines and Torres Strait Islanders and Australian museums, and First Nations/Native Americans and museums in Canada and the United States have set the standard for new relationships and forms of research. These have been born out of indigenous critiques of museum curation and representation, and from a growing sense of frustration by scholars and museum professionals with many of the same issues. They are given impetus by the growing expertise of indigenous peoples at pursuing their agendas, both locally and on the world stage, and by changing political relations between their communities and settler societies. Lobbying for and implementing changes in museum practice have (even where staff are co-operative) involved much conflict and tension within museums because of the challenges these changes create for curatorial authority, as well as for the essential functions of museums. Nor have such changes been evenly adopted across North America and the Pacific: they have emerged out of endeavours between particular museum personnel and particular source communities on a project-by-project basis.

Collaborative projects between museums and geographically distant source communities have been much more sporadic. The extensive face-to-face interaction between community members and museum staff necessary for relationship-building and central to these new processes is even more expensive and logistically difficult when the museum is in England and the source community is in the Torres Strait. Combined with a sense of political distance from source communities that such situations lead to, these factors have made museums in the United Kingdom and Europe slower to adopt the new attitudes and processes associated with community-based research that museums in the Pacific and North America have begun to assume are necessary, even though costs in these countries are also often restrictive (for example, if the museum is in New York City and the community is in Alaska). In the United Kingdom, while there has been a long tradition of social history curators developing consultation procedures with diaspora communities (e.g. Poovaya Smith 1991; Giles 2001), curatorial authority and institutional procedures have not shifted much at all as far as overseas communities are concerned: for example, source community members are not necessarily consulted when research or exhibition proposals are submitted, exhibit labels are written, or catalogues published, whereas these have become fairly common procedures in Canada and Australia. In these places, too, as Ames remarks in his contribution to this volume, funding for research and exhibition development may now be dependent on approval from the source community, which is not the case in the United Kingdom or Europe (and see, on such differences in praxis, Peers 2000, 2001; King 2001). Nevertheless, individual curators and institutions have initiated change, usually on a project level. Anita Herle's article in this volume describes the development of an exhibition commemorating the 1898 Cambridge University Expedition to Torres Straits, which deliberately incorporated a high level of Islander input. The essays by Anthony Shelton and Eithne Nightingale and Deborah Swallow provide overviews of other projects in British museums which have used overseas curators and diaspora community members in Britain as links to source communities. These three pieces give a sense of the distinct stance of British museums on collaborative research, and a range of strategies being used to deal with the difficulties imposed by the daunting spaces, both geographical and intellectual, between museums and source communities.

Diversity in museums and source communities has been an important factor in the process of developing new relationships between them. The changing nature of what constitutes a heritage institution means that these relationships do not always involve traditional museums with ethnographic collections (which themselves range from university museums to national museums), but may also involve local museums with social history collections, tribal keeping houses, cultural centres, or eco-museums founded and maintained by the local community. Lissant Bolton's essay in this volume examines this diversity by exploring the development of heritage facilities in the Pacific. Furthermore, just as the nature of museums is diverse, so is that of the communities involved in these new relationships. Communities are not homogeneous, and source community members inevitably represent a range of perspectives. Museums entering into research projects need to deal with this diversity and ensure that different community voices are represented on project teams.

ARTEFACTS AS 'CONTACT ZONES'

One of the most frequently referenced articles documenting some of these changing relationships has been James Clifford's 'Museums as contact zones' (1997b) which begins by describing a consultation session, and the tensions that emerged in a museum space as it became evident that the museum's agenda for consulting with a Native American group – to gain knowledge about its collections – was being ignored as the source community members used the opportunity to pursue their own agendas. While we have chosen not to reprint this article (it is reprinted elsewhere), it is a useful starting point from which to consider the meanings of material heritage to source communities today, as well as the relationships that can be created around artefacts. The term 'contact zone', borrowed by Clifford from Mary Louise Pratt (Pratt 1992), refers to a 'space in which peoples geographically and historically separated come into contact with each other and establish ongoing relations' (Clifford 1997b: 192). Pratt located this in the context of unequal colonial relations, which would equate to the traditional relationship between museums and source communities, but it could equally be taken to mean relations within source communities, where the histories and politics of the past several centuries have often led to gaps in knowledge across generations. Artefacts function as 'contact zones' – as sources of knowledge and as catalysts for new relationships – both within and between these communities.

Artefacts in museums embody both the local knowledge and histories that produced them, and the global histories of Western expansion which have resulted in their collection, transfer to museums, and function as sources of new academic and popular knowledge. As 'sites of intersecting histories' (Edwards 2001: 2), artefacts have overlapping, but different, sets of meanings to museums and source communities – and tend to be interpreted very differently by each group. Particularly for indigenous peoples, for whom the effects of colonisation have produced rapid and wrenching change, museum artefacts represent material heritage and incorporate the lives and knowledge of ancestors. They are also crucial bridges to the future. For peoples whose way of life has changed dramatically but whose identity rests on historical cultural knowledge, artefacts offer the possibility of recovering a broad range of cultural knowledge for use in the present and future. Some of that knowledge may have been deliberately suppressed by policies of assimilation, or lost as a result of dislocation from familiar landscapes. Still, knowledge surrounding historic artefacts tends to live on in source communities even without their presence, sometimes for many decades, and can be reinvigorated and used for new purposes when those artefacts are encountered again. Aldona Jonaitis describes such a scenario in the volume that accompanied the American Museum of Natural History exhibition *Chiefly Feasts: The Enduring Kwakiutl Potlatch* (Jonaitis 1991), recalling the responses of Kwakiutl people to the Museum collections: the evocation of song, of story, of dance, of laughter (Jonaitis 1991: 68). Jonaitis's work foreshadowed that of Clifford (1997) and Ann Fienup-Riordan, whose moving account of the visit by Yup'ik elders to a collection of Yup'ik material culture at a German museum describes both their determination to take home the knowledge embedded in the objects, but also the way that the objects, even in that very foreign context, triggered songs, stories, memories, biographies, histories, laughter, and traditional social behaviour. As Fienup-Riordan notes, what the group sought was 'the return of the knowledge and stories, the history and pride'; they saw the artefacts as 'opportunities to affect the future' (Fienup-Riordan 2002 and this vol.).

For source community members, gaining access to their material heritage is vital. Work with museums has enabled communities dealing with the legacy of colonisation to engage with objects and images in ways that bolster cultural identity and foster healing. Artefacts prompt the re-learning of forgotten knowledge and skills, provide opportunities to piece together fragmented historical narratives, and are material evidence of cultural identity and historical struggles. They also prompt the transmission of cultural knowledge across generations: the songs and stories evoked by the artefacts documented by Jonaitis, Clifford, and Fienup-Riordan might not have been told within their local communities if not prompted by the sight of the artefacts to which they were tied. Within museums, source community research with collections and consultation for exhibition developments provides opportunities to articulate perspectives and narratives denied by the dominant society. In other instances, through loans or repatriation, objects and archival collections leave museum buildings and are reincorporated into source community life so that the knowledge they embody can be transferred across the generations (Tapsell 1997 and this vol.). Repatriation may, in fact, be thought of as one end of the spectrum of actions which result from the changing relations between museums and source communities.

Photographs, whether of people or of artefacts, have the same capacity as artefacts to evoke knowledge, spark lively debates on the identity and stories of the people or makers involved, and the cultural knowledge and intention encoded in them, and function as links between past and present. Accordingly we have included a section in this anthology on projects that link communities with archival photographs and film footage of their ancestors or of artefacts in museums. Though such projects, known as photo-elicitation or visual repatriation, raise their own sets of problems which overlap with other kinds of collaborative methodologies, they are proving to be a meaningful way for museums to give back to source communities and to build relationships of trust (see A.K. Brown 2001; Brown and Peers, in prep.; Kingston this vol.; Peers and Brown 2002; Stanton this vol.).

The stories that emerge when copies of film or photographs are shared with the communities in which they were taken are often local histories that have been denied by official narratives constructed by Europeans (Bell this vol.; Binney and Chaplin this vol.; Edwards 1994). The sight of these images can trigger the telling of counter-narratives, often for the first time in generations, and are used as visual proof of a community's account of past events. (This can, of course, be a very difficult and emotional process for source community members who find themselves facing distressing histories.) This work also leads to conversations within communities about issues such as cultural identity, the uses of historic knowledge in the present, the shifting meanings of artefacts, and the nature of change and cultural continuity. In some indigenous communities, working with historic artefacts and photographs becomes part of a strategy to preserve the emotional, psychological, cultural, and physical health of members through the dissemination of knowledge about identity and history. Educational materials designed by community members which utilise museum and archival resources, for instance, have become a means through which people can learn about the diversity of materials available to them and about how the histories related to these resources are relevant today. Such projects include curriculum materials produced by the Kainai Board of Education to address social issues such as drug and alcohol abuse based on interviews with elders and historic photographs (Fox 2001) and a CD-ROM, *Our Grandmothers' Voices: East Cree material culture in museums* (Oberholtzer 2001), which presents images of historic northern Cree beaded artefacts, and associated information, for use by beadworkers in northern Cree communities. Some museums are also developing educational programmes aimed at indigenous school children which provide them with an opportunity to explore their own culture and history, and to learn about museums more broadly (e.g. Alger and Welsh 2000; Christal *et al.* 2001; Kahnapace and Carter 1998). In turn, such work has brought new sources of knowledge into the museum, has re-attached information to artefacts, and has re-vivified museum collections: objects gain fresh meanings and acquire new interest for the public when viewed through the eyes of source community members (Clifford 1997: 188–91; Dunstan 1999; Philp 1998a).

Recognition of the very personal connections that can be made between families, communities, images, and artefacts has also made museum professionals aware of the ways in which museums are expressions of Western culture, and has helped them to re-think the intentions and procedures of their institutions to become more responsible to source communities. Poignant (1996: 12), working with photographs, found herself cutting up copies of prints in order not to show images of recently deceased people to their close kin; archivists and curators are working with source communities to find mutually acceptable solutions to curating sacred and sensitive information and artefacts. Following consultation, access to these materials may be limited: sensitive information is generally not placed on publicly available catalogues, and researchers may require permission from elders or community councils to study or publish certain collections (Edwards this vol.; Macaulay 1999; Rosoff this vol.). Some of the most successful solutions have emerged from projects involving the hiring of source community members to assist in-house and to act as liaisons between their communities and heritage institutions (Rosoff, Stanton this vol.). Such projects have been very little published about, however, and the museum profession requires opportunities for training in such new attitudes. Museums have their own traditions of knowledge about the items in their collections, their own professional culture, their own ways of caring for and classifying artefacts, and their own goals of education and entertainment that they wish to realise from their collections in their work with the public. By and large, these differ dramatically from the perspectives and goals of source communities. Involving and sharing power with source community members means that staff must unlearn much of what they know, or think they know, about collections and museums, and begin to see these from very different perspectives. Fienup-Riordan's account (this volume) of Yup'ik elders reordering and correcting attributions of a Yup'ik collection in Germany according to their own detailed knowledge, only to have the museum staff place things back in their long-established but incorrect order and categories, hints at some of the issues, problems, and implications of cross-cultural work within museum institutions.

In many cases, museum staff have made a commitment to collaborative work, most often through exhibition development, but also through the involvement of source community members in developing new storage and conservation practices. On such initiatives, we have included Nancy Rosoff's paper on the integration of Native American perspectives into collections management policy at the National Museum of the American Indian (see also Clavir 2002). Beyond specific procedures, however, is a willingness to seek community involvement at as many levels as possible. The selection of artefacts for display, the writing of label text, the enhancement of database entries, the storage and conservation of collections, the establishment of procedures for approving research projects involving museum collections, the design of special storage facilities for sacred/sensitive materials and human remains, the development of educational programmes, the selection of gift shop stock, the choice of logo designs, are all areas where source community members should be consulted and where their input is invaluable. These are specific points at which overlapping museum and source community rights in historic artefacts can and should be recognised. To involve community members in these ways does take additional time and money. But for museums committed to addressing issues of access and ethics, to exploring a new model in which they are forums for discourse between peoples (Ames 1991: 14) – in which they act as contact zones – it is critical that such involvement begin.

RELATIONSHIPS AND POWER; LEARNING AND UNLEARNING

To do this, of course, rests on establishing relationships between museums and source communities, a process in which we all have much to learn. At the core of the new approaches presented in this book is a series of crucial issues including power and authority, commitment, control, and learning. Without addressing these, new relationships and outcomes between museums and source communities cannot develop. As noted earlier, museums and source communities bring very different goals and needs to a working relationship. They almost certainly have different expectations about how matters will proceed, about the appropriate division of labour and credit, and about the nature of authorship or control. A museum's obligations to its publics, to its governance structure, and to the museum profession may be quite different to the community, kinship, and cultural obligations felt very keenly by source community consultants. Combined with the cross-cultural factors involved, partnerships are prone to strains resulting from these differences. It is all too easy to misread a partner's intentions and perceptions from one's own perspective, or to interpret community input as fitting easily into existing museological practice. Margaret Hanna, a curator at the Royal Saskatchewan Museum, Canada, who was involved in the redisplay of its First Nations gallery in the early 1990s, for example, writes candidly about the 'patience and persistence' needed to overcome deeply entrenched attitudes of some staff, who were committed to 'the traditional view of the museum world', whereby the curators were the experts and 'asking the spiritual leaders was a nice formality, but we didn't really have to follow their advice if it didn't fit with our plans' (Hanna 1999: 44). Hanna observes that as the gallery developed, attitudes changed; staff learned to listen and sought ways to get round some of the bureaucratic and institutional constraints.[1]

For such change to happen, relationships of respect and trust must develop between museum staff and community members, and for this reason, in the process of working with members of other cultures within the museum space, relationships are foregrounded at least as much as the artefacts themselves (Bolton this vol.). Conaty's essay on Glenbow's Blackfoot Gallery (this vol.) explains that the efforts of community members and museum staff over the past decade to nurture mutual trust *before* the gallery development process got underway were essential to the project. In developing relationships, museums may have to put their agendas aside temporarily to first address community concerns regarding, for instance, the handling of secret-sacred objects or the disposition of human remains, before community members agree to participate in projects such as exhibition development. Shifting priorities in this way reflects community desires to see issues of importance to them effectively dealt with and is also, of course, a test of the institution's commitment to the community, rather than to its own needs. One of the most important elements of the new way of working with source communities is that trust-building is considered integral to the process, and creating respect or healing the effects of the past is seen as being as important as co-writing labels or enhancing the database.

In the process of developing relationships and dealing with community needs, larger issues must also be addressed. Clifford's description of Tlingit elders examining historic artefacts in the Portland Museum of Art focused on the elders' call for the museum to support the families whose material heritage it held, 'to act on behalf of Tlingit communities, not simply to represent the history of tribal objects' (Clifford 1997: 193). Museums have claimed they are neutral spaces, and have tended to resist lending political support to source communities; Clifford, however, notes that, 'when museums are seen as contact zones, their organizing structure as a *collection* becomes an ongoing historical, political, moral *relationship* – a power-charged set of exchanges' (1997: 190). One of the effects of working with source community members is realising the political nature of museums, their histories, and their functions, as well as the need to acknowledge and address these dynamics when creating new relationships.

None of this is easy to do in practice. Some of the core dynamics of new approaches pose great challenges which are often not realised by museum staff until well into a project. For many source communities, collaboration means full and equal partnership in all stages of a project; it is a recognition of their expertise and their attachment to objects that are central to their culture, and their participation will often be based upon expectations of community benefit. Furthermore, the more a community invests in a project, the greater their expectations for continued involvement will be. Though many relationships begin with a specific project (the creation of a new gallery, or collections research), community expectations are that such projects are vehicles to developing long-term relationships, while museums may assume their responsibilities are over when the project ends. Project teams need to give thought to what happens once the exhibition opens or the initial project concludes: what are the long-term goals for the relationship? Who sets these goals? Who is intended to benefit from the partnership? How best can museum and community partners make use of a relationship which starts very tentatively, and then deepens and strengthens as participants get to know one another, work through problems, and enjoy the successes of collaborative projects? At one level, this work involves allocations of money, time, and human resources which are too significant for one-off projects; at a more fundamental level, it is about changing the attitudes and goals of museums so that they are committed to long-term relationships involving mutual support and learning.

Conaty's contribution to this volume describes how the primary goal of Glenbow's Blackfoot community team was to develop a gallery in which their children could learn about their culture and history from the perspectives of their own people. In comparison with needs such as this, a museum's goals for a collaborative project may appear more superficial and be based upon the need to gain knowledge of collections or a desire to 'do things the right way' and gain political credibility. Such goals may be achieved by what communities regard as a 'hit and run' policy, whereby the museum comes in search of information and then leaves to work on its projects, but is less prepared to address the community's needs (Lorne Carrier cited in A.K. Brown 2000: 242). Museums and source communities need to accept that while they may have some shared goals, others will simply be different, requiring compromise. Similarly, working with source communities may illuminate the multiple agendas that are played out within museums, for instance, balancing the conservation needs of an object with its cultural use (Bernstein 1992a; Clavir 2002).

With notable exceptions (Kreps 1998; Dunstan 1999), most of the existing case studies of museum/source community collaboration have focused on the positive benefits for both partners and have tended to skim over the problems encountered and how these were overcome. There are fairly obvious reasons why this has happened, largely relating to confidentiality. However, this has led to serious omissions in the literature; methodological, institutional and cross-cultural difficulties have been glossed over, despite the fact that such challenges are inherent in this kind of work. Furthermore, few writers have been prepared to comment on those situations whereby their hopes for collaboration have failed, due to insufficient resources, lack of planning, problems communicating, or disagreements within the community. Indeed, there are times when a collection or a museum's history may have so many negative associations for a community, that it simply is not possible for that community to work with the museum.[2]

Typically, anthropology curators are the interface between the museum and a source community, while few other museum employees may be involved in co-managed projects. This can be interpreted by source community members as a sign of a museum's lack of institutional commitment, putting the researchers in a difficult position if their efforts to engage their institution in a closer relationship with the community fail. Gift shop managers, educational programmers, conservators, registrars, and administrators should all ideally have some involvement in a collaborative project and be prepared to think through the implications of relationships as well as to support innovative projects administratively. Their participation heightens institutional awareness of the legitimacy and importance of cultural protocols when developing new relationships (see Fienup-Riordan 1999: 353–4), for instance sponsoring feasts and giving gifts as well as honoraria to source community partners, in addition to the more traditional costs involved in museum work.

Many staff, and many institutions, who have learned to cope with such new dynamics, have found them rewarding and stimulating. One of the most important elements of new relationships between museums and source communities is the extent to which they promote learning and growth for the museum profession. By viewing collections through the eyes of source communities, museum staff are able to think more broadly about the meanings of objects and their continued significance for communities today, alerting them to new possibilities for interpretation. As the roles are reversed and museum staff find that they are being educated by community members, they begin to see in a new light the assumptions embedded in traditional museum training, and become open to alternative ways of doing things. This is particularly so for those staff who have been privileged to attend ceremonial events involving objects that, at some point during their social lives, have been part of the museum's collection. Seeing artefacts in their cultural context, hearing stories of frustration and pain caused by inappropriate scholarly inquisitions or museum representations in the past, understanding a community's dreams for the future, all make clear the importance of developing new ways of thinking and of working.

CONTEXTS AND LITERATURES

Developments between museums and source communities have been part of a broad pattern in the social sciences of questioning relations between scholars and those whom they study. Anthropology has proved something of a lightning rod for such questioning, and many scholars have felt the need to move away from a praxis based on colonial relations of power to one in which power is more equitably shared. At the same time, source communities have begun to insist that their participation in research and exhibition projects is conditional on forms, goals, and outputs of work which are acceptable to them as well as to the museum or scholarly researcher. Various forms of community-based research are part of this new way of working between museums and source communities. Applied and advocacy anthropology are part of this new approach, as are participatory action research and collaborative research, in which forms of research and their outcomes are mutually determined and controlled by researcher and source community alike (Hall 1979; Ryan and Robinson 1990; Warry 1990, 1998). The essays in this volume represent responses to several related literatures that emerge from these academic and museological contexts. Some of this material is difficult to access: the still-emerging nature of work between museums and source communities means that much is yet unpublished, and other materials have been produced either for in-house use by individual museums or are only known within a particular nation. This Introduction, together with the references in the essays in this volume, provides an opportunity to highlight some of these works.

One of the most powerful bodies of literature to which the essays in this volume are related has critiqued museum representation and the historical relations of power it embodies. These works include James Clifford's essays 'Histories of the tribal and the modern' (1988), 'Four Northwest Coast museums: travel reflections' (1991), 'Paradise' (1997a) and 'Museums as contact zones' (1997b), which address the complex relationships between museums, their audiences, and their collections. Other critiques include Coombes's *Reinventing Africa* (1994), Barringer and Flyn's *Colonialism and the Object* (1998) and several case studies in Phillips and Steiner's edited volume *Unpacking Culture* (1999). These explore how objects have been used by scholars to construct notions of indigenous identity, culture and history for consumption by audiences in the West. Such analyses have drawn on parallel works in ethnography which have problematised the history of relations between anthropologists and the peoples they have traditionally studied and the role of colonialism in those relations (e.g. Clifford and Marcus 1986; Fabian 1983; Stocking 1985, 1986) and explored the often problematic relations of power inherent in these histories. These have extended, in museum contexts, to the ethnographic tendency to turn a blind eye to the realities of the present in favour of the idealised pasts of their subjects – part of a broader pattern of scholars fulfilling their intellectual and career needs rather than their research subjects' often more pressing ones, and a pattern against which the new relationships are reacting.

Indigenous museum professionals and other source community voices have made important contributions to these critiques, and have especially questioned the right of museum staff to represent their communities in Western academic modes. They have expressed concern at the re-contextualisation of their objects according to Western values, and have pointed out the political meanings and implications of museum displays. This literature is still emerging as a genre, but there are powerful pieces by writers such as Deborah Doxtator (1985, 1988), Gerald McMaster (1992, 1993), Gloria Frank (2000), Richard W. Hill (2000), James Nason (2000), Richard Handler and Eric Gable (1997), Paul Tapsell (1997, 2000), Deborah Eldridge (1996) and Henrietta Fourmile (1990), which convey a range of source community responses to traditional ethnographic museum practice and attitudes (and see also interviews in Clavir 2002). Indigenous curators are also publishing on their approaches to museum work and on the changes they are making within their own institutions, whether they work in mainstream museums or community-managed facilities (Mauger and Bowechop 1995; Tamarapa 1996), and while this body of work is still slender, it is very much welcomed to provide guidance for the museum profession.

Another branch of the literature has emerged from source communities' protests against traditional museum practice and particular exhibitions. The heated and highly publicised conflict surrounding the Lubicon Lake Cree's 1988 boycott of *The Spirit Sings* exhibition in Canada – a protest, in part, against an exhibition that was firmly focused on the past whilst being funded by a corporation felt to be damaging First Nations communities in the present – made visible the rifts between First Nations peoples and museums in Canada, as well as within the museum community. Other exhibitions, such as the Royal Ontario Museum's 1990 exhibit, *Into the Heart of Africa*, which was perceived by many in the African-Canadian public to have racist overtones, have proven equally contentious for related reasons (Butler 1999; Harrison 1993; A.L. Jones 1993). Responses to such conflicts have led to the creation of working groups in several countries which have made recommendations for change in museum practice designed to meet the needs of source communities and to encourage better working relations with them. In Canada, for instance, following the controversy over *The Spirit Sings*, a joint Task Force was established by the Canadian Museums Association and the Assembly of First Nations, which met with representatives of museums and First Nations communities to 'develop an ethical framework and strategies for Aboriginal Nations to represent their history and culture in concert with cultural institutions' (Task Force 1992). The resulting *Report* suggested recommendations to make museums more accountable to First Nations communities, relating to issues of access to and interpretation of collections, the repatriation of human remains, and increased training opportunities for Aboriginal staff (Task Force 1992; Nicks 1992).[3] Similarly, Museums Australia has produced a policy document that explicitly states that Aboriginal and Torres Strait Islander people have rights to self-determination in matters relating to cultural heritage and that museums have obligations to support them.[4] The document goes beyond repatriation of secret/sacred objects and human remains and outlines ways in which museums can incorporate indigenous Australian and Torres Strait Islander perspectives into their daily management and exhibition strategies (Museums Australia 1996). More publications, which both reflect and explain the new ways of thinking about and working with collections, are needed by museums as a starting-point to begin developing relationships with source communities. For museums that are geographically distant from some of their source communities, such documents are especially valuable resources, revealing as they do the new standards and expectations, and consolidating existing experience as a springboard for learning and change elsewhere.

In order to address the challenges raised by critics, many museums, especially in North America and the Pacific, have generated institutional documents and policies that encapsulate the guidelines of the national strategy documents referred to above and recognise indigenous interests (e.g. Kawharu 2002). A number have developed community advisory councils which advise museum staff on a range of issues such as selecting objects for loan to other institutions, assessing shop stock, and providing suggestions for educational programming (Conaty 1996). Policies that are developed in conjunction with source communities allow both partners to negotiate their different understandings and expectations, reducing the possibilities for misunderstandings. They also ensure that museums put into writing assurances that they will adhere to the wishes of the community involved, a point that can be extremely important in developing trust where none has existed before. Some museums are beginning to make these policies available in abbreviated format on their websites, or on request, a move that is helpful not only to indigenous groups planning research, but also to museum professionals seeking guidance on drafting policies for their own organisations.[5]

The implementation of new curatorial processes cannot, however, be done on the basis of documents alone; it requires consultation with source communities. Curators who ask whether, for instance, small bags of tobacco should be placed with some Native American or First Nations collections as offerings to show respect, or whether one should burn sweetgrass or other purifying herbs before handling these artefacts, need to understand that such procedures can only be respectful when they are performed by people who have been trained by the source community, who have begun to understand community perspectives and histories at a deep level, who have built relationships and trust with members of the source community, and who have been authorised to act by community elders (Rosoff this vol.). The actions taken within the museum storeroom need to happen within the context of relationships in the present with the community: the consultation, the human interaction, the willingness to learn, and the investment of time, effort, and money are far more important, and genuinely respectful, than gestures learned from books.

These relationships are the most important manifestation of the new curatorial praxis, but the process of establishing them has not received much attention in the critical literature. Nor has the concept of 'source community' and its special needs in and rights to material heritage held in museum collections been a focus in the literature. The one volume that stands out as a forerunner to the present work in exploring some of these concepts is Karp, Kreamer, and Lavine's anthology *Museums and Communities: the politics of public culture* (1992), which explores museum/community relationships. In an essay in that volume, 'Audience, ownership, and authority: designing relations between museums and communities', Steven Lavine observed that by 1992 'many museums [had] taken up the challenge of responding to their various constituencies and relating to them more inventively; many have even begun to reimagine who those constituencies might be' (Lavine 1992: 137). A number of the essays in that anthology presented projects based on partnerships of various kinds between museums and local communities. This volume builds upon Karp, Kreamer, and Lavine's work by providing an overview of recent literature on relations between museums and *source* – not necessarily local – communities, a development which has intensified since *Museums and Communities* was published.

THE ROAD AHEAD: VOLUME ORGANISATION

The essays in this volume explore several themes: actual relationships between museums and source communities and how these have developed; the potential of artefacts to be links between museums and source communities; and changing attitudes within the museum profession about such work. This book is arranged into three parts, each dealing with different manifestations of this broader range of developments.

Part 1 explores the museum as a field site or contact zone when source community members enter it for purposes of consultation and collaboration. Edited by Trudy Nicks (Curator of Anthropology at the Royal Ontario Museum, Toronto, and co-editor of the report by the Canadian Task Force on Museums and First Peoples, entitled *Turning the Page* [1992]), the articles in this part show what happens when the museum becomes an arena for cross-cultural debate, learning, and contest.

Part 2 considers case studies using one particular methodology as an example of the range of benefits and developments that can occur when museums begin working with source communities. This section, edited by Elizabeth Edwards (a specialist on the entwined histories of anthropology and photography and Curator of Photographs and Manuscripts at the Pitt Rivers Museum, Oxford University), considers visual repatriation, in which images of ancestors, historical knowledge, and museum artefacts are returned to source communities and are used as foci for interviews in which source community members share narratives about culture and history. Such work facilitates the recovery and preservation of cultural and historical knowledge, permits researchers to address theoretical and community-based interests, and provides copies of photographs for community use. It also challenges museum and archival professionals to be aware of the meanings of images and artefacts to source communities, and the implications of these for collections management.

Some of the most difficult, but ultimately useful projects, to have occurred in the context of shifting relationships between museums and source communities, have focused on the development of particular exhibitions or the re-display of existing galleries. In Part 3, Ruth Phillips, formerly Director of the Museum of Anthropology at the University of British Columbia, explores the ways in which such projects have challenged established attitudes and practice within museums. This part overview and the articles within it discuss developments in exhibition practice, which include working with advisory committees, developing ceremonial and political procedures for seeking assistance from source communities, changes in exhibition development and implementation, and the theoretical implications of such developments for museums.

As editors selecting articles to include in all three parts, we have noted that relationships between museums and source communities have changed most dramatically in countries where indigenous populations now live amongst settler-founded, modern nation-states, such as Australia, New Zealand, Canada, and the United States. Much of the literature on changing relationships has emerged out of experiences in these countries, and we have therefore included a number of articles from these areas. Material from elsewhere in the world has been included to show how similar issues may develop in very different political and museological contexts. Nor are all the articles focused on relations between museums and indigenous peoples, although again, much of the existing work arises from precisely this set of relationships. Finally, since the volume editors are based in the United Kingdom, and conscious of the different dynamics affecting the desire of museums in the United Kingdom and Europe to participate in changing relations with source communities which may be half a world away, we have included several articles that address situations in which the museum and the relevant source community are physically separate.

The greatest difficulty in selecting articles to include has been the lack of material written by source community members themselves, and to us, the least satisfactory element of this volume is the imbalance of voice represented in the articles and section introductions. That there should have been so much to choose from written by non-Native museum staff, and so little by source community members, is in itself revealing of the different goals and constraints of both parties: museums may wish to demonstrate their willingness to adapt and to facilitate meeting the needs of source communities for intellectual and political reasons, but only some museums – the larger ones, and often the university museums – will have the staff resources and impetus to publish about their projects and experiences. Source communities, particularly indigenous communities, may be battling with a range of more pressing issues concerning health, housing or land claims, and are more concerned about effecting change or achieving particular goals in projects to meet their community's needs than with communicating their experiences to museums, a point made by Paul Tapsell, a Maori museum professional, in his thoughtful Afterword, which reviews many of the issues raised across the other essays from a particular source community perspective. We can only hope that over time, more work will emerge from source communities and be more widely published: we need to hear these voices. In the meantime, we offer this volume as a statement of changing attitudes, of developing experience, and of knowledge still emerging.

Laura Peers
Alison K. Brown
Oxford, 2002

NOTES

1   For discussion of this project from the perspective of a Plains Cree participant, see Goforth (1993).
2   Laura Peers (Peers, 2003) has written about such a project dealing with children's hair samples taken at schools in an Ojibwe community in Minnesota in the 1920s which have since been part of the collections of the Pitt Rivers Museum, University of Oxford, and are sensitive to the Ojibwe for cultural and historical reasons. While community members were pleased to be contacted and told about the collection, and asked for advice about its curation, they have not so far been willing either to work further with the museum or to request repatriation of the hair.
3   In the United States, the process of negotiating the Native American Graves Protection and Repatriation Act (NAGPRA, 1990) and the effects of that legislation in enforcing consultation between museums and Native Americans has produced similar results, though in a more confrontational way.
4   This statement is closely related to parts of the draft Declaration of the Rights of Indigenous Peoples, which affirm the rights of indigenous peoples to their heritage and traditions, and urges states to take appropriate steps to ensure the preservation of these. Work on this important document has also assisted indigenous source communities to codify their feelings regarding material heritage and outside institutions which curate it.

5   Examples of museums which provide on-line guidance of this nature include the Museum of Anthropology at the University of British Columbia, and the Australian Museum's Aboriginal Heritage Unit.

Part 1

MUSEUMS AND CONTACT WORK

INTRODUCTION

Trudy Nicks

In a global context where collective identity is increasingly represented by having a culture (a distinctive way of life, tradition, form of art, or craft), museums make sense.

(Clifford 1997b: 218)

Museums have a dual role. They display a past that demands respect in its own terms, but they display it in a present that is characterized by obsessions of its own.

(White 1997: 34)

As institutions largely defined in the colonial environment of the nineteenth and early twentieth centuries, ethnographic museums have seemed to face an uncertain future in a world in which indigenous peoples were actively pursuing goals of self-identification and self-determination. In the latter decades of the twentieth century, indigenous peoples around the world challenged the right of museums to tell their stories and to hold collections of objects obtained from their ancestors. Exhibitions marking anniversaries of first arrivals of European explorers on foreign shores – the 500th anniversary of Columbus's arrival in the Americas, the 200th anniversary of Cook's arrival in Australia, and the 500th anniversary of Bartolomeu Dias's landing on the Cape of Good Hope – received hostile receptions from the modern descendants of the indigenous peoples 'discovered' on these voyages (Simpson 1992: 30). Some exhibitions, notably *The Spirit Sings* mounted by the Glenbow Museum for the 1988 Calgary Winter Olympics, were criticized for glorifying the past and ignoring the contemporary problems faced by indigenous peoples (e.g. Clifford 1997b; Simpson 1996). Other exhibitions, notably *Into the Heart of Africa* mounted at the Royal Ontario Museum in Toronto, Canada (hereafter ROM) in 1989, were criticized for focusing on the colonial history of collecting and interpretation rather than on celebrating African achievements (Butler 1999a, 1999b). At the same time, indigenous peoples around the world began actively seeking to regain ownership of the objects made and used by their ancestors, and to regain the very remains of those ancestors held in museums. All of these activities occurred within the context of a broader social, political and economic activism which has led, at the international level, to recognition by the United Nations that indigenous people have the right of self-determination, and, in consequence, the right freely to determine their political status and to pursue their economic, social and cultural development (Alfredsson 1989; Magnarella 2000: 36).

RETHINKING MUSEUMS

The challenges by indigenous peoples have encouraged an assessment of the positioning of museums within Western colonial culture, in much the same way that the discipline of anthropology itself has had to come to terms with its own colonial ties (Asad 1991: 314; Herzfeld 2001: x). In museums, this reflexive approach is leading to a shift from abstract classification and tracking survivals of pre-contact cultures to a focus on the social relationships represented by collections and by the museum as institution (Handler 1993). There is a growing appreciation of the necessity to understand objects in terms of the human interactions – the stories, songs, and activities – that give them meaning (Cruikshank 1995; West 1994: 54). There is also a growing acknowledgement that museum collections brought together under conditions of colonialism are embedded in power relationships, and that politics and morality are as much a part of museum history as they are present-day issues (Clifford 1997). For their part, indigenous peoples are challenging the focus on preserving objects and arguing the need and the right to have access to museum objects for purposes of cultural renewal and well-being. All of these trends have brought indigenous peoples into museums in unprecedented numbers, and, at the turn of the twenty-first century, their presence has begun to influence both institutional purpose and praxis.

The chapters in this part are case studies in the evolving relationships between indigenous peoples and the museum world. They describe developments in what James Clifford (1997), following Mary Louise Pratt, has termed a 'contact zone'. The concept of the contact zone specifically addresses issues surrounding human relationships in colonial encounters. As originally defined by Pratt (1992: 6–7), a contact zone represents 'the space of colonial encounters, the space in which peoples geographically and historically separated come into contact with each other and establish ongoing relations, usually involving conditions of coercion, radical inequality, and intractable conflict.' Clifford argues that thinking of museums as contact zones provides a way of understanding, and addressing, the concerns of contemporary indigenous peoples. As long as museums are thought of 'as collections of universal culture, repositories of uncontested value, sites of progress, discovery, and the accumulation of human, scientific, or national patrimonies', that is, as end products or witnesses of colonial achievement, we will continue to marginalize non-Western peoples and deny them agency and legitimacy in the past and the present (Clifford 1997: 213).

Contemporary relationships, which can range from contestations over the interpretation and ownership of collections to the possibility of collaboration and shared authority, make sense when seen against a background of colonial histories. Clifford acknowledges that reactions from within communities may be diverse, and that it is necessary to take account of different histories of contact, of agency as well as exploitation, and of creative intercultural borrowing (transculturations) that have been part of historical relationships. He also acknowledges that there are many constraints, such as budgets, curatorial control, restrictive definitions of art and culture, community hostility and miscomprehension, that militate against easy change in museum practices. But he argues that approaching museum work as contact work provides the understanding and context necessary to begin to grapple with the real difficulties of dialogue, alliance, inequality and translation which will be part of any change (Clifford 1997: 213).

TRANSFORMING MUSEUMS

The case studies presented here are examples of a growing body of literature that documents the kinds of changes that are occurring as indigenous peoples enter and use museums. These changes are representative of the new directions encouraged through national museum policies (Task Force 1992; Griffin 1996) and national legislation (Museum News 2000). In this introduction I discuss three themes that emerge from these sources. The first theme concerns changes in the status of indigenous objects in museums and in the purpose of anthropology museums. The second theme deals with changes in museum practice, and the pressures and strains these may cause as institutions endeavour to address the needs and interests of indigenous peoples. A third theme considers some of the implications of contact work for the curatorial role within museums. The present discussion focuses on 'back-of-house' activities and does not consider the very significant trends related to exhibitions and other public representations of indigenous cultures and histories in museums since these are considered elsewhere in this volume.

CHANGING PERSPECTIVES ON OBJECTS AND MUSEUMS

Anthropological collections were amassed to preserve a record of disappearing indigenous cultures. Even as the notion of vanishing peoples has waned, museums have still sought to preserve objects in perpetuity through the application of the best available Western scientific technology. As museums work with source communities, the focus on object preservation – as central purpose and guideline for practice – is being challenged by those who feel that the primary purpose of a museum should be the preservation of indigenous cultures. The most thorough decentring of the object preservation focus is seen in those museums controlled by indigenous peoples. Lissant Bolton (this volume) notes that Aboriginal Australians favour the idea of a Keeping Place, 'where objects are kept until needed for use', over the traditional museum focus on long-term preservation. In other museums, the object preservation ethic is giving way, in varying degrees, to more open and inclusive practices that take into account indigenous interests and needs. The status of objects within museums thus changes as a result of contact zone work. Museums now accept that many contemporary indigenous groups see objects as living entities, some of which may retain spiritual power sufficient to endanger museum workers and visitors alike. The significance of objects is no longer restricted to past contexts of manufacture, use, and collecting, but now takes into account the demonstrated meanings they may have for indigenous communities in the present and for the future (A.K. Brown 2001; Fienup-Riordan and Bolton this volume).

CHANGING MUSEUM PRACTICES

It is no longer sufficient to treat indigenous objects as inert relics or bits of art to be arranged according to abstract typologies in standardized storage facilities. Taking account of indigenous practices and interests serves to decentre the dominance of scientifically based museology by making us aware of the assumptions and values inherent in Western practice (Kreps 1998: 3). Appropriate care for living entities that have continuing meaning to source communities requires attention to indigenous practice, and this has implications for methods of caring for collections based on Western science. Gillian Flynn and Deborah Hull-Walski (2001) describe recent changes in storage practices at the National Museum of Natural History in Washington, DC, which reflect the varying needs and concerns of the worldwide indigenous communities represented by the collections. The changes accommodate the respect due to sacred and ceremonial items, the need to allow living entities to breathe, and the need to restrict access to sensitive materials. Incorporating indigenous practices at the museum has included performance of a ceremony by Cheyenne traditional religious leaders to reduce the threat posed by the spiritual power of a sacred buffalo head. Bolton (this volume) likewise describes the use of ritual specialists to control the power inherent in some Melanesian objects. At the Woodland Cultural Centre, a First Nations-run institution on the Six Nations reserve at Brantford, Ontario, the directors have enlisted the assistance of members of the Iroquois community as care-givers for the powerful False Face Society masks in their collections (Tom Hill, pers. com.).

Scientific methods aimed at long-term conservation of objects are being modified to take account of indigenous concerns and curation methods. Conservators now seek to preserve the cultural information which is part of an object, as well as to stabilize it, and may forego any treatment for objects meant to deteriorate as part of ritual practice (Flynn and Hull-Walski 2001: 38–9). In conservator Miriam Clavir's words, 'the question of how preserving "the physical object" balances with preserving "the cultural object" can be said to represent a reconceptualization of the norms for ethnographic conservation' (Clavir 2002: xxii). Indigenous people may argue for the priority of cultural concerns, but Clavir's research indicates that there is also appreciation of the value of scientific methods of preservation, particularly as these might 'serve the use (in its many forms) of the object in their communities' (ibid.: 246).

Some indigenous needs and practices strain the ability of museums to accommodate. Pest control in storage rooms is an ongoing concern with implications for indigenous practices of making offerings and ceremonial feedings which often involve organic materials. Offerings and ceremonial feeding are permitted at the National Museum of Natural History as long as organic materials are suitably contained (Flynn and Hull-Walski 2001: 36). Other museums request that ritual foods be frozen to kill insect eggs that may be present (Clavir 2002: 247). The past use of poisonous substances to prevent pest damage to objects is a source of contention. For indigenous people, the application of poisons to objects that they consider to be living entities is incomprehensible. Items treated with poisons may continue to remain dangerous for handling or ceremonial use even after being cleaned, presenting difficulties for indigenous peoples and museums alike. From a preservation standpoint, loans of objects outside of museum contexts are problematic. Museums may make objects available to be present at ceremonial events (Flynn and Hull-Walski 2001: 38). Some museums loan objects for ceremonial use (Rosoff this volume) but such practice is still the exception.

Meeting the needs of indigenous peoples requires other changes to facilitate greater access to collections and associated documentation. Space needs include sufficient room for private viewing, discussion and ceremonial activities by groups of people. In the absence of appropriate ventilation, it may be necessary to override fire protection systems to permit smudging ceremonies. Museums can also provide space and resources for indigenous peoples to work on projects not directly involving collections, such as language recovery and training, and for community meetings (Kwa'ioloa 1997: 153).

Ideally, collections records and organization would be coherent in terms of indigenous terminology and categories, but this remains a future goal for many, if not most, institutions. On the positive side, the need to accommodate indigenous access and standards of care has resulted in improved standards of documentation and record keeping for museum collections (Giesen 1999: 3). With computer databases it is possible to integrate new information and terminology, and even to reorganize collections records according to indigenous categories, with minimum expense and effort. Now that electronic images and databases are the norm, museums need to consult with source communities to decide which images, and what data, should be restricted from public access.

There are constraints, as Clifford has noted, on how readily museums can implement new practices, especially if change requires new resources. In institutions with broad mandates, for example both natural and human history, budgets may have to stretch to accommodate special storage needs for collections ranging from faunal specimens preserved in alcohol to sacred or gender-sensitive indigenous objects. And even the best-intentioned policies for accommodating the needs and interests of source communities can fall foul of the bureaucratic processes of a large institution. The timetable for an exhibition project in which the Native-run Woodland Cultural Centre and the ROM were to collaborate as equal partners in fact ended up being controlled by the collections management processes of the ROM. Waiting for the ROM process proved to be a frustrating experience for the Woodland Cultural Centre which, as a much smaller institution, was accustomed to operating less formally and much more quickly (Nicks 2002: 156). Constraints inevitably result in delayed or restricted access to collections and documentation, which in turn become continuing sources of frustration for communities.

Reconciling issues of ownership represents a complex and difficult part of contact work. The first reaction of museums to challenges from indigenous communities has often been fear that mainstream museums would lose the right to hold or exhibit indigenous materials. Thus far legislation including the Native American Graves Protection and Repatriation Act (NAGPRA) passed in the United States in 1990, and policies developed by national museums associations in Canada (Task Force 1992) and Australia (Griffin 1996), have been fairly conservative with regard to the outright return of museum collections to indigenous communities. Some collections have been, and more will be, returned to communities, with the greatest emphasis placed on human remains and classes of objects deemed essential to the continuation of traditional cultural practices and identity. A major repatriation issue for museums is the question of who, or which community, is the appropriate recipient for material. Except where an individual can prove clear legal title, general practice favours returns to the source community for an object or collection. The process of repatriation is complex and needs to be transparent to all parties involved. To do otherwise runs the risk of playing the interests of indigenous groups against each other, with serious, negative consequences for the museum and the groups involved. As a case in point, the 1998 release of Midiwewin material from the University of Winnipeg anthropology museum to the Three Fires Society based in the United States, without consulting the original source communities of Pauingassi, Jackhead and Little Grand Rapids in northern Manitoba, has resulted in acrimonious public debate and potential legal problems with no easy resolution in sight (Singleton 2002).

Communal vs. individual ownership rights clash when museums seek to comply with copyright laws. Western law is biased in favour of individual rather than communal rights to ownership. Contemporary native artists, including those whose works are based in indigenous knowledge and tradition, are usually familiar with copyright agreements and are comfortable with claiming individual ownership. But many native people who create more traditional forms of art and artefacts, see themselves as working within a communal knowledge system. For them, being asked by a museum to sign a copyright document is to make an impossible claim.

CHANGING CURATORIAL ROLES

The traditional curatorial role changes considerably in the context of contact work. The isolated scholar and manager becomes a facilitator and a collaborator who shares, rather than represents, authority. Essays in this volume repeatedly note the need to be sensitive, to be flexible, and to be respectful in dealings with source communities. As a facilitator, the curator can assist in finding or creating jobs and training internships for members of source communities. The responsibility to source communities involves a good deal of time spent in providing access to collections and associated research and documentation. In recent years the ROM Anthropology Department has hosted workshops for members of the Toronto urban Native community. For many of the younger people in attendance, the workshops provided a first opportunity to see and to learn from objects related to their own cultural histories. These workshops have also helped to demystify museum practice. In 1996 the ROM, as a collaborating institution, hosted a group of over 20 beadworkers from the Tuscarora Nation in upstate New York as part of the research process for an exhibition entitled *Across Borders: Beadwork in Iroquoian Life* which toured museums in Canada and the United States between 1999 and 2003. The Tuscarora beadworkers examined over 400 examples of Iroquoian beadwork in the ROM's collections. For many of them it was a rare opportunity to examine, and record for their own future use, nineteenth-century examples of beadwork.

Negotiating arrangements to share the care and use of collections with source communities has become an increasingly important part of curatorial work in Canadian institutions as a result of the inclusion of material culture in land claims cases initiated by a number of First Nations across the country. While claims agreements legally cover only those museums that report directly to federal or provincial governments, in fact the arrangements being negotiated in these contexts are being used as precedents for dealing with non-government museums.

Some apparently simple approaches to sharing collections have turned out to be starting points rather than final solutions. 'Visual repatriation' of collections by way of photographs or digital images is one way in which museums have sought to return information to communities, but it may not be sufficient to meet indigenous needs or interests. The people of the Tr'ondëk Hwëch'in Nation in the Yukon Territory of Canada were pleased to receive digital images of objects from their community in the ROM collections. They subsequently requested that the museum bring the clothing illustrated to their community so that they could make a detailed study of construction methods, and a loan was arranged for this purpose (Ken Lister, pers. com.). The opportunities for developing arrangements are constrained only by the imagination and resources which can be brought to bear by the parties concerned. But it is necessary to recognize that co-management and co-ownership arrangements have long-term implications for resources, especially time and budgets, that curators, museums, and communities must be prepared to honour if they are to succeed.

MUSEUMS AS TRANSCULTURAL SPACES

Museums have proved to be adaptable mechanisms for post-colonial purposes. Mainstream museums, through working with indigenous peoples, have learned to understand ethnographic collections as records of human relationships within native cultures and between native and non-native groups and are being transformed in the process. Indigenous peoples have become museum-literate both in the sense of learning to negotiate with colonial institutions – NAGPRA has given Native Americans new tools of language and procedure (Museum News 2000: 47) – and in the sense of adapting museums to their own purposes of cultural revitalization, self-identification, and self-determination in a complex, increasingly urban and global world (Bruner 1996; White 1997; Yellowhorn 2000). Indigenous peoples around the world are creating their own museums, sometimes enlisting the services of professional consultants from the West to help design buildings and exhibitions and to train staff. This process of change across and between interconnected cultures is the transculturative experience that Clifford references in his discussion of museums as contact zones (Clifford 1997: 201–2; Gupta and Ferguson 1997: 28). Arguably, both sides have come to share a concept of culture as heritage and as project.

CASE STUDIES

The four chapters in this part of the book are important contributions to a growing literature on the evolving relationships between the indigenous peoples of the world and museums. As case studies they demonstrate how different experiences of colonialism are played out in the contact zone represented by museums.

Ann Fienup-Riordan describes the mutually powerful experience of reuniting members of a source community with collections in museum storerooms. For the Yup'ik elders from Alaska who travelled to the Museum für Völkerkunde in Berlin to see objects collected from their region over a century earlier, the experience elicited cultural knowledge and performance in much the same way Clifford (1997) has described for North West Coast elders who visited the Portland Art Museum. Fienup-Riordan's account of the visit provides a glimpse of Yup'ik social relations as evoked by contact with the Berlin objects. The Yup'ik responses to the Berlin collections clearly demonstrate that, for source communities, objects are far from frozen in time but rather have continuing lives. They are connections to a past with continuing relevance to the present, and they are seen as having significance for the future well-being of Yup'ik culture. For the museum, the Yup'ik elders' visit added to and corrected extant documentation. The elders' response to the objects added a way of understanding them that, in Fienup-Riordan's words, 'the original collectors never imagined'.

Fienup-Riordan outlines useful guidelines for museum behaviour in a contact zone situation. For a successful encounter, she argues, community members need to be provided with enough working space to examine multiple objects simultaneously, they need to be able to touch objects, and they need the time and privacy to explore. In short, museum staff need training which sensitizes them to people as well as training directed toward the preservation of objects. Fienup-Riordan sees visits to collections as opportunities for source communities to conduct their own fieldwork through which they can learn about the collection process as well as collections. These visits can serve as acts of 'visual repatriation' that enable them to 're-own the knowledge and experiences embodied in objects'.

Fienup-Riordan mentions almost in passing that the Yup'ik project included recording the sound made by objects in the Berlin collections. With this comment she reminds us that there is still a Eurocentric bias toward the visual and the verbal in museum representations, abetted by conservation agendas. These senses are not necessarily the most relevant ones to the ways in which objects 'work' in indigenous cultures. It is the sound of the drum that communicates with the supernatural world; and the physical contact with a sand painting that imparts its curative powers. If museums preclude expression or experience of these senses, then the human relationships which give the objects meaning are likewise obscured.

The chapters by Bolton and Rosoff offer a comparative perspective on progress made by indigenous peoples of the Pacific and the United States in gaining control over the management and interpretation of museum collections. Bolton's chapter provides a striking example of the importance that different contact histories have had to the responses that contemporary communities make to museum settings and representations. For Australian Aboriginal communities, which were extensively disrupted by the colonial experience, 'instituting some form of control over how museums use collections of Aboriginal material has been of considerable importance in asserting the vigour of their population and in reversing the assumption of colonial authority'. In Melanesia, where the colonial experience was less disruptive to traditional culture, the response has been less focused on re-possessing objects than on using museum settings to promote ongoing cultural knowledge and performance. For Melanesians, the management of heritage sites rather than collections has become an important function for museums.

At the Smithsonian's National Museum of the American Indian (NMAI) the collections of the former Heye Foundation in New York City have become the foundation of an institution run by Native Americans. Rosoff details how collections management issues have been defined and effected at the NMAI. In part, these issues follow the imperatives set out in the NAGPRA legislation passed by the United States government in 1990. In accordance with NAGPRA, the museum is concerned with the repatriation of human remains and funerary objects, and sacred and other objects belonging to the 'cultural patrimony'. The NMAI is concerned with merging conservation and traditional approaches to collections care, and to that end is holding formal consultations with Native people on care and handling issues. The museum also lends sacred materials for ceremonial use on a case-by-case basis, and, according to Rosoff, without detriment to the preservation of the objects involved. As with Fienup-Riordan's chapter, these contributions underline the active dialogue and trust that are essential for productive contact zone encounters. The NMAI work on more inclusive approaches to collections conservation will be of great value to all museums entrusted with the care of indigenous collections.

The chapter by Swallow and Nightingale on the development of *The Arts of the Sikh Kingdoms* exhibition adds the dimension of an immigrant source community far from their geographical homeland. The main issue for the Sikh diaspora community in England is social inequality, and the Victoria & Albert Museum (V&A) thus becomes a contact zone in which to negotiate cultural recognition, legitimacy, and value. The authors provide a valuable account of a museum moving from custodianship of significant Sikh art and historical treasures to active collaboration with the source community as represented by Sikh immigrants. The experience described has been very significant for the V&A. The art and design museum gained valuable assistance in research, in fund-raising, in marketing the exhibition, and in visitor support services from members of the Sikh community. (As one of the venues for the travelling version of this exhibition, the ROM also received strong support from the Toronto Sikh community.) The Sikh participants found the association with the V&A opened doors into other collections, both in the UK and in India. The project is notable as well for the effort made to continue the relationship between the V&A and the local Sikh community beyond the exhibition project. While such projects are important steps forward in working with communities, the authors note that they still represent marginal change in practice for the host institution. Compared with the Bolton and Rosoff chapters, it seems that change in core policies and management will proceed quickly only in institutions in which indigenous communities have a significant degree of managerial control. The practice of including source communities in museum projects is valuable, but it is only the start of an incremental process of change.

COMMUNICATING CONTACT WORK TO VISITORS

The chapters in this section are good examples of the kind of rethinking that Clifford has argued is basic to overcoming difficulties of dialogue, alliance, inequality, and translation in the relationships between indigenous peoples and museums (Clifford 1997: 213). They are part of a growing literature which includes important works on the topics of interpretation and repatriation (for example, Butler 1999a; Greenfield 1989; Jessup and Bagg 2002; Karp and Lavine 1991; National Museum of the American Indian 2000; Simpson 1996) and on the complex histories of cross-cultural interaction reflected in ethnographic collections (for example, R.B. Phillips 1998; Phillips and Steiner 1999; Steiner 1994; Thomas 1991). In an era when museums are equally focused on connecting with general publics by catering to their various interests and physical comforts, it is necessary also to communicate to these visitors that objects and collections are representations of complex and ongoing human relationships rather than souvenirs of exotic others and exotic ways. If museums are to be agents of social change, as many argue they must (Rankin and Hamilton 1999), then they need to translate their contact work into effective means of replacing colonial representations of passive indigenous peoples with representations that make explicit the agency with which these peoples have always engaged their own and other worlds.

1

YUP'IK ELDERS IN MUSEUMS

Fieldwork turned on its head

Ann Fienup-Riordan

This chapter describes efforts begun in 1994 to bring Yup'ik elders in direct contact with museum collections gathered from their region 100 years ago to simultaneously preserve their knowledge and make it available to scholars and Yup'ik community members. The museum artifacts that provided our focus were the 7,000 objects collected by Johan Adrian Jacobsen from Alaska in 1882–3. Housed in Berlin's Museum für Völkerkunde (now the Etnologisches Museum), they constitute the largest unpublished collection of Yup'ik artefacts anywhere in the world, including detailed ethnographic and linguistic information. Bringing information about a major collection home to Alaska is an act of 'visual repatriation' that we hope will illuminate the world view of its creators. Yup'ik elders working side by side with anthropologists and museum professionals can help us better understand the artefacts Jacobsen collected from their area. These are first steps in the two-way process of Yup'ik people owning their past and museum curators realizing the full value of the contents of their attics.

INTRODUCTION

Fifteen years before the outset of the Jesup North Pacific Expedition, Adolf Bastian, director of Berlin's Royal Ethnological Museum, commissioned a 30-year-old Norwegian jack-of-all-trades, Johan Adrian Jacobsen, to travel to America's northwest coast and collect for his museum. Aware that the Geographical Society of Bremen was sending the Krause brothers to the Pacific Northwest, Jacobsen set his sights on Alaska.[1] He was especially interested in slate blades, nephrite (jade) amulets, and other 'stone age' tools, and hoped to bring home evidence of ancient Eskimo adaptations (Jacobsen 1884, 1977; Krause 1956).

Arriving in St Michael in 1882, the year after Edward Nelson (1899) left, Jacobsen (1977: 159) continually complained in his correspondence that 'Mr Nielsen' already had gotten all the good stuff. In fact, plenty remained for Jacobsen, and he returned to Berlin in 1883 to great acclaim. His collection of 6,720 objects, a third from Yup'ik communities on the coast of the Bering Sea, was displayed in a special exhibit for Berlin's Anthropological Society, and Crown Prince Friedrich came to view it. This was the first of many trips Jacobsen made for the Royal Museum, which today houses more than 15,000 objects collected by him from all over the world (Fienup-Riordan 1996: 219–26).

Jacobsen spent the following winter in Berlin cataloguing his collection, but his lack of academic training earned him a cool reception among museum professionals. Franz Boas visited the museum and perused Jacobsen's accession records, complaining about inaccuracies and exaggerations (Thode-Arora 1989: 52). In part because of these limitations, Jacobsen's collection remained largely unpublished until the Second World War, when most of it was thought to have been destroyed during the bombing of Berlin (Westphal-Hellbusch *et al.* 1973). In fact, the Soviet Army took much of Jacobsen's material (along with other museum collections) by train through Poland to Leningrad when they retreated from Berlin. In 1978 these collections were sent to the Leipzig Museum for Ethnology in East Germany and, after the fall of the Berlin Wall, returned to the Museum für Völkerkunde (Hopfner 1995).

I first visited the Museum für Völkerkunde in 1994, looking for Yup'ik masks. There I was stunned to find the staff busily unpacking this extraordinary Yup'ik collection, second only to Nelson's in size and scope, yet with accession records still handwritten in old German script and almost completely unpublished (Dissellhoff 1935, 1936; Hipszer 1971). I spent my brief stay in Berlin busily photographing masks. But along with photographs, I brought home a desire to return to Berlin and dig deeper into Jacobsen's treasures.

YUP'IK ELDERS TRAVEL TO GERMANY

After the mask exhibit opened in Anchorage in 1996, a team of Yup'ik elders and community leaders and I set to work planning for that return visit. The National Science Foundation funded our project through a grant to the region's non-profit corporation, the Association of Village Council Presidents. After a year's preparation, including a four-month battle with Passport Services,[2] our seven-member 'Yup'ik delegation' set out from Anchorage on 5 September 1997. The group included Marie Meade as interviewer and translator, Andy Paukan, mayor of St Marys, as videographer, four elders representing the different areas of the region – Wassilie Berlin, Paul John, Annie Blue, and Catherine Moore – and me as photographer and guide. We spent three weeks working at the museum. As in the mask exhibit (Fienup-Riordan 1996: 23–30), what we sought was not so much the collection's physical return to Alaska, but the return of the knowledge and stories, the history and pride that they embodied and that, we hoped, we would be able to bring home.

From the beginning the Yup'ik reaction to learning about the existence of Yup'ik collections has been gratitude and pride. Andy Paukan stated it well:

> I'm thinking that coming to Germany to examine these objects will make it easier for us to explain our culture to our young people and to our children. We will be able to tell them things with no reservations. Our work will make it easier to prepare teaching material about our culture for our younger generations, our children, our grandchildren, to our peers and even our own parents and grandparents. With this work, our roots and culture will come closer to us.

This attitude toward collections as opportunities to affect the future was the primary reason elders and regional leaders supported this project and agreed to travel so far and work so hard. While in Germany they saw themselves not as sightseers or solitary researchers, but as representatives of the Yup'ik nation. The elders who travelled to Berlin were the recognized 'professors' from their regions and were chosen both for their ability and willingness to share what they knew. Their detailed knowledge was impressive. They spoke in collections not for my benefit or for that of the scholarly community, but to enlighten and empower their descendants.

To understand the magnitude of their trust and dedication, you should know that three of the four elders speak only Yup'ik. Two are in their eighties and the others in their seventies. Yet they made a 24-hour plane trip, crossing 10 time zones, to a place with unfamiliar sounds and sights and foreign food. The first morning we were there, I remember teasing 81-year-old Wassilie Berlin, calling him my *uicungaq* ('dear little husband', or teasing cousin). This endearment has often worked to break the ice with elders. Instead of laughing, he looked at me seriously and said, 'No, you are my daughter'. He said this in part because, since we had met, I had served him like a daughter. In the weeks that followed, he changed his mind. He and the other elders sometimes called me their mother because, along with Marie, I cooked and cared for them. Catherine confided how scared she was when I went out of sight, and I realized the depth of their dependence. I was humbled one morning near the end of our trip when Paul John, the acknowledged leader of our group, said that we had been chosen by God to do this work. Although we had fun on our trip, this was very serious business.

ELDERS' WORK IN COLLECTIONS

Our work in the museum began with a brief tour of the storage room where 14 large cases with glass doors held the Yup'ik collections. Each elder wore a cotton *qaspeq*, and we stood together and sang 'Tarvarnauramken', a song describing the traditional act of purifying oneself with smoke. This song had closed the Yup'ik mask exhibit *Agayuliyararput (Our Way of Making Prayer)* in Anchorage, and subsequently opened the exhibit in each of its Lower Forty-Eight venues, including New York, Washington, DC, and Seattle. Following the 'blessing' song, Annie Blue led us in the Lord's Prayer. Three weeks later our work ended with a feast and another prayer as we joined hands in a circle with the German museum staff we had come to know. Our group embodied not only geographic variation but all three religious denominations active in the region – Catholic, Moravian, and Russian Orthodox.

Between prayers we looked at all 2,000 objects, one by one. Our major hurdle at the museum was not the German language, but their organization in which 'Eskimo' and 'Arctus' are comprehensive categories. We were fortunate that although Yup'ik and Iñupiaq collections were mixed, most objects from Alaska, Canada, and Greenland were stored separately by type (e.g., net sinkers, spear points). They had not, however, been divided by Alaska region (Yukon, Kuskokwim, Coastal, Bristol Bay), which, as it turned out, would have been a disaster for our regionally diverse group. When presented with a group of bows, for example, the elders would comment in turn on those from their area, being careful to mention the differences from bows of other areas. The separation between men's and women's things that I had anticipated did not take place. For example, Annie and Catherine knew almost as much about the use of bows and arrows as did Wassilie and Paul; conversely, Paul and Wassilie spoke eloquently about the making of sinew, technically 'women's work'.

Group dynamics followed Yup'ik protocols. We had a number of English-speaking visitors during our stay, but we did our best work when discussions were carried out in Yup'ik. The balance between men and women was critical. Because of his full-time teaching job in St Marys, Andy Paukan originally planned to return home after the first week. It became clear that if he left then the other men would follow him, as he was the only man among them who spoke English and, as their roommate, provided an irreplaceable measure of security. Because of the value Andy placed on this work, he agreed to stay. Had he not done so, the whole trip would have fallen apart.

Formal Yup'ik etiquette dictated our roles as speakers and listeners while working in collections. As the eldest man, Wassilie spoke first, followed by Paul as the recognized expert orator with, as Andy liked to say, 'a mind like a computer'. Paul directed his explanations primarily to Marie, Wassilie, and Annie, while Catherine (raised at the Catholic mission of Akulurak and consequently less knowledgeable about some traditional practices) often took a back seat. In cases where Paul knew more about an object than Wassilie, he would still listen to Wassilie before giving a full explanation. When we looked at something that both men were familiar with, Paul would often tell Wassilie to go ahead and talk about it. That 'talk' took a range of forms, including names, personal experiences, actions, stories, and songs (Figure 1.1).

Figure 1.1 Wassilie Berlin 'hunting' in Berlin. Andy Paukan and Uli Sanner in the background. September 1997. (Photograph by Dietrich Graf, courtesy Etnologisches Museum, Berlin)

NAMES

The detailed vocabulary associated with the collected objects was a major point of interest. When looking at a box of harpoon points, elders sorted them by named type: *nuusaarpak* (three-pronged fish or bird spearpoint), *kukgar* (attachment to the spearpoint on a seal-hunting weapon thrown with a throwing board), *kukgacuarat* (small spearpoint), and *kukgarpak* (large spearpoint). Not only were there *akitnat* (arrowpoints), but *meq'ercetaat* (arrowpoints used for hunting), *nuiret* (points for bird or rabbit spears), and *umit* (stone arrowpoints used during warfare). A large needle used to string salmon heads had a special name, as did a rock used as a tool for decorating clay pottery. The comment '*Ayuqluni*' (It's the same) let us move relatively fast through boxes of objects of a type we had already discussed.

During our second week we were confronted with two boxes, each holding a mixture of kayak and harpoon parts. Paul and Wassilie carefully separated them, gave each a name, and described their use, placing kayak parts in one box and harpoon parts in another. When I looked the next day, the museum's collection manager had reordered the ivories according to the original confusion, since that was the way they had historically been located in storage. Fortunately, we had recorded the information about the objects' function so that the elders' ordering could be replicated if and when the museum staff chose to do so.

Regional differences in design and designation were points of great interest. When presented with a box mixing Yup'ik and Iñupiaq ivory spear points (*talutet*), the elders picked out ones from their area to comment on, ignoring those of their northern neighbours. Although technically the handiwork of Yup'ik speakers, things from Unalakleet were dismissed as Iñupiaq and were not investigated.

Pre-contact regional hostilities were referenced. The third day we looked at a box of spear throwers (*nuqat*). I lay them out on the table, and each elder picked up those made from his or her area. Annie Blue chose the *nuqaq* made by the warlike Aglegmiut, and playfully pretended to use it as a gun to shoot Paul and Wassilie across the table.

Elders made old things familiar in their comments, emphasizing similarity between past and present over difference. Paul John designated an ivory story knife (*yaaruin*) a 'cartoon-*alriit*'. Catherine called a bladder water bottle (*mervik*) a 'Yup'ik thermos'. And when looking at ivory pieces, Andy commented, 'I guess our ancestors forgot to patent these gas hose connectors'.

PERSONAL REFLECTIONS: THE PAST MADE PRESENT

Jacobsen's diverse collection also evoked a wide range of personal experiences. Wooden bowls were tremendously evocative. For example, Wassilie took up a young boy's bowl, like one he had used as a child, and related the *inerquutet* (rules) from his area about what could and could not be placed in it. Looking at a large wooden snow shovel, Paul John recalled that a young man would shovel for four years before he would 'graduate' (become a good hunter). After four years he would see a seal head emerging from the path he had been clearing. Again and again I heard the traditional rules for living I had recorded in *Boundaries and Passages* (1994), but in this context they were organized dramatically around real objects and activities, rather than didactically around ideas of what it meant to be a 'real person'.

The elders continually used objects to make points in an ongoing conversation among themselves. This was never more striking than on the fourth day, when we looked at a model dance house. Its delicately carved ivory figures and unusual costumes drew no comment, but Andy and Paul both gave long explanations of the tiny drum model. In brief, they said that the drum holds the elders and all that is good, but that half of the Yup'ik people today are outside this drum. I was listening to a political statement about what it meant to be Yup'ik in the modern world which would certainly be re-stated in public hearings back in Alaska.

Equally eloquent was a 10-minute description of a wooden dipper by Paul and Wassilie. Wassilie first described the dipper's use, followed by Paul's detailed account of the drinking restrictions imposed on young boys to make them fleet and strong. Wassilie then described the face designs painted on the inside bottom of drinking containers, which reminded Paul of the story of the boy who was told to look into a water bucket where he observed the face of an old man. This, his grandmother told him, was his own image, as he was destined to live a long life. Wassilie then told of a woman whose husband was lost on the ice. She told her son to look into the water bucket, and there he saw an image of his father in his boat, foretelling his safe return. Paul John concluded reflectively, 'If we had continued to channel these customs to the present time, we would still have our own shamans that would be able to do that kind of work for us ordinary people.' All this from three ounces of old wood!

The group hotly debated which personal experiences were worth recording. For example, while looking at a large wooden bowl (*qantaq*), Catherine Moore began to describe a similar bowl that had belonged to her father. Andy objected, saying that we should focus exclusively on objects in Jacobsen's collection, while Marie insisted that Catherine's comments were important. This issue came up several times and was never resolved.

Moreover, the handling of the objects was savoured as a personal experience that would be talked about for years to come. In the process the elders noticed everything; for example, an ivory story knife carved for a 'lefty' and a restored axe with the blade put on backwards. In three weeks we examined more than 2,000 items – feeling each grip and point, looking down the line of each arrow, opening each tobacco box. Our German hosts gave us space to work, permission to touch, and privacy to explore, without which our work could never have gone forward.

During a lunch break Paul John observed Peter Bolz, the Museum's North American curator, moving his hands in enthusiastic explanation, and he called Peter 'a real dancer'. In fact, all the elders danced through the collection – chopping with axes, shooting arrows, digging for mousefood, shovelling snow, mixing *akutaq*, and making fire with the bow drill. Among the most dramatic explanations was Annie Blue's preparation of snuff tobacco. Assembling seven tools from different parts of the collection she first pretended to cut, pound, and strain the tobacco, mix it with ash, and then sniff it into one nostril, sneezing and wiping the water from her eyes when she was done. Her presentation was so realistic that the group later questioned whether today's young people should be shown the video, lest they want to revive the custom.

Needless to say, we played with all the toys, including tops, darts, balls, and an ivory spindle spun in a bowl in a game called *caukia*. When we looked at an eagle-feather dance wand (*nayangan*), Wassilie walked around the table and stood Catherine up, telling her to sing the *taitnaur* 'asking song'. Then he quickly left the room and returned carrying his coat as a gift, showing his muscles, and dancing to the beat. In fact, every day I had the overwhelming feeling of attending a dance festival. Unlike the mask exhibit *Agayuliyararput*, where exploring collections had paved the way for a major series of events (Fienup-Riordan 1996), this was the event, not mere preparation. A book might be the result, but the action was here and now.

SONGS AND STORIES

Just as the objects evoked names, remembrances, and dramatic displays, they also conjured a multitude of stories. The numerous bows and arrows started an avalanche of war stories that continued through lunches and long evenings at the hotel. When Annie Blue saw a cutting board, it reminded her of the story of the woman who turned into a bear by dressing in a bear skin with a board behind her back to take revenge on her unfaithful husband Picartuli. When we looked at spear heads, Andy asked Paul to describe the detailed division of a seal after the hunt.

My favourite story was when Annie Blue held a Nushagak carving (IVA5353) in front of her while she related an account of the creature *paalraayak*, named in Nelson's *The Eskimo about Bering Strait* (1899: 444), but until now a mystery. Thanks to Bill Fitzhugh and Susan Kaplan (1982), who asked me what a *paalraayak* was years ago, my ears pricked up when I finally heard the answer.

> They have mentioned *paalraayak*. And recently, I think it was the year before last, it was mentioned that there was such a creature in the area behind Assigyugpak. It was said that *paalraayiit* were able to move around underground. . . .
>
> One spring there was a couple who were up in the mountains hunting squirrels in the area of Assigyugpak. In the past people were told not to go in the area behind Assigyugpak. Since the younger generations don't pay attention to the teachings of the old, they have begun to travel around in that once-restricted area. . . .
>
> One day when the couple went up in that area behind their spring camp, they saw an animal that looked like a land otter behind them. It was said that *paalraayiit* look like land otters. I'd like to look at that carving while I tell you this story.
>
> The animal they saw resembled a land otter like this, and its face looked like a land otter's face, but as they observed it, it would disappear into the ground and come back up again. And as the couple continued on, the sled they were pulling began to sink into the ground.
>
> Normally, the ground in the spring is still frozen hard. As the couple walked and their feet began to sink into the ground, a person suddenly emerged out of the ground near them. A total person appeared right in the direction of their camp as they were heading towards it. And the land otter they had seen disappeared into the ground.
>
> It was said that *paalraayiit* were attracted to *caagnitellrianun* [people experiencing puberty, death, childbirth, miscarriage, etc.]. *Paalraayiit* resided in the mountains. There are many mountains in our area as you know. Since there were many mountains, the *caagnitellriit* were restricted from roaming in them. . . .
>
> It was said that when *paalraayiit* came to a person, they swam all over his body. And many came swimming up and down in front of his nose . . . Once they've entered a person, the person would soon be destroyed.

They were *paalraayiit* for many years, then they'd turn into *amikuut*. Out on the lowlands they'd see their tracks. When I was a girl I heard people talking about seeing their tracks. I'd hear them say that they saw some strange cracks in the lowlands back there. They'd say that they were tracks of *amikuut*.

Back when we observed the *eyagyarat* [traditional taboos], they told us not to roam in the mountains during that time. It was said that the *paalraayiit* were attracted to *caagnitellriit* . . . And later on in life, the person would begin to suffer from bodily ailments. They throw sharp stones at the *caagnitellriit*. They'd suffer from that later on in life and die.

(10 September 1997, Tape 2b)

Annie Blue's account meant different things to those assembled in Berlin. For me, it was exciting to hear her solve a long-standing scholarly riddle. But Annie's motive for telling this story was not academic. As she made plain in her telling, rules guided a young person's actions in the past, and we ignore these rules today at our peril. She wants the younger generation to hear her stories and gain awareness of their history so that they can avoid very real dangers in the world today.

Later an enormous king salmon net made of braided willow bark inspired Paul John to tell the story of a king salmon swimming upriver, choosing which net to enter based on its condition. Like Annie's story, Paul's tale was not intended as remembrances of the past as much as advice for the future.

Academics like myself were not the elders' primary audience. Rather, I was the mother, the guide. Yet listening, I learned much that would be of great interest to both the Yup'ik and academic communities. For example, I learned that dog faeces was a common binding agent in shaping clay pots. Paul John described how aged seal blood was used as glue, and how carvers collected and dried sea foam to use as sandpaper to polish wooden bowls. Examining two small carved faces with chin labrets, he explicitly stated the connection between humans and animals which I had always hoped to hear (Fienup-Riordan 1990). He said, 'The Nunivaarmiut used these ornaments on their chins. It was said that these represented walrus tusks. When men wore them they were pretending to be walrus.'

Later we looked at a large mask with five-fingered hands projecting from its side (Fienup-Riordan 1996: 79, 180–96). Wassilie Berlin recognized it as a representation of *qunguq* reaching its hand out of the sea and putting it down on the ice. According to Wassilie, the hole in the hand was where the hunter aimed his harpoon. Wassilie's comment constitutes the most explicit explanation of this iconographic feature that I have ever heard.

Objects also evoked disclaimers about what they were not. For instance, Paul John looked at one carved figure (IVA3677) and said, 'This figure doesn't represent Qupurruyuli. But let me mention it since it suddenly came to mind.' He then continued with a rare account of Qupurruyuli, the woman of the sea with flowing hair, who created a pathway through the ice for the hunter who owned her as a power source (see also Fienup-Riordan 1994: 258):

When the travelling companions became curious, they looked and saw a pair of human hands in front of his kayak visible from down below. And since the hands were extended like this, the ice in the front was being moved to the sides, making a pathway for the kayak to glide through. The upper part of the person's long hair was visible above the water with the bottom part down below. And when they looked down from their kayaks they saw the rest of her hair in the water. Since Qupurruyuli was a woman, her hair was very, very long. They all continued to move forward in the ice.

Then just before they came out into the open water, the person behind the leader accidentally bumped into the tail of his kayak. Then suddenly the ice jammed up in front of them. But, since they were close to the open water, they dragged their kayaks through the ice the rest of the way.

Since this figure suddenly reminded me of that story, I've just recounted it. The man who had Qupurruyuli as a power source was able to use it when he was in trouble in the ocean. He was able to help not only himself, but also his travelling companions using his Qupurruyuli.

(11 September 1997, Tape 3a)

Not all stories inspired by the collection were deemed appropriate to be told. While looking at bags made of raven skins, the men remembered a raven story so embarrassing that they could not talk about it in front of us women lest it make us uncomfortable when we had intercourse with our husbands. The women later agreed that they 'did not mind not hearing it'.

Among the most moving accounts was Wassilie's and Catherine's description of a small drum (apqara'arcuun) used by men and women in private. Holding the drum in front of their face, they would hit it from the front to summon their avneq (lit., 'other half', felt presence) with song. All had observed this when they were young and remembered the power of these private ritual acts.

Along with stories, Jacobsen's collection also evoked many songs. A loonskin hat for the sweat bath brought out a song about a loon, complete with its call. Holding two stuffed squirrels from Nushagak, Annie Blue told a story about squirrel and ptarmigan singing a slow-style ingula song. Wassilie sang the arrow song of the famous warrior Apanuugpak while we looked at slate blades. In fact, objects made of slate were particularly poignant as they had been used before these elders were born.[3]

We even recorded the sounds of the objects, holding up a caribou-tooth belt to record the teeth tinkling against empty bullet shells or shaking a pair of thumbless dance mittens to hear the wooden dangles. Marie's response to one song was, 'That's a good one, we'll have to bring it back.' Just as objects evoked songs and stories, we sometimes treated songs and sounds as objects to take home.

Last but not least, we told jokes. When we looked at a large wooden bowl, Paul said off the record that it was Apanuugpak's homebrew pot, but said he wouldn't say that on the tape because it wasn't true. When examining a fishskin bag with delicately inset raven's foot designs, Paul quipped, 'They represent our impending trip to Germany. It's exactly what happened recently. Here is the jet plane and here are its tracks.' When we looked at a double bowl with a handle (IVA3902), Wassilie designated it an iqvarcuutet, a device for gathering berries, one side for blackberries and the other for red. Looking at a similar bowl (IVA4217), Paul said it was a bowl for twins, and Wassilie added that one side was for pee and one for poop. This Yup'ik ribaldry brought on peels of laughter in the privacy of collections. When we were in public, however, Wassilie was constantly putting his finger to his lips in a futile attempt to hush us giggling women. Catherine agreed that we should not laugh in the presence of strangers, as they might think we were laughing at them.

ELDERS' REFLECTIONS ON THE BROADER SIGNIFICANCE OF COLLECTIONS

We looked at many rare things while in Berlin: thumbless gloves worn by a young girl during her first menstruation, an eagle-feather hood, a painted bladder, and ice skates carved in the shape of puffins. Yet I think the elders were not as impressed by what they saw as by what they heard from our hosts and from each other. Along with sharing what they knew, each elder eagerly listened to companions, learning as well as teaching. In the middle of our trip Andy said that he was reminded of what his father had taught him – that when you die you are still learning. And we were learning first and foremost from each other.

Wassilie spoke eloquently on the last day of our visit. He expressed his gratitude to Jacobsen, who lived in such a harsh environment so far from home to collect these objects. He also expressed his gratitude to the museum for the good care they were giving these things. He was impressed by the meticulous organization of objects and glad that they would be there for his children's children to observe, 'Gosh, I'm so grateful for what he did. If he hadn't collected them, they would have disappeared long ago. Not one of the items would be visible now if our counterparts, the white people, hadn't collected them.' Most of all he expressed gratitude to his fellow group members for all they had taught him. He had not realized how much there was to learn from these old things, and he was grateful that he had been chosen to come. Later he added that he would like to do this kind of work again, although he hoped he would not have to travel so far.

Catherine also expressed her gratitude, as well as her desire that the things we had learned be brought home, 'I'm thankful that we came here even though it's far from home. My hope is that if these things of our ancestors were seen by a group of our people, or if they were used to educate our young people, that they would begin to stimulate their minds.'

Andy Paukan, the teacher, also spoke of his desire that what we had learned would be brought home for the benefit of the younger generation: 'Our work seems to have opened up times ahead and filled it with information. . . . With this work, our roots and culture will come closer to us.' Yet his pride was mixed with regret. He concluded, 'Evidently, [our ancestors] lived a clean life. Their life was very good. By looking at their work, I envy them.'

A determined leader as well as an eloquent orator, Paul John's words on his last day in Berlin were perhaps the most pointed and far-reaching, moving beyond the walls of the museum. Doing his first fieldwork in a non-English-speaking country, he had been observing the German people, and he was impressed, 'Here in Germany, I see that people truly live according to their tradition. I see that they have kept their ways and traditions.' He contrasted their cultural integrity to the situation back home in southwestern Alaska.

> When I think about our home, I feel sad realizing that we Yupiit are not holding on to our traditional ways. And through my observation of this land and its people,

I've realized that by not holding onto our traditional ways, our home and its people have become confused about their own identity.

Since our ways are confused and our minds are not in harmony, our culture has become weak. If pictures of the things we saw here were seen by our descendants, it might help to reunite the people. And our descendants might begin to believe in themselves and their culture. Perhaps they will soon desire to live like their ancestors and begin to unite in their ways and thinking.

Even though I've heard about the vast ocean, I had not pictured it in my mind before. And since I came here, by looking at the time difference I now believe that we indeed have reached the other side of the ocean. When night comes to our families back home it would be morning here. Our places are so far apart.

Though we live far apart, we've realized that people here have held onto their culture, and though this place is populated, life here is pretty quiet . . . and we haven't seen any disturbance or problems between people. . . .

God indeed created many tribes of people with our own traditional ways and beliefs which were to be practised until the end of the world.

Finally, Paul spoke about how our work in the museum might help to remedy this situation.

When we were looking at the objects that were once used by our ancestors, I began to realize that they were persevering and hardworking people. They had total control of their lives and were self-reliant. Evidently, they took total responsibility for their lives even though it was a very difficult lifestyle. Though they didn't have excellent tools, their workmanship was so fine. The fact that they had taken care of themselves could be seen by their work. Western-made material was totally gone from their work. Gosh, our ancestors took charge of their lives, truly living in their traditional culture. . . .

Since we have no understanding, we've abandoned our cultural ways. But those of us that came here have been granted more understanding regarding our people. We have a better understanding that we should retain our cultural ways until the end of the world. . . .

My vision is this. Many of us seem to have been in the dark for many years. And now, stories and information about our roots have emerged from this unknown, faraway place across the ocean. Now that the knowledge is out, I hope our work together will be written and be presented to our people. I hope that the pictures of our work will be shared with the people. And if it's possible, I hope the objects would be exhibited in the villages or at a museum in Bethel. . . .

If our people begin to see them and begin to understand the culture of our ancestors, they might begin to believe and gain pride in their own identity. I envision our people gaining more faith in their own identity by seeing the objects or seeing their pictures or reading about them in books. My hope is that our work will bring our people closer to their own culture.

Much more important than any specific information they evoke, Paul sees collections as tools capable of teaching self-reliance and pride to young people who have grown up as second-class citizens in an English-only world. Knowledge is power, and it is Paul's strong hope that young people use this long-hidden knowledge as ammunition in their battle to take control of their land and lives.

Since our return, these elders have been honoured in different ways. Catherine Moore's family gave her a surprise birthday feast on her return to Anchorage. Paul John has publicly described his experiences, eloquently stating how looking at these old things has increased his understanding of his own people. Togiak threw a village-wide potluck dinner for Annie Blue on the Friday following her return, after which she showed the pictures she had taken with her pocket camera and described her experiences. In October she was flown into Anchorage to receive the Alaska Federation of Natives' 'Elder of the Year' award, including a beautiful wristwatch which she joked she would keep on German time.

CONCLUSION

The subtitle of this chapter, 'Fieldwork turned on its head', refers to the project's reversal of the traditional fieldwork paradigm in cultural anthropology. Whereas anthropologists are known to travel to distant lands to study the resident natives, in this case native elders travelled to one home of anthropology – the museum – to do their own fieldwork, coming to their own conclusions about the value of the ethnographic collections they explored. Archaeologists and material culture specialists within anthropology have always done research in museum storerooms, and Franz Boas, Alfred Kroeber, and George Byron Gordon are but a few anthropologists who had indigenous people working in their collections. The thrust of their work was to increase non-natives' knowledge and understanding of native peoples, but in this case it is the natives who seek an understanding of both collections and the collection process so that they can use them for their own ends.

Our project is neither the first nor the only one of its kind. Bernadette Driscoll (1995) travelled to European and Canadian museums with Canadian Inuit seamstresses in the 1980s to study Inuit clothing styles and the terminology and symbolism associated with them. This fieldwork triggered a renaissance in clothing manufacture in some Canadian communities (see also Issenman 1985, 1990, 1991). In the early 1980s Susan Kaplan (pers. com. 1998) invited North Greenland Inuit to work in the museum, and continues to work with Labrador Inuit using the Peary-MacMillan Arctic Museum and Arctic Studies Center collections. In the 1990s the repatriation movement has prompted increased access to and scrutiny of museum collections by members of various native groups, often in collaboration with museum professionals. For example, Deanna Kingston (forthcoming) has worked with King Island elders in the film archives of the National Museum of Natural History, while Steve Loring and Aron Crowell of the Smithsonian's Arctic Studies Center have explored NMNH collections with a number of Alaska Natives.

Yup'ik elders' work in the Museum für Völkerkunde is an example of what I have described elsewhere as 'visual repatriation' (Fienup-Riordan 1996: 23–30). As in Yup'ik elders' comments on masks and mask-making in preparation for the *Agayuliyararput* exhibit, their primary concern was not to reclaim museum objects but to re-own the knowledge and experiences that the objects embodied. And, as in the mask exhibit, instead of resentment at what has been lost and taken from them, elders expressed profound gratitude toward both the collectors, without whom the objects would surely have been destroyed, and the museums, who so carefully preserve these objects today. While repatriation and struggles for the physical control of objects remain contentious issues, Yup'ik elders' work in collections provides a lesson in how native access to collections can work to everyone's benefit.

There is a lesson here for museology as well. During recent decades, museum professionals have become more specialized, often training in curation and conservation rather than anthropology or history. They are not researchers themselves, and their primary responsibility is to the objects, not to the people whose ancestors made them. Their focus on the care and protection of objects can have disastrous consequences for visiting indigenous groups. I have accompanied Yup'ik elders on visits to museums thousands of miles from home and watched as their days in collections shrank to hours as they waited for museum handlers to access objects, present them one at a time, and remove them before going on to the next piece. In contrast, our German hosts provided ideal circumstances to explore collections, giving us the space, time, and privacy we needed. As a result elders moved into collections, owning them in ways more restricted access would have made impossible.

Although a number of indigenous people have made short visits to the Museum für Völkerkunde's world-famous ethnographic collections, ours was the first native group to carry out a systematic study of an entire collection. Staff members were initially concerned both for the safety of their collections and wary of native efforts to reclaim them. They were, however, willing to allow the visit, and their respect for these indigenous researchers grew as the days went by. Our workspace was in a large, well-lit, open hallway between the museum's storage room and exhibit space, and passing staff members often stopped to watch the elders' animated interactions with collections, ask questions, and share in their excitement. Moreover, elders' expressions of thanks reassured them that it was not the objects that elders coveted but the opportunity to use them both to teach and to learn. Not one object was broken or damaged during our three-week stay. Instead each was enriched with myriad bits of information, stories, and songs.

As I boarded the plane to Berlin, exhausted by efforts to get passports for elders with multiple names and dates of birth, I vowed that I would never again try to take elders to objects. A week later, however, I knew absolutely that it was worth the effort. Ironically, though fragile objects like grass socks and gut-skin parkas will endure in museum collections, elders will not. If we do not bring elders into museums over the next decade, we will lose an opportunity to understand collections in ways that Jacobsen and his contemporaries never imagined. More important than any specific information, in the hands of community leaders throughout southwestern Alaska this knowledge of the past has the potential to shape the future.

ACKNOWLEDGEMENTS

I want to acknowledge my friend and teacher, Jim VanStone, as the inspiration for this article. Jim was originally invited to travel to Germany with our group, not as an outside expert but as an elder among elders. A bad back prevented him from making the trip, and I especially wanted him to share in the high points of our expedition.

Jim is a renaissance anthropologist of the first order, and his interests are among the most diverse of any Arctic scholar I know. From our first meeting in Chicago in 1974, when I was an energetic student completely lacking in the experiences he already possessed in abundance, he has never failed to offer sound criticism and good advice. On my draft dissertation he politely inquired, 'Are you sure red salmon run before kings?' No other colleague has given me more encouragement, a debt I can acknowledge but never repay.

Work in Germany was made possible by a grant from the National Science Foundation, Office of Polar Programs, and the Rockefeller Foundation. The project could not have gone forward without the help of the Museum für Völkerkunde, especially their curator for North American Ethnology, Peter Bolz. The translations were prepared by my associate, Marie Meade, who has been a full partner in this research project. Thanks also to Igor Krupnik for the invitation to present these preliminary results at the Jesup Centenary Conference at the American Museum of Natural History in November 1997.

Finally, thanks to Susan Kaplan, Allen McCartney, my husband Dick Riordan, and, of course, Jim VanStone, for their many useful comments on an earlier draft of this paper.

NOTES

1   In fact, the outset of the Krause expedition was a major reason that the Royal Museum was able to secure funding for Jacobsen's expedition. Berlin high society had no intention of being bested by Bremen.

2   I mention this battle to alert future researchers to problems I encountered while obtaining passports for Yup'ik-speaking elders. Our negotiation with Passport Services was more than difficult. In the end neither Paul John nor Catherine Moore could receive a regular passport as neither could produce two qualifying documents with the same name and date of birth. Both had baptismal certificates and recorded birthdates in Catholic mission records, but as Paul John was a much-loved only child with a multitude of names and Catherine was born during the 1918 influenza epidemic, following which her parents died and she was adopted, names and dates in these official records were conflicting. Thanks to the intervention of Senator Ted Stevens' office, both elders received temporary passports, but otherwise neither would have been able to make the trip.

3   This is a real strength of Jacobsen's collection, as he had intentionally sought out 'ancient things'.

2

THE OBJECT IN VIEW

Aborigines, Melanesians, and museums

Lissant Bolton

There is a cartoon by the New Yorker cartoonist Charles Barsotti that shows a man in a suit and tie standing before a glass display case, looking with respectful awe at the single small pot within it. The caption reads, 'The wonder of it all' (Figure 2.1). This cartoon sums up something that I greatly value about museums: the way in which objects can open horizons of knowledge and imagination that are rich and moving. Through

Figure 2.1 'The Wonder of It All'. (© The New Yorker Collection 1986 Charles Barsotti from cartoonbank.com. All Rights Reserved.)

the practices of collection and public exhibition, museums have developed a discipline of looking – a way of retrieving meaning from objects. This meaning is comprehended imaginatively by each viewer and often depends on the object as a conceptual opening through which the viewer can pass to apprehend another time or another place. Museums, in this sense, are about the pleasure of eye and mind, and as Barsotti suggests, such seeing and imagining often incorporate awe and wonder at the object, at other times and other places.

The discipline of looking is a particular cultural practice, one that has crossed many national boundaries but which belongs to a specific Euro-American tradition. Its distinctive character is that it depends on the disconnection of objects from the contexts in which they were made and used. It is because the objects are disconnected that they can represent, and thus become a way to imagine, those contexts. The objects become, as Roy Wagner puts it, 'strategic relics' (1981: 28).

Different traditions of museology place different constraints on this process of imagination. Art museums usually provide a minimum of information and context for the object, allowing visitors free rein in their engagement with the object (albeit as art). In art museums the 'wonder of it all' approach predominates. The practices of ethnographic and history museums are different. The principle by which ethnographic collecting operates is that objects are collected on the assumption, or with the intention, that their significance in the situation in which they were collected will be retained. As a consequence, ethnographic museums usually impose a particular set of meanings on objects through label text and illustrations, presenting these meanings not as interpretation but as fact.

Changing theoretical developments in anthropology and related disciplines have been influential in altering understandings of museum collection and display. In recent years debates about the connection between object and meaning have become part of the discourse of museology and museum anthropology. As these disciplines have become increasingly sophisticated, the idea that the meaning of the objects to their original makers and users can be retained in any straightforward sense has been called into question. The small pot in Barsotti's cartoon is accorded honour by being placed alone in its glass case, an invitation to the viewer to look at it with awe. Its journey across time and space from its maker to the case gives it a significance as a survivor, which it could not have had to its maker. The meaning of objects is affected by their context: as objects are moved from context to context, their significance changes. The way in which the meaning of objects is affected by their immediate context is an increasingly recognized problem in ethnographic collection management and display.

With the development of these ideas has come also the recognition that such meanings are rarely without moral and political dimensions. Objects are collected and displayed in specific political and intellectual environments. Much early ethnographic collecting was made with the assumption that objects and information were all that would remain of certain communities. The objects were to represent a people and a way of life that would soon no longer exist. The earliest recommendation that an Australian institution collect ethnographic material, for example, seems to have been George Bennet's 1832 suggestion that the Australian Museum collect artefacts and skulls 'as lasting memorials of an extinct population' (cited in Specht 1979: 141). Bennet assumes that the settler community had a moral and intellectual right to document the very people whose society their own was understood to be destroying.

There is also often an explicit political purpose in the display of ethnographic collections. Flora Kaplan's edited volume *Museums and the 'Making of Ourselves'* demonstrates how, for newly independent nations, the gathering of objects can contribute to a notion of national unity. In her introduction Kaplan argues, 'Each country uses its museums to represent and reconstitute itself anew in each generation' (1994: 4). Thus Emmanuel Kasaherou, then director of the Musée Territorial de Noumea, wrote about the development of the Jean-Marie Tjibaou Cultural Centre, a French colonial initiative that opened in 1998 in Noumea, New Caledonia, that it was being built 'to use our past Kanak roots as a base from which to develop a new evolving culture which includes the whole population of the country' (1995: 32).

Although such changing theoretical developments have been influential in altering understandings of museum collection and display, by far the most important factor in bringing changes to ethnographic museum practice has been the influence of indigenous communities. In the last two decades indigenous Australians and Melanesians, among others, have entered museums and brought with them a series of ideas about the meaning of objects that have unsettled and irretrievably altered the ways in which ethnographic collections can be imagined and understood. This impact is not singular in its effect. The engagement between indigenous communities and museums has taken many forms and had many consequences.

This chapter looks at some of the alterations to museum practice introduced by indigenous involvement by considering the way indigenous Australians and Melanesians have engaged with the idea, and the reality, of museums. I have a specific relationship to this material. Raised in the Euro-American tradition of museum-going and thereby educated to perceive the wonder of it all, I have spent a good deal of my working life in museums. I was an ethnographic collection manager at the Australian Museum in Sydney for many years, my employment spanning the period during which that museum began to employ and to refer to indigenous Australians in dealing with its Aboriginal collections. In 1989 I also became a voluntary staff member and adviser to the Vanuatu Cultural Centre. I was brought up, so to speak, in a Western professional museum context and have learned another perspective through interaction in the museum with indigenous Australians and Melanesians. The changes and the debates that I discuss here are matters in which I have myself participated to some extent, and my participation has inevitably coloured my understanding of these processes.

The diversity of indigenous perspectives on museums can be illustrated with two quotations. The first is from the recommendations of the UNESCO regional seminar held in Adelaide in 1978, at which indigenous Australians spoke forcefully about their desire for access to public collections of Aboriginal material culture in Australia. They argued for 'the important role that owners and leaders of particular cultural traditions can have in giving life to existing collections of lifeless objects' (Edwards and Stewart 1980: 13). The second quotation comes from Lawrence Foana'ota, director of the Solomon Islands Museum, 'Some people . . . still regard [the museum] as a dumping place for old, meaningless, and dead objects that no longer have any value or use to the communities in the provinces' (1994: 100). Both statements suggest that objects have no life when they are disconnected from the people who can give them meaning. The Adelaide recommendation urges a reconnection to resuscitate the objects, while the Solomon Islanders described by Foana'ota see the museum as a place to put objects that are past their use-by date, objects that have no further significance to their makers and users.

The assumption of settler superiority and authority set out in George Bennet's suggestion that the Australian Museum collect Aboriginal material as 'lasting memorials' was the assumption behind ethnographic collecting in Australia for many decades. For indigenous Australians, instituting some form of control over how museums use collections of Aboriginal material has been of considerable importance in asserting the vigour of their population and in reversing the assumption of colonial authority. A turning point was the Adelaide UNESCO seminar, which was co-organized with the recently founded Aboriginal Arts Board. The seminar itself arose out of changes in the political and social climate in Australia and was fuelled in part by the referendum of 1967. Indigenous delegates claimed the right of Aboriginal people to influence the management of objects used to represent their communities and the presentation of their knowledge and practice in exhibitions. They focused on the need for the employment of Aboriginal staff to manage Aboriginal collections and for greater indigenous involvement in the development of exhibition and education programmes, and they raised concerns about the management of secret/sacred or restricted objects and the management and reburial of collections of Aboriginal human remains. Jim Specht, who attended the seminar for the Australian Museum, says that indigenous participants 'repeatedly criticized Australian museums and their boards of management for their insensitivity, arrogance and exclusiveness' (Specht and MacLulich 1996: 31). The proceedings include a long list of recommendations (Edwards and Stewart 1980).

Crucial to the Adelaide seminar, and to the ongoing transformations that have developed from and beyond it, is the concept of cultural property. In popular usage today, the idea of 'culture' is often framed primarily in terms of ownership and rights. The relationship between indigenous people and museums is politicized by ideas about culture as ownership, and these ideas are embodied in the term 'cultural property'. This term developed within UNESCO, and it is defined, somewhat laboriously, by the 1970 UNESCO *Convention on the Means of Prohibiting and Preventing the Illicit Import, Export, and Transfer of Ownership of Cultural Property*.[1] UNESCO defines cultural property at the level of the state and refers to it as property designated as important by the state itself. As this term has come into common use, however, at least in museums, it usually operates with reference to much smaller groups, which are usually designated as 'traditional owners'. Cultural property is spoken of as belonging to traditional owners – that is, to the makers and users of the object or to their descendants, descent being loosely defined so that it can refer to a specific family or an entire ethnic group.

This idea of cultural property has had a significant impact at a conceptual level within Australia. It challenges the settler assumption of a moral and intellectual right to speak about the knowledge and practice of indigenous peoples. Instead, it allows that the descendants of the makers and users of ethnographic objects have a moral right to determine the meaning and often, in consequence, the use of those objects – or at the very least to prohibit certain meanings and uses. This moral right applies even where the legal ownership of the objects lies in other hands – specifically, in the hands of public institutions. That is to say, the right is often observed by museums in their practices of collection management and display, even where it has not yet been formally enshrined in the institution's policies. The relationship between acceptance of the idea of cultural property and the adoption of formal policies that acknowledge it is a complex one.

For most objects in ethnographic collections, details of provenance and producer are not known, and therefore the concept of cultural property is applied generally, the right to speak about objects being allocated to all the people who could be classified as belonging to the group from which the makers and users come. In the Australian context, this means that any indigenous Australian is understood to have a greater right to speak about any Aboriginal object than any non-indigenous Australian. The consequences of such an approach are profound. The political and emotional needs of indigenous Australians with respect to objects have a very considerable force. Museum collections have become one of the loci of Aboriginal reclamation of a traditionally derived identity and, more specifically, of the reclamation of cultural autonomy.

Australian museums have by now accepted most of the recommendations from the Adelaide seminar and have made many changes in the way they operate. All museums in Australia now recognize the moral rights of traditional owners with respect to collections of secret objects. Respecting Aboriginal sensitivities about this material, no museum now displays, or allows research access to, Aboriginal secret material, even when very little is known about the individual objects. This development involves a radical alteration in museum practice, since the objects are no longer available for display or for other kinds of research. Most museums have further accepted the principle that if specific traditional owners can be identified, a secret object should be returned, in actual and legal transfer. These returns are made possible where there has been no radical break in the meaning of these objects to their owners – where the meaning of the specific object is remembered. That is to say, while the significance of the object is altered by its sojourn in a museum storeroom, to its owners it holds continuing significance, which can be taken up again upon its return to them.

All major museums now employ Aboriginal staff, so much so that in some instances, such as that of the Museum of Victoria, the majority of the Indigenous Studies Department staff are Aboriginal. Most museums defer to Aboriginal consultative or advisory committees in making decisions about exhibition and education programmes, as well as about collection management. No museum in Australia now displays or allows research access to Aboriginal human remains or secret or restricted material, and significant numbers of objects in both categories have been returned to their traditional owners.[2] This transformation has been formal in the Museums Australia policy statement *Previous Possessions, New Obligations* (1996), a document intended to guide museums in framing their own procedures for dealing with indigenous Australians. In the introduction, the president of Museums Australia, Des Griffin, declares, 'This . . . policy is intended to recognize the fact that Aboriginal and Torres Strait Islander peoples have a right to be involved in all aspects of care, management and presentation of their culture' (1996: 2).

As well as becoming involved in state museums, many Aboriginal communities, especially those in rural southeastern Australia, have also set up their own small museums and cultural centres, which range from displays in Aboriginal community offices to purpose-built small museums such as the one in Shepparton in Victoria. A number of communities have modified existing buildings for the display of Aboriginal material, such as the Nungera Museum at Maclean in northern New South Wales, which was established in an old bank building in the mid-1980s. In 1998, for example, there were in New South Wales eight community museums and another four shopfront displays set up in community offices and the like; an Aboriginal centre at Wallaga Lake, which operates tours and other programmes for the tourist market; and a centre at Foster concerned with issues of archaeological heritage. Aboriginal community museums are established through the medium of Aboriginal land councils or other incorporated bodies, and are funded from state and federal funding bodies. The Aboriginal and Torres Strait Islander Commission is a strong source of funding support for such projects.

Until the last few years, Aboriginal communities in northern and western Australia took a different approach to museums. In a context in which objects are still being made and used, local priorities have focused on the storage and protection of important objects, leading to the foundation of Keeping Places, where objects are kept until needed for use. Over the last three or four years, however, Margaret West, of the Northern Territory Museum, reports (pers. com. 1998) that there has been a trend toward the development of more conventional museums with conservative, object-based displays. The Djomi Museum at Maningrida, the Bukularrnggay Museum at Yirrkala, and a Wadeye community museum at Port Keats have all been assisted by the Regional Museums Program of the Northern Territory Museum to develop exhibitions designed largely for visitors. West comments that in all cases the local community concentrates their interest not on the objects but on photographs, both archival photographs and photos of living people. Local people are not, she says, as interested in looking at objects that are still being made in the community. In the case of both the museum at Port Keats and the one at Bathurst Island, collections focus as much on repatriated archival material such as photographs and publications as on objects. Both of these museums were founded with the assistance of church groups, and they have a historical emphasis and act as a community resource centre.

Major state museums provide training and support services to all such regional initiatives, partly as a result of financial assistance to them from the Aboriginal and Torres Strait Islander Commission. The Australian Museum, for example, now has an Aboriginal Heritage Unit with two indigenous Australian staff who visit and assist New South Wales Aboriginal communities involved in cultural preservation and provide various training options for community members involved in regional museums and cultural centres. One of the problems that indigenous community museums of this kind face is that there are few objects known to derive from these areas in either public or private collections. Most state museums have established loan programmes, which enable objects to be returned to the region and community from which they are understood to come on temporary or semi-permanent loan. This process returns objects not only to communities but also, significantly, to a place.

Of course, by no means all members of Aboriginal communities are interested in local museums and cultural centres. Such small museums are often the result of the driving interest of one or several community members, and if that person or group withdraws from the project for some reason, support from the wider community is often insufficient to sustain it. The Nungera Museum at Maclean, for example, was largely the initiative of a woman named Joyce Clague, and when she ceased to be involved in the project, the museum died. The fluctuations of interest in community museums may also reflect a political reality: the establishment of a museum and the return to it of Aboriginal objects deriving from the local region asserts Aboriginal control over Aboriginal identity. These actions do not involve ongoing engagement with either the museum or the objects, and contemporary museological preoccupation with conservation, research, and display may be of little interest to the local community. The meaning of the objects has to do with their ownership and control and location, and once these are obtained, their individual significance may often not be important.

Within major museums, Aboriginal staff and advisers also sometimes redirect attention away from the existing ethnographic collections. One of the objections that indigenous Australians have consistently made against museums has been that Aboriginal society is presented as if it were timeless, as if it existed in a nonspecific ethnographic present on which the European incursion has made little impact. Many museums were founded to capture the disintegrating image of this timeless present, and for this reason, most museums refused to collect objects that obviously incorporated European goods and concepts. Indigenous Australian have consistently pressed museums to present images of their contemporary concerns and preoccupations. One of the Adelaide seminar recommendations encourages established museums and art galleries to 'mount exhibitions and special displays detailing contemporary Aboriginal and Torres Strait Island issues and aspirations and Aboriginal cultural and social history of the recent past' (Edwards and Stewart 1980: 13). The 1996 Museums Australia policy document sets out this same emphasis on contemporary Aboriginal experience in more forceful language, 'Aboriginal and Torres Strait Islander cultures must be presented as vital, living, diverse and changing' (1996: 8, point 4.3).

These objectives achieved one expression in an exhibition that opened at the Australian Museum in March 1997, *Indigenous Australians: Australia's First Peoples*. This exhibition was designed largely by Aboriginal people; both museum staff and members of New South Wales Aboriginal communities were consulted on the exhibition's content, which focused primarily on the post-contact history of Aboriginal people and on such issues as stolen children. The museum's important ethnographic collections do not feature to any significant extent in the displays. Far more important to NSW Aboriginal people is the opportunity to present their own image of themselves in an institution that formerly presented only its account of their lives and concerns.

Developments at the Museum of Victoria follow a similar trend. The Indigenous Cultures Program in this museum operates a number of projects not directly related to material culture. These include community language workshops and family history and photographic research programmes. Gaye Sculthorpe, head curator of the Museum of Victoria Indigenous Cultures Program, says that there is less Aboriginal community interest in objects than in these other programmes (pers. com. 1998). Many Aboriginal objects deriving from what is now Victoria are, however, on loan to Aboriginal community museums within the state. Displays at the Museum of Victoria itself are concerned especially with twentieth-century Aboriginal history, and object acquisitions reflect this focus. In 1996, for example, the museum acquired a truck used by a boxing troupe that comprised Aboriginal and non-Aboriginal boxers.[3]

Up to the end of the Second World War, expatriate concern about the disappearance of Melanesian local knowledge and practice led to the making of collections for European and Australian museums rather than to the founding of museums in the region. Only gradually, as these places took on a coherent image as distinct entities (as colonies and incipient nations), did regional museums appear. A museum was founded in Papua New Guinea in 1954, in Vanuatu in 1956, and in the Solomon Islands in 1969. The exception is the New Caledonian Museum, founded in 1863. All these institutions were founded by expatriates and were staffed mainly by expatriates until each country achieved independence. As in Australia, the indigenous community did not begin to enter these museums as staff, or even as visitors, until the late 1970s. In Melanesia, the employment of local staff in the museum was part of the process of acting upon independence.

Melanesian museums, like those in Australia, have become a focal point for the negotiation of ideas about culture and cultural heritage. But the concept of culture has entirely different political implications in Papua New Guinea, the Solomons, and Vanuatu than for indigenous Australians. Independence restored political autonomy at a time when many rural Melanesians were living in a way that was consistent with their precolonial knowledge and practice. They suffered less of a radical break with their past, even though much has changed. Although developments such as the growth of urban and political elites are creating increasing rural alienation, indigenous culture is not at present a locus of political protest. Melanesians are not asserting their identity in opposition to the state by claiming the objects in the national museum as their own cultural property, nor is there any protest against the presentation of local knowledge and practice through exhibitions. Museums are a focus for the presentation and negotiation of ideas about cultural identity at a state level, but they are generally not important to the wider population.

This situation has come about partly because of the way in which the idea of 'custom' has been formulated in the Melanesian nations. In common usage the terms used in the Melanesian pidgins – *kastam* (PNG), *kastomu* (Solomon Islands), and *kastom* (Vanuatu) – refer not to objects but to knowledge and practice, to dances, songs, stories, indigenous medicine and magic, and so on. Public occasions that celebrate custom tend to be arts festivals and regional shows of various descriptions, reinforcing this perception. Objects are not featured in these contexts except as body ornamentation and dance props. Most of the objects that continue to be made and used in village contexts are not objectified as 'custom'; rather their meanings are a product of their immediate context.

If one problem facing Melanesian museum staff is the indifference of the wider population, another is the difficulty of reconciling local conditions and concerns with international museum practice. International organizations such as UNESCO and the International Council for Museums are active in the Pacific region, organizing and funding conferences and training courses for regional museum staff. Most Melanesian museum professionals have become skilled in the language of museum curatorship, but struggle to find ways to implement it with minimal resources of funding and equipment and in a context where international museum standards often make little sense. The Museum of Victoria's head curator Gaye Sculthorpe commented that in Australia, Aboriginal museum staff are beginning to develop a new and distinctive style of indigenous curatorship (pers. com. 1998). In some ways another style of indigenous curatorship is also developing in the Pacific. If Aboriginal curatorship is built on the principle of the reconnection between object and traditional owner, Melanesian curatorship is developing around the idea of an ongoing, uninterrupted connection.

In general, Melanesian museums hold few old objects in their collections. With the exception of the PNG Museum, which has acquired significant numbers of objects through repatriation, especially through the repatriation of the MacGregor Collection from the Queensland Museum, most items in their collections were acquired within the last three decades. Often the objects in the museum are the sorts of objects that are still being used, or are at least remembered, in the places from which they come. This means that those Melanesians who *are* interested in the museum see the objects in it as connected to recent or even present-day local knowledge and practice.

This idea of an ongoing connection is, for example, made explicit in attitudes and actions toward spirits and spiritual power. The idea that the objects in museums have dangerous spiritual powers that have to be controlled is widespread in Melanesia. In 1989, when I went to Vanuatu to catalogue the Vanuatu Cultural Centre's collection, staff arranged for a renowned sorcerer, Aviu Koli, to perform a ritual to 'kill' the power of the objects that my colleagues and I would be handling, lest we be endangered. The objects were alive with spiritual power that needed to be controlled. The centre's staff told stories of the objects restless in their glass cases at night, stories told to me with a rueful uncertainty about whether they would or could be believed. In this case, even if the specific meaning of objects to their original makers and users might not be known, a meaning was knowable by means of an occult insight that was itself part of local practice. At a meeting of Pacific region museum staff that I attended in 1995, this same issue caused delegates (especially those from Melanesia) considerable concern. They discussed at some length the danger that unrecognized spiritual power inherent in objects could and did cause curatorial staff in their own institutions and in museums elsewhere. Emmanuel Kasaherou, director of the Musée Territorial de Noumea, wrote in 1995, 'Even today there are many Kanak people who are uneasy when viewing traditional objects with supposed magical powers which could be dangerous to the viewer. With these ways of looking at traditional objects, the purpose of the museum is hard to understand' (1995: 31).

Melanesian museum staff are also often frustrated or bemused by the distinction that sets objects – material culture – apart from other aspects of local knowledge and practice. Another significant concern raised consistently at meetings of Pacific region museum staff is the management of sacred sites and other places of importance. Anthropological research increasingly recognizes the importance of places in the construction and remembering of knowledge and history in Melanesia. For regional museum staff, this issue arises at a more practical level as they see places destroyed by logging and other forms of development. Thus Soroi Eoe, director of the Papua New Guinea Museum, writes:

> Museums should . . . serve as development catalysts by assisting governments to forge their development projects in ways that better serve the people of both today and tomorrow . . . Particularly important is [museums'] involvement in multi- and bilateral aid programmes, which through mining, lumbering and drilling projects currently in operation in the Melanesian states . . . are responsible for the large-scale deforestation of enormous tracts of wilderness and the destruction of villages resulting in the displacement of their inhabitants.
>
> (Eoe 1991: 3)

That heritage site management is a responsibility of the museums in PNG, the Solomon Islands, and Vanuatu[4] is a reflection of the degree to which museums in the region are responsible not just for objects but also for cultural heritage preservation in general. The imperative to preserve objects can pale in significance when compared with the imperative to preserve places. The conflict between the development preoccu-pations of national governments and the museum's concern to sustain indigenous knowledge and practice causes great difficulty, and often a great deal of discouragement, for museum staff. In such a context, again, the preservation of individual objects can seem less critically important.

In other words, in Melanesia, as at the Museum of Victoria and other Australian museums, staff are initiating programmes of cultural revival that are not directly focused on objects. The most locally active and successful Melanesian museum is the Vanuatu Cultural Centre, and its success seems to derive in significant measure from the fact that it does not emphasize object-oriented activities. Rather, the institution has concentrated on recording oral traditions using audiotape and videotape, on promoting arts festivals, and on the maintenance and revival of local languages and rituals. The museum's efforts in these areas have been achieved through the development of a group of voluntary extension workers, known as fieldworkers, rural ni-Vanuatu[5] who work in their own villages and districts to 'document and revive' local knowledge and practice. Until the opening of a new museum building in Port Vila in 1995, the Cultural Centre paid far less attention to its collections and exhibitions than to these programmes.[6]

When the new museum building was opened, museum staff allocated to several fieldworkers cases in which to set up displays. Each worked with friends or colleagues from his own area. They were given no instruction in exhibition theory or design and no direction about display content. They were merely given the assistance of a ni-Vanuatu carpenter, who could make supports and mounts for objects, and then left to their own devices. Sometimes the fieldworkers chose to display newly made objects brought from the islands – in one case contemporary body decorations from a traditionalist enclave on Tanna, in another a newly revived form of textile, barkcloth from Erromango. Fieldworkers from Ambrym took fern-tree figures in the existing Cultural Centre collections and restored and repainted them.[7] The opening of the exhibition was immensely successful, with some thousands of visitors on opening day alone. Significantly, no labels were attached to these objects; instead, fieldworkers stood beside the displays to explain them. The museum became a kind of performance space in which ni-Vanuatu affirmed and expressed their contemporary knowledge and practice to each other.

The story of the opening exhibition of the new Vanuatu museum illustrates a further issue, which is the conflict between programmes directed at local people and programmes directed at tourists. Melanesian museums find it consistently difficult to provide resources for tourists while at the same time addressing a local audience. This conflict is evident at the most basic level, such as the arrangement of objects in exhibitions and the content of and language used in display labels. The opening exhibition in Vanuatu would have made almost no sense at all to any tourist who came in the door. There is no need to re-state here debates about the relationship between tourism and the ongoing integrity of indigenous cultural practice; rather I shall simply observe that these issues are of concern to Melanesian museums.

The concerns arise not least because, if programmes of national development affect museums through issues of site preservation, they also affect them through the issue of tourism. Governments the world over are inclined to the misapprehension that museums can help to make money from tourists, and governments in Melanesia are no exception. Nelson Paulius, representing the PNG minister of culture and tourism, said to a 1989 gathering of Pacific region museum staff:

> International tourists who visit Papua New Guinea and other Pacific island nations are fascinated by, enjoy and wish to buy our colorful and artistic arts and crafts. . . . In Papua New Guinea, our Department of Culture and Tourism will continue to encourage provincial and local governments as well as cultural groups to establish museums and cultural centres which will facilitate the performance of songs and dances and preserve traditional artefacts.
>
> (Paulius 1991: 11)

There have been some attempts in Melanesia, especially in PNG, to develop community museums and cultural centres in rural areas. Like Aboriginal community museums, these entities are often established because of the interest of one or two individuals and are dependent on the continuing interest of those individuals for their survival. Funding for these initiatives sometimes comes from national and provincial governments or from external funding agencies of various kinds. In many cases, these initiatives are designed with the intention of attracting, educating, and obtaining money from tourists, as Paulius suggests they should, but tourist numbers are rarely sufficient to sustain them, and many of them appear and disappear over a period of only a few years. Brief accounts of many of these appear in Eoe and Swadling's edited collection *Museums and Cultural Centres in the Pacific* (1991).

The situation in New Caledonia is somewhat different. One of the consequences of the signing of the Matignon–Oudinot Accords in 1988, by which France and New Caledonia agreed to move toward a referendum for independence in New Caledonia, was the foundation of the Agency for the Development of Kanak Culture (ADCK), an organization funded by the French government and created to develop and promote Kanak culture. The main project of the ADCK has been the development of the Tjibaou Cultural Centre, a remarkable building designed by Renzo Piano and constructed at a cost of 320 million French francs, which opened in 1998. The ADCK has both French and Kanak staff, but it is distinctive in the region in producing publications that refer to the Kanak population as 'they' rather than as 'we'. The emphasis of the Centre is on fusion, both of the old with the new and of the different cultural elements within New Caledonia. The Tjibaou Cultural Centre's website sets out as a goal of the institution:

> to be the principal point of interchange with other cultures existing in New Caledonia, making it the 'reference culture' by offering the Kanak inheritance as part of the general cultural heritage of the whole population of New Caledonia and, on this basis, proposing elements of common cultural reference in which artistic creation can take root.[8]

The Tjibaou Cultural Centre is also intended to be a cultural focus for the whole Pacific region, although the extraordinarily generous funding that supports the institution, as well as the European-influenced style of its programmes, sets it apart from other museums in the region. It will be a very considerable tourist attraction in its own right. The relationship it might have with rural Kanak has yet to be established.

This approach by the Tjibaou Cultural Centre runs counter to developments in the rest of the region, most particularly in the matter of staffing. In Australia it is increasingly difficult for museums to employ other than indigenous Australians to work with Aboriginal collections, and although Melanesian museums sometimes employ non-Melanesian staff on contract, their policies are to employ local staff only. As already discussed, the emphasis on indigenous staffing has led to new models in the management of ethnographic collections in the region.

Indigenous interests in museums can best be summarized in terms of contemporaneity. Although by no means all members of their communities are interested in museums, where Aborigines and Melanesians do have this interest, their interest is in using the collections, and the institutions, to address contemporary issues. Aboriginal people assert autonomy and authority through the control of collections, using museums as a venue in which they can develop wider cultural programmes. For Melanesians, museums are a vehicle through which they seek to preserve and promote local knowledge and practice. The orientation to the present is a component of what is happening in Barsotti's cartoon – the small pot in the drawing is a conceptual opening to a world that the viewer imagines and wonders at through his own present understandings and for his own present pleasure. The difference is in the attitude toward the objects themselves. Indigenous curators are interested, or not interested, in the objects in museums in the context of their present concerns. They are not necessarily interested in the objects in and of themselves.

The present director of the Vanuatu Cultural Centre, Ralph Regenvanu, expresses such ideas clearly, writing about the impact of a Swiss-French touring exhibition that was shown in Vanuatu in 1996. *Arts of Vanuatu* contained a selection of objects from the museums of Europe and was extremely successful. It was visited by more than one-third of the population of Port Vila, Vanuatu's capital, a percentage that most Western museum directors can only dream about. Regenvanu emphasizes the degree to which the ni-Vanuatu interpreted the objects in the exhibition in terms of their present concerns:

> It is the narrative, visual and material records of our traditional cultures which now provide the wellspring from which contemporary cultural identity in Vanuatu can be reassessed, contemporary artistic traditions strengthened and new and truly indigenous forms of expression created.
>
> (Regenvanu 1997: 11)

Soroi Eoe, director of the PNG Museum, expresses the same ideas in another form, 'Museums should go to the people and take an active interest in their problems' (Eoe 1991: 2).

The new models of indigenous curatorship in Australia and Melanesia are a stimulating and important development within the wider disciplines of museum curatorship and museum anthropology. They contribute to the overturning of political injustices and improprieties and bring new meanings to the objects in museum collections. The fundamental change that these models bring, however, is a shift in focus away from objects themselves. This is a very important change, and it needs to be recognized and acknowledged. The discipline of looking, which involves wonder at the object itself, is becoming in this context a thing of the past. A tradition of Euro-American scholarship is not so much disappearing as becoming, in this arena, difficult to sustain. Barsotti's cartoon may itself be becoming a way to think about another time and another place.

ACKNOWLEDGEMENTS

Many people provided information for and commentary on this chapter. I would like to thank in particular Elizabeth Bonshek, Mark Busse, Philip Gordon, Klaus Neumann, Mike O'Hanlon, Gaye Sculthorpe, Jim Specht, and Margaret West for their assistance.

NOTES

1   The UNESCO definition reads: 'For the purposes of this convention, the term 'cultural property' means property which, on religious or secular grounds, is specifically designated by each State as being of importance for archaeology, pre-history, history, literature, art or science and which belongs to the following categories: . . . (f) Objects of ethnological interest'.

2   The South Australian Museum is presently host to the federally funded National Skeletal Provenancing Project, which is directed by physical anthropologist Colin Pardoe. The aim of this project is to research unidentified Aboriginal human remains so that they can be returned to the correct social group for reburial.

3   Sculthorpe discusses the importance of presenting Aboriginal history in museums in her 1993 article 'Interpreting Aboriginal history in a museum context', *Museums Australia*, (1991–2), vols 2–3: 49–56.

4   Heritage site management is the responsibility of the Archaeology Department of the National Museum and Gallery in Papua New Guinea, the National Sites Survey of the Solomon Islands Museum, and the Vanuatu Cultural and Historical Sites Survey, a department of the Vanuatu Cultural Centre.

5   'Ni-Vanuatu' is the term used in Vanuatu to refer to the indigenous citizens of that country. Other constructions, such as 'Vanuatuan', are never used.

6   A number of publications discuss the Vanuatu Cultural Centre projects. The *Oceania* special issue *Fieldwork, Fieldworkers* discusses the impact of the fieldworker programme on research in Vanuatu in a number of different disciplines (Bolton 1999). See also Sam 1996, Bolton 1996, and Rodman 1998.

7   This restoration caused horrified fascination among Australian Museum materials conservators, who were running a conservation training course for Cultural Centre staff at that time.

8   Quoted from the Jean-Marie Tjibaou Cultural Centre Web site, *http://www.noumea.com/neacom/jmtjag.htm#A3.1.*

3

THE ARTS OF THE SIKH KINGDOMS

Collaborating with a community

Eithne Nightingale and Deborah Swallow

Museums can impact positively on the lives of disadvantaged *individuals*, act as a catalyst for social regeneration and as a vehicle for empowerment with specific *communities* and also contribute towards the creation of more equitable *societies*.

(Sandell 2002: 4)

In 1999 the Victoria and Albert Museum mounted *The Arts of the Sikh Kingdoms* to coincide with the 300th anniversary of the 1699 founding of the Sikh *khalsa* (fellowship of the pure)[1] by Guru Gobind Singh, the tenth and last Sikh Guru – a central event in the history of the Sikhs. The exhibition was an externally visible dimension of an ongoing programme of activity and dialogue between the Museum and South Asian individuals and communities which had started some decades earlier and continues today(Figure 3.1).

In her speech of welcome at the opening of the exhibition by HRH the Prince of Wales, the V&A's chairman spoke of the background and purposes of the exhibition:

> The V&A's links with the Sikh community and their art and culture are long and close. The Museum is privileged to have in its care the Golden Throne of Maharaja Ranjit Singh. Its rich collection of works of art associated with the Sikhs inspired W. G. Archer, when Keeper of the Indian Department, to challenge the prevailing views of the time and draw attention to the strength and vitality of Sikh painting. The Museum has maintained this tradition of scholarship and presentation, collaborating on Sikh exhibitions at Gunnersbury Park and Bradford . . . The project has provided exciting opportunities to enrich our relationships with the Sikh and the broader Asian communities in the UK, and with our professional counterparts in India and in Pakistan, in Europe, the USA and of course here in the UK. Without them the show would not have been the same, and we have incurred many debts of gratitude.

The speech flagged significant aspects of the project – its roots in older relationships and events, its timeliness, the international collaborations that made it possible, and the significance of its community dimension. It went on to note the importance of key objects lent by the Royal Collection and the support of other lenders and sponsors. Finally it outlined the plans for the exhibition to tour to the Asian Arts Museum, San Francisco,

Figure 3.1 Bhangra dance performance by the Jugnu Bhangra group from Gravesend on the entrance steps of the Victoria & Albert Museum, 29 May 1999. (Photograph, Hajra Shaikh, Victoria & Albert Museum)

and the Royal Ontario Museum, Toronto. But inevitably the speech could only skim the surface. This chapter attempts to look in more detail at the project, exploring the way in which a series of cross-cutting relationships with the Sikh community took shape and continue today.[2]

The V&A is Britain's national museum of art, design and the decorative arts. Founded following the Great Exhibition of 1851 as a centre of excellence and as a source of inspiration for Britain's designers and manufacturers, its declared mission is to educate and inspire generations of audiences about art and design. Amongst the Museum's collections however are materials acquired at an earlier period, and for different reasons. In 1880 the South Kensington Museum took over from the India Office a large section of the former Indian Museum (itself the descendant of the Museum of the East India Company). Besides many items acquired at international exhibitions, these collections also included objects taken at the annexation of the Panjab in 1849, notably the Golden Throne of Maharaja Ranjit Singh, the last great independent Sikh ruler. These iconic objects became the core of a larger collection of material relating to the Sikh cultural tradition, including a substantial collection of paintings of the Sikhs acquired in the twentieth century, the subject of the first ever monograph on that subject (Archer 1966), written by W. G. Archer, Keeper of the Indian Department and a former Indian Civil Servant.

Sikh connections were maintained and developed. Robert Skelton (Keeper, 1977–88) recognized the need to make the V&A's 'Indian' collections more accessible to the

UK's growing South Asian community. Skelton championed the 1978 exhibition, *The Arts of Bengal*, at the Whitechapel Art Gallery, London, which subsequently toured to Manchester in 1980 and also mounted a small exhibition of Sikh artefacts at Gunnersbury Park (1981). In 1983, following the V&A's 1982 Festival of India show, *The Indian Heritage*, a general exhibition of Indian art was sent to Bradford (Bradford Art Galleries and Museums 1983). In Bradford, Nima Poovaya Smith developed further collaborations with national institutions, a highlight being the 1991 exhibition on the arts and culture of the Sikhs entitled *Warm, Rich and Fearless* (Khushwant Singh *et al.* 1991) which also toured to other venues.

In 1990 the Nehru Gallery of Indian Art was opened, a dedicated post in South Asian arts and community education was established,[3] and community projects such as the 'Mughal Tent Project' were initiated (Akbar 1999). The 1995–6 exhibition, *The Peaceful Liberators: Jain Art from India*, drew a considerable Jain audience and 1997 (the 50th anniversary of the independence of India and Pakistan) saw two major exhibitions – *Shamiana: The Mughal Tent*, and *Colours of the Indus: Costume and Textiles from Pakistan* (Askari and Crill 1997).

In 1992 Dr Narinder Singh Kapany, a San Francisco-based Sikh businessman, expert in fibre-optics and alumnus of Imperial College, who had set up The Sikh Foundation, had been shown the Nehru Gallery by Susan Stronge. A regular visitor to the Museum, he asked whether key objects could be lent for an exhibition and conference in San Francisco which would celebrate the Foundation's 25th anniversary.[4] Short notice meant that the V&A could not lend artefacts, but Susan Stronge spoke at the conference at the Asian Art Museum of San Francisco, Kapany mounted an exhibition of books and artefacts from his own and other private collections, and an idea was born.

Over the following years the concept of an international exhibition, led by the V&A and with Susan Stronge as its curator, but with San Francisco as a partner and tour venue, gradually took shape. Kapany insistently drew the Museum's attention to the significance of the tercentenary of the founding of the Sikh *Khalsa*, which would have its main focus at the festival of *Vaisakhi*[5] in April 1999. The Museum was persuaded that an exhibition on Sikh subject matter, held at this time, would help to achieve the Museum's objective of reaching South Asian audiences. A time slot in the spring and early summer of 1999 was agreed.

The focus of the exhibition was a matter of some discussion. The V&A's role as a museum of art and design, and the particular nature of Sikhism, meant that a focus on the Sikh religion was ruled out at an early stage. Sikhism, from its inception, rejected religious imagery. This narrowed considerably the range of material available or appropriate for an art exhibition. The religion permits paintings of the Ten Gurus, but no portraits of the Gurus exist which are contemporary to their lives. Those of later dates vary considerably in quality, the best material was difficult to access, and it was felt that an exhibition based solely on paintings would have had limited appeal. Susan Stronge therefore proposed a broader theme. The exhibition would concentrate on the courtly arts of the Panjab, and would adopt an innovative approach – presenting a story of the Sikhs in nineteenth-century Panjab through works of art, with a major focus on the greatest of the Sikh rulers, Maharaja Ranjit Singh.

In order to weave the Sikh religious theme into an exhibition with a mostly secular theme, the opening section was conceived to concentrate on the holy City of Amritsar and the Harmandir (Golden Temple), which had been rebuilt by Ranjit Singh. It would then look at the artistic heritage of the Panjab and examine both the significance of the Mughal cultural legacy and Lahore as a royal capital, and the arts of the Hindu kingdoms of the Panjab hills – both of which had profoundly influenced the styles of the Sikh court. Then it would focus on the court of Ranjit Singh, looking at the Mughal emblems he adopted, at the Sikh military tradition, and at the role Europeans played at his court. Subsequent sections would explore life outside the court, the death of Ranjit Singh, the Anglo-Sikh Wars and the annexation of the Panjab and Crown property. The final sections would deal with two contrasting themes in the much-neglected period following British annexation of the Panjab in 1849 – the first time any exhibition had dealt with this subject matter. One was of particular relevance to Sikhs in Britain – the history of Ranjit Singh's son and the last Sikh king, Maharaja Dalip Singh,[6] who had been brought to Britain as a young man, had become part of Queen Victoria's family circle, but had died an exile in France having late in life recognized the loss of his Panjab and Sikh inheritance. The other would deal with the kingdoms, the courts and the continuing traditions of the Panjab from 1849 to 1900. The range of objects was to be large – from works on paper and photographs to metalwork, weapons, jewellery, textiles, woodwork and musical instruments.

The project would involve many partners – as object lenders, academic contributors and community participants. The exhibition would assemble some of the most important works of art associated with the Sikh kingdoms in the nineteenth century. Approximately half would come from the V&A's collection, but loans would be needed from public and private collections in India and Pakistan, France, Ireland and the US, and other UK sources including the Royal Collections.[7] In nearly all cases requests met a favourable response. The accompanying book would include chapters by well-known scholars and writers from the UK and the US, France, India and Pakistan.[8] The research and work of soliciting these loans and written contributions brought the curator and others into close association with individual Sikhs and Sikh organizations in all these countries.

The subject matter was complex. The sections of the exhibition that preceded the presentation of the court of Maharaja Ranjit Singh explored the significance of Lahore as an earlier royal capital, of the Mughal cultural legacy, and of the arts of the Hindu kingdoms of the Panjab hills, in order to demonstrate better the significance of the work created under Sikh patronage and inspiration. Focusing on antecedents and presenting the Sikh contribution in this broader context was likely to challenge some popular understandings of the uniqueness of the Sikh tradition amongst the Sikhs themselves. There were also other sensitivities. Key objects – the focus of the central section of the exhibition – were items taken by the British at the annexation of the Panjab. These included works of art in the Royal Collection – the so-called 'Timur Ruby', owned by several Mughal and Iranian rulers before Ranjit Singh, which had eventually come to London in 1851 as part of the Lahore State Property; the emerald and diamond belt of Maharaja Sher Singh; one of the original enamelled gold settings of the Koh-i-nur diamond[9] – and of course the Golden Throne of Ranjit Singh in the V&A's collection.[10]

The V&A's reputation as a custodian of key Sikh objects meant that there had always been visitors to see the Golden Throne. Sikh organizations and individual Sikhs regularly sought information about these and other Sikh heritage items believed (erroneously in the case of sacred relics) to be in the collection. The V&A always gave as much access as possible to the reserve collection and the archive. Once it became known that the

V&A was planning an exhibition for 1999, interest grew still further. Two young second-generation UK professional Sikhs who had developed a deep interest in Sikh military history, soon found the V&A. Although familiar with museums and libraries, Amandeep Singh Madra and Parmjit Singh only approached museum staff after they met a relative of one of the Indian Department's curators and thus met Susan Stronge. Stronge, in turn, sought advice from them on issues relating to the military section of the exhibition.

It was clear that the V&A needed the support of the wider Sikh community if the exhibition and education programme were to be successful. Susan Stronge contacted Bhai Mohinder Singh and Britain's largest Sikh *gurdwara* – the Guru Nanak Nishkam Sawak Jatha (UK) in Birmingham. The GNNSJ played an important advisory role and later provided contemporary photographs and commissioned a video[11] for the exhibition. In the meantime, the search for funds to support the exhibition was underway. The subject matter was not attractive to major corporate sponsors and approaches therefore initially concentrated on the community itself. A fund-raising gala event (entitled *By the Five Rivers*) was arranged by a ladies' committee, chaired by a Sikh, Mrs Surina Narula, but including women from across the whole of the UK South Asian community and representatives of all the South Asian religions. This raised a substantial sum for the exhibition[12] and increased awareness of the project within the Asian community.

A major partner was the Maharajah Duleep Singh Centenary Trust (MDSCT), a UK Trust, formally launched in 1993 to mark the centenary of the death of Maharaja Dalip Singh. The Trust was the first to focus on a theme associated with Sikh historical heritage. The use of the striking portrait from the Royal Collection by Franz Winterhalter of the young Dalip Singh as the front cover of the catalogue of a major National Portrait Gallery exhibition (Bayly 1990) had brought the image of the maharaja into the wider public arena. Fourteen thousand gathered for the first Anglo-Sikh festival in 1993 in Thetford, near the site of Dalip Singh's former home and burial place at Elveden, signifying the immense interest in Dalip Singh himself. In 1994 the MDSCT commissioned David Jones, keeper of human history at Ipswich Museum and an expert on Dalip Singh's life, to undertake research on Anglo-Sikh history. His report cited the V&A's collections as a central source, and the Trust made contact with the V&A.

In March 1998, Susan Stronge and Hajra Shaikh, the Museum's South Asian Arts and Community Education Officer, met the Trust's project co-ordinator, Harbinder Singh Rana, to explain the Museum's plans. The Trust, emphasizing the need to explain the exhibition's secular theme in advance of the opening, advised on ways to reach the Sikh audience, on audience expectations, and how to assess and pre-empt religious or cultural sensitivities. Hajra Shaikh began research on UK Sikh groups and organizations, drawing together existing contacts, information on *gurdwaras*, other Sikh organizations, local authority networks and contacts established at Sikh events.

In August 1998, V&A staff attended their first major Sikh event – the unveiling of an equestrian statue of Maharaja Dalip Singh at Thetford, organized by the MDSCT. This event, attended by over 11,000 members of the Sikh community from across the country, offered a unique opportunity to network and publicize the exhibition. An open-air stall and accompanying mobile poster display featuring key objects and introducing people to the main themes of the exhibition was mounted next to a tented display of photographs and objects arranged by Amandeep Singh Madra and Parmjit Singh. A Panjabi speaker and dual language (English/Panjabi) leaflets helped communication with older people. In December, 40 people from Birmingham, Coventry, Essex, Kent, London, Middlesex, Nottingham, Slough, Warwick, Watford and West Midlands attended a session for volunteers willing to disseminate information within the community. There was a lively sharing of views. Targeting schools with both Sikh and non-Sikh children was of particular concern. The Museum learned about additional marketing and outreach possibilities and those attending were given 'volunteer packs' with information on the Museum and the exhibition, with posters and slides of artefacts. The V&A approached the ten UK local authorities with the highest Sikh population. Many offered to promote the exhibition using their own and local Standing Advisory Councils for Religious Education (SACRE) networks and mailing lists. Information on Sikh websites and press and media enquiries were passed to the Press and Marketing departments of the V&A.

Over the following months, and during the April *Vaisakhi* celebrations, activities increased. V&A staff attended celebrations in Hounslow, Slough, Gravesend and Birmingham, distributing information, developing and sustaining partnerships. They gave slide talks to other interested Sikh and non-Sikh groups across the country and took part in the regional launch the MDSCT hosted for local media and community organizations at Birmingham Museums and Galleries. The mobile display developed for Thetford, featuring large poster images of the Golden Throne and the Akali turban, proved popular and triggered demand amongst Sikhs for similar displays to be held at community venues both during and after the exhibition.[13]

Consultation and networking with the community were key to clarifying the objectives, content and mode of delivery of the exhibition's education and events programme. Working with colleagues in the Education Department, Hajra Shaikh aimed to develop a fully inclusive programme, encouraging participation from both Sikh and non-Sikh individuals and groups. The family programme included Sikh storytelling, demonstrations of turban-tying and handling sessions of Sikh-related artefacts. Demonstrations of *phulkari* embroidery, miniature painting and metal-inlaying took place at weekends. A highlight was a performance of *Vaisakhi* festival music (*kirtan*). There were presentations to different interest groups – a sign-interpreted talk which attracted Sikh deaf visitors and an exhibition tour for blind and visually impaired visitors. And there was a two-day international conference on the visual culture of the Sikh Kingdoms of eighteenth- and nineteenth-century Panjab. Performances of *bhangra* (Punjabi folk dance) and *gatka* (traditional Sikh martial art) were spectacular. The latter, with men, teenage and young boys yielding swords precariously near the torso or limbs of adversaries, elicited great excitement. Both attracted casual visitors as well as the large groups who came from the Midlands and North of England. A programme of pre-booked events – jewellery making; *phulkari* embroidery; calligraphy using *Gurmukhi* script; table drumming; and storytelling in Panjabi /English – targeted the South Asian community. In all, over 10,000 people attended the events and education programmes.

A unique feature of the exhibition was the voluntary help provided by a network of young Sikh men and women. Volunteers developed and managed a 'Sikh helpdesk' each weekend throughout the exhibition. Although set up primarily for and by Sikh visitors, many non-Sikh visitors also asked for information. As Susan Stronge explained:

> For me, the presence of the Sikh volunteer helpdesk set up by Navleen Kaur was one of the most rewarding aspects of the exhibition. The cultural background to

the paintings, textiles, weapons, and other things on show, was complex and not easily understandable by visitors unfamiliar with the detailed history of the period. For those unfamiliar even with the experience of going to museums there were additional problems. The volunteers put an enormous effort into helping people. Inside the exhibition, volunteers explained whatever they felt necessary, or were asked about, and were so approachable that Western visitors frequently asked them all kinds of questions not related to the show – particularly on aspects of Sikhism, and why Sikh men wear turbans, for example.

Support from the Sikh helpdesk and a rota of V&A staff were crucial in welcoming and helping first-time visitors, including coach-loads organized by Sikh *gurdwaras* and other organizations from across the country. Numbers of 200–300 were not uncommon.

Simply meeting coach parties and escorting them through the Museum to find the exhibition, for example, meant [the volunteers and rota staff] spending Saturdays or Sundays taking people from the entrance where coaches could park to the exhibition, which happened to be at the other end of the Museum. On the way they pointed out the lunch room and garden and then everyone was escorted back again.

(Susan Stronge)

The schools' lunch room and garden came into their own as picnic areas as many groups brought their own communal meal.

Over 200 visitors[14] were surveyed during the last two weeks of the exhibition, and 35 of the 150 Sikh and other South Asian groups who attended the exhibition returned questionnaires.[15] Sixty-three per cent of the individual visitors surveyed were Sikh. Of these, 73 per cent were first-time visitors to the V&A and 41 per cent were first-time visitors to any museum or gallery. For the groups the figures were 74 per cent and 59 per cent percent respectively, reflecting the significant role that the *gurdwaras* and other organizations played in organizing coach-loads of first-time visitors from both the Midlands and North West.[16] The survey also revealed that the *gurdwaras* and the poster had been the most important means of communication about the exhibition.[17] The poster had been an area of debate early on in the campaign. In one of the first mock-ups, a designer unwittingly overlaid the Golden Temple at Amritsar with a coating of red and a Mughal sword which, to the Sikh community, could have signified both the tragic massacres of 1984 at this important centre of pilgrimage and the martyrdom of Sikh gurus by particular Mughal emperors. Other designs focused on the rich abundance of jewels – a subject which might have attracted a general audience, but would not have signified anything particular to the Sikhs. The final design, illustrating Sikh horsemen, was distinctively Sikh, and many members of the community requested copies.

POSITIVE IMPACTS OF MUSEUMS AT INDIVIDUAL AND COMMUNITY LEVELS

In a recent article Richard Sandell posits a framework for museums to counter social inequality:

Museums can impact positively on the lives of disadvantaged *individuals*, act as a catalyst for social regeneration and as a vehicle for empowerment with specific *communities* and also contribute towards the creation of more equitable *societies*.

(Sandell 2002: 4)

As statements from visitors (obtained in surveys and pers. coms) reveal, the exhibition and related events certainly had an impact on *individuals*:

Inspirational and interesting, makes you proud to be a Sikh.

(P.S. Golar, Hounslow)

Absolutely brilliant.

(Kumar Singh, South Africa)

So so unique, at every level. People were excited from the historical point of view . . . most of them just thought it wonderful to see these things.

(Amandeep Singh Madra)

It built up expectations within the Sikh community:

Very good. The best exhibition I've seen. Well done to all those who made this possible. I hope it can stay here permanently.

(Shaminder Singh Bitta, Bedford)

Excellent exhibition. Surely this success points to a permanent Sikh gallery at the V&A.

(Kamaljit Singh, Bradford)

Its perceived and actual importance to young Sikhs and the reinforcing of cultural identity was transparent:

I liked the exhibition, it was well overdue. It's very good for my children.

(Jasvir Gill, London W6)

In San Francisco alone two young Sikhs that had shaved off [their beards and cut their hair],[18] both at different times saw the exhibition, then went to their best friends and asked for a turban. They wanted to be a Sikh again.

(Narinder S. Kapany)

Individual benefits, however, went both ways. Staff in the Museum drew on the expertise of individuals like Amandeep Singh Madra and Parmjit Singh, who initially were unclear about the Museum's expectations:

We were surprised . . . what do they want with us? We met Sue and Neil more to find out what was going on than to contribute. Sue told us about the exhibition and asked for help with one thing . . . to find out about the Anglo Sikh wars from the Sikh perspective. It was very perceptive of her to ask about this. And all early faxes from May to August in 1997 were about that very question.

Neil then took us to Battersea [an off-site store] and we went through arms and armour. We both filled in each other's gaps, able to point out little things. In these early meetings it was more a case of us being happy to be able to contribute to this sort of thing, while everyone else in the community was talking about 1999 events . . . many of them not likely to happen. We realised that the V&A project would happen and was a good place to put our energies.

(Amandeep Singh Madra)

Each side overcame misconceptions of the other, sharing expertise for mutual benefit:

And we met the people in metalwork [Simon Metcalf] and textiles [Lynda Hillyer] conservation. It was a strange session . . . we were being asked to read inscriptions in Persian, which we didn't know anything about. But they were also asking how the Akali turban worked. Did it have a chin strap (a question we'll always remember)? Each of us was finding out what the other knew, coming from different angles and getting to know each other. Later we went to India and made a video of an Akali tying his turban and putting on the *chakkar* [quoit worn round the turban] and we showed it to the conservators when we came back in December.

(Amandeep Singh Madra)

Involvement with the V&A, in turn, opened doors here and abroad:

We were proofreading and writing bits and pieces for Sue. The network mush-roomed. . . . Suddenly we were legitimized and put in touch with other people who were approaching her, like Jeevan Deol. Sue was a conduit for wonderful contacts. We were asked to go to the Armouries. Doors opened. We wouldn't have known how to do that, would have struggled. Writing and cold calls might not have had the same result.

This was true not just in UK, but in India itself. There are difficulties within the community – a certain level of suspicion. When you come out of that and are allied to an institution, doors do open and they see you on your merit. In India that worked. You have to know someone who knows someone. It helped a lot for us. We don't have upper-class contacts.

(Amandeep Singh Madra)

The V&A found itself contributing to a growing network:

In July we were introduced to Harbinder and in October to Narinder at the MDSCT dinner at Wentworth. We had [independently] got some funding from the Arts Council to put our photographs [of military Sikhs] together. Sue introduced us to Harbinder over the phone. And he suggested that we have a display at the dinner . . . Our networks didn't come into play until much later . . . when the exhibition opened. [At the beginning . . .] the other way round it was phenomenal.

(Amandeep Singh Madra)

The display at Wentworth brought Amandeep and Parmjit wider attention, and led directly to the Sikh Foundation's support for the publication of their book (Madra and Singh 1999).

There is no doubt that members of the Sikh community, in the UK and abroad, believed the exhibition contributed to enhanced respect and appreciation of the arts and culture of the Sikhs and encouraged the community's active participation:

> Our organization extends our thanks for enhancing the image of the Sikh community at the most appropriate historical event of the formation of the *khalsa*.
>
> (The Council of Sikh Gurdwaras in Birmingham)

> As our relationship with the V&A grew, we progressed from being infrequent and passive observers of such institutions to being active participants/ partners. The collaboration had allowed us the opportunity to give expression to the latent interest and talent, which clearly existed within the Sikh community. In many ways, this shift is in itself representative of the way in which the community has and is 'evolving' within the UK since its first arrival in the mid-1950s. As it has grown and flourished, so it has become more assertive and aware of its own cultural identity in relation to the host community. The 'insularity' which so marked the formative years of the diaspora has given way to a new and bolder readiness to interact and progress.
>
> (Harbinder Singh Rana)

The exhibition may have been effective in increasing Sikh audiences, bestowing cultural authority and contributing to enhanced self-respect within the Sikh community, but how significant was the exhibition and related programming in effecting change at a societal level? The concern to target schools, expressed at an early stage, was rooted in the belief that younger people's attitudes to diversity could be more effectively influenced. This is clearly a driving concern of the Maharaja Duleep Singh Centenary Trust, the Sikh Foundation, and other Sikh individuals and organizations.

> We would like the Sikhs, and equally important non-Sikhs, and particularly the younger generation, to become a lot more aware of the history, culture, philosophical and religious background of the Sikhs.
>
> (Narinder S. Kapany)

This desire for cultural recognition, legitimacy and value is often rooted in concerns about inequality and racial prejudice in society.

> This new approach in many ways demonstrates a shift in focus away from the original colonial and post-colonial movement of the Sikh diasporas to the emergence of modern UK subjects with mobile and dual identities. An earlier, purely 'eastern' perspective has given way to a more pragmatic approach which sees the UK as being the 'home' to British Sikhs. As such, that heritage earlier invoked by Sikh objects in the UK was no longer purely representative of a colonial era but increasingly recognized as being part of a new future in which the demands of tolerance and diversity transcended the inequalities and injustices perpetuated by history.
>
> (Harbinder Singh Rana)

The inter-relationship between the societal and the cultural are clearly explained in the Parekh Report on the future of multi-ethnic Britain:

Acts of racism, racial violence, racial prejudice and abuse do not exist in a vacuum. They are not isolated incidents or individual acts, removed from the cultural fabric of our lives. Notions of cultural value, belonging and worth are defined and fixed by the decisions we make about what is or is not culture, and how we are represented (or not) by cultural institutions.[19]

It is difficult to gauge the long-term effects of museum initiatives in counteracting racism. There are very few examples where the impact on visitor behaviour perceptions and values has been researched, although some museums are starting to attempt this (Kelly and Gordon 2002: 160).

The exhibition was very well received[20] but interesting issues were raised. Some felt that there should have been more assistance with interpretation.

Maybe it was more to do with the labelling, this problem of understanding. Panjabi language would have helped. People missed a lot . . . I was able to talk about some of the objects with people that I went with, to add richness to objects . Maybe there should have been that thing that a lot of American museums do quite well – a talking tour [audio-guide].

(Amandeep Singh Madra)

Others felt that colour and atmosphere should have been more in keeping with Sikh tradition or that Sikh members dressed up in traditional attire could have been used as interpreters.

Language was an important issue. The experience of outreach had suggested that it was important to provide information in both Panjabi and English, as many older members of the community in particular would be able to access the Panjabi text more readily than the English. By this time the exhibition design and planning were far advanced. The project team was not convinced that dual language text panels or labels were the solution to the problem and there was no allocation in an already tight budget. Several things were done. The text panels were translated into Panjabi and incorporated into a dual language leaflet (sponsored by the Metropolitan Police) which was handed out at the exhibition. The 'events and education' leaflet and several education events were dual language, and Hajra Shaikh gave informal talks in Urdu to Sikh visitors who needed help with interpretation of the objects. This limited approach failed to satisfy all:

Also everybody could not read English, so Panjabi should have been available.
(Guru Nanak Sikh temple, Wolverhampton)

To have Punjabi labels on the exhibits as the leaflet doesn't follow the route.
(Anon: visitor survey)

There was also comment on the exhibition's content. Some asked why there was such emphasis on the Mughal antecedents of royal Lahore. Others found it difficult to understand why, in the *Khalsa* tercentenary year, the V&A was mounting an exhibition which included very little on Sikhism itself, despite the Museum's attempts to explain the rationale of the exhibition.

The Sikh exhibition was good but we thought that a lot more to do with Sikhs could have been on show – paintings of our gurus.

(Anon: visitor survey)

To explain the significance of 1999 and the *Khalsa*, and to communicate Sikhism as a contemporary faith, the gallery through which visitors approached the exhibition had a display of photographs of Anandpur Sahib,[21] the site in Panjab where Guru Gobind Singh founded the *Khalsa*. A video presentation on Sikhism[22] was shown in a dedicated area at the end of the exhibition, while photographs[23] showing the *Vaisakhi* celebrations at Anandpur Sahib in early April 1999 were mounted in the exhibition as soon as they were available.

The first section of the exhibition itself was simple, focusing on Amritsar and the Golden Temple. It had been hoped to represent the ten gurus visually and to convey the importance of the scriptures in Sikhism. This presented a challenge. It had proved difficult to locate and secure loans of individual portraits of all the Sikh gurus of sufficient artistic merit. At the last minute, key paintings sought from India were not lent. There was no question of including the Guru Granth Sahib in the exhibition. The holy book of the Sikhs, which was compiled and edited by the fifth guru, Guru Arjun Dev, in 1604, has been the object of the greatest reverence since 1704, when guru-ship was conferred on it.

As the manifest body of the Guru, the book is treated with the highest respect and veneration. It rests on cushions or quilted mats, draped in silk and brocades, with a canopy hanging over it for protection. Sikhs bow to the Guru Granth and sit on the floor before it; they remove their shoes and cover their heads in its presence.

(Singh 1999: 38)

The exhibition did, however, include a nineteenth-century Dasam Granth[24] volume from the British Library, with illustrations depicting the Ten Gurus. The Dasam Granth, a compilation of texts attributed to Guru Gobind Singh, has a different status from the Guru Granth Sahib, although in the eighteenth and nineteenth centuries it was generally treated with the same reverence. The Museum had sought advice as to whether it would be appropriate or acceptable to display the Dasam Granth in the exhibition, open at the illustrated page, and had been reassured that it did not have the status of the Guru Granth Sahib. The previous appearance of this particular volume in Bradford's touring exhibition, *Warm, Rich and Fearless*, was a decisive factor. The Museum made the decision to include it, in a separate showcase. However, its inclusion did cause some unease and resulted in a few comments from Sikh visitors. Most were reassured once the Museum explained that it had consulted religious leaders and academics before the show, although some still felt that other advisers might have had different views.

PROJECT: 'CULTURAL DIVERSITY AND THE V&A'

One of the frequent criticisms of museums is that they rarely sustain community interest after major events with intense community involvement. It was partly for this reason that the Museum made a bid to the Heritage Lottery Fund for a project entitled 'Cultural

Diversity and the V&A', which aimed, amongst other things, to establish ways of sustaining Sikh community involvement after the exhibition. One idea was suggested by a group which had visited the exhibition:

> To have more workshops and space them out bi-monthly so as to keep the interest going.
>
> (Woking Asian Women Association)

Such proposals contributed to the idea of a Sikh history group. Other initiatives included the development of learning resources and handling collections and a web site.[25] An independent initiative, the hosting of a Sikh heritage desk at the V&A, suggested by the Maharajah Duleep Singh Centenary Trust, worked in tandem.

The Sikh history group was originally envisaged as a small group, which would collect and possibly publish oral history. However, this evolved after consultation with individuals who had been involved with the exhibition[26] into a wide-ranging and intellectually challenging series of lectures. Working with Hajra Shaikh to devise the programme, the core team contacted speakers and marketed the initiative through their own networks. Many exhibition volunteers were again involved. The lecture room had a capacity of 70 and the talks were soon oversubscribed. An additional one-day conference was arranged at short notice to permit one speaker from India, Gurmeet Rai, to talk to a wider audience about the conservation of historical sites in the Panjab. The success of this initiative led to a second lecture series which explored more contemporary themes, such as Sikh architecture in the West and contemporary Sikh female artists. Meanwhile Amandeep Singh Madra and Parmjit Singh, now formally incorporated as the UK Punjab Heritage Association, successfully applied to the Heritage Lottery Fund for funds to develop the lecture series for the UK regions.

One issue was how to reach the target audience. Some Museum staff thought publicity for the lecture series should be included in general V&A leaflets. The organizers perceived problems. The V&A mailing schedule was committed months in advance and was not aligned with the more organic process needed if the community were to play a part. They feared that seats might be taken up by the V&A's traditional white, middle-class audience.[27] A predominantly Sikh audience, they felt, would ensure an environment where individuals could speak openly – whether about interpretations of history or about heritage conservation policy and practice in India. Certainly the involvement in planning the lecture series contributed to a feeling of ownership, both of the series and of the V&A:

> After the early talks people wrote or said to me, 'We can't believe this. It's almost as if the V&A belongs to us. We realize that national institutions are for us.' The V&A has a reputation among second-generation Sikhs as being very progressive.
>
> (Amandeep Singh Madra)

Another strategy adopted to sustain the interest of the Sikh community was the development of a web micro-site. The site (*http: //www.vam.ac.uk/vastati/microsites/ 1162_sikhs*) covers aspects of the exhibition, the lecture series, selected V&A objects from the Panjab and an online storytelling activity, thus exploring material and themes that the V&A cannot currently present by traditional means. Questions and answers on Sikhism include details of the ten gurus – which had been perceived as an omission in the exhibition. This appears therefore to have potential for expanding the interest in Sikh heritage so clearly demonstrated in the response to the lecture series among the UK Sikh community and the wider Sikh diaspora familiar with the web.[28]

Another project responded to community interest in exploring religious themes. Adult and community education staff developed a touring photographic exhibition project (Sacred Spaces) for communities of diverse faith – Buddhism, Hinduism, Sikhism, Jainism, Islam, Judaism and Christianity – to explore connections between Museum objects and their own sacred spaces. It was in this context that a group of young Sikhs, many of whom had volunteered on the Sikh helpdesk, explored more specifically religious or cultural themes such as the significance of the 5Ks,[29] *gatka*, the equality of men and women, the concept of service (*Kar seva*), and the celebration of festivals. This exhibition has been loaned both to Sikh organizations and to organizations concerned with inter-faith issues.[30]

The V&A has also continued to engage with the expanding activities of the MDSCT, many now involving other national and regional organizations (e.g. an annual lecture on Sikh military history at the Imperial War Museum, advising English Heritage on Sikh community issues at Osborne House, and mounting an exhibition at the Wellington Arch to commemorate the role played by Sikh soldiers in the two world wars). The Trust's 2001 dinner to mark the bicentenary of the founding of the Sikh kingdom by Maharaja Ranjit Singh was held at the V&A. The Museum now co-hosts a Sikh heritage desk which supports activities such as the development of an Anglo-Sikh heritage trail that will identify and connect every location in the UK – from the Isle of Wight to Perthshire – which reflects the shared history of the Sikhs and Britain.

CONCLUDING REMARKS

The V&A's work seems to have impacted positively on individuals, communities and, possibly, on society at large:

> As cultural institutions within the UK seek to engage with and reflect the diversity of modern Britain, the V&A's work with the Sikh community has set a precedent which demonstrates the positive benefits of proactive engagement.
>
> (Harbinder Singh Rana)

The V&A has tried to listen to and learn from individuals, communities and organizations, entering into partnerships where people have increasingly taken on responsibility for ensuring that what was on offer was enriching, enlivening and did not offend. Individuals and community groups have taken on advisory roles, contributed videos, photographs, initiated fund-raising, set up helpdesks, and determined marketing strategies. Single events have snowballed into series, individual connections into longer-term networks. The exhibition idea itself came from the community, but meshed with a V&A intention and moved forward. The lecture series led to an independent lottery bid and a regional programme. The concept of the Sikh Heritage Desk provided a focus for networking between the community around the country and national cultural institutions. Has the V&A in fact gone some way towards sharing and relinquishing power?

Can those who run or work in national institutions relinquish some of their power in order that others may exercise some? Is it possible that a large museum or archive can resist seeing itself as a 'centre for social change', instead becoming a matrix of groups that combine as partners? Can established, high status institutions readily adapt to the interests and needs of a local community based project that wishes to approach them to take on the role of delivery partner, rather than lead body?

(Young 2002: 205)

This was no locally based community project, however: it operated at international, local community and individual levels. The exhibition moved on from London to equally successful showings in San Francisco and Toronto, where it was reconfigured to include collections from local sources. And in the UK, the network includes *gurdwaras* and community groups from Slough to Birmingham, Gravesend to Bradford.

The 600,000 strong Sikh community in the UK perceived the V&A's 1999 *Arts of the Sikh Kingdoms* exhibition as a landmark event. Not only did it admirably capture and reflect the mood of British Sikhs as they celebrated a historical milestone, but it also established a precedent and model of how national institutions were progressing from a role of mere custodianship to proactive engagement with diaspora communities.

(Harbinder Singh Rana)

For the V&A the future offers practical challenges:

Maybe things can be loaned for local display as some people find it difficult to travel.
(Singh Sabha Gurdwara, Southampton)

A mobile exhibition for Sikh *gurdwaras*.

(Sikh Union, Slough)

There are other challenges. How can the Museum both sustain this work and start work with other communities under-represented within the V&A? Is one criterion of success to transform visitors to unique events and programmes such as *The Arts of the Sikh Kingdoms* exhibition project into general V&A visitors? Or is the issue more complex? Is there, as Lola Young sees (2002: 205), a danger of a 'concentration on marginality that leaves those at the centre unexamined and unchanged'? She rightly contends that the challenge is to 'connect with the disconnected and the alienated, but not in ways that say come and be like us' (ibid.: 211). How can the experience of working with the Sikh community transform not merely the margins but also the very heart and centre of the institution? This is the transformation that remains the most fundamental challenge.

NOTES

1 In 1699, Guru Gobind Singh established the *Khalsa* or 'fellowship of the pure', choosing the five founding members of the *Khalsa* by means of a test to determine the strength of their

commitment to the faith. The founding was solemnized in a ceremony of initiation which included sipping *amrit* (sweetened water) stirred with a double-edged sword, symbolizing the One Universal God.

2 The authors are particularly grateful to Susan Stronge and Hajra Shaikh for their contributions to and comments on this paper, and to Amandeep Singh Madra, Harbinder Singh Rana and Narinder Singh Kapany for their commentaries on the project.

3 Funded by the Paul Hamlyn Foundation.

4 The Foundation, in San Francisco, California, supports Sikh studies through conferences and publications (see, for example, K.N. Singh 1995, and K. Brown 1999, both published in collaboration with the Sikh Foundation). It supports exhibitions and is working to establish permanent displays of Sikh art in major public museums. It also promotes the conservation of Sikh monuments.

5 Traditionally, *Vaisakhi* is the first day of the month of *Vaisakh*, according to the Bikrami calendar. This was an important time for celebrations among Panjabi farming communities even before *Vaisakhi* 1699, when Guru Gobind Singh founded the *Khalsa*.

6 The spelling Duleep is also commonly used.

7 Stronge (1999: 6–7) lists all lenders to the exhibition. The Surveyor of the Queen's Works of Arts and Director of Royal Collections responded positively immediately.

8 For list of authors and contributors see Stronge (1999: 6–7, 256).

9 The Koh-i-nur diamond was owned by the Mughal emperor, Shah Jahan, and remained in Mughal possession until taken by Nadir Shah of Iran in 1838. It then fell into the hands of the Afghan ruler, Ahmad Khan, and passed from him to Shah Shuja. Shah Shuja, ousted from the throne of Afghanistan in 1812, was imprisoned in Kashmir. His wife offered the diamond to Ranjit Singh to free Shah Shuja. The diamond became part of the Sikh treasury and was in this setting in 1849. The diamond itself was re-cut and is now part of the Crown Jewels, set into the crown worn by the late Queen Mother at openings of Parliament.

10 Made (1820–30) by a leading Muslim goldsmith of the Lahore court. Shipped to London for the Indian Museum by the East India Company after annexation. In 1879 transferred to the South Kensington Museum (later renamed the V&A) where it has remained ever since.

11 The provision of the video represented a substantial financial donation by the GNNSK.

12 The Museum is also grateful to individual donors, the Metropolitan Police, and the Malaysian Commonwealth Studies Centre, Cambridge.

13 For example, at Gravesend, Harrow, Warwick and Portsmouth.

14 A sample of 211 respondents, including 100 weekday and 111 weekend visitors.

15 These groups represented 2,240 people. Three groups were over 200 (the largest 266), seven groups were over 100, and 25 groups less than 100.

16 Of individual visitors, 18 per cent came from the Midlands, 10 per cent from the South East and East Anglia, 4 per cent from the North West, 3 per cent from Wales and the South West. Of the groups 26 per cent came from the Midlands, 9 per cent from the South East, 6 per cent from the North West.

17 Of the individual visitors – Sikhs and non-Sikhs – 31 per cent had heard of the exhibition through the *gurdwara*, 9 per cent through the V&A poster, 25 per cent through the newspaper and 23 per cent by word of mouth. Of groups, 21 per cent had heard of the exhibition through the *gurdwara*, 16 per cent through the poster, 14 per cent through mailing from the V&A, 12 per cent through word of mouth and 11 per cent through a community/Sikh newspaper.

18 The injunction not to cut the hair is one of the five external symbols (known as the five K's) which Guru Gobind Singh introduced to mark out a Sikh. The others are the *Kara*, iron bracelet; *Kachhera*, short breeches; *Kirpan*, sword; and *Kanga*, comb. Together they symbolize an individual's transformation to a more complete humanity.

19 The Commission on the Future of Multi-Ethnic Britain (2000: 159), as quoted in Sandell (2002: 10).

20 Individual survey: 46 per cent better than expected, 45 per cent as expected, 6 per cent worse than expected, 3 per cent had mixed feelings. Group survey: 50 per cent better than expected, 35 per cent as expected, 15 per cent worse than expected.

21 The photographs, taken in 1998, showed the Sikh faithful preparing the temple for the 1999 celebrations.

22 Specially commissioned by the GNNSJ (UK).
23 Kindly supplied by Pushpinder Singh Chopra.
24 A compilation of texts in Braj, Hindi, Persian and Panjabi, attributed to the tenth Guru, Gobind Singh, and consisting of devotional works, a biography of the Guru, narrative tales, praises of weapons, and legendary accounts of the gods and goddesses.
25 Other strands of the bid were to encourage the return of audiences with whom the V&A had previously worked, to work with new communities under-represented at the V&A, including the African Caribbean community, and to promote intercultural work.
26 Amandeep Singh Madra and Parmjit Singh, with Cambridge historian, Jeevan Deol, supported by Jasprit Singh.
27 As had been the case with an 'Arts of India' course which had been advertised through the V&A's normal channels.
28 Evaluation of the website will demonstrate whether it sustains the interest of exhibition or lecture audience or attracts a different audience.
29 See note 18, above.
30 Including local education authorities and the chaplaincy of Brixton prison.

4

INTEGRATING NATIVE VIEWS INTO MUSEUM PROCEDURES

Hope and practice at the National Museum of
the American Indian

Nancy B. Rosoff

Objects are alive and must be handled with respect. This chapter will examine how
the National Museum of the American Indian (NMAI), Smithsonian Institution, is
attempting to implement this and other Native philosophies in the care of its collection.

Since the NMAI was established in 1989, the museum staff have been consulting
with Native people concerning the nature and function of the museum. As a result of
these consultations, NMAI is beginning to integrate Native world views into standard
museum practices. This integration is mandated by the museum's Mission Statement
and Collections Policy, which encourage 'the direct and meaningful participation of
Indian people' in all aspects of the museum's activities. In addition to providing detailed
procedures for documentation, acquisition, repatriation, exhibition, care and handling,
and other museum functions, the Collections Policy 'respects and endeavors to
incorporate the cultural protocols of Indian people that define: cultural and religious
sensitivities, needs, and norms; the utilisation of cultural knowledge and information;
and restrictions outlined by specific tribal groups' (NMAI Collections Policy 1993: 166).

Out of respect for the sensitive nature of many of the issues being discussed, most
tribes mentioned in this essay are not identified by name. In instances where tribes are
named, museum staff have received permission from these groups. Some Native
American staff members agreed to be interviewed on condition that their comments
remain anonymous; their comments are cited as 'personal communication' (pers. com.).
The reader should also bear in mind that the examples presented in this chapter do not
reflect the beliefs held by all tribes. In fact, the traditional care practices being carried
out by NMAI are handled on a case-by-case basis and are constantly changing, reflecting
the fluid nature of collaboration. Today we are not sure if these practices are still
appropriate, and further consultations are needed. The complex and highly sensitive
issues presented in this chapter underscore the fact that collaboration between the
museum and Native groups is an ongoing process that will continue well into the next
century and beyond.

HUMAN REMAINS AT NMAI

Of paramount concern to Indian people is the presence of human remains in museum collections (see Bernstein 1991; Boyd and Haas 1992; Ladd 1993; Leicht 1989; Parker 1990; Tabah 1993). NMAI's highest priority is the deaccession and return of all human remains in the collection. As George Horse Capture (Gros Ventre), Deputy Assistant Director of Cultural Resources at NMAI states, 'At the very least, society's ethics calls for us to do what we can to allow these remains to return to the earth so they might continue their cycle' (Horse Capture 1994).

It was initially challenging, however, just to get an exact count of the number of human remains in the museum, a number that kept increasing as staff members continued to encounter human remains in collection storage areas. According to Ray Gonyea (Onondaga), NMAI's former Repatriation Coordinator, when he started working for the museum in 1993, he was under the impression that there were only a handful of unresolved human remains cases. But as repatriation and collections management staff worked in the collections, they continued to find human remains that were not listed as such in the museum's inventory records. According to Gonyea, 'it was as if [the human remains] knew that there was a chance to go home and didn't want to be left behind and so were making themselves known' (Gonyea 1994a: 6).

In order to resolve once and for all the question of the number of human remains in the museum's collection, NMAI staff conducted a shelf-by-shelf search of the collection over a two-week period in May 1995. A physical anthropologist was hired to verify the human attribution of unidentified bones. By the end of the survey, a total of 524 human remains, including those listed in the museum's original inventory records, were identified.[1] Most of the new discoveries were remains of cremations and skeletal parts, some as small as a dime. The early catalogue records of NMAI's precursor, the Museum of the American Indian, Heye Foundation (MAI), often listed an artefact without noting that human remains were associated with it: for example, a ring proved to be on a human finger bone; and a ceramic vessel contained cremation remains. These early cataloguing practices indicate that human remains at that time were considered less important than their associated artefacts.

All the human remains found in the shelf-by-shelf search were consolidated into one room, approximately 10×12ft in size, which was designated as the Human Remains Vault. The remains were removed from old crates and other containers, and all artificial materials such as plastic covers and mothballs were discarded. As each human remain was wrapped in muslin, it was sprinkled with a mixture of sage, sweetgrass, tobacco, and cedar.[2] All four plants were used, according to Gonyea, since it is not known which plants were sacred to these individuals. All human remains that had been separated from their funerary containers at the time they were accessioned were reunited. The remains were rehoused in acid-free boxes with cedarwood chips as packing material to cushion them for the journey home. An effort was made to use only natural or organic materials so that nothing would interfere with the return of these human remains to the earth (Gonyea 1994b, 1994c).

As of today, 227 human remains have been deaccessioned, 161 of which have been returned (Repatriation Office 1996: 2). The Repatriation Office still has to complete the final steps to return the remaining 66 deaccessioned remains (ibid.).[3] 'Deaccessioning' is the procedure used to record the removal of an accessioned object from the collection. Such removal, also referred to as 'disposal', implies the relinquishing of legal title. An object cannot be repatriated until it is legally deaccessioned from the collection (NMAI Collections Policy 1993: 174–5).[4] As of August 1997, the Repatriation Office has 13 repatriation reports in preparation. In 1995, NMAI's Board of Trustees, as a commitment of support to the repatriation process, established a trust fund in the amount of US$170,000 to cover the costs of additional staffing to speed up research and writing of reports (Repatriation Office 1996: 5).

In addition to staffing limitations, the repatriation process is slowed by the complex and varied customs of burial and treatment of the dead among the many tribes involved. While some tribes welcome the return of their human remains, others have indicated that while they claim cultural affiliation, they are unable, for various reasons, to receive the remains, and the museum has to consider other arrangements.[5] One tribe claimed their ancestors but requested that they be placed in the custody of another museum, a disposition that was culturally appropriate for this particular tribal group (B. White, pers. com.).

The issue of what to do with undocumented and unaffiliated human remains is also complicated. NMAI decided to bury a group of 31 such human remains with the assistance of a Native American tribe in upstate New York; burial took place in the tribe's cemetery. The museum's board of trustees took the position that these remains were entitled to a decent place of rest (Gonyea 1994b).[6]

> We felt that they should be buried by Native American people in the first place. Native Americans would know the appropriate ceremony, the appropriate way, the appropriate attitudes for reburying human remains, and sending them once again on their way to the other side. And we wanted a reservation too because they have pretty much fixed boundaries . . . the risk of them being dug up again was a great concern. Pot hunters will certainly not go on reservations, at least not around here because our reservations are not that big . . . the people are right there and they can sort of act as the guardians for these remains as they return to the earth.
>
> (Gonyea 1994c)

SACRED OBJECTS AT NMAI

Sacred objects are another important category of object that NMAI's Repatriation Office has identified for repatriation.[7] According to Richard Hill (Tuscarora), Assistant Professor at SUNY Buffalo, repatriation enables Native people 'to use those objects of power that they feel are important in the expression of the[ir] cultural identity and spiritual concerns' (Sackler et al. 1992: 61). Each Native group is to determine which objects are sacred to it, if the objects are to be repatriated, and if not, how the museum should care for and exhibit them.[8] George Horse Capture eloquently describes the complexity of defining sacred material:

> Sacredness in the Indian world is like the early morning dew, it falls over everything. Nothing is exempt, everything is sacred. But there are degrees of sacredness, places where the dew only lightly touched, and others where the dew heavily coated. These are the areas of intense sacredness, of power. The bottom line is that we have to go

back to our communities for these answers, to the elders. We are going to have to deal with them. If they say we can't show it, we can't show it.

(Morris 1994: 1, 3)

Since NMAI was established, the museum has been consulting with Native people regarding the appropriateness of exhibiting and publishing images of potentially sensitive material. For its three inaugural exhibitions and companion publications – *Creation's Journey*, *All Roads Are Good* and *This Path We Travel* – the museum contacted and received permission from elders and religious leaders to include some sacred objects and funerary goods in the exhibits and publications. In order to exhibit some of the sacred material, the museum complied with the traditional care recommendations made by the appropriate Native groups. For example, containers with tobacco and cedar were placed within exhibit cases containing Mimbres bowls and Osage ribbonwork blankets. A medicine pouch of tobacco, which was originally part of a Delaware Me'sing or bear skin, was placed inside the outfit when it was exhibited.

After carefully gathering information regarding the traditional care of its collections, NMAI has begun to implement the following traditional care practices at its present storage facility in New York: the Human Remains Vault is smudged with a mixture of tobacco, sage, sweetgrass, and cedar every week; drawers containing sacred materials such as bundles have been flagged so that people know where this material is and can show it proper respect; during the full moon, the sacred Crow objects in the Plains vault are smudged with sage. As one Native American staff member pointed out, 'we are not performing any ceremonies, we are just trying to take care of these things in the best way that we can' (pers. com.). This statement characterizes the situation quite well because there are no pan-Indian ways of dealing with all the Native cultures represented in NMAI's collection. Until we receive specific instructions from a tribe, we leave the care of the collection to the discretion of Native staff members to treat the objects in the most respectful way possible according to their own cultural knowledge and customs.

As tribal delegations visit the museum to see their group's cultural materials prior to a repatriation request, any traditional care information that they are willing to share is recorded, and when possible, implemented. For example, a Plains Cree delegation from Saskatchewan, Canada, said that the proper procedure for storing a war bonnet that once belonged to a particular warrior was to place it on top of the other objects in the drawer because of its power. This recommendation was implemented, and a male staff member who was allowed to accompany the Cree delegation when they examined the medicine bundles and other sacred materials said that they smudged the sacred objects with sweetgrass and then placed a folded piece of white cotton cloth in the drawer (Mark Clark, pers. com. 1994).

Museum staff members must establish relationships with Native people that are based on mutual trust because Indian people will not share traditional care knowledge with museum professionals unless they feel assured that such knowledge is respected. One Native American staff member believes that tribal delegations visiting NMAI have been more forthcoming with traditional care information because they see that there are people on staff who care about 'doing the right thing' (pers. com.).

MERGING CONSERVATION AND TRADITIONAL CARE

The collections and conservation staff are also looking at new methods for deterring or eliminating active insect infestation in culturally sensitive objects. Current standard museum treatments such as plastic bags, freezing, and low-oxygen atmospheres may be inappropriate for certain objects because they might 'suffocate' a living entity. Therefore, the staff have begun investigating traditional Native American fumigation techniques such as regular smudging and the use of certain aromatic botanical substances in sachets. Before proceeding with any method, consultation with appropriate tribal representatives is initiated (Drumheller and Kaminitz 1994: 59). Also, the repair and stabilization of culturally sensitive and sacred objects are usually not undertaken by members of the Conservation department unless they are able to get permission from the Native group concerned (Kaminitz 1994). The department is experimenting with procedures that satisfy both Native communities and professional conservation standards.

LENDING SACRED MATERIALS

The NMAI Collections Policy contains a provision for lending sacred objects to Native people for the practice of their ceremonies on a case-by-case basis (NMAI Collections Policy 1993: 182). Tribes request sacred objects to manifest their spiritual beliefs and to perform ceremonies that benefit their communities. Some tribes feel that they are fulfilling a responsibility to utilize cultural materials as they were intended. For example, in June 1996, the Confederated Tribes of Siletz Indians of Oregon borrowed dance regalia for their Ceremonial Dance House Dedication, and then again for their Summer Ceremony the following year. According to Robert Kentta, the tribe's cultural resources protection specialist, they could have used the regalia presently owned by the community, but it was important that the older regalia be danced because it was made for that purpose – that was its intended use. Community members and the museum, as the regalia owner, came together to fulfil this responsibility (Kentta, pers. com. 29 August 1997).

Susan Heald, NMAI's textile conservator who accompanied the loan in 1996, said that Bud and Cheryl Lane (the Dance Maker and his wife) assisted in repairing and stabilizing the regalia. Cheryl Lane also made sure that the most experienced dancers wore the older museum pieces because they danced most smoothly. Heald said that the dancers looked magnificent in the old regalia, and that observing the ceremonial use of the pieces in their traditional context more than justified the flexibility required in carrying out the museum's standard loan policy and handling requirements. She wrote in her journal:

> I am learning that if you are going to take collection items back to their communities, you have to be flexible, be sensitive, be careful not to offend. Listen carefully to the people and to the objects and be guided by them. It's all about respect and trust.
>
> (Heald 1996: 6–7)

None of the Siletz dance regalia was damaged as a result of its ceremonial use, and some pieces returned to New York in improved condition because they were stabilized for dancing. The experience was a positive one for everyone involved.

NMAI'S CULTURAL RESOURCES CENTER

NMAI has also sponsored formal consultations with Native people regarding traditional care and handling issues. The purpose of these consultations was the development of an architectural programme for NMAI's Cultural Resources Center in Suitland, Maryland, designed as the museum's research and collections storage facility. In March 1992, several Native museum professionals were invited to the museum's research branch in the Bronx for a two-day conference on traditional care and handling. Three comments made during the consultations illustrate Native curation concerns.

Ed Ladd (Zuni tribal member, Museum of New Mexico) made the following statement regarding the care of masks: Zuni masks must be fed once or twice per year by their people, male and female: to let the museum's staff do this would be to neglect our responsibility and would not do any good (Venturi, Scott Brown & Associates 1993: 436). Greig Arnold (Makah tribal member) described how Makah headdresses should only be seen when they are danced:

> Once we have a headdress out on the floor and it is being danced, the person with that headdress is supposed to put it on right away and come out – he is that thing, whatever it is that he is doing. If he is wearing a thunderbird or if he is wearing a wolf, he is that on that floor. As soon as that song is over and that energy is gone, he comes off and then transforms. Then he is back to who he is as a person or she is as a person. All that gear is then put away and stored after that, not to be seen until it is danced again.
>
> (Venturi, Scott Brown & Associates 1993: 438)

Bob Smith (Oneida tribal member, NMAI) spoke about storage requirements for Iroquois Medicine or False Face masks:

> At one time . . . the masks were actually buried with the individual. But the way I understand it and the way these masks are up here now [in storage at the National Museum of the American Indian] . . . that isn't the way that they would be stored; you wouldn't hang the mask face out. If the mask was to be hung, it would be facing towards the wall and it would be covered. The proper way of storing the mask would be to store it face down, because if you store a mask face up, it connotes something that is dead or dying.
>
> (Ibid.: 441)

As part of the architectural programme for the construction of the Cultural Resources Center, the Smithsonian Institution hired Wendy Jessup & Associates to determine the space and storage needs of NMAI's collection. Jessup & Associates assembled a team that included Native consultants in order to ensure that traditional care would be incorporated into the museum's future collections storage facility. For six weeks in 1992–93, Jessup & Associates sponsored a 'traditional care' survey of the collection in order to identify culturally sensitive materials and specify their special storage needs. In their final report, the authors acknowledged that the survey was purely preliminary, and that to be truly comprehensive and accurate they would have had to consult with representatives from every tribal group. Nevertheless, three recommendations were incorporated into the design of the Cultural Resources Center;

1 objects are alive and must be handled with respect (Wendy Jessup & Associates 1993: 1013);
2 taboos must be respected regarding the placement of men's and women's objects. For example, among the Crow and Blackfeet, men's objects must be hung and stored above the women's. For the Makah of Washington and the Shuar and Achuar of eastern Ecuador, male and female objects cannot be stored together (Rosoff 1992: 5–6). Among other groups, women are not allowed to touch or even be near the men's objects (Wendy Jessup & Associates 1993: 1013);
3 some tribes such as the Cheyenne object to people walking above their sacred and ceremonial objects so the area containing such items should ideally be located on the top floor of the building (ibid.: 1014).

The Jessup traditional care survey, in concert with other Native American recommendations, is the kind of commentary that NMAI is in the process of gathering about its collection, but the process is slow, and implementation is complicated by the fact that tribal preferences are not uniform. In addition, traditional care information available to museum staff comes primarily from repatriation visits.[9] This means that except for the museum's early consultations, the staff is learning more from tribes who can make the trip to New York (Angela Pearce, pers. com., 22 August 1997). Some Native American employees expressed frustration with the process of addressing the traditional needs of the collection as they saw them, and in 1995 they established an unofficial museum working group called the Traditional Care Committee to address their concerns and make recommendations. While this working group does not make policy, it is beginning to consolidate the traditional care information received from consultations and tribal visits.

Sometimes it is not feasible for museum staff to implement certain traditional care practices. Angela Pearce (Apache), a graduate fellow in the Conservation Department and a member of the Traditional Care Committee, points out that when tribal representatives come to the museum's Research Branch in the Bronx and see the facility, they can tell if it is possible or not for museum staff to implement their suggestions:

> They may tell us what the best thing would be for an object – to be stored alone, to be in a certain type of container – but will often add, 'but what you're doing is okay', if not ideal. So it's not really traditional care in the true sense, but an evolution of new traditions for museums. With more tribes starting their own collections, they have a better understanding of the limitations posed by a museum environment.
>
> (Pearce, pers. com., 22 August 1997)

How will the museum address the many different ways in which Native people respect and care for their own cultural materials, especially in light of the fact that NMAI's collection of over one million objects is hemispheric, has a temporal range of tens of thousand years, and represents some 600 tribes? There are many challenges that NMAI will face as staff members learn how Native people respect and care for their objects, and as the staff strive to integrate methods of traditional care with standard museum practice. The goal and hope for NMAI's future facilities, such as the museum on the Mall in Washington, is that they will be welcoming places that incorporate the special spiritual requirements of all Native people.

ACKNOWLEDGEMENTS

I would like to thank Bruce Bernstein, George Horse Capture, Mary Jane Lenz, Betty White, Lee Davis, Clara Sue Kidwell, Ray Gonyea, Angela Pearce, and members of the NMAI Collections Management, Repatriation, and Conservation Departments for their assistance in preparing this essay. A version of this essay was presented at the annual meeting of the American Anthropological Association, Atlanta, Georgia, 30 November to 4 December 1994.

NOTES

1 Of the 524 catalogue entries for human remains, 73 catalogued remains no longer exist in the collection because at some point they were given away, transferred, discarded, or exchanged (Repatriation Office 1996: 1–2).

2 According to a Native staff member, sage, sweetgrass, tobacco, and cedar are the four main plants that the Creator gave to Indian people so that they can stay in harmony with themselves, their environment, and the Creator. When these four plants are burned (called smudging) the smoke becomes a prayer and offering to the Creator and to other spirits (pers. com.).

3 Betty White, NMAI's former Repatriation Manager, points out that once a research report is written and the object is deaccessioned, determining who should receive a repatriation is at least half of the process. It is often necessary to contact all potentially affiliated groups, wait for their responses, and follow up with further correspondence. When there are competing claims, consensus is difficult to achieve and the process becomes even lengthier (White, pers. com., 22 August 1997).

4 Also see NMAI Collections Policy in Tabah (1993: 176–9) for information pertaining to repatriation procedures. The Board of Trustees is still in the process of evaluating the draft repatriation policy prepared by NMAI staff.

5 Tribes may not be able to receive human remains for a variety of reasons, such as taboos against handling the dead, burial rites that are specific to individual clans and families, and a lack of reburial ceremonies for remains excavated after their initial burial (White 1997).

6 This approach to reinterring non-culturally identifiable human remains is also discussed in the report of the Panel for a National Dialogue on Museum/Native American Relations in Tabah (1993: 120–1).

7 As of August 1997, NMAI has repatriated 194 religious/ceremonial and communally-owned objects, but human remains will continue to be given first priority until they are all deaccessioned and returned (Repatriation Office 1996: 4).

8 For further discussion about sacred objects in museum collections, see Blair 1979; AIRFA Task Force 1980: 19–23; Powell 1989; Hall 1989; Mibach and Wolf Green 1989; Boyd and Haas 1992; Sackler *et al*. 1992; Ladd 1993; Tabah 1993.

9 As of September 1997, for repatriation visits, NMAI's Repatriation Office finances round-trip airfare, local travel, and three nights in a hotel for two people.

Part 2

TALKING VISUAL HISTORIES

INTRODUCTION

Elizabeth Edwards

LOCKED IN 'THE ARCHIVE'

Photographs are amongst the most potent of museum objects. In cross-cultural terms they have an enormous and twofold potential. They are an evidential source within the communities they depict, inscribing complex layers of cultural information and knowledge, and an important site of negotiation for the development of long-term collaborative relations between museums and communities. At the same time, to engage with this potential has major implications for museums holding collections of photographs. This is especially so for those in western European anthropology museums, for whom source communities are often not, in geo-political terms, part of their local constituency, but who, as the theme of this volume insists, are part of a wider ethical community whose rights to collections cannot be ignored. My particular perspective is that of a white, educated, middle-class curator trying to find equitable and workable solutions to sometimes seemingly intractable problems. Working with a photograph collection that has a global reach, I have seen the issues considered here evolve over the years and have developed an acute awareness of the differing sensitivities, demands and expectations peoples bring to photographs. Consequently this part introduction is an overview of complex issues, which work themselves out variously in different cultural situations, but at the heart of which lies the very nature of photographs themselves.

As a class of objects, photographs – and indeed film – are not straightforward. Photographs, especially of the kinds that have historically entered European and American museum collections, are almost always, for better or worse, a site of intersecting histories – the visual legacy and historical deposits of sets of encounters and relationships. They emerge from a multiplicity of shared experiences, from the violent and intrusive to those of friendship. Nevertheless, photographs and their archiving have been produced and controlled through sites of authority of the collecting society – archives, museums, universities. Their interests have been privileged in the way in which photographs have been curated, displayed and published, creating specific regimes of truth to the exclusion of others (Edwards 2001: 185–6).

The nature of photography itself is intrinsic to this powerful process. Through their mutability, photographs are able to create stories, distort identities and appropriate cultures.[1] As a result, photographs have been immeasurably powerful in creating, distorting and perpetuating ideas about culture. The endless reproduction of images constitutes a form of visual appropriation and imperialism, constructing, for instance, a range of 'Indians' from the barbarous savage, through the romantic 'vanishing race' constructions of Edwards S. Curtis, to the mysterious keepers of planetary secrets. As Paul Chaat Smith wrote, in response to this resolute photographic exoticism, 'Heck, we're just plain folks, but no one wants to hear that' (Chaat Smith 1995: 9). Consequently, at one level, demands for the control of photographs have not been simply about access to knowledge of what is portrayed in the photograph, but rather photographs themselves have become symptomatic and symbolic of people's desire to control their own histories and their own destinies.[2] The nature of photography itself is integrally connected with both indigenous resistance to it and concerns about it. The combination of capture and trace become symbolic of the space between the collector and the collected, the photographer and the photographed, the museum and the source community – the asymmetries of power and the spaces in which source communities are locked, dispossessed, disenfranchised, silenced, marginalised and appropriated (Harlan 1995: 20). Indeed, expressions of political empowerment have been expressed through the photographic metaphor of 'reclaiming the shadows'.

Before considering further the relationship between photographs, telling histories and the specific social relations of visual repatriation and re-engagement, it is necessary to explore further the nature of photography itself as a medium, for it prescribes the power of photographs for source communities, both positively and negatively. Photography draws much of its power from its indexicality, the chemical trace of light reflected off the physical reality which was in front of the camera. It is this tracing of indigenous lives which constitutes the enormous potency and political impact of the symbolic sucking of a life force for source communities. Through this process, photographs translate the flow of lived experience into a series of stilled, muted fragments of space and time, defying diachronic connections and separating the image from its real-life subjects. The past is transported in apparent entirety to the present: in Barthes's famous phrase – the 'there-then' becomes the 'here-now' (Barthes 1977: 44). Film, whilst sharing some of these characteristics, has a very different narrative effect. The length of quotation from the flow of life being longer, it gives the sense of real time rather than fractured time. It also lacks the intense performative qualities of photographs. The stillness of photographs invites certain ways of weaving stories around them – a point to which I shall return.

As I have suggested, both photographs and films, despite appearances, seldom have closed meanings. Rather, meanings are mutable and arbitrary, generated by their viewers and dependent on the context of their viewing, their relationship with written or spoken 'texts', and the embodied subjectivities of the viewer. The trace of the past is thus ascribed different meanings by different people, interests shifting in time and space. Such shifts from, for instance, mission, to museum, to community, constitute a social biography for photographs through which 'a culturally constructed entity [is] endowed with culturally specific meanings and classified and reclassified into culturally constituted categories' (Kopytoff 1986: 67). Photographs are ultimately uncontainable; they carry an incompleteness and unknowability. There is seldom a 'correct interpretation': one can say what a photograph is *not*, but not absolutely what it is. Consequently meanings emerge that are perhaps diametrically opposed to, for instance, colonial intentions of the photographs. As Binney and Chaplin demonstrate in their chapter, photographs record parallel realities. This infinite recodability of photographs is the site of fracture and re-engagement and is fundamental to visual repatriations. Visual repatriation is, in many ways, about finding a present for historical photographs, realising their 'potential to seed a number of narratives' (Poignant 1994/5: 55) through which to make sense of that past in the present and make it fulfil the needs of the present. Yet this cannot be done in any essentialising way. As both Bell and Kingston's chapters demonstrate, these processes cannot be homogenised but constitute complex and sometimes contradictory contexts within communities as narratives inflected with age, gender or lineage for instance, are woven with and around photographs.[3]

The cultural production of meaning applies not only to individual or community readings, but to the construction of whole 'visual economies' through which photographs become meaningful. An idea that overlaps with that of social biography, Poole has defined 'visual economy' as the political, economic and social matrices in which photographs operate and which pattern their production, circulation, consumption and possession, encompassing both the modes of production and those individuals who use the images (Poole 1997: 9–13). 'The Archive' is a construct within a broader visual economy, formulating certain ways of absorbing, ordering and presenting photographs. Thus, as I have suggested, 'The Archive' has become paradigmatic of the processes that have silenced indigenous voices. Collaborative visual repatriation thus requires the recognition of differently valid 'visual economies' in which 'The Archive' is decentred, and the visual economy extended and refigured through inclusion, recognition and liberation of the 'indigenous voice'.[4] I shall return to these possibilities in my last section.

Traditionally, museums have collected photographs as transparent and unproblematic raw data, to explain objects or extend the knowledge of culture from which objects were extracted. There was a limited appreciation of the extent to which photographs were legitimate concerns to their subjects or could provide significant insights into these concerns (Holman 1996: 118–19). Work on photography, theories of realism and the politics of representation over recent decades, combined with a radical shift in thinking about photographs and source communities, have made such a position untenable. One might conceptualise this shift as one from the 'public' (determined by 'outsider' concerns) to the 'private' (determined by the 'insider') because the way in which photographs can be said to move from one to the other has much to do with their reading as historical data and their insertion into different visual economies . 'Public' photographs remove the subject matter of the image from its contexts, so that meaning becomes free-floating, externally generated and read in terms of symbol and metaphor. The traditional constitution of 'The Archive' has functioned as a public reading of photographs, open to many meanings about culture but at the same time operating within a disciplinary paradigm that reified and objectified the subject matter as both 'data' and archetype. As a result it is possible for a photograph to stand for 'The Nuer' or 'The Inuit'. Photographs have been, through this process, instrumental in the construction and appropriation of cultures and people's lives within Western scientific and museological discourses.

On the other hand, 'private' images are those read in a context contiguous with the 'life' from which they are extracted: meaning and memory stay with them, as in family photographs, for example (Berger 1980: 51–2). This links precisely with a key concern about photographs for source communities. Concepts of public and private differ, of course, from culture to culture.[5] In many cases, photographs of ceremonial activities have been perceived as violating private space and incorporating it in different systems of meaning and value (Holman 1996: 114–15).

In the light of this model, visual repatriation might be defined as the conscious shifting of photographs from a 'public', 'outsider' to 'private' and 'appropriate' spaces. Photographs that were created as colonial documents, and which became 'ethnographic' records through their entanglements within specific institutional structures, become family history, clan history or community history. None the less, while returned to the same locations, photographs are at some level returning to very different social relations. Communities are faced with what is known to them from their own ways of remembering, through the eyes of an outsider, with very different resonances. Conversely, photographs might destabilise an idealised past and thus the foundations of identity. Such transformation and translations are not necessarily straightforward or painless. Notwithstanding, photographs enter a new stage of their social biography, operating in different visual economies, with all the potential that suggests. Perhaps this is no more vividly illustrated than in the different outsider/insider readings of Curtis's photographs of Native American peoples. Curtis has been presented by Western critics as the archetypal constructor and manipulator of Native Americans (e.g., Lyman 1982) yet to many Native Americans he respects their beauty, power and history, qualities focused not on a universalised stereotype but on real, remembered individuals (Clifford 1997: 127–9; Lippard 1992: 23–6, Tsinhnahjinnie 1998: 44, 53).

If the collecting and control of photographs have been embedded in unequal power relations, so equally have been the theory and analysis of photographs and photography. These have, in their turn, inflected curatorial practices. These theories are located within the dominant Western concerns with realism, subjectivity and individual and in Western modes of historical truth, narrative and identity. While the ontology of photography (as outlined above) is essential to it, the understanding and cultural application of those characteristics cannot be assumed to be general. For instance, portrait photography may have very different cultural meanings in cultures with very different constructions of personhood. To analyse these through Western ideas of individuality and portraiture risks misunderstanding a culture's relationship with photographs at a profound level.

One of the most potent Western theories has been the association of photography with death and loss, as developed in the theoretical writing of Walter Benjamin, Roland Barthes and through the metaphor of photography in, for instance, Proust's writing. These ideas have inflected both photographs and 'The Archive' as places of loss. While the link between photographs and 'what has been' is probably universally recognised, it is equally likely to be actually used in very different ways (Poignant 1996: 10). Re-engagement and re-cognition of the kind discussed here have the cultural potential for being not only about loss, but instead empowerment, renewal and contestation:

> That was a beautiful day when the scales fell from my eyes and I first encountered photographic sovereignty. A beautiful day when I decided that I would take responsibility to reinterpret images of Native people.
>
> (Tsinhnahjinnie 1998: 42)

On one register, there is loss, a cultural dispossession, as photographs both inscribe and signify the difference between then and now. However increasingly, as this volume argues, archives and museums are becoming not only places of exclusion and disappearance but also spaces of contested histories and contesting practices, negotiation, restatement and repossession (Ames 1992; Clifford 1997; Simpson 1996). If we are really going to explore the intersections represented in photography, perhaps we need to destabilise those theories and find other tools, encompassing indigenous world views, with which to think about the specifically cultural nature of photographs.[6]

The theoretical and practical shifts emerging from wider issues of cultural politics of representation, identity and sovereignty, have gradually opened spaces for 'indigenous counter-narratives' (Douglas 1999). These processes have resulted in fragmenting the authoritative and monolithic power of 'The Archive', but at the same they demand a re-evaluation of the importance of visual records. The basic questions that inform the way we think about photographs and must inflect curatorial practices are surely:

- What kind of past is inscribed in photographs?
- Whose past?
- What is the affective tone through which the photographs project the past into the present?
- What are the intellectual, curatorial and administrative processes required to open photographs to other readings?

Such strategies move beyond the surface level evidence of appearance, so that

> if it can be recognised that histories are cultural projects, embodying interests and narrative styles, the preoccupation with the transcendent reality of archives and documents should give way to dispute about forms of argument and interpretation.
>
> (Thomas 1997: 34)

It is this latter strategy that clears the space for different readings and the absorption of photographs into the 'lives' from which they were extracted.

PHOTOGRAPHS AND HISTORIES[7]

Thinking through the nature of photographs helps us to see what is happening when people engage with historical photographs. Equally, it is important to think through the relation-ship between photographs and telling histories, because such an understanding helps to reformulate approaches to museum collections and to create a deeper understanding of the processes underlying visual repatriation. In much writing on the relevance of photographs as a memory salvaging tool, the methodology has been conceived in the traditional relations of photo-elicitation, and work with source communities is often glossed as such. However, photo-elicitation emerged from the classic power relations of anthropology, its methods and goals, and was developed as a methodological tool to trigger memories and glean cultural information. Despite the acknowledgement of some dialogic quality to such encounters – they 'sharpen the memory' and give a 'gratifying sense of self-expression' (Collier 1967: 48) – the concern was largely a one-way flow from informant to ethnographer. This is clearly, but inadvertently, articulated by Collier: 'questioning the native [with] the photograph can help *us* gather data and enhance *our* understanding' (ibid.: 46, added emphasis). However, between ethnographers' use of photographs and how communities interpret them 'lie inconsistencies which shed light on our historical enterprise' (Niessen 1991: 419). What happens in this space between is crucial. The re-engagements considered here are very differently premised, for the relationships, goals and outcomes of such encounters have changed radically. The emphasis now is on shared approaches, the acknowledgement of sensitivities, an access defined by source communities and the recognition of boundaries– that in such exercises photographs will be reabsorbed into social spaces where the ethnographer cannot and should not go. Crucial to this model is that photographs, and indeed film, are active and dynamic, that they are interlocutors in the process of telling histories.

This dynamic model constitutes photographs not as passive images in which communities merely recognise an ancestor or a now deserted settlement. It is more than simply responding to images through a sharpened memory. Photographs are active in the dialogue, become social actors, impressing, articulating and constructing fields of social actions and relations, as Stanton (this volume) argues, powerful stimuli for the maintenance of indigenous knowledge. This is clearly expressed by Gordon Machbirrbirr, Burarra photographer at the Maningrida Bilingual Literature Production Centre, Arnhem Land, Australia:

> It's like a life coming to you. Like you have your life coming back. . . . I have never seen my ancestor, but I would like to see them in the photo you know, and say 'Ah yeah, this is my grandfather' . . . and when you look at the photo and say 'Aah' and you think that the spirit of that person came to the life, and lived.
>
> (Cited in Poignant 1992: 75)[8]

Photographs allow people to articulate histories in ways that would not have emerged in that particular figuration if photograph had not existed: 'Understanding . . . photographs is a process of reaching out for what is finally absent, rather than grasping the presence of new "truths" ' (Lippard 1992: 20). Importantly, photographs can contest dominant inscriptions of the past, for instance as Binney and Chaplin argue (this vol.), photographs vindicated Maori Tūhoe people's perceptions of a police assault at Maungapohatu which had been 'buried under an orchestrated litany of lies' in the official account.

Nonetheless, assumptions about these processes are based on Western expectations of the relationship between photographs and memory: expectations and, consequently, uses and readings that prefigure approaches to photographs in certain ways, 'universalis[ing] an interest in certain modes of historical narrative . . . a step taken in the name of democratising history . . . [which] curiously affirms the generalised authority in certain ways of establishing a command of the past' (Thomas 1997: 45–6). Similarly Niessen, who worked with photographs of museum textiles in Sumatra, has argued that there is a peculiar faith that photographs will function in certain ways:

> This is an aspect of our own mythology about who we are in relation to 'the other'. Photographs do not perpetrate this relationship but are manipulated in its service and as such act as an extension of ethnographic authority.
>
> (Niessen 1991: 429)

Such a position might thus obscure differently constituted relations between the photograph and the past, where inscriptions in photographs might not accord with an historical conscious-ness that is not necessarily defined around the same events or chronologies that have been assumed to inform photographs. Obviously, alternative perceptions of the past will instigate different readings of images. However, there is a tendency to universalise not only the authority of certain modes of historical narrative (Thomas 1997: 46–9) but also assumptions of the qualitative expectation of photographs as natural conduits for memory based on a universalised notion of realism and visual inscription.

How photographs actually insert themselves into communities varies radically according to culturally specific visualisations of the past, ideas of verification and expression of historical events and transmission of historical knowledge. Arguably photographs, however ubiquitous, superimpose a preconceived model of seeing and articulating the past that is in direct contrast with other patterns of remembering (Connerton 1989: 19). While the realist nature of the photographic image suggests access to unmediated historical truth, the patterning is that of the outsider: fragments of a community's past experience deemed relevant and significant by investigators. Is there a danger that photography's realist claims state categorically an appearance of the past that might, in historical 'reality' or oral historical perception, have more fluidity? As I suggested above, translation into 'private' space is not always comfortable. However, an increasing number of collaborative projects between museums, archives and libraries, projects of self-representation or critical analysis from indigenous scholars and others, point to creative intersections of global and local. Responses will be culture-specific, an intersection not only of traditional indigenous modes for visualising history, and the influences, absorptions and refigurings of the outpourings of a globalised media,[9] but also of differing degrees of engagement with the possibilities and politics of the power of photography.

Photographs and peoples perform histories together. It is important to realise the extent to which empowered narratives, realised through photographs, are experienced as real, true or even relevant within a particular moment (Morris 1994: 7). Photography not only functions at a micro-level of clan or family, it also links to larger political narratives. As Bell demonstrates, for instance, photographs are entangled with the assertions of identity in the local communities' negotiation with Malaysian logging companies operating in the Purari Delta, Papua New Guinea.[10] Photographs, re-activated and re-engaged with, thus emerge as important in contrasting and overlapping historical configurations in the multiple articulations of cultural identity, as well as formal histories, of emergent nation-states in a global forum.

However, photographs and film cannot be dissociated from other modes of historical narrative. The textual domination of Western histories has tended to constitute the 'visual' as a separate and indeed often problematic form – and this is mirrored in institutional structures and practices. It is clear from all these essays that photographs do not necessarily operate as a separate or discrete category in the way in which they are perceived, rather they are integrally related to the oral, spoken or sung, the danced and to other material objects that carry historical meanings. Orality, in particular, penetrates all levels of historical relations with photographs, not simply in terms of verbalising content, but in the way the visual imprints itself, is absorbed and is played back orally as photographs have stories told about them weaving their way through conversations. Photographs are also described in terms of orality: 'Photographs can speak. They can whisper or shout. They can lie' (*Lost Identities* 1999). As Poignant noted at Maningrida, 'the interpretation of photographs seemed no more than traditional oral modes of representing the past' (1996: 8), the community consensus was that photographs were like bark paintings – they had stories (Poignant 1992: 74). People not only talk about photographs, they talk with them and weep over them. Binney and Chaplin (this vol.) describe how '[t]he group photograph of Rua's arrest on 2 April 1916 was crumbled and stained with tears'. Likewise, an old woman from Banada, D'Entrecasteaux Islands, Massim District, Papua New Guinea sat on her lineage's stone platform in the village, holding a photograph of a long-dead kinsman, and cried a soft mourning lament (Edwards 2001: 101).[11] In Arnhem Land, Frank Gurrmanamana sang *yuluk* (Stingray tail) to a photograph depicting the painting of this pattern, at the same time using the photograph as a clapping stick (Poignant 1992: 76). What is key to all these examples is that the photographs were not only perceived as active in the flow of information, but that they were, from the beginning, embedded in local structures that privilege the oral in relation to photographs. Indeed, the significance of the oral is given metaphorical shape in the frequency that 'silence' – the absence of voice or sound – is used to described the archival suppression and alienation of source community interests: 'Many photographs . . . are silent. When individuals, events or details are not known, photographs do not have voices' (*Lost Identities* 1999).

Yet this 'orality' is also highly regulated and its structures will inflect responses to photographs. This is another aspect of photographs being absorbed into other ways of telling. For instance, in traditional Australian contexts, speaking rights are carefully controlled; knowledge itself being a form of property. Violating those rights of speaking is a form of theft (Michaels 1991: 260). Bell's essay describes a different source of regulation – the reluctance of I'ai people to tell certain histories in public as jealousy of one's ancestral claims might attract sorcery. Such a situation will structure responses to photographs in a given situation, and in the case of the I'ai people, this resistance to assert histories was seen as one of the causes of their failure to harness the riches offered by the logging companies. It was precisely the tensions over who controlled the photographs which became important in Niessen's fieldwork in Sumatra:

> Men . . . resisted my power as the holder of the stack of photographs . . . Was this because they . . . could not comment at great length on the textiles as women could? . . . [A]ccording to local custom, the power to dominate the interview should have been in their hands rather than, literally mine.

> (Niessen 1991: 421)

Speaking with photographs, despite perhaps its apparent informality and the excitement of recognition, must thus be seen as a regulated response embedded within social structures.

In this context, some consideration must be given to the materiality of photographs because it is integrally linked to the ways of telling, for one is telling histories not just with images but with objects that are images. While on one hand this is linked to the social biography of the photographs, more important in the context of collaborations and visual repatriation are the material forms through which people actually have access to photographs and how they respond to them. The narrative contexts articulated in response to Hubbard's film, described by Kingston (this vol.), are in some ways conditioned by the presentational form that constitutes the filmic experience. Photographs also have a material performativity, a phenomenological relationship with the viewer, not simply of content, but as active social objects. As such, the past is projected actively into the present by the nature of the photograph itself and the act of looking at a photograph, focusing on an object. This is important because it points to the significance of material forms in which communities actually view material and use it: sitting around, passing the photographs from one to another, perhaps in ways that express traditional social relations of history telling. Bell (this vol.) describes how at Mapaio he handed photographs first to male elders, after which they were passed down through the hierarchy. Poignant reports Jacky Nabuliya, a Maningrida elder, explaining the photographs in detail to his daughter, after which the photographs were passed back away from the women and taken to the other side of the yard by the young men of the family, in accordance with the community's complex social avoidance rules (Poignant 1992: 73).

The fact that photographs could perform within various and sometimes incompatible histories within the community was given material expression at Maningrida, as Poignant explains: 'soon I was doing all manner of unexpected things – such as cutting the print in half to separate the figures' (1996: 12). This not only separated the living from the dead but, where possible, complied with the avoidance rules of the community.[12] Photographs as material objects are also tactile and physical like a real person or thing. They are handled gently. As Bell describes, people traced the object in the photograph with their finger as they spoke about it. Such experiences are very different from looking at images as slides blown up in a darkened space or clustering around a computer screen to view a CD-ROM. Indeed, as the Kimberley Website Project (discussed by Stanton) revealed, few people, especially amongst the elderly, were comfortable with new technologies but instead were keen to have photo albums of prints. Different representational forms will elicit different responses and mediate the way in which photographs participate in social relations.

Nonetheless it is the indexicality of photographs – 'that it was there' – and random inclusiveness of the medium that have such potential. Photographs give information a kind of equivalence or equality, with the trivial and the significant intertwined and shifting places. 'Photography is a vast disorder of objects . . . Photography is unclassifiable because there is no reason to mark this or that of its occurrences' (Barthes 1984: 6). A function of a photograph's recodability it is that the disorder of objects forms routes into other disorders 'the big black plums and cherries that grew there, the Saturday services held there' (Binney and Chaplin this vol.). While responses of indigenous communities may appear forensic readings of the surface trace – 'this is what they wore', 'this is my grandmother', 'this is the old meeting house that burned down when I was a boy' – it would be a mistake for either communities or commentators to see them simply in these terms. As I have suggested, the processes operating within this are more extensively empowering. Narratives grounded in the forensic open the spaces for radically different articulations and thus visual repatriations. For instance, a local reading of a photograph of fishing in Mud Bay evoked commentaries by three men from Bwaidoga, D'Entrecasteaux Islands.[13] The reading was cued by a reading of the landscape inflected through land-use: fishing grounds, rocks, gardens and land reverted to bush were all enumerated. This was more than merely a detailed local reading, it shifted the significance of the photograph from both its formal and ethnographic centre – men fishing with large *lata* (square nets) – to a totally different centre, the distant wisps of smoke, indicating gardening activity. It projected significant, emotionally invested attitudes on to the photographs and triggered a history inscribed by means other than 'shown in the image'. Only through reference to local readings of land did people enter the story (Edwards 2001: 99–100).

In a similar fashion, Bell describes how the formal centre of a photograph of a colonial building was unremarked upon, despite all one might take it to stand for. Instead people described food-gathering activities and food in the surrounding land. These are not merely forensic descriptions of what is in the photograph; rather, photographs are absorbed into established ways of inscribing the past, initiating a local, historical refiguration of the images which emphasises social relations, networks and social expectations. Through photographs identities were re-asserted, and associated with control of the land, and hence the means to produce food and therefore wealth and status.[14] Layered historical inscriptions emerged – land, memory that links individual and social identity, and photograph. Similarly, as Kingston demonstrates, Hubbard's film was absorbed into the naming of kin which structures King Island ways of telling histories– Alex Muktoyuk made no less than 506 observations in this connection. Here we see the points of intersection of different ways of telling history, in which the photographs established a dynamic within the community, setting up a network of interlocking memories and narratives which increased the potential for interactive engagement.

ELIZABETH EDWARDS

FROM 'THE ARCHIVE' TO 'LIVING ENTITY'[15]

If photographs have this enormous potential to build bridges and articulate histories, where does this leave the museum? The historical performances described in these essays have major implications for museums and the way in which they curate, and for relationships developed through these strategies. To start with, issues of stewardship are especially complex with photographs. The nature of photographs and their reproducibility raise particular problems but at the same time a multitude of collaborative possibilities. As cultural objects they are largely non-indigenous, especially in the historical period. However, in terms of content they do indeed embody indigenous interests, and are subject to the same special claims, needs and rights of source communities in relation to access to material heritage (Powers 1996).

The reproducibility of photographs and their complex cross-cultural origins make them a useful first step in collaboration from which other initiatives emerge, and thus particularly appropriate for working through the issues that permeate this volume. At the same time they defy the usual arguments on restitution and repatriation. Importantly, the reproducibility of photographs and film and modern technical facilities enable collaborative interactions with material to take place, not in the museum space, where it is all too easy for institutional agendas to re-assert themselves when they are least wanted, but in local communities. Cultural knowledge and thus appropriate relationships with photographs become embedded within the relationship between space and social being. Visual repatriation enables photographs to be engaged with in 'private space' and a social space which is in some way contiguous with that from which the photographic moment was extracted – where emotions stirred by photographs are supported in their own cultural environment.

Perhaps the first step is to decentre the idea of 'The Archive'. Many critiques of Western museums have been premised on a broadly Foucauldian model of the appropriating discourse, the objectifying practices and, in the case of photographs, the 'colonial gaze', which have concentrated on the unequal power relations out of which photographs emerged. While these ideological structures undoubtedly pertain at a meta-level and are key to contested authorities, at the same time to see photographs only in these homogenising terms, denies precisely the space from which challenges might emerge. It denies the possibility of parallel realities and indigenous agency in what is inscribed in photographs[16] – that photographs might have other meanings and perform in different spaces. 'The Archive' has become, especially in post-structuralist disciplinary critiques, a stereotype of its own, a dead controlling space in which photographs 'gather dust' in the sense of being removed from active social contexts both in institutions and in communities.

However, Barthes's 'there-then becoming here-now' is not necessarily universally desirable or unproblematic. The conceptual frameworks of preservation of photographs, as for other forms of museum objects are, in many cases, alien to indigenous communities. For example, in some Pueblo societies it is not necessarily appropriate to preserve things beyond their natural life span (Powers 1996: 135), something photographs do supremely well. Nevertheless as the essays here demonstrate, the photographs in 'archives' are far from dead if we allow them the space to operate on other registers. Like other classes of object, the museum/archive stage is perhaps only a phase in the social biography of an image. The 'life history' in the title Wúrdayak/Baman Life History Photo Collection is significant because it established new community parameters for using the photographs: in Gordon Machbirrbirr's words 'The photo is still there . . . their life in that picture' (Poignant 1996: 15). Likewise Donna Oxenham, who has been involved with numerous visual repatriation projects as discussed by Stanton (this volume), sees the photographs, films and sound recordings as 'living entities' because of their importance to indigenous families searching for information about their families and their histories. Indigenous identities are not necessarily locked into the periodisation of past, present and future which is implied in the Western concept of 'the archive' of 'past records', rather all three exist in the here and now – like photographs (Oxenham, pers. com. 2002).

To develop successful collaborations and visual repatriations, photograph collections demand the same level of ethically engaged curatorship as other classes of objects. This is well established, especially in North America, New Zealand and Australia (e.g. the Berndt Museum in Western Australia discussed in Stanton's chapter), where the interests of local communities are enshrined in museum policy documents; or at the Museum of New Mexico, where photographs are specifically identified in the museum's policy of Sensitive Cultural Materials (Bernstein 1992c: 2).

If collaboration implies an active dialogic relationship around collections, then it is one that must permeate all levels of the curatorship of photograph collections. Access is a key concern, both in terms of intellectual access and the practicalities. Henrietta Fourmile expressed it forcefully:

> What use is it to me to have my Yidindji and Kunggandji heritage . . . invaluable cultural resources such as family histories, photographs, language tapes and mission records down south [of Australia]? I didn't even know these things ever existed until I was thirty years of age.
>
> (Fourmile 1990: 59).[17]

On the part of the holding institution, it requires curatorial skills to facilitate re-engagements and repatriations through appropriate procedures and tools, such as open access databases and print-out catalogues in appropriately framed language. As Smallacombe has argued, however helpful and supportive individual curators might be, the welter of finding aids and indexes, too often written in an alienating or offensive style and language, merely stresses alienation and dispossession (Smallacombe 1999: 3–4). Again, there are an increasing number of protocols, consultative committees and documents emerging for '[t]here needs to be nothing less than a total paradigm shift away from Eurocentric approaches to categorisation and description' (Byrne 1995: 7).

Community ideas of how photographs should be accessed are crucial indicators to the way in which curatorial approaches might be developed. Within communities this will be framed through local concepts of appropriateness. For instance, in accordance with local structures of knowledge and ideas of appropriateness, Zuni leaders removed photographs of religious significance from the series deposited at the A:shiwi A:wan Museum (Holman 1996: 109) . At Maningrida, Gordon Machbirrbirr was guardian of the 'Die Bodies File' which accumulated personal and community photographs of the recently deceased; after the period of mourning had elapsed, the bereaved could request prints so that photographs could be used in a shared process of mourning (Poignant 1996: 10).

Consultation between museums and communities about suitable formats is also important. The demand for locally accessible formats for Hubbard's film was the impetus for Kingston's work with King Island community (Kingston this volume), and similar demands were the impetus for the Kimberley Website Project (Stanton this vol.). There are many projects facilitating access and visual repatriation emerging at all levels of museum and community collaboration; some examples suggest the range and scale of this work. In terms of access there are digitalisation, copying programmes and the development of CD-ROMs and other educational materials for school use, for example those being developed by Brown and Peers with the Kainai Nation, of southern Alberta, Canada (see Brown and Peers in prep.). It is important that sets of prints are in a usable form, for instance Poignant's prints for the Wúrdayak/Baman Photo Collection were reproduced as good-quality photocopies which were laminated so as to withstand constant handling (Poignant 1992: 75). In the exhibition, *Lost Identities*, which has travelled to First Nations communities throughout southern Alberta, 'shadow images' which could be annotated by community members were placed alongside photographs, building up identities and comments. Access to information is equally important, for instance the Museum of Victoria has produced a catalogue of over 2,500 photographs of Aboriginal peoples in their collections which was distributed to local communities to improve knowledge of collections, and on which communities could make their own descriptions (Partos 1996). The National Anthropological Archives, Smithsonian Institution, which provided copies of its holdings for Native American communities, has a newsletter, *Smithsonian Runner*, to keep interested parties informed.[18]

The accumulated force of such work cannot fail to impact upon photograph collections and their associated curatorial practices. The information and commentaries from source communities resulting from visual collaborations can provide a firm base for informed curatorial decisions in the museum. For museums, it is necessary to understand photograph collections better, not simply in terms of 'knowing more about' and better description of content, but, as suggested in the first two sections of this chapter, to understand the *significance* of their collections in broader theoretical, historical and cross-cultural perspectives. This in turn saturates curatorial practice, opening up unimagined ways of thinking with photograph collections and interpreting them in the museum space.

As Stanton's chapter demonstrates, documentation is key to this process, but because of the evidential and realist insistence of photographs, it is easy to think at the descriptive level only. Research on the history of photography can establish a firm base for collaboration between museums and sources communities. For instance, research can identify linked groups of photographs molding a narrative and establishing 'long quotations' which have greater density for source communities, in turn extending their narratives. It can also establish the parameters of a photographer's particular vision – to what extent were images the product of the photographer's 'gaze'? To what extent did the agency of communities imprint itself on the photographic record (Poignant 1994/5: 57)? Different kinds of photographs – commercial, scientific, journalistic, mission – will carry different resonances, for instance Indian school portraits will always carry painful recollections near the surface (McMaster 1992). We are dealing with historically saturated images which will, to a greater or lesser extent, carry such baggage with them. Yet, as experience at the Berndt Museum shows, a diversity of sources brings potential density to visual histories (Stanton this volume). Museum-based research can give source communities another set of tools with which to make their own assessments of material. Documentation and collections history break the monolithic model of 'The Archive', for they show not only how categories such as 'the ethnographic' are established and function, but also how they dissolve. Visual repatriation and collaborations are active players in these serial dissolutions and should be recognised as such: on the one hand, a new and active stage in the social biography of the museum object; on the other, a photograph becoming a 'living entity'.

Access by non-community users raises a further set of issues. Various agreements on appropriate curatorial procedures have been in place in Australian, New Zealand and North American museums for some time, with, for example, restrictions being placed on material of religious significance, and access by non-indigenous researchers requiring the permission of the community. Similar to the removal of 'secret' material from the museum at Zuni, in some Australian museums, some material of a ceremonial nature can only be accessed by initiated men. However, such protocols have not, on the whole, filtered through to European museums. Certainly restrictions are in place on certain categories of material at the request of communities, for instance the Pitt Rivers Museum makes certain images available for research use 'at the print' only; they are not available for copying or publication as the latter would be inappropriate. At the National Museum of the American Indian photographs of religious or ceremonial significance can only be exhibited, published or reproduced for public or private use with the permission of the culturally affiliated group, the onus of contact being on the researcher. Such policies bring into sharp focus the conflicts between different forms of knowledge and concepts of 'appropriate' and how they conflict with 'open access' archive policies (Powers 1996). Hopi photographer Jean Fredericks voices the dilemma from the indigenous point of view:

> [P]rivately many Hopis approve of photography and want pictures of their families and celebrations, just like anyone else. Publicly, many feel they have to adopt a political position against photography . . . This is to protect their privacy.
>
> (Cited in Lippard 1992: 22)

General concerns have been raised by Holman (1996), Friedman (1998), Isaac (2002) and others about modes of knowing and the fundamental contradictions between local forms and their translation for wider audiences. For instance, the incompatibility of content and form; questions of authority; and locally motivated appropriations and refigurations, ideas of appropriate and informed consent, impact in research protocols, rules and guidelines on what can be used and how it might be disseminated and levels and access established. As Byrne has argued, 'Appropriate handling does not mean censorship. It means sensitivity to the contexts in which information agencies operate, the scope of their services and the nature of the communities they serve' (Byrne 1995: 10).

These categories are not straightforward, however, and it is not always possible to have specific guidelines or even lists of images which are 'okay' or 'not okay' because of the complex ownership and dynamic nature of knowledge within communities. While traditional knowledge might be characterised as unchanging, it remains dynamic in the way that it operates within contemporary situations (Michaels 1991: 265–6), hence the 'carpet case' discussed by Stanton. Further it is not always appropriate to discuss details, for to do so would be intrusive and indeed the construction of 'rules' might in itself be construed as a violation of indigenous authority and autonomy (Powers 1996: 131; Michaels 1991: 262). Consequently guidelines demand not so much a set of procedures as a shape of imaginative and responsive interpretations of appropriateness in any given set of relations, balancing the needs and legitimate rights of museums, source communities and other users (Powers 1996: 129). It is from such a situation that discussion groups have emerged at, for instance, the Museum of New Mexico (Bernstein 1992b) and the Museum of Indian Arts and Culture, Santa Fe. As Powers has stated, 'Such an exchange requires honesty and willingness to listen as well as speak' (1996: 136). This includes not only curators and representatives of source communities but other users of collections.

Indigenous concerns are often not only about access to the content of a photograph as such but especially about the use made of images (Holman 1996: 116). One of the problems here is the way photograph collections have been perceived in relation to other classes of object. Within many institutions, their function has been either as a source of raw data to explain other classes of objects (Edwards 2001; Porter 1989) or as a 'picture library'. Both approaches are antithetical to the kind of collaborative approaches advocated here. This is especially pertinent at a time when, in British museums and elsewhere, mantras of a politically driven and parochial concept of access merge with the illustrative and commercial potential of the 'picture library'. Put bluntly, this places curators not as mediators, facilitators and co-workers, but as brokers in a global image market, selling other people's family photographs as commodities or as 'infotainment'. Such a position threatens the integrity of work with source communities, not only in relation to photograph collections but in all aspects of an institution's relations with source communities. Ideas of informed consent, appropriate access and the ethics of release (Gross et al. 1988) are developed in relation to Western photographic practices and are not therefore an appropriate basis for making decisions about photographs in the contexts that we are considering here.[19] Here the indexicality of the photograph and curatorial ethics come together. Again, community concerns which emerge through collaborations are important in defining curatorial parameters and practices. Nevertheless, my own experience confirms Powers' claim that most demands for inappropriate access and use emerge from ignorance rather than ill-will (1996: 130). If it is part of the duties of a curator in an anthropology museum to 'educate' on cultural diversity and different world-views and to facilitate and mediate access to collections in this context, thereby balancing the needs of different users and collections, then discussing the issues openly is part of that process. In my experience users are both interested and co-operative.

Ethical curatorship also implies that photographs as material objects should be treated with respect, and that photographs should be looked after properly. The significance of the indexicality of photographs is again paramount and thus storage and access must account for responses to that indexicality. Visitors should be shown photographs in a way that shows care and attention, not left to rummage through a filing cabinet. This was brought home to me by a visiting representative of a Tasmanian community who commented that whatever the other wrongs of the situation, they were pleased to see photographs of their people so well looked after and respected. While my discussion here has been concerned with field photography, similar arguments should be extended to that overlooked category of photographs in the museum, photographs of objects. Although the degree to which the properties of an object transfer to its photographic representation is culturally specific (Michaels 1991: 268), in many cultures artefacts are family property, kin, extensions or manifestations of people or spirits and should be treated accordingly. This was forcefully demonstrated by representatives of the Haida Nation visiting the Pitt Rivers Museum Photograph Collection, whose response to nineteenth-century photographs of Haida objects was as focused and engaged as that to portraits and field photographs. Indeed, at the National Museum of the American Indian, photographs of objects of religious or ceremonial significane are subject to the same restrictions as photographs of the activities themselves.

In displays, historical photographs (or indeed any photograph) should not be used iconically, decoratively or unproblematically to 'explain' objects or to evoke a generalised affective tone (Edwards 2001: 184–9). Rather photographs should be subject to explanation themselves, intrinsic to the narrative on their own terms through the mediation of source communities.[20] Used consultatively, photographs can be used to 'people' source community voices within museum displays; again their indexicality becomes key here. This was done very successfully in *Torres Strait Islanders: An Exhibition to Mark the Centenary of the 1898 Cambridge Anthropological Expedition to the Torres Strait* in Cambridge (1998), which emerged from a long collaborative and consultative project with contemporary Torres Strait Islanders (see Herle this vol.). At the Horniman Museum, London, new portraits were used to extend contemporary African and diaspora voices in the *African Worlds* galleries (see Shelton this vol.). In communities themselves, of course, exhibition photographs perform in a totally different way, but they are becoming increasingly common at many different levels, often as a result of collaborations with museums. For instance, photographs from the Smithsonian were exhibited at the A:shiwi A:wan Museum and Heritage Centre at Zuni; *Lost Identities* was organised collaboratively by Alberta Community Development and Museums Alberta; and the Pitt Rivers Museum exhibition prints of Jenness's 1911–12 D'Entrecasteaux photographs were given to and exhibited at National Gallery of Papua New Guinea (Edwards 2001: 102–3).[21] Exhibitions remain key events through which communities can learn of the existence of photographs and re-engage with them, both as prelude and outcome of other historical activities.

CONCLUSION

An increasing body of work, from academic work to community projects, suggests the enormous potential of photographs for opening alternative histories and giving different forms of expression to telling histories. Photography can do this precisely because it invites also a subjective, internalised response, even a purely emotional response, that references different experiences and opens a space for their articulation. The space exists for recoding and absorption. There are inside ways of responding to culturally specific actualities that work through photographs, and inside ways to which the museum cannot and should not have access. For the photographic relationship is not about acquiring information for the museum but to let go of meanings so that photographs fulfil the potential of their infinite recodability. In this they bring forward many associations, both painful and pleasurable, that were invisible in the European record but still active within individual and collective memory. If, as Bruce Bernstein has argued in relation to North American collections, 'Indian people can help transform artifacts into meaningful cultural materials, alive, full of context and style, and interesting to scholars and non-scholars, Indian and non-Indian alike' (1992: 8), then the same applies to photographs.

ACKNOWLEDGEMENTS

I should like to thank all those colleagues who have commented on this essay and fed me so much relevant material, Alison Brown and Laura Peers who bravely invited me to write this piece and have given so much constructive advice; Gwyneira Isaac, Donna Oxenham and Joanna Sassoon. They have all greatly enriched my understanding of the issues.

NOTES

1 Indeed the very language of photography – photographers and subjects – is drawn from political systems in which one group dominates another (Michaels 1991: 272). This is, of course, part of a much larger process (see, for example, Desai 2001).

2 Resistance to photography has a long history (see Lyon 1988). For instance, by the early twentieth century many Native American communities, especially in the South West, USA, had prohibited photographs at ceremonials. Today permits are still required for any photographic activity in order to protect the privacy of communities as they themselves constitute it. The very real fear of photography 'stealing the soul' has become a clichéd Western primitivist explanation for any indigenous resistance to photography. However, the belief, whether literal or metaphorical, has an indisputable base in the context of the issues discussed here, for photography and the control of 'The Archive' might be said to steal the power of communities to determine their own historical voice.

3 A photographic and oral history project in Kenya, with Luo people, undertaken by Johanne Agthe and Dr Joseph Oluoch, revealed tensions between generations. The older people were sometimes uncomfortable with the 'primitive' appearance in early twentieth-century photographs, whereas the younger people were more at ease with such a record (Agthe 1994 and pers. com.).

4 This is in itself not unproblematic. As a number of post-colonial theorists have argued, the 'Other' has always spoken, but dominant tools and structures have not heard, have not been willing to hear or have merely reinscribed the voices in their own forms.

5 The law usually upholds Western notions of privacy that do not accord with indigenous concepts of rights to privacy and informed consent. For an example of such a case, see Faris's discussion (1998: 248–53) of Lilly and Norman Benally (Navajo Nation) vs. Amon Carter Museum, New Mexico, concerning their rights to privacy in relation to the publication of Laura Gilpin's famous photograph *Navajo Madonna*.

6 For a detailed discussion of 'decolonising' research methodologies, see Smith (1999).

7 Here histories/historical are used in the broadest possible sense, not a confined Western sense (see Smith 1999: 28–35).

8 Roslyn Poignant worked at Maningrida, Arnhem Land, Australia in 1992 . She undertook a major project of visual repatriation and community history around the photographs made by her late husband, distinguished documentary photographer, Axel Poignant, in 1952. There were numerous community members who remembered the six-week encounter (Poignant 1996).

9 Most modern communities have TV, a video store, access to a camera, video or digital media to record their own family and community events, and ideas of the real are inflected through this experience.

10 Ballard records a similar entanglement in Irian Jaya (pers. com.).

11 The photograph was taken by Diamond Jenness 1911–12 and was part of a small visual repatriation project undertaken by anthropologist Michael Young in 1992 with photographs from Pitt Rivers Museum, University of Oxford (Edwards 2001: 93–101).

12 Poignant also notes that there was sometimes the quiet illicit pleasure of scrutinising a photograph of one's tabooed kin (1992: 73).

13 As told to Michael Young.

14 As in many Melanesian societies, status is gained through the competitive production, display and disposal of food crops.

15 I am grateful to Donna Oxenham for providing me with this particularly apposite phrase.

16 An increasing amount of work points to the disintegration of this model (see Edwards 1998, 2001; Poignant 1994–5, 1996; Peterson and Pinney (2003)). However, it is at the same time important not to overstate this argument and deny the very real power disparities that made the act of photography possible and thinkable in the first place.

17 Attention to archival material has been especially focused since 1992 when Recommendation 53 of *The Royal Commission into Aboriginal Deaths in Custody* emphasised the need to 'provide access to all government archival records pertaining to the family and community histories of Aboriginal people to re-establish community and family links with those people from whom they were separated as a result of past policies of government' (quoted in Smallacombe 1999: 2).

18 There is sometimes a tension between the demands of a museum's financial-monitoring and income-generating systems and the needs of collaborative projects. While these costs can be written into grant-funded projects either by museums or source communities, one must not overlook everyday access and the need to have the flexibility to waive fees, produce prints at cost or provide other cheap or free copies of photographs.

19 While the judicious use of collections is not necessarily inappropriate, photograph collections seen as picture libraries are dominated by concerns of marketing departments and auditors who see photographs solely in terms of commodity, rights, permissions and fees on a global image market.

20 For a detailed examination of the reception of a single photographic exhibition in different institutional spaces, from the metropolitan to the local community, see Kratz (2002).

21 Local newspaper/newsletters also play an important role in raising consciousness of historical photographs. For example *The Namibian* ran a 'Picturing the Past' column once a fortnight throughout 1997 and 1998 in collaboration with the National Archives of Namibia, stimulating a massive interest in visual history (Hartman *et al.* 1998: 8–9).

5

TAKING THE PHOTOGRAPHS HOME

The recovery of a Māori history

Judith Binney and Gillian Chaplin

The act of taking back to their communities some early twentieth-century photographs of Māori elders unlocked both history and memory. This article analyses the creation of two very different books based on photographs and the oral histories that were narrated to the authors.

In 1977 the photographer Gillian Chaplin and I, a historian at the University of Auckland, set out with a box of early photographs into one of the centres of the Māori world: the Tūhoe people of the Urewera. We were seeking the followers of the prophet Rua Kenana Hepetipa who died, after predicting his own resurrection, in 1937. We hoped that those who had lived with him at Maungapohatu, the City of God he had created for Tūhoe, might be able to help identify the unknown faces in an extraordinary series of photographs taken between 1908 and 1937, which we and our co-author Craig Wallace had been gathering together. We expected nothing more. Instead, we found that the photographs unlocked memory. They brought forth so many associations of grief, pain and pleasure that our encounters with Rua's people became for us a transforming experience. The photographs conveyed a past that had not died in individual memories, but which had been suppressed in the European-recorded historiography. They became the means by which a people's history was recovered and their particular understanding of it brought into the world of light. In 1979 we first published the results, *Mihaia: the Prophet Rua Kenana and his Community at Maungapohatu* (Binney, Chaplin and Wallace 1979).

Some of the people to whom we had brought the photographs were not literate. But they could read the photographs, and they read them with an attention to detail that revealed their precise and very personal knowledge. Few of them had ever seen any of the photographs before. Bringing the photographs was as if we were bringing the ancestors, the *tīpuna*, to visit. Some of the oldest people talked directly to the photos. As Mrs Makere Hose had said to Michael King, when he took the portrait of the old lady Rehara Maki to her in 1968, 'Ah. It's a long time since we've been able to look at each other. It's a long time since we've been able to talk' (King 1985: 37). Our visits similarly became a reunion between the living and the dead.

When we brought the photograph of Rua's first wife, Pinepine Te Rika, taken in Auckland in 1916 (Figure 5.1), to Harimate (Materoa) Roberts, whom Pinepine had reared from a child, Harimate sang a lament to the portrait as if it were Pinepine. 'Hello Mum', she said. And then she talked about her. Pinepine was the one to whom Harimate told her dreams:

Figure 5.1 Pinepine Te Rika, Auckland, 1916. (F-74756 1/2, E. Murphy Collection, Alexander
    Turnbull Library, National Library of New Zealand/Te Puna Mātauranga o Aotearoa)

I always tell her, and she always ask me, 'Well girl, what's the meaning?' . . . 'Look
Mum, I dreaming I've been picking up charcoal for my *kai. E kai haere ana au i te
ngārehu* [I am eating charcoal].' . . . And she says, 'Why girl, why?' And I say to
her, 'Everything you say to us is come, right now. The people is start selling
Maungapohatu. . . .'

For Harimate, Pinepine was the woman from whom she acquired her knowledge,
and the photograph possessed for her a portion of Pinepine's *mauri*, or life force.
Pinepine had been a *tapu* woman: 'that's our Holy Mother, her' (Roberts 1978).
Therefore the photograph was also *tapu*. For Rua's daughter, Te Akakura, born of
another, younger generation, seeing the photographs of the old people of Maungapohatu
was an experience which brought her immense pleasure, living as she had in Auckland
city since the late 1940s. 'Who are you?' she would say to faces that she knew from her
two brief years in Maungapohatu (1926–28), 'Who are you? I remember you!'

Ancestral photos could also carry some painful associations. The group photograph
of Rua's arrest on 2 April 1916 (Figure 5.2) was crumpled and stained with tears on
more than one occasion. It had to be reprinted several times. It recalled for everyone
the 'war' of the police assault at Maungapohatu, and the bitterness that remained
because of the injustice that the community had experienced. Bringing this photograph
spurred people to discuss their knowledge with ourselves, the outsiders. Their accounts

Figure 5.2 Rua's arrest, 2 April 1916. His eldest son Whatu is handcuffed to him. The other men arrested are Maka Kanuehi, Pukepuke Kanara, and on the right, Awa Horomona and Tioke Hakaipare. Photo by A.N. Breckon. (F-28072 1/2, C.C. Webb Collection, Alexander Turnbull Library, National Library of New Zealand/Te Puna Mātauranga o Aotearoa)

had been buried under an 'orchestrated litany of lies', erected by the senior police witnesses at Rua's trial in 1916, and which had remained the orthodox account ever since. We provided the opportunity to re-open the history.

The photographs generated dialogue between us that otherwise would not have occurred. Happiness and sadness mingled in the conversations. Ira Manihera, a Ringatū *tohunga* (priest), told us that he had lived at Maungapohatu for about four years during the First World War, but he never returned after the police assault of 1916. Yet looking at the photographs of the community brought back to his mind the great opening of the meeting house Tane Nui a Rangi in 1914, when Te Arawa came through, and Rua talked, and they all had 'good *kai*' (in a world where starvation was a reality). He thanked us for coming to see him, because we had revived for him such joyful memories (Manihera 1978).

From these many dialogues, history was reconstructed. We had found some major clusterings of photographs. The first was a series taken in April 1908 – and added to during Christmas 1908 – by George Bourne, who worked for the *New Zealand Herald*. They included the photograph of Rua's first meeting house, Hiona or Zion (Figure 5.3). It is probably this photograph more than any other that has etched Rua's movement in the popular imagination. The house was spectacular, its circular shape and painted

Figure 5.3 Hiona, Rua's court house and meeting house, April 1908. Back: Te Akakura Ru; Te Aue Heurea, Rua's fourth wife; Rua; Whakaataata, Rua's eldest daughter with Pinepine; Mihiroa Te Kaawa, Rua's fifth wife. Middle: ? Whirimako Ereatara, Rua's seventh wife; Pinepine. Lower: Wairimu (Martha Vercoe), Rua's sixth wife; Pehirangi Kanuehi, Rua's second wife. (Photograph by George Bourne. C6221, Auckland War Memorial Museum)

designs being derived from the ancient tiled mosque in Jerusalem, the Dome of the Rock, which was frequently reproduced in nineteenth-century biblical engravings as the Temple of Solomon. Rua adopted the images of the club and the diamond for himself as the coming King and Messiah. Halley's comet, a warning of a new age, was added (it was due to appear in 1910), and two monograms of unknown significance were placed on either side of the lower entranceway: CA and AV Bourne photographed Rua and nine women standing on the steps and upper entrance into Hiona. Very few people to whom we showed the image could remember the meeting house, because it was pulled down by Rua on his return from prison in 1918. The iconography of the diamonds and the clubs was understood by only a few men. But most could identify the women, whom Bourne had presumably grouped for the photograph. They included Pinepine, and Rua's *rangatira* (chiefly) wife, Te Akakura Ru. This photograph was one of our starting points for the recovery of another history, that of the women of Maungapohatu.

Perhaps the most spectacular of Bourne's photographs of Rua's wives, with whom he was fascinated partly because of their plurality, was that taken on Christmas Day 1908 (Figure 5.4). It was a photograph whose power touched everyone to whom we

Figure 5.4 The women dressed in white for Christmas day, 1908. Te Akakura Ru leads, carrying the washing pails for the *wāhi tapu* area. The others are Pehirangi, ? Mihiroa. Pinepine, Wairimu (at the back), Waereti Irohia, Rua's tenth wife; Whaitiri, Whatu's wife; Te Aue; – . (Photograph by George Bourne. C5881, Auckland War Memorial Museum)

took it. It led to discussions about the relationship between the women, and the dominant role of Te Akakura, who is shown leading them forward. She is carrying pails for water, to place at the entrances to the inner *wāhi tapu* (the inner *tapu* sanctuary of the *pā*) so that people could sprinkle themselves both on entering and leaving to prevent their contamination. This photograph helped to open up an understanding of both the ritual and domestic structuring of the community.

Bourne himself seemed to have been unaware of the significance of a photograph he took of a group of young men in April 1908 (Figure 5.5). He merely called it 'a group of Ruaites at home' and commented on the various methods they had of dressing their long hair (Taipo 1908: 498). The men were young, and they were visibly poor; but they were also the Levites, the teachers of Rua's faith. If Bourne grouped these young men for his photograph, they had themselves organized who was to be in it for their own purposes. They had not only consented; they had also controlled its message for themselves.

The second clustering of photographs were taken by another *New Zealand Herald* photographer, A.N. Breckon, in 1916. The *Herald*'s reporter, John Birch, had been tipped off by the police of the intended armed expedition against Rua, and the two men were able to travel with the police from Auckland to record the events. Their presence

Figure 5.5 The Levites, April 1908. They are: Back: Pita Te Taite, Pinepine's elder brother; Teka Hekerangi; – ; – ; Tuhua Pari; – ; Tauru Tuhua. Middle: Tatu Haropapera; Wharepapa Hawiki. Front: Te Wairama Taoho. (Photograph by George Bourne. C5882, Auckland War Memorial Museum)

was intended to glorify the crowning episode in the career of the Commissioner of Police, John Cullen, but the photographs recorded crucial elements in the assault that ran counter to the sworn evidence of the senior police and Birch. They substantiated the Māori witnesses' statements. One critical photograph (never published) was that of armed police guarding the women, whom the police claimed they had never restrained (Figure 5.6). The long shadows indicate that several hours had passed since the morning's shooting. Another photograph, which was reproduced in the newspapers, was in fact an artificial reconstruction posed after the shooting was over. This we learnt by taking it to one of the policemen, Tom Collins, who had been there, and who turned out to have posed for the photograph (Figure 5.7). It had served, by being repeatedly re-published, to perpetuate the popular version of the assault as the 'brave police under ambush'; the oral testimony placed it in a very different context of calculated image-making on the part of the police.

Undoubtedly the key photograph was that (almost certainly) snapped by the police doctor, Rex Brewster (Figure 5.8). It verifies the Māori witnesses' statements that Rua did not resist arrest at all, but threw up his arms to the mounted police, who had ridden

Figure 5.6 The women under guard. Two policemen stand beside them, one with a drawn revolver in his hand. (Photograph by A.N. Breckon. John B. Turner private collection, Auckland)

straight onto the *marae* (enclosure), and called out '*Taihoa*' (Wait). This photograph was never presented by Rua's defence counsel, although it was found among his papers. Brewster was by then absent at the war and, presumably, the photograph could not be used in evidence without his having identified it, even though its existence was mentioned in court.

The photographs also offered a means of testing the written sources. Because they freeze a moment, they record that moment in ways that human memory and written words do not. Memory and words both elaborate and select. If, as Susan Sontag has said, photographs artificially fragment continuities (Sontag 1978: 22, 156), they can also sometimes provide critical details. Thereby, as in this case, although they cannot create a 'moral position', they can reinforce it (ibid.: 17). Rua's arrest and trial were a perversion of justice; the photographs provide evidence to confirm that judgment.

The third clustering of photographs were taken by Presbyterian missionaries in the years after 1918. Less spectacular visually, being mostly of the Brownie box camera variety, they still recorded central aspects of the community's ritual revival and physical reconstruction. Again, they were able to be read for information that none save the Iharaira (the Israelites), Rua's followers, possessed. The blurred and badly angled

Figure 5.7 The police posing behind the tree stump. Tom Collins identified the three policemen in the marked inner portion, which was reproduced in the *Auckland Weekly News*, 13 April 1916, as John Garvey; himself (both armed with revolvers); and John Reilly, a police marksman, armed with a rifle which cannot be seen. This uncropped version was found among Rua's defence counsel, J.R. Lundon's papers. (Photograph by A.N. Breckon)

portrait of four women in cloaks (Figure 5.9) records a particular occasion; it is not just a poor snapshot. It was taken on the day of 'bringing in the flowers', when Rua gave the 'meaning' of their chosen flowers to each of the women present. The future of each participant was foretold through her choice. It was, therefore, a day all remembered.

The photographs also gave us a means of testing our informants. For in explaining who individuals might be, informants also quite often explained their own relationship with them. Some people were confident, some cautious. Confidence usually reflected the degree of knowledge, but occasionally it shielded a bluster. By consulting widely from family to family, we came to know the networks of relationship and who were the more accurate informants. We came to understand many private histories.

One of our most important visits was the occasion, in January 1978, when we returned to Maungapohatu with two of Rua's daughters, Te Akakura and Putiputi. The experience was profound for both women, and their very different responses to visiting their father's derelict home at Maai are captured in Chaplin's photograph (Figure 5.10). Te Akakura, the city-dweller, was the elder daughter of Rua and of his pre-eminent wife, whose name she bore. Her pride and her powerful personality can be seen, for as her father had told her, 'You are of your blood'. Puti was the daughter of Rua's second wife, Pehirangi

Figure 5.8 Whatu (left), Rua (with hands outstretched), and his second son Toko (right) who was shot by the police in the assault, waiting for the police on the *marae*. The police commissioner, John Cullen, is turning to look back at the mounted police behind him. This would appear to be the moment when Rua put up his hands and called out '*Taihoa*', as the Māori witnesses described. (Photograph probably by Dr Rex Brewster. Lundon collection)

Kanuehi. Pehirangi was a quiet woman, who in the 1920s ran a little shop selling sweets and cigarettes at Maai. Puti's sadness is due to her recollection of the many years she had lived at Maai, both as a child and as a young married woman. She spoke of the memories that came flooding back: the big, black plums and the cherries that grew there; the Saturday services in front of the house, when her father and the Levites sat on the veranda before the congregation; and all the people who had lived there (Onekawa 1978). The photograph taken that day of the two sisters was seminal for us, for it came to stand not only for our great debt to Rua's children but also for our growing awareness that private histories can reveal a larger history. This photograph was the seedbed of our second book, *Ngā Mōrehu: the Survivors* (Binney and Chaplin 1986).

If *Mihaia* was about the recovery of history, *Ngā Mōrehu* was about the making of history. It contains the oral narratives of eight women whose lives interconnect and form part of the living history of the Ringatū faith. Here the use of photographs was of a significantly different kind. Most were private photos, that is, they were personal portraits of family or community occasions, *hui* or *tangi*. As published, they are collated to illuminate the particular histories generated by each oral account. For Māori oral histories are essentially family histories; they belong to particular *whānau* or *hapū*.

Figure 5.9 Bringing in the flowers. The women are Whakaataata, Matatu Mahia, Te Aue, Pinepine. (F-30896 1/2, Sister Annie Henry Collection, Alexander Turnbull Library, National Library of New Zealand/Te Puna Mātauranga o Aotearoa)

Figure 5.10 Te Akakura and Putiputi, Rua's daughters, at Rua's house at Maai, 21 January 1978. (Photograph by Gillian Chaplin)

It is therefore misconceived to amalgamate them with other family histories, for all have their own purposes, linking the family into the larger tribal or religious history. *Ngā Mōrehu* attempted to retain this structure of orality and the photographs were integral to it. Chaplin's portraits of the individual women were taken in places that they themselves chose because of their particular associations. The women stand out as they are, undramatized by special lighting effects or technical manipulation. The historical photographs reproduced in the book did not unravel the past, for those photos were usually known to the women or, if not, confirmed what was known. The photographs were therefore a living part of memory: they did not unlock memory as the previously unknown photographs had done for Rua's people.

Sontag has said that photographs are 'not so much an instrument of memory as an invention of it or a replacement' (Sontag 1978: 165). She argued that it is not reality that they make accessible, but rather images. However, the unknown images we brought to the elderly Māori people of Rua, who had been marginalized not only from European society but also to some extent in their own world in later years, confirmed for them their reality. They recorded in particular and significant detail a past that affirmed what they were waiting for: the coming of Rua as the Messiah. The photographic images had recorded that past in a series of moments whose meaning they could bring alive. It was a history which until then had had little or no acknowledgement in the outside world.

In essence, the importance of photographs to all Māori who hold traditional values is that they record the images of their ancestors. They exist as a bond between the living and the dead. Portraits of dead kin are hung in the meeting houses to which they belong, so that the continuity, the line of descent, the *iho*, is retained. Photographs are the contemporary extension of the ancestral carved figures, who support the meeting house and the living, and they have been used in this manner since the late nineteenth century. Photographs of the dead kin are brought out at *tangi* and placed by the *tūpāpaku* (the body). They are addressed during the speeches as if the person himself were present. In 1908 an uninvited photographer, as Bourne was, was regarded initially with suspicion at Maungapohatu and labelled *Taipo*, goblin or magician; but he was soon able to be accepted for Māori purposes. He was invited back to celebrate Christmas. Seventy-one years later, at the launching of *Mihaia* at Tuapo, Rua's family *marae* and resting place in the Bay of Plenty, the unlettered Paetawa Miki, guardian of Maungapohatu and one of Rua's followers, spoke with pleasure about the photographs. They and the details they contained were, for him, the book, and as he said, 'This is a book I can read'.

NOTE

This essay was prepared in connection with *In Our Image*, an exhibition proposed by the National Art Gallery of New Zealand.

6

LOOKING TO SEE

Reflections on visual repatriation in the Purari Delta, Gulf Province, Papua New Guinea

Joshua A. Bell

In a recent meditation on reading and writing histories (to which my title alludes), Dening (2001: 32) comments,

> The first mark of my history, the first reading I make, are always shaped by the transience of the moment in which they were made. . . . It belongs to times that are so long or short or broken or continuous as the human experience that sustains it.

While of different ontological status, photographs, one of the marks of the intersecting histories on which I am working, share the same social embeddedness (Morphy and Banks 1997). Outside of the museum or archive and brought back to the field of their original production, visual repatriation (Fienup-Riordan this vol.) or photo-elicitation (Collier and Collier 1986) has emerged as another aspect of photographs' social lives (Appadurai 1986). Used productively to re-engage indigenous communities, visual repatriation can generate counter-narratives to the once monolithic, colonial and disciplinary histories that the photographs themselves often helped to create and sustain. In the process, visual repatriation helps untangle the knots that bind these histories, their narratives and the assumptions invested in them (Binney and Chaplin this vol.; Edwards 1994; Poignant 1996). In this chapter, I discuss the role of two photographic collections in eliciting narratives about past and present social transformations experienced by individuals and communities in the Purari Delta of Papua New Guinea and address what local communities receive from visual repatriation. Moving through a series of examples, I explore the range of responses, problems and mutual benefits in conducting such a project. In doing so, this chapter points to the productive ways photographs can be used to create new links between museums and host communities.

While the collections used in this project have distinct trajectories, both emerged out of the anthropological attempt to document the inhabitants of the Purari Delta during the first half of the twentieth century. Currently housed in the University of Cambridge Museum of Archaeology and Anthropology (UCMAA), the first collection was created by Dr A.C. Haddon and his daughter, Kathleen Rishbeth, while in the Territory of Papua (hereafter Papua) for three months in 1914 (Rishbeth 1999). The second collection, taken by F.E. Williams in 1922 during the eight months of his first assignment as Papua's governmental anthropologist, is held in the National Archives of Papua New Guinea (NAPNG), and the National Archives of Australia (NAA) (Young and Clark 2001).[1] Produced at the height of the region's popularity among European anthropologists, both sets of photographs became objects of distinction[2] whereby people, material culture and views were collected and later classified as part of a developing colonial visual economy (Edwards 2000; Poole 1997; Thomas 1991).

Following Edwards' observation that 'the mutability of [photographs'] meaning[s], contain their own future, because of the near-infinite possibilities of new meanings to be absorbed' (2001: 6); it is not surprising that these two collections continue to function as objects of distinction, albeit for local purposes. The photographs are currently being absorbed into an evolving critique of Malaysian industrial logging in the Purari and into negotiations surrounding the ambiguities of chiefly hierarchy, clan history and resource ownership. They have helped revitalize inter-generational communication by giving aspects of the past a new *presence*. In so doing the collections have become new loci for the transmission of stories, traditions and life histories (Binney and Chaplin, this volume; Poignant 1996: 5). This, however, is not a straightforward process, but involves personal as well as clan rivalries and is overshadowed by the threat of sorcery. Ownership, which has always been reckoned through one's ancestors' actions (glossed here as history), has become an arena of intense dispute because at its heart it is also a debate about identities. Not surprisingly, my role in bringing the collections did not escape local scrutiny and was framed as part of the return of a mythical lost younger brother's descendant. I will return to this facet of my experience by the way of a conclusion, because it highlights local expectations about what my research and potential partnerships with the collections' holding institutions can do for the Purari's communities.[3]

SITUATING THE PURARI: METHODOLOGY AND LOCAL REACTIONS TO VISUAL REPATRIATION

The Purari Delta comprises a 1,300 square mile area of channels and sago swamps and is located along the country's southern coast, 200 miles west of Port Moresby, PNG's capital. The inhabitants of the region's 20 villages, who number approximately 10,000 people, belong to six interrelated but self-described 'tribes': the Baroi, I'ai, Kaimari, Koriki, Maipua and Vaimuru (Petr 1983). Speaking dialects of the same non-Austronesian language (H.A. Brown 1973), they share a common bundle of cultural practices whose current configuration is the result of the interplay between local and foreign agents (missionaries, labour recruiters, anthropologists and government officials) over the last century. Like other coastal Papuan societies (Knauft 1993), each tribe is divided into *ravi* (longhouse), that form hamlets within villages and which are composed of several *airu* or *ava'i* (exogamous patrilineal clans) of various mythic origins. The province of men, the *ravi* before their abandonment in 1946 (see below), were a principal site for the reproduction of society and its associations with *imunu* (ancestral spirits) (Haddon 1919; Holmes 1924; Maher 1961; Williams 1923, 1924). While the *ravi* are now absent, they remain, alongside the clans, one of the primary units of identity within each tribe.

For this project I worked with 58 of the Haddon photographs and 76 prints from the Williams' collection, both sets constituting the full known range of each collection's images of the Purari. Given the random inclusiveness of photographs, and not knowing what type of image would provoke responses, I brought all the images I could locate, regardless of subject matter (Edwards 1994: 12). Both collections' visual content can be broken down into three overlapping categories:

1   snapshots or posed 'scientific reference' (Edwards 2001: 133–81) images of individuals or groups (sometimes containing Europeans);
2   photographs whose subject matter is material culture (architecture, canoes and portable objects);
3   landscape photographs which include villages, government stations, and or natural features.

These categories are of my own making and were not used as an organizing principle when presenting the collections. Indeed, as I soon discovered, much of what I thought was the principal subject of a photograph, turned out to be inconsequential details for locals. Both the Haddons and Williams were consistent with their geographic attribution, which made it possible to divide the photographs on the basis of village and tribal group. During interviews, unless asked, I presented images only from the interviewee's tribal group. This cut down on what would otherwise be an unwieldy number of photographs for people to process. I showed the photographs in a binder in no particular order and I took care to let viewers decide the rate at which images were viewed.

Each photograph was scanned directly from a study print or a laser photocopy and then printed from a computer. While I attempted to print each photograph only with its accession number, due to the inferior quality of some laser copies and a lack of time, I resorted to using scans of Williams' plates from his 1924 monograph with their original published captions. As captions too often influence how we see an image (Barthes 1977), by excising them I tried to provide villagers with the least mediated image possible. I created a separate index of published and unpublished captions for reference. The presence of these few captions had a definite effect on how the photographs were collectively understood. Early in my stay, while showing Paul, a retired agricultural officer of some social standing among the I'ai, the entire Williams' collection at his request, he noted the discrepancy between named portraits of Koriki men versus unnamed portraits of I'ai men (in each collection women if pictured make up a small fraction of the portraits).[4] While in this case the presence of the captions was an artefact of my doing, the fact that Williams provided names of his Koriki subjects may reflect his greater familiarity with them.[5] The difference in named and unnamed portraits, however, may also just as easily be a product of spoiled plates, the damage occurring either while attempting to take photographs or develop them.[6] While I tried to explain these vicissitudes, Paul insisted that the fault for the anonymous I'ai portraits lay not with Williams but with the men themselves.

He understood the lack of names to be symptomatic of the long-standing fear among the I'ai of publicly disclosing their histories and, therefore, indicative of the men's lack of concern for their descendants' welfare.[7] Sorcery, caused by jealously of one's ancestral claims, stands as the greatest impediment to the I'ai's public assertions of histories. This past and present inability, Paul concluded, lies at the root of their current problems receiving recognition by the two Malaysian logging companies, Turama Forest Industry (TFI) and Rimbunan Hijau (RH), operating in the Purari interior.[8] In 1995, while I'ai clans formed Incorporated Land Groups (ILGs), the registered bodies through which customary resource tenure is legally recognized, they have yet to receive any of the royalty payments that began to flow to other tribes' registered ILGs in 1999. Owned by clans, history has always been a discourse about identity. Receiving money is seen as a national and international confirmation and legitimization of a clan's history and thus identity. This lack of recognition has compounded the normal regional contestation of history to the extent that the I'ai have been all but paralysed. Among the Koriki, it was asserted that having to form ILGs helped break down *vupu* (laws) about the public discussion of histories. As Koivi, a young man explained, the registry process 'showed us [the younger generation] how important history is'. Many Koriki elders viewed such statements cynically, arguing that history's new 'importance' for younger men relates to its perceived efficacy in obtaining money through the ILGs. In contrast, I'ai elders looking through the collections frequently expressed the need to overcome their longstanding problem and, as one urged, '[we] must reveal the whole hidden history because it may be the last time someone comes to record our ancestral history.' An elder added that if given 'correctly', then development would finally come to the I'ai.[9]

In what now can only be seen as an ironic twist of history given present preoccupations, an indigenous push for economic self-sufficiency following the Second World War led by an I'ai man named Tom Kabu, disrupted the cultural mnemonics through which chiefly hierarchy and clans' histories were principally reproduced (Connerton 1989). In the name of business, the Kabu Movement (1946–69) broke up villages and resettled people for cash cropping. In order for 'the light' to enter and so as to become like *urupu kape a'a* (white-skinned people), the *ravi* were abandoned, clay pots replaced by aluminium, carvings left to rot at the old villages, and rituals phased out.[10] As part of this restructuring and signalling the movement's wider horizons, Kabu instituted European-style homes, adopted Hiri Motu as a *lingua franca* (Dutton 1985), and introduced the Baha'i faith. Through his business activities Kabu introduced new avenues for social advancement that helped erode the traditional hereditary leadership structures.[11] While unsuccessful in achieving its long-term goals, the movement created new structures of feeling that ushered in different perceptions of time and culture, which still have a deep resonance today (Maher 1961, 1967, 1984).

Paul's underlying insistence that the photographs were *proof* prefigured most reactions to the collections. With all the groups with whom I conducted visual repatriation, the photographs were equated with surviving ancestral heirlooms which, individually owned, have emerged as reinvigorated markers of identity, history and resource ownership (Bell 2001). As one young I'ai man remarked while showing me an ancestral *ua* (pig tusk), 'We keep this as our *eve uku* (hand mark), as I said earlier, evidence. We have evidence of what we say, not the word only.' Using similar rhetoric, Omaro, a middle-aged Koriki man, told me before I left his village following a visual repatriation session:

> A lot of these photos are helping us prove who our *amua* [class of chief] are. Photos like this help us identify who the *amua* were, because now many people are claiming to be *amua*. If you have more photos like these, please bring them.

Alongside these heirlooms, the photographs are understood to be not only *from* the past, but also through their indexicality they are *of* the past, thereby providing evidence that supersedes otherwise contestable oral claims. As 'certificate[s] of presence' (Barthes 1984: 87) the collections give the past tangibility, a past for which most of whose material markers and thus verifiability have disappeared.[12] The collections' overseas origin also lent them an aura of power that complemented the heirlooms' mythic origins. The incorporation of the collections echoes Stewart's argument (1984: 184) that 'we need and desire souvenirs of events that are reportable, events whose materiality has escaped us, events that thereby exist only through the invention of narrative.' Through their images of *koi* (stylized carved representations of ancestors), individuals (assumed chiefs) and the *ravi*, the photographs both generated and were invested with these narratives. However, the desire to claim the images as markers of the narrator's clan meant that I often had to preface their viewing with the photographs' geographic origin. However, as the project progressed, I became less concerned with truth registers, which at one level are, in any case, culturally specific, and realized that the collections' importance and value lay in their ability to inspire the public and private performance of oral histories (Edwards 2001).

People responded to the collections with overwhelming enthusiasm. As a result I typically had to carry out first a public, and often chaotic viewing of the images. During these meetings I handed photographs, as local protocol dictated, to male elders first, who then passed them to the gathered younger men, followed by the women and children. The cacophony of responses necessitated the reliance on taping sessions, which I later translated and transcribed. This allowed me to record some of these sessions' spontaneity. After these meetings, I moved to more controlled group interviews where elders gathered surrounded by interested individuals. At elders' request, I then set up individual interviews during which we discussed the photographs in a more private setting.[13] What emerged during this process was the nature of public versus private historical discourses. In multi-clan settings, personal reminiscences and topics deemed appropriate for public consumption, such as rituals, songs and the construction/use of objects were discussed. Alone or surrounded by immediate family, discussions also consisted of the latter but incorporated genealogies and thus personal connections to land or chiefly status. Individuals whose identity was publicly puzzled over, in private were pronounced with much conviction. In these settings heirlooms were displayed alongside the collections, and individual photographs were more readily incorporated into personal histories.[14] While recognizing the nuances of these two discourses, they both compose the 'plural frames of history' (Edwards 1994: 12) which the photographs provoked and participated in during their re-inscription.

People aged 65 and older responded the most enthusiastically to the collections, as they were the last generation to have experienced the *ravi*, its ceremonies, and the Kabu Movement. It is principally with these male and female elders that the most productive dialogues emerged. They were the only individuals capable of making cultural sense of the images. Photographs of individuals, such as Williams' *Three Iari Men* (in which men adorned in shell valuables, and holding bows stand in front of a backdrop) provoked various responses when publicly viewed. Principally addressing each other and then their audience, elders named each object worn, how they were made or obtained, their use and what status these objects conferred; thus restoring the objects to their former social, political and economic nexuses. Today such items, if they exist, are generally relegated to the inside of a suitcase. Their cultural pride reawakened, many elders left the gathering, only to return wearing their own shell valuables and items of traditional adornment, much to the amusement of all. In very concrete terms, this photograph and others like it allowed elders to perform otherwise neglected aspects of their identity. For many, the pasts presenced by the photographs overwhelmed them emotionally. Within the context of this image, one elder, Mailau, wiping his eyes remarked, 'I just saw olden time decorations and my eyes are forming tears.' For most, the photographs showed objects and scenes that had been absent for over 50 years. It was common to hear the lament *sori* (sorry) repeated under people's breath. Other concurrent discourses also emerged. Another elder, named A'ape, held up the same photograph stating, 'This is how our ancestors used to be! *Voa dipi dipi* [not very good].' Elders often invoked Tom Kabu, who, depending on the narrator's inclination, was either praised or vilified for destroying their traditional culture; an action that many attribute with causing the current state of confusion regarding resource ownership and chiefly hierarchy. In contrast, younger men openly laughed at this and other such photographs, commenting in regard to this particular image that the people photographed must be Africans. While the cultural distancing exhibited in this comment can be a common feature of visual repatriation (Niessen 1991: 420), in this context I believe the young men's remarks are not indicative of contemporary Christian concerns, but rather reveal the degree to which, for them, the past is a foreign country (Lowenthal 1985).

What is lost in this account so far is a discussion of how people physically engaged with the photographs. As I remarked earlier, images of personal adornment induced people to go find and wear their own such objects. Similarly, photographs of the *ravi* and particularly the *aiai'imunu* (mother ancestral spirits) masks prompted both male and female elders to sing. Worn by men, these masks were danced as part of an annual ritual that celebrated and renewed ties with the spirits. On more than one occasion elderly women demonstrated how, as young girls, they danced with their arms raised around their clan's *aiai'imunu* while mimicking the cries of their clan's *opa* (totems). Men, who as young adults wore the masks, related how they were worn and their personal experiences of dancing them. An image of the exterior of the I'ai *ravi*, Aikavalavi, caused its male elders to recall in detail the building of the last *ravi*, which they witnessed in the late 1930s. They spontaneously began pounding the floor to the rhythm of the hand drums and performed the songs of the *ravi* opening, as well as the songs sung during the *aiai'imunu* festival. The photographs were also touched, with the outline of people and objects traced by fingertips and, in more private settings, held intimately while crying. Similarly, as in the case of a photograph of a re-modelled Koriki skull taken by Williams, Karara an elder of the village of Kairimai, lifted and held up the photograph for the assembled onlookers as he explained the lapsed memorial practice surrounding this object (Figure 6.1).

Viewers also reinscribed the photographs with former patterns of movement and relationality. Individuals spent a lot of time attempting to locate where a photograph was physically taken. This was pronounced while examining *A Scene in Iari*, the discussion of which revealed aspects of social geography alongside the histories inscribed in the relationship between the environment, objects and people. The photograph's foreground depicts several women closing off a creek with an *uru* (a fishing weir) while across the river, on the opposite bank, sits the village's government rest house, surrounded by trees. I thought that this photograph would stimulate discussion of colonialism and

Figure 6.1 Engaging with photographs in the Koriki village of Kairimai, 2001. (Photograph by Joshua A. Bell)

while people did talk about government patrols and regulations, these narratives were a secondary concern.

Older women focused on the photograph's foreground, revealing aspects of their social orientation to the environment and in food-gathering activities. Among other things (the creek's name, the height of the tide, etc.) they remarked on the shifting nature of fishing technology. Previously women's work, today fishing is no longer defined as such. Similarly, nylon nets that were introduced in the 1970s have largely replaced *uru*. This shift has brought with it subtle changes in the social aspects of fishing, specifically the movement away from communal to more solitary fishing practices. In contrast, the men focused almost exclusively on the photograph's background: the trees. Identifying individual trees, such as *kemu* (tulip, *Gnetum gnemon*) and *imara* (breadfruit, *Atrocarpus altilis*) the trees' owners were also named despite the 80 intervening years since the photograph was taken. Besides being a major food source, trees are the inherited property of men (women once married use the trees belonging to their husband's clan) and are an important marker of male status. Trees were and still are a major source for local material culture – canoes, houses, carvings, tools, rope, etc. (Williams 1924). The men also focused specifically on three *ipa'a* trees (erima, *Octomeles sumatrana*). They recalled each tree's personal names, as well as the names of their deceased owners, when each tree was cut down, by whom, and for what purpose, and also what was consumed at the ensuing feast. These are not just inconsequential details but are rather indicative of the multiple layers of people's engagement with their environment (Hirsch and

117

O'Hanlon 1995). Most large trees are believed to be the site of *iri imunu* (tree spirits), who must be appeased through feasting before their homes are cut down. Supernatural beings, *imunu* are likened to humans but dwell invisibly in the environment in trees or specific locations in rivers or the ground. When seen they are usually in the form of various animals (crocodiles, pigs, birds, cassowary), whose *ruru* (skin or covering) they can wear. Clans trace their origins to a specific *imunu* (Maher 1974).

The two collections' images of *ravi* interiors, besides eliciting similar details of movement to those elaborated while looking at *A Scene in Iari*, in the process also elicited ancestral narratives. Many of the traditional objects stored in the *ravi* were also types of *ruru* worn by *imunu*. *Koi*, one such object, were displayed as part of an accumulated ensemble of materials a clan kept in their section of the *ravi*. Individually named and owned by a clan's male members, *koi* were used to instruct initiates as to their clan's origins. Not only did *koi* represent ancestors, their stories and thus tracts of land and water, but they also represented their owners and their patrilineal lines of descent (Maher 1961; Williams 1924; cf. Beier and Kiki 1970). Alluding to these chains of significance, a Koriki woman named Varia had to excuse herself while looking through the Haddons' images of Koriki *ravi* interiors because, as she remarked, 'the sight of so many *koi* makes me feel sad for those that have died.' Her comments encapsulate local articulations of what many argue is a common Melanesian cultural theme, the intersection of people and the material world, such that people are understood to be composites of accumulated actions (Strathern 1988). With the return of the collections, these sets of relationships have now become rearticulated through viewing the photographs. The collections can be thought of as a new 'skin' in which the dead, spirits and their histories can dwell and circulate.

FRAMES FOR THE FUTURE: PHOTOGRAPHS AS CONTAINERS OF HISTORIES

My arrival in the region was framed as the current phase of a myth in which I was positioned as the descendant of an I'ai ancestral hero, Kairi Arikinumere. With his elder brother Mailau, Kairi descended from the sky and together they assembled the dispersed clans that would become the I'ai. However, in the course of giving these people *vupu* (laws), a disagreement arose between the brothers and Kairi left for the West. However, this was not before prophesying that either he or a descendant would eventually return to help the I'ai. My interest in history, as I described my research, but more importantly my possession of the two photographic collections, confirmed this genealogical connection for many. It was hoped that with the photographs I would help ensure their successful resource ownership negotiations and thus herald development's arrival (Bell 2001). As Luktehaus (1995) found during her research on Manam, such ancestral linkages prompted by photographs can help establish an intense relationship with people quickly, but it also surrounds one with an aura of strangeness and power (Niessen 1991). Using the pervasive Melanesian idiom of kinship, it raises the often uncomfortable question of what a researcher can and will do for their host community (cf. Kirsh 1996; Tuzin 1997). While the articulation of these expectations may make one personally uncomfortable, as they did in my case, I believe as researchers we need to take these relationships and their obligations seriously. This does not mean we should play the role of a returning ancestral hero, but we do need to think about what we, and the institutions we represent, can do for host communities. These may not be easy questions but they are issues we must come to terms with. Of course, the return of photographs, in this case the very items that helped shape the construction of my genealogical connection to Kairi, is one way in which to re-engage with host communities. As the various chapters in this volume show, the benefits that can and do emerge out of this process of re-engagement are multiple.

As 'a third party' (Collier and Collier 1986: 105), the photographs allowed me to ask specific questions regarding objects depicted (their use, construction, names, etc.), which otherwise would have gone unasked because of their absence in the contemporary situation. It also gave me a visual frame of reference with which to understand narratives and then, in turn, use these to question informants about the specifics of their experience. This material will be incorporated within each holding institution's existing databases for the collections, as well as in the PNG National Museum and Art Gallery. Unfortunately, the combination of a lack of a cultural centre and the tropical environment's harsh treatment of paper, which rots in the humid climate, has meant that at present I have not deposited copies of the collections locally. Copies of my work will be available, however, as eventually will the photographs, once local storage conditions improve. Through these various levels, the material that evolved out of this visual repatriation project will be preserved and will hopefully become part of a sustained dialogue and resource for future generations in the Purari.

Locally, these photographs have become sites through which traditions were revisited, contested and publicly discussed, thus giving elders a chance to share unspoken aspects of their individual and collective histories. With their ability to inscribe landscapes, architecture, people and portable objects, the collections preserve these otherwise transient forms of historical inscriptions. Through giving the past a new presence, the collections have illuminated realms of experience that in the current environment may have otherwise gone unmentioned. Despite some elders' beliefs that the present generation's interest in the past revolves around its potential efficacy in achieving personal wealth available through the logging ventures, I feel that the discussions surrounding the collections went beyond being motivated only by politics. The density and range of the genres of oral histories, the different levels of their enactment – song, dance, dialogue, the display of heirloom and non-heirloom objects – and the excitement that they generated both in their narrators and in their audiences, point to the extent that these meetings were not just about histories but also about the celebration of cultural identity. Thus in the face of perceived cultural loss that has been internalized in the region's historical narratives and sense of self, the collections have provided a means for the expression of cultural identity which for many has been dormant. By helping elicit these elders' enactments of their histories, the two collections have created a space through which elders' memories and experiences could be channelled and illustrated for the present generation. Visual repatriation has given the elders something to 'hang' their stories on. In doing so, the photographs, like ancestral heirlooms, act as a proof of the past, supplementing and stimulating oral narratives. As one enthusiastic young I'ai man remarked after one session, 'I don't know about the rest of you, but I am learning. I have never heard such stories!' Both publicly and privately the collections have facilitated the transmission of histories and thus hopefully their continued reproduction.

Aptly described as 'a transforming experience' (Binney and Chaplin, this vol.), visual repatriation creates spaces wherein the host community, researcher and holding institution can revisit and rework intersecting histories as they are embodied and displayed in their various by-products. In returning photographs taken by our anthropological ancestors of their ancestors, both the fieldworker and host community can re-engage in dialogues that began long ago: dialogues which at the time they were begun may have been unequal because of existing colonial structures, and which have remained unfinished. The resulting conversations 'open up these objects' stratigraphy' (Seremetakis 1994: 7), enabling the critical reappraisal of how we have represented our mutually entangled histories, of which they are a product. The resulting collaboration can then be used critically to examine the genealogies of our narratives about host communities, the roots of which in the particular case of the Purari, partially lie in the photographs and the ideas they helped their authors generate (Haddon 1920; Williams 1923, 1924), and which still influence our constructions today (Knauft 1993; Maher 1961; Newton 1961). Visual repatriation is a step in the process of reinvesting host communities with a degree of agency and a voice in what we write about them.

Visual repatriation highlights how photographs, and indeed all ethnographic objects, are containers of histories (Neumann 1992: 16), not only of a biographical nature, but also in the sense of their ability to elicit and thereby contain within their frames multiple narratives, histories of the past, present and future. In discussing our relationship to objects, Wagner suggests that in learning to use objects, we learn to use ourselves in new ways; 'we admit into our personalities the whole range of values, attitudes, and sentiments – indeed creativity – of those who invented them.' Objects 'are "invested" with life . . . they partake in the self, and also create it' (Wagner 1981: 76–77). What I would like to suggest is that with visual repatriation, in the interchange that transpires as we meet to look and talk, in the process we are learning to see. By this I do not mean that we learn to see in the sense of the narrow confines of a photograph's contents but rather, as I have discussed throughout this chapter, we learn to see the wider sets of relationships not only within local communities between people, landscape and objects, but also the relationships that bind together the institutions we represent with the host communities with which we work. Visual repatriation enables the re-visioning of these relationships, their histories and, as such, the future direction of their partnership. In this sense, visual repatriation helps return to photographs some of the 'transience of the moment in which they were made' and thus helps us to look, see and write histories that do justice to the 'human experience that sustains' (Dening 2001: 32) them and their objects.

ACKNOWLEDGEMENTS

The material presented here is part of my dissertation research on past and present social transformation in the Purari Delta. At the time that this paper was written, I had completed 12 months of fieldwork. As in the case of any long-term project, I am indebted to many people and institutions, however any omissions or errors are my own. Research on the Haddons' collection began in 2000 under the auspices of a Crowther-Beynon grant administered by the University of Cambridge Museum of Archaeology and Anthropology (UCMAA). I would like to thank Anita Herle and Sudeshna Guha of the

UCMAA and Godfrey Waller of the Manuscripts Reading Room in the Cambridge University Library (CUL). In October 2000, with the help of travel grants from Dartmouth College and Hertford College, University of Oxford, I first went to the Gulf Province with Robert L. Welsch and Senior Technical Officer of the Papua New Guinea National Museum and Art Gallery, Sebastian Haraha. Sharing his enthusiasm for the Gulf, Robert L. Welsch has graciously given me both practical advice on fieldwork as well as for my work. Sebastian Haraha's family generously shared their home, which helped ease transitions between the Purari and Moresby. During my initial trip in 2000 I began working with copies of the Haddons' collection. Before returning to the Purari, the staff of both the National Archives of Australia (NAA) and the National Archives of Papua New Guinea (NAPNG) helped me obtain copies of the Williams' collection. Field research for my dissertation resumed in March 2001 and finished in November 2002. A 2001 Crowther-Beynon grant and a dissertation grant (GR6700) from the Wenner-Gren Foundation provided funding for this phase of my research. I am grateful to PNG's National Research Institute (NRI) and the National Museum and Art Gallery for helping facilitate my research and for providing in-country affiliation. As my project has unfolded, my supervisors Michael O'Hanlon and Elizabeth Edwards have given me insightful feedback that has helped me tease out different nuances of my field material. I am also grateful to the editors of this volume for asking me to submit a chapter and then for dealing with the various difficulties that arose in its long-distance editing while I was in the field. My greatest debt is to the communities of the Purari, particularly the villages of Mapaio, Kinipo, Kairimai and Baimuru, whose residents took the time to sit, look, see and discuss the Haddons' and Williams' collections and the histories they found in them. I am grateful to the Rove and Aukiri family for their acceptance, hospitality and support. *A'ai ovara miki.*

NOTES

1 The Haddons' photographic collection is housed in the UCMAA, while their notes are in the Haddon papers kept in the CUL. I did the majority of my work with the F.E. Williams' notes in the NAPNG where the originals exist (copies exist in the Mitchell Library, Sydney) and primarily worked with the photographs from the NAA collection.
2 I have adapted this term from Fabian's term 'commodities of distinction' (1998). Primarily the term is meant to highlight photographs as *objects* (cf. Edwards 1999a, 2000, 2001) and thus move away from the tendency to see them merely in terms of what they visually signify. It also foregrounds how, as objects constituted by anthropological notions of the ethnographic (Fabian 1983), photographs helped map differences (both real and imagined) onto the region.
3 The interviews carried out for this research were conducted in a variety of languages – principally I'ai (each tribe refers to the vernacular by its own name), Tok Pisin and English. While Motuan is still widely used in the region, its use is declining in the Purari Delta and elders, those most conversant in Motu, preferred that I speak with them in their vernacular. I am indebted to Kaia Rove for teaching me the nuances of I'ai and for helping me in its translation. When used in the text, I'ai terms are italicised followed by their glossing in English.
4 Williams took 24 portraits while in Purari. While only eight of the 14 Koriki portraits are named, no record remains of his eight I'ai subjects' names. In comparison, I could only locate references to the identities of one group photographed in the Haddons' set of 14 portraits, specifically of two of the native police force that accompanied the Haddons.
5 From his field notes, it is possible to reconstruct that Williams worked in I'ai villages for approximately 31 days from 13 April to 20 May 1922. Over the course of three trips (25 May–13 June; 3–14 July; 9–24 August 1922) he worked for 48 days with the Koriki.

While the difference in time spent between the two groups is 17 days, more significant is that Williams worked among the Koriki towards the middle and end of his fieldwork, presumably when he was in a better situation to understand the local social situation. This is reflected in his field notes by the greater density of ethnographic details (genealogies, relationships between participants in initiations, etc.) that he gathered on the Koriki in comparison to the I'ai.

6 Williams is unfortunately silent regarding when and where he developed his photographs and only infrequently referred to his photography.

7 In I'ai oral histories surrounding Williams it is narrated that men at the time feared telling him all their traditions, practices and histories because they believed that if they did, they would be removed from the village and punished. This may have been a result of the presence of at least one Papuan policeman, who served as Williams' guard, cook and translator (Williams 1924: 119, 236). In his field notes, Williams does remark on a reluctance to discuss certain topics, particularly headhunting and the meanings of certain objects, but this reticence was widespread and not particular to the I'ai.

8 The Purari's west bank falls under TFI's jurisdiction, while RH operates on the river's east bank.

9 The new forms of wealth – the ability to consume store-bought food, dinghies, money, outboard motors and water tanks – made accessible by the logging are frequently talked about as development.

10 The Kabu Movement affected the customs of the region's tribes differently (Maher 1984). Its long-term impact is complicated by the presence of religious missions, such as the Seventh Day Adventists and the Pentecostal Christian Revival Church.

11 Consisting of two classes, *mari* and *amua*, leadership was a combination of ascribed and achieved status. The sphere of the *mari* was the *ravi*, wherein he oversaw the efficacy of ritual objects and practices. The *amua* ensured the various practical steps necessary to accomplish these activities and oversaw the organization of raiding parities and of feasting (Maher 1961, 1967, 1974; Williams 1924).

12 I do not mean to understate the importance that features in the landscape (i.e., stones, trees, waterways) play in the narration of history and in its reproduction (Rumsey and Weiner 2001). As I argue below, photographed landscapes emerged as one of the principal vehicles for the inscription of histories. However, like heirloom objects, landscapes can and have changed or disappeared over the successive years of resource exploration and as part of the Purari's naturally shifting delta environment (Petr 1983).

13 While presented as a smooth process, this pattern of meetings emerged organically as a result of local anxieties about histories. For example, I quickly learned that discussions of ancestral things, and thus the photographs, could not be done at night because it was precisely during these times that sorcerers most frequently roamed. All my meetings were thus confined to the day.

14 Despite their perceived similarities, some people differentiated between the photographs and heirlooms. Ropo, an old I'ai man, commented in private 'I have *eiri* [dog's teeth] and *ua* [pig's tusk]. What I brought is *history*. I thought what you had brought was older but it isn't. What I have is *eni'i miki omoro* [lit. old real talk]. What you brought human beings were doing, but what I know is [from] *imunu* [ancestral spirits] time.'

7

REMEMBERING OUR NAMESAKES

Audience reactions to archival film of
King Island, Alaska

Deanna Paniataaq Kingston

Visual anthropologists have long cautioned that photographic images are not objective recorders of reality. Rather they are subject to the biases and purposes of the cameraperson. I shall not labour this point. Instead, I wish to shift the focus from the photographer and remind readers that the audience's own biases affect how they view and make meaning from photographic images. To demonstrate this point, I shall describe the comments elicited from members of the King Island Native community who viewed archival film images of King Island from 1937 to 1938 in order to show how they reflect the audience's experiences and interests. Thus, not only are moving images manipulated and shaped by the filmmakers, but the interpretations of moving images are manipulated and shaped by the audience. These comments and reactions were elicited at different times and reflect a change in the context and motivations of the people viewing the films.[1]

For the first audience, I shall describe my own viewing of Father Bernard Hubbard, SJ's unedited footage of King Island, Alaska, based upon my knowledge of them in 1993 and on my status as a King Islander who grew up in Oregon. This is reflected in the grant proposal that I wrote to the National Science Foundation (NSF) to conduct an oral history project. The second audience is my maternal uncle, Alex Muktoyuk. He came to the Human Studies Film Archives at the Smithsonian Institution in late November/ early December 1993 to annotate Hubbard's unedited footage. His annotations were transcribed in 1997 and were analyzed for this article. Finally, I shall report how the King Island elders reacted to the film as they participated in an oral history project funded by NSF in July 1995. Before I do this, though, I must first describe the photographic record and its photographer, Father Bernard Hubbard, SJ, a Jesuit priest. In addition, I shall discuss the short edited films he made of the King Islanders in the late 1930s and early 1940s.

BERNARD HUBBARD, SJ, AND THE PHOTOGRAPHIC RECORD OF THE KING ISLAND COMMUNITY

Santa Clara University Archives estimates that it has between 2,500 and 4,000 still photographs of the King Islanders taken in the winter of 1937 and 1938. The Human

Studies Film Archives at the Smithsonian Institution has about 40,000 ft (or about 20 hours) of unedited, silent film footage from the same time. The man who created these images was a Jesuit priest, Bernard R. Hubbard, SJ. Ordained in 1923, Hubbard received a teaching position at Santa Clara University, a Jesuit college in southern California, in 1926 (Renner 1987: 2). However, Hubbard was not happy in the classroom setting. A colleague reported that Hubbard, ever eager to be in Alaska, submitted final grades for a class before he gave the final examination. 'When the dean pointed this out, Hubbard feigned great surprise, and declared that he had indeed made an error – he had given the dean the wrong set of grades' (Murray Scarborough 1993: 18). Based upon this behavior, Hubbard's superiors released him from teaching duties.

Instead, in support of the Catholic missions in Alaska, Hubbard conducted annual summer 'scientific' expeditions for almost 30 years, which he funded by traveling throughout the United States and lecturing to public audiences about his experiences. Apparently, though, Hubbard's expeditions were scientific in name only, being an excuse for his real love of exploring the great outdoors. As one of his colleagues wrote, 'the overall scientific value of his 30-odd expeditions to Alaska was not great' (McKevitt 1979: 248). An example of Hubbard's science is included in a eulogistic newsreel in which the narrator explains that Hubbard proved his 'theory' that the Eskimos were a recent migration from Asia by going with the King Islanders on a 1,000 mile boat voyage to Point Lay, where the King Islanders and the people of Point Lay could speak the same language. Obviously, Hubbard's finding that the King Islanders could speak the same language as the people from Point Lay is not enough proof that they are recent migrations from Asia and shows how superficial Hubbard's science was. His true calling, apparently, was as a lecturer. Because of his showmanship, charm and skill as a photographer, Hubbard became a household name after his experiences and photographs were published in the *Saturday Evening Post* in 1932. By 1937, he was the highest paid lecturer in the United States (ibid.: 246–8).

Hubbard is best known for his work on King Island. Although it is unclear why Hubbard decided to change the topic of his expeditions from geology to anthropology, Murray Scarborough (1993: 26) suggests that this shift 'allowed him to escape the criticism of those who had demonstrated their disapproval of his work. It also may have offered new, exotic material to market to the public'. Although he documented almost every aspect of life on King Island, a significant percentage of Hubbard's work focuses on the King Islanders as pious Eskimos. Nearly one hour of the 20 hours of film shows the King Islanders dragging the statue of Christ the King up to the top of the island, mixing the cement for the base of the statue, and the dedication ceremony presided over by Fathers Lafortune and Hubbard. It seems a shame to me, a King Island descendant, that over five per cent of Hubbard's film record is devoted to these monotonous scenes of the statue of Christ the King. However, as Hubbard was eager to promote himself, it makes sense that he fully documented the gift of the statue that he brought to the island. Renner reports that, in his later years, Hubbard felt that the two happiest days of his life included 31 October 1937, when he dedicated the statue on King Island, and the day he presented to Pope Pious XII a replica of the statue carved in walrus ivory by a King Islander (Renner 1987: 3).[2]

To further demonstrate that the King Islanders were pious and religious, we can turn to Hubbard's lectures on King Island which he delivered after his return. Since the money he raised from the lectures funded his forthcoming expeditions as well as the mission in Alaska, he could continue doing one of his favorite activities (exploring) while he fulfilled his obligations as a Jesuit priest. This is stated succinctly by Murray Scarborough, who writes that,

> It would be impossible to say with certainty whether Hubbard promoted so hard so that he could get back to Alaska, or whether he went to Alaska so that he could be a promoter. He appears to have enjoyed both roles to some degree . . .
>
> (Scarborough 1993: 24)

So, in his lectures, Hubbard focused on the success of the Alaskan missions. For instance, in a handbill that advertised his lecture at Constitution Hall in Washington, DC, entitled 'Cliff Dwellers of the Far North' (Anon, n.d.). Hubbard impressed upon his Catholic audience the King Islanders' devotion to Catholicism. This handbill describes the King Islanders as

> a people who have preserved their racial integrity and traditions dating back to ancient times, yet are *religious*, are educated, are naturally refined. . . . [Although they acknowledge] their Chief as civic leader, doctor, dentist, midwife, yet they bow to the *spiritual guidance of the Jesuit Missionary* who has lived with them for 38 years.
>
> (Ibid., added emphasis)

Finally, the handbill states,

> The pictures are full of strange contrasts. . . . Eskimos seeming wild and primitive as they execute their tribal dances in weird masks and ceremonial costumes, and the same Eskimos *humbly kneeling at the foot of the bronze statue of Christ the King.*
>
> (Ibid., added emphasis)

Obviously, Hubbard emphasized to his audiences that the King Islanders were good Catholics.

In addition to the almost 4,000 still photographs and 20 hours of film, Hubbard created three film shorts of King Island: *Arctic Springtime*, *Winter in Eskimo Land*, and *Eskimo Trails*, where he discusses everything from the inhabitants' diet to winter activities to their travels. In these films, Hubbard seemingly wanted to dispel previous myths and stereotypes about Eskimos and about Alaska. For instance, in *Arctic Springtime*, Hubbard shows that the King Islanders ate an abundance of food resources, including walrus, seals, sculpins, cod, puffin and murre eggs, greens, crabs, and salmon and black berries, not just the raw fish of popular stereotypes. In addition, his editing and narration demonstrate that Alaska was not a frozen wasteland, but rather a place filled with natural resources. Similar points were made in the other two edited film shorts, apparently to convince his lecture audiences throughout the United States about the advantages of living in Alaska. He continued to urge audiences to move to Alaska after his death. In a eulogistic newsreel about Father Hubbard entitled 'The Glacier Priest', the narrator states:

A new project was born. He would go on a lecture tour to break down the notion that Alaska was a frozen wilderness. He would spread word of the opportunities that awaited settlers in the North. The project succeeded. Years later, Father Hubbard visited the new Alaskan settlers. He saw kids playing in modern grounds like kids in any other part of America.

Hubbard not only discussed the success of the Alaskan missions, he also dispelled stereotypes of Eskimos and of Alaska.

Regardless of Hubbard's editorials about King Island life in his lectures and film shorts, the filmic record he created of King Island life in 1937–8 is a comprehensive one. As testimony to Hubbard's activities, Father Lafortune wrote in his journal that Hubbard immediately started photographing on King Island when he arrived: 'One can hear the click of the camera at any hour. What is commonplace to me is wonderful to Father Hubbard' (Renner 1979: 102). Wendell Oswalt, an anthropologist who spent considerable time in Alaska, wrote:

> The photographs are of outstanding quality; the images are consistently sharp, and the composition is superior. . . . Furthermore, the Hubbard Collection is superior to others [Lomen Brothers and Curtis] because of the vast number of pictures and diversity of subject matter it includes. It is no doubt among the most comprehensive photographic collections documenting Eskimo culture change during the 1930s.
>
> (Oswalt 1983: 1)

Dorothy Jean Ray, an ethnographic expert on Bering Strait cultures stated the following:

> I find this [the Hubbard Collection] to be the broadest coverage, in both areal extent and diversity of subject matter, of any collection with which I am acquainted. . . . In view of the changes that have taken place since Hubbard was on the [King] island, these photographs are of inestimable value, and record a way of life that is gone.
>
> (Ray 1984: 1)

Bogojavlensky and Fuller also discuss the significance of these images:

> The ethnographic and historical significance of these photographs is enormous. In 1937, King Island was essentially an intact, ongoing indigenous Eskimo society based on the hunting of marine mammals and season summer trading by skinboat along the mainland coasts. To our knowledge, no comparable photographic record of an aboriginal sovereign state in all of Arctic ethnology exists.
>
> (Bogojavlensky and Fuller 1973: 66)

Thus, despite himself, Hubbard created a photographic record of the King Islanders that is of significant anthropological value.

Although Hubbard's choice of photographic images of the King Islanders was rather self-serving, as shown in the examples above, I believe he genuinely enjoyed the King Islanders. My uncle, Alex Muktoyuk, tells of a time in 1959 when Hubbard gave my uncle and another King Islander a warm welcome when they visited him at Santa Clara University. (At the time, they were living in Oakland, California under the Indian

Relocation Act.) In addition, when Father Hubbard was the guest on the old television program, *This Is Your Life*, Ralph Edwards, the host, surprised Hubbard by sending for Charlie Mayac (Hubbard's favorite King Islander) to come to California to appear on the show. The archived copy of the program shows that Hubbard was very pleased to see Charlie Mayac again.

MY VIEWING OF HUBBARD'S UNEDITED FILM FOOTAGE OF KING ISLAND

In the 1980s and early 1990s, Hubbard's film was deteriorating in a basement storage area at Santa Clara University (SCU) and the SCU Archives was afraid that they would deteriorate too badly. In the meantime, the King Island community began lobbying Santa Clara University to transfer the film to Alaska, so that it could be closer to the people depicted in the images. The primary concern of the King Island community was to gain immediate access to the images of themselves, their now-deceased relatives, and life on King Island. In 1992, they drafted and passed resolutions asking that the film be sent to Alaska to an organization called the Alaska Moving Image Picture Association. Concerned that the Alaska association lacked significant funds to conserve and transfer the film to video, SCU Archives approached the Human Studies Film Archives about the possibility of depositing the film at the Smithsonian Institution. Before doing so, since the King Island Native Community, the King Island Native Corporation, and the Bering Straits Native Corporation all passed resolutions that requested immediate access to the film, the Human Studies Film Archives (HSFA) agreed to transfer the film to video as soon as the film had been deposited in their archives. In addition, they agreed to make video copies available to the King Islanders. In summer 1993, Santa Clara University transferred this film to the HSFA and put it on a temporary deposit of 50 years.

In the meantime, plans were made to bring me to the HSFA to start working with this filmic record because of my own interests in King Island culture and heritage. As stated above, I am of King Island descent although I grew up in Oregon. (My mother went to Chemawa Indian School, a Bureau of Indian Affairs boarding school in Salem, Oregon.) Part of my duties were to catalog the King Island portion of the film, but upon receiving the film at the Smithsonian, we discovered that Santa Clara University had previously created an accurate shot-by-shot description of it. Thus, my efforts turned toward writing a grant proposal to use the film in some way. In order to pinpoint what kind of project I might do, I began viewing the film after it had been transferred to video format. I remember being very keenly interested, both emotionally and academically, in the images. How cool it was finally to see what life on King Island was like! I started to get a sense of the terrain of King Island, especially with the steep cliffs and rocky hillside where the village was located. It was also exciting to see the houses on stilts, the different plant and animal species they used for subsistence, the techniques used in butchering and preparing meat, what King Islanders wore at the time, and how babies were carried. I was most fascinated with the scenes of dancing, including scenes where they used masks. I knew intellectually that some of the people in the film were close relatives, but not knowing what they looked like, I didn't spend time looking at faces. I was much more interested in the activities, particularly since I had grown up in a completely different environment and culture.

Based upon this viewing of the images and upon on a statement by Bogojavlensky and Fuller, who brought copies of the still photographs to the King Islanders in 1970, I decided to write a grant proposal to conduct an oral history project using the film as a memory aid. Their statement was:

> The photographs are an incomparable aid to memory and stimulated a great deal of discussion, thus retrieving information which would have been lost forever to all other forms of ethnographic and historical inquiry.
>
> (1973: 66)

But since Hubbard's film record of King Island contains over 20 hours of footage, I decided that I should concentrate my efforts on just a portion of the film that I could use in a research project. Based on my knowledge of and participation in King Island singing and dancing traditions at the time (cf. Kingston 1996), I decided to use images of King Island singing and dancing traditions in an oral history project.

In 1993, the King Island community still existed as a distinct community in Alaska even though they had been displaced from King Island for 30 years and were scattered throughout Alaska and the lower 48 states.[3] My own family – and that of my uncle's in Portland, Oregon – are examples of this displacement. My cousins, my siblings and I were taught that we were King Island Eskimos as opposed to just 'Eskimos'; thus, the distinctiveness of the King Islanders was firmly imprinted into our identities from the time we were children. By 1993, however, my primary experience of King Island life and culture involved singing and dancing traditions since I was actively learning them at the time. I felt that the only way I could claim to be a King Islander was because I knew King Island songs and dances. This explains why the images I was most interested in were the scenes of dancing.

I carried my interest in King Island dancing traditions into a grant proposal to the National Science Foundation (NSF), where I expressed my hope that the King Islanders would be able to identify the dances depicted in the Hubbard films. Since the film was silent, I hoped that the songs to the dances would be remembered, and then revived by the King Island community. My hope was strengthened by the fact that the King Islanders have continued these traditions, which is in contrast to many other Eskimo communities in Alaska. Fortunately, NSF funded this project. Beginning in July 1995, after assembling the dance footage of Hubbard's film on two one-hour video cassettes, I gathered the elders in Nome to view the film and asked them to tell me what dances were being performed and to sing the song that accompanies the dance. This was only moderately successful: of the two hours of footage, the elders could only remember the songs to three or four of the dances. In addition, they remembered two other dances, but not the words to the songs that accompanied them. For a long while after the project, I considered it a partial failure since I had hoped that several dances no longer performed would be revived. I was also disappointed because it seemed that dancing was not as important to the elders as I thought it would be. Again, my viewing of the images reflected my own interests and experiences as a King Islander.

THE VIEWING OF THE FILM BY ALEX MUKTOYUK

My maternal uncle, Alex Muktoyuk, was born in 1941. By this time, non-Native people had been wintering on King Island since 1929, when both the Bureau of Indian Affairs (BIA) school and Father Bellarmine Lafortune's Catholic church were built on the island. Lafortune had converted most King Islanders to Catholicism by 1920 (cf. Renner 1979; Kingston 1999: 128–44). Thus, King Islanders in my uncle's generation grew up with a very strong Catholic presence on the island as well as with the requirement of attending the BIA school. In addition, my uncle voluntarily left King Island several times from the late 1950s to the mid-1960s for education or job opportunities. However, he also grew up hunting birds and walrus, gathering eggs in the rocky cliffs, and dancing (cf. Kingston 1996: 25–6). I would characterize his experience as participating almost equally in both Western and traditional Iñupiaq society. Since 1969, my uncle has lived in Portland, Oregon, where he is an avid Portland Trailblazer (professional basketball team) fan.

Uncle Alex spent approximately five days in late 1993 viewing Hubbard's unedited footage of King Island. In that period of time, he annotated approximately half of the 40 reels of film. He was instructed to talk about what he saw in the film as well as to identify people. In 1997, I had the opportunity to transcribe his annotations for the Human Studies Film Archives and I have just analyzed those transcripts for this chapter. From having transcribed them several years ago, my sense was that about half of the time, he did talk about the kinship and naming relationships in the film, but the other half of the time, he talked about the activities depicted in the film. The analysis reveals that Uncle Alex discussed kinship or naming relationships about 506 times, whereas he discussed activities and scenes about 620 times. In other words, for the most part, my initial hunch about what my uncle emphasized in his viewing of the images was correct. What follows are excerpts from these transcripts.

First, here are comments Uncle Alex made of the different scenes depicted in the film:

1   Yes. [laughs] A lot of people on that boat. That's how we actually went to Nome in the spring. In those *umiaqs*, and there would be about a foot, the top of the boat would be about a foot above the water. The rest of it was covered by canvas, previously, they used old walrus skin to keep the water out, but later on, they started using canvas. [silence for 12 seconds] Looks like this was taken in the springtime because you can see the ice already melting, a cutter might have picked up the people and taken them to Nome, or Father Hubbard might have gone there, I don't know. You can see the edge of the ice, some air space by the edge of the ice, that means it's being melted (Tape 93.1.1–2RV, Side A: 6).

2   Right, right. And, [the wind] the hunters are hoping, this time of the year, the hunters are hoping it'll blow from the north . . . Because that's, that's where the animals, such as seals and polar bears could come from, and with the ice that drift[s] from the north, uh, come the bears and the seals, and, and, occasionally, a walrus, while walrus are very plentiful in the springtime, they're migrating north and they're resting, usually resting on the ice packs, but in the fall, when they start to migrate south, there's no, there's not very much ice, so they swim back, and so it's harder to get the walrus then. But the north winds will bring in all the rest of the animals

that the hunters go after. [silence for 15 seconds] The island is located 40 miles from the closest part on the mainland, and in the wintertime, it's surrounded by ice and it is isolated from the rest of the world for approximately nine months. And, later on, when the bush planes started coming around the Northwest, the bush planes would come once in a while, and only they have a flat piece of ice to land on, ski planes (Tape 93.1.1–2RV, Side B: 5–6).

3   This man is wearing a waterproof raincoat sewn entirely out of walrus intestines. . . . The walrus's intestine is very, very long, hundreds of feet, and maybe even yards, and what they did when they dried it was to attach it to one end of the village and spread to the other side of the village and let it hang to dry. There was another use for the intestine, it was used for water container for the hunters when they're out on the ice. We didn't have canteens in those, so what they would do when they were hunting was fill the tube of intestine, dried intestine, with snow and melt it with their body heat for drinking water. Almost the entire part of the walrus was used (Tape 93.1.1–3RV, Side A: 3–4).

4   These boys are gathering dead grass as it is used for insulation of houses. Whenever somebody was building a house, the boys went up the hill to cut this grass, dead grass, for the insulation of the houses. . . . They build the outer wall, and the inner wall and they are separated by the width of the two-by-fours, in-between is an empty space, so they stuffed this grass in between the walls (Tape 93.1.1–4RV, Side A: 3).

5   The island is oftentime, oftentimes covered with fog. Here it is rolling in from the north. This fog is very damp and very cold. You can see the shore ice still clinging on to the rocks on the island. It has started to break up, the rest of the pack ice has been drifting away. [silence for 13 seconds] This is the vessel as seen from the village on King Island. The shore ice is still there. And, the fog bank is farther on on the horizon. [silence for 6 seconds] Wintertime on King Island. There is no open water on the ice right now (Tape 93.1.1–7RV, Side A: 1).

These comments give an idea of my uncle's annotations of the activities and scenes depicted in Hubbard's unedited footage. I do remember asking him to talk about what he is seeing, but I do not think my request is the only reason he discusses them. He is also keenly aware that he has been disconnected from these activities because he lives in Oregon, so he is reliving these activities as he views them. He recounted similar pastimes in an article he wrote for *Alaska Magazine* (Muktoyuk 1986a, 1986b), in which he stressed how much he missed both the food and the activities on King Island.

As for the identification of kin and namesakes in the film, Uncle Alex was also detailed. Examples are below:

1   This is my mother, Clara Ahgiavinnaq Muktoyuk . . . The baby is called Angnatuq, I don't know what the baby's name is. They, my parents had adopted this baby, but the baby died in infancy (Tape 93.1.1–2RV, Side A: 1–2).

2   Right, and in the foreground is my grandmother, my mother's mother, Sakkana, in between Sakkana and the statue is Ellanna . . . No, her name was Ellanna and

she was my sister-in-law's mother, Edward Muktoyuk's mother-in-law. You can see Paniataaq, there in the extreme right corner, right top, right-hand top corner, that's Paniataaq, my uncle Philip Tatayuna's wife, and for whom you were named after. You meaning Deanna Kingston (Tape 93.1.1–2RV, Side B: 2).

3   That looks like Kokuluk, John Kokuluk, let's, yeah that's John Kokuluk. I named my son after him, Kokuluk. It was the custom of the Northwest Alaska Inupiat that when a person dies, either the relative or somebody in the village has a baby, they, they would name that child after their relative, or somebody who had died recently. And that way the name stays on and it was an ancient belief that they were the reincarnation of that person because that person is gone and now has come back in the form of, uh, a little kid, uh, and it was not necessary which sex the baby is, whether it's a boy or a girl, it can be named after anyone that the parents decide to name their kids after. For example, my name, given name is Allughoq, after my grandfather (Tape 93.1.1–2RV, Side B: 2–3).

4   My grandfather was Allughok and I was named after him. And, my grandmother's name is Kalaġina. And, also, one of Gabriel's daughters is named Kalagina (Tape 93.1.1–19RV, Side A: 2).

5   This is, the lady to the left is Clara Sirloac. And, the lady on the far right is my aunt, Theresa Koyuk. [silence for 15 seconds] Iqthliq was her given name. [silence for 10 seconds] The lady on the bottom left is Agnes Konnuk. [silence for 12 seconds] This, the lady in the foreground is my grandmother, Sakkana. . . . She was my mother, Agiavinnaq's mother. . . . Sakkana was married to Angnazungaq (Tape 93.1.1–20RV, Side A: 4).

I also remember asking my uncle to identify people if he could. However, he volunteered the extra information, such as how he was related to a particular person or who someone was named after. This indicates that this knowledge of the kinship and namesake relationships was also important to him.

REACTIONS OF KING ISLAND ELDERS

Earlier in this chapter I mentioned that I considered the Hubbard Oral History Project a partial failure, since the elders failed to identify many of the songs and dances in the Hubbard film.[4] However, after reflecting on the results of the project, I realized that it was more of a success than I had initially thought. In the grant proposal, I stated that this oral history project would elicit from King Island elders their conception of their identity and history in their own words. When thinking in these terms, then, this project was a success. For what the King Island elders considered particularly important was not their singing and dancing traditions, or even the activities or scenes depicted in the film, but rather an accurate recording of their intricate kinship and naming relationships. Thus, my own emphasis on singing and dancing traditions is at fault, and thus, what I set out to do was only partially accomplished. However, when you consider how the King Islanders think of themselves and their community, then I consider the project a success in that the elders recorded what was most important to them.

I should state that, at the time of the project, most of my contacts with the King Island community (aside from my Master's degree fieldwork with my uncle, Alex Muktoyuk) consisted of some correspondence and a telephone call or two. When I asked the community permission to do this project in April 1995, I also asked the community what else they would like to have researched. One of my cousins, Yvonne Muktoyuk, who is a couple of years older than me, requested the following:

> I would like you to make a database or something of King Island Eskimo names. I don't know many names myself and I know if my parents weren't around, then I wouldn't be able to name my kids anything. So, try to get all the Eskimo names of the people in the film.[5]

Realizing that my cousin's request was important, I asked the elders to identify everyone in the film and to tell how individuals were related to contemporary community members.

Rather than being a chore, as I expected, this request fell right along with what community members felt was more important. For instance, I will give one elder's reaction to seeing the unedited film. When Clara Tiulana first sat down to watch (14 June 1995), she exclaimed:

> I get excited when the, when the pictures show, I get excited seeing my relatives in there. That was what I was telling Francine [Taylor]. I get excited and words get in my, stuck in my throat. I get excited inside. It's like they were with me, something like that, I don't know how to explain it!

This was not an isolated reaction. King Island elders were always thrilled to see themselves as well as their relatives in the footage; whenever someone they knew came up, they always pointed that person out first and how they were related to them. Of the 500 pages of transcripts of the project, based on the 21 hours of audiotapes, over 70 per cent of the conversations discuss Eskimo names and kinship relations of the people depicted in the film. In addition, they would inform me how I was related to particular individuals. In one case, when I asked who a particular woman was, they exclaimed, 'YOU!' It turns out that the woman in the film was my *atqin* or namesake. As noted above, the Iñupiat believe that a person carries with them the spirit of the deceased person they are named after, so the person in the film really was me since I carry that woman's spirit within me. Thus, they were incorporating me into the King Island community, by showing how I was connected both to them and to other people. Their reactions show that the King Island elders are much more interested in seeing themselves and their relatives and namesakes who are no longer alive. I believe this reflects the fact that the activities they see in the film are just normal, everyday activities, very much like driving a car or eating cereal are for me, activities that do not deserve much comment.

But the question arises: why are kinship and naming relationships so important? The answer has to do with the role these relationships have in traditional Iñupiaq society. Iñupiaq kinship was additive, meaning that one's web of kin relationships was readily expanded, either through marriage, trading partnerships, naming and adoptions (Bodenhorn 2000: 135). The purpose of such practices was essentially to increase the numbers of potential kin who would be obligated to help out in a time of need or famine, to create a trading relationship for goods one did not normally have access to, or to have access to travel through or use someone else's territory.[6] Thus, King Island elders know the intricate details of who is related to whom, to the point that they'll say things such as, 'You should call me auntie because my grandmother and your great-grandfather were brother and sister.' In other words, they will figure out how one is related to themselves, even if the connecting close relationship is three or four generations in the past. So, the elders, when viewing the film and seeing themselves and other deceased relatives, concentrated on reporting the intricate kinship and naming relationships, because it was traditionally important to do so and they want this information to be recorded for future generations.

CONCLUSION

In order to analyze and interpret photographs and film, Collier and Collier use the analogy of reading texts; they instruct researchers to 'read' the images and to organize the photographic data in sequential order, much like the pages of a manuscript (1986: 115, 179). I believe that they do this purposefully for they acknowledge that:

> Both visual communication and visual evidence confront the literacy-biased value system of modern Western society. We are compulsively verbal both in our communication and thought. Our memory image is codified and now computer-organized. There is small room in our literate society for visualization.
>
> (Ibid.: 154)

I, too, will use this literate analogy because in order to make sense of these three different viewings of Hubbard's film, I have based the point I wish to make on the work of Greg Sarris, who has analyzed Native American texts. Sarris argues that:

> So much of what we do as readers of texts is unconscious. We aren't aware of all the cultural and personal influences that determine how we read; we aren't aware of our self-boundaries and how we work to tighten or widen them in our encounters with texts.
>
> (Sarris 1993: 92)

Later, he asserts that the 'truth' that critics (and other readers) of oral and written Indian literatures bring to their reading of the literature:

> is contingent upon their purposes and biases as readers and their particular relation-ship with the worlds of what they read or otherwise learn about Indians and with the worlds of the written texts they study. . . . At some level or at some point in the encounter and interaction between critic and text, there is a dialogue of sorts.
>
> (Ibid.: 128)

Scholars of filmic audiences also use this literate analogy. Banks specifically calls ethnographic films 'socially constructed texts' in which meaning is 'derived from the interaction between the audience and the film text' (1996: 130). Martinez (1996: 81) reiterates this analogy when he states that. 'Readings [of film texts] are always heterogeneous activities, they engage multiple perspectives in perceptive, encoding, interpretative, ideological, and imaginary practices.'

This chapter points out that different generations of King Islanders view Hubbard's images in different ways. My generation, having grown up off the island and immersed for a large part of our lives in Western society, is more interested in the activities we have heard about from our parents and grandparents. Since we do not know what deceased relatives and namesakes look like, the identification of people in the film is not a priority. My uncle Alex, on the other hand, did know some of the individuals, and because he grew up believing in the central role that kinship plays in traditional Iñupiaq society, he reported the kin and namesake relationships. However, he was also aware of the activities in the film that he and the King Islanders no longer do because he has lived outside Alaska for over 30 years. So, when he viewed the film, he discussed these activities in detail because he was aware of the great cultural changes that have happened in the community. Elders, in contrast, tended to gloss over the activities and concentrated almost solely on the identification of kin and namesake relationships, since they were so important in traditional society. My research, then, shows that the meanings that viewers obtain from a film not only derive from the film itself, but also from the cultural make-up and context of the viewers themselves: their gender, age, social status and ethnicity affect their interpretations as well as the intentions and motivations they bring to a viewing (cf. Ruby 1996: 193–5). Photographs and film, then, are not static objects that have only one interpretation. Rather, the viewers' experiences imbue images with multiple interpretations.

ACKNOWLEDGEMENTS

This article was made possible by the support and assistance of several institutions and individuals and I would like to thank them here. First, I need to acknowledge the entire King Island Native Community for making this research possible and for supporting my efforts to document our history and culture. Although I do not have room to give the names of individuals, know that I thank all who helped and facilitated my work. In addition, I would like to thank the Aboriginal Studies Circle and Heather Norris Nicholson of The University College of Ripon & York St John for supporting my participation in the conference, *Screening Culture: Constructing Image and Identity*, for which I originally wrote this article. Also, through a program with the Smithsonian Institution, British Airways generously donated the airfare for my trip to England. I am very grateful to the National Science Foundation which funded the research for this paper under Award Number 9400929. In addition, initial research into Hubbard's film of the King Islanders was funded by the Human Studies Film Archives (HSFA) and the Arctic Studies Center (ASC), National Museum of Natural History, Smithsonian Institution with special thanks to John Homiak, Director of the HSFA, and William Fitzhugh, Director of the ASC. Understanding Hubbard's purposes in creating this photographic record was made considerably easier by the work of Caprice Murray Scarborough, who painstakingly went through Hubbard's papers at Santa Clara University. My research here rests upon her foundation. I wish to thank Stephen Loring of the Arctic Studies Center, Smithsonian Institution, for making editorial comments and suggestions on an earlier draft of this paper; and to David McMurray, Oregon State University, for furnishing additional references; and to Adrienne Kaeppler of the National Museum of Natural History, who encouraged me to be the Project Director, instead of a Research Assistant, of the NSF grant. I also wish to thank the volume editors (Alison Brown and Laura Peers) for giving me the opportunity to rework this article in order to incorporate more information, and to Elizabeth Edwards, for guidance in the rewrite. Finally, I want to thank Cathleen Osborn-Gowey, an Oregon State University Ethnic Studies student, who efficiently analyzed my uncle's annotation for this article.

NOTES

1 Although I did not intend such an analysis when I started the project, Martinez (1996: 87) called for research in which 'the horizons of expectations and reception of particular texts [films] by concrete viewers at different historical circumstances' are analyzed. Not only is Martinez interested in the viewers' historical context, but also in their cultural context, which includes consideration of such things as gender, age, and ethnicity of the viewer (ibid.: 81–2; cf. Ruby 1996: 193–5; Banks 1996: 119), the 'discourses of power and knowledge affecting producers, viewers, and the pro-filmic event itself' and the 'agency and intentionality of the viewers' (Martinez 1996: 72), as well as a 'consideration of the interaction of actual viewers with the discursive positions in the text' (ibid.: 74; cf. Banks 1996: 130).

2 Hubbard's pride in his accomplishment is not without merit. The statue of Christ the King is still an important part of King Islanders lives. Many remember stopping at the statue to pray on their way to the top of the island. And, in 1995 or 1996, King Island community members wanted me to find out who made the statue so we could replace the crown that had blown away in winter storms several years before.

3 King Island has been uninhabited since the mid-1960s. This is due to many factors, but the primary one is that the Bureau of Indian Affairs closed the school on King Island in 1959, forcing many King Islanders with school-age children to move to Nome permanently (Kingston 1999: 182–202).

4 Although the project was only a partial success as far as the film was concerned, Hubbard also created some sound recordings on reel-to-reel tape. These recordings were transferred to audio cassette-tape and given to the community in the autumn of 1994. By the following summer, two of the songs had been reincorporated into the King Island song and dance repertoire.

5 Most King Islanders of my generation seem most interested in the activities and scenes depicted in the film. However, my cousin's comments also reflect a concern with naming practices linked primarily to a concern with potential culture loss through the loss of names, and not so much to the implied obligations that namesake relationships hold for older King Islanders, discussed later in this section.

6 Although, as Bodenhorn (2000: 136) notes, 'The expansive potential of adding on relatives of course does not mean that all kinship links are permanently active. The universe of potential kin is much larger than one could maintain if one were to satisfy the obligations that kinship entails: shared food, labor, company, child care, political support, and so forth.' In other words, this detailed information was good to know in case it was needed, but more often than not, these relationships were not activated.

8

SNAPSHOTS ON THE DREAMING

Photographs of the past and present

John E. Stanton

History, it is said, is in the eye of the onlooker: Indigenous artists provide a special eye on the past. An elder from the Western Desert region of Australia once likened it to me as 'a snapshot on the Dreaming'. 'It's like your camera', he said, 'It's an image for the future, when it will [then] be something of the past' (Malcolm Shaw (Ngaanyatjarra language), pers. com.).

The Berndt Museum of Anthropology holds an internationally renowned collection of contemporary and historical Australian Aboriginal cultural materials, as well as collections from Papua New Guinea, South-east Asia and Central Asia. These collections have been assembled over the past 60 years, initially by the late Ronald and Catherine Berndt, and subsequently by staff and students of the Department of Anthropology at the University of Western Australia, associates of the Museum, and through an active purchasing programme to acquire contemporary materials.

The focus of the Museum has, however, long been on Aboriginal Australia, and this emphasis is reflected in the strength of its collections and the significance that these have, both locally and at a regional level. These collections comprise ethnographic items and works of art (which are undifferentiated by the Museum), sound recordings, photographs and motion pictures (including cine and video recordings in a variety of formats).

The Berndt Museum of Anthropology also holds one of Australia's most extensive collections of contemporary and historic photographs, focusing on Aboriginal communities from the western half of the continent, which defines the Museum's collecting mandate. The earliest photographs date from the late nineteenth century and have been augmented by photographs donated by staff of government departments, former mission stations, and the like. However, it is the collection of photographs taken by Ronald and Catherine Berndt, commencing in the early 1940s, which represent the core of the Museum's holdings and now provide an extraordinarily important resource for the appreciation of Australian cultures in all their diversity. Indeed, among this multiplicity of experiences, photographic and sound collections retain a cultural significance beyond their unique immediacy. The images of the past represent a powerful stimulus for the present: as historic recordings, they empower the present and engage the future.

The Museum's active programme of acquiring photographs from a diversity of sources has seen the development of an extensive network among Aboriginal communities and their constitutent families. Together with non-Indigenous researchers, teachers and others, they contribute to the essential documentation and re-evaluation of these photographs, and their incorporation into the contemporary social milieu. Active in the Museum's current exhibition and research programmes, Aboriginal community members inject their own perspectives and insights through both their interpretation of these images and through their participation in their exhibition, enriching the Museum's verification and the history of the photographs themselves. New technologies are providing the means of enhancing the context and meaning of such recordings of Aboriginal societies and the knowledge and experience with which they are associated. The Web is extending this process further.

The emergence of collaborative roles between Museum staff (comprising both Aboriginal and non-Aboriginal persons), and local and regional Aboriginal community organisations and family groups, promotes the Museum's long-term commitment to the contemporary interpretation of earlier visual records, from the perspectives of both producer culture and repository institution.

MUSING WITH THE COMMUNITY

The Museum's collections of photographs and sound recordings serve as a springboard to the development of original initiatives. They engage with and secure the active participation of Aboriginal regional and local organisations from whom the collections have been obtained – the 'communities of origin', as these have been termed.

The manner in which the Museum itself came into being is directly relevant in this respect, since its rationale created an environment within which these engagements would take place. It was established formally by the University Senate only in 1976 in order to house, in perpetuity, the extensive collections made by the late Ronald and Catherine Berndt that were held at that time in the Department of Anthropology. The Berndts had founded the Department in 1957, the first in a Western Australian university and only the third in the country. They had brought with them, primarily as research and teaching resources, the extensive collection they had assembled during field research while associated with the University of Sydney.

The Museum collections have since grown from some 1,600 objects and 200 photographs to over 10,000 ethnographic items and 26,000 photographs today. Several substantial donations have complemented the active acquisition programme, which focuses on contemporary items. The donation of historic photographs and sound recordings by both Indigenous and non-Indigenous sources has enhanced greatly the earlier collections made by anthropologists, and those in related disciplines. These have great significance to present-day Aboriginal communities living throughout Western Australia, the Northern Territory, and South Australia, in particular.

The Museum has always maintained an active research profile, and sees its ongoing exhibition programme (and, particularly, its community outreach programme) as a vital means of communicating the results of this research to a wider population than that of the University alone. It currently employs six curatorial staff, including three Indigenous Australians – two women and one man – two of whom are employed under a grant from the Aboriginal and Torres Strait Islander Commission (ATSIC) to work on the Museum's current major project, *Bringing the Photographs Home*.

Indigenous Australians increasingly perceive museums as partners – potentially at least, if not in fact – in the preservation of heritage. This has provided heritage institutions both with fresh challenges and new opportunities. Responses to these demands for closer collaboration have varied: some museums have retreated, fearful of issues such as repatriation, for example. Others, unfortunately, have seen federal funding to assist repatriation as simply a means of creating additional employment opportunities rather than of enhancing dialogue, until they have come to a sudden realisation that the funding is being driven essentially by bureaucratic timelines and outcomes, rather than by Indigenous desires, intentions and cultural perspectives. Other museums have sought actively to recruit Indigenous staff and provide culturally relevant mentoring programmes that support Aboriginal aspirations. Some museums, like the Berndt, have tried to combine a number of strategies to develop more fully their existing policies of enhancing engagement and the promotion of Indigenous interests.

It is clear that Australia's museum communities can and do play a crucial role in the promotion and advocacy of contemporary Indigenous Australian cultures. For specialist museums, the issues and priorities are more readily identified and acted on than may sometimes be the case elsewhere. As museums grow and transform themselves with the passing of time, they must position themselves to reflect on these changes and the implications that they have for broader institutional goals and aspirations. The Berndt Museum has benefited from the maintenance of pre-existing and extensive linkages with Indigenous communities throughout the state and beyond, often extending over several generations. These connections have grown out of bonds between communities and anthropologists that sometimes span several generations: they have guided the Museum both in its historic performance and will continue to do so in its future efflorescence. Different projects focusing on elements of the Museum's holdings, such as the historic photographic and sound recording collections, richly support this role.

The Museum's active engagement with Indigenous communities has refined the expansion of collaborative research and exhibition programmes and has enabled it to establish an enviable role within the broader Australian setting. Cited for its example of best practice in its ongoing relationships with Indigenous communities by the national University Museums Review Committee (1996), the Museum has maintained a continuing commitment to extensive consultation and the development of collaborative projects across the western half of the continent. Of course, best practice is always difficult enough to achieve – let alone sustain. There are still many issues both to identify and to address and these will constantly be changing over time. The transformational processes incumbent on today's Australian museums have already been enunciated in policies codified by the national body, Museums Australia (1993), itself influenced by parallel processes in Canada and, less relevantly, the United States of America, where legislated policies have perhaps inhibited flexibility in terms of response and the development of relationships between museums and constituent communities. The theme is consistent, however. Museums must install strategies within their respective organisational structures if they are to address adequately these changing contexts and expressions (Fourmile 1991).

STRATEGIES OF THE CONTEMPORARY

For the Berndt Museum, this has meant maintaining our commitment to focusing on contemporary issues, in order to understand the historic. Two principal factors have clarified this approach, both of which provide a degree of consistency and coherence in the execution of the Museum's charter, as well as a quantifiable response to community needs.

The first factor was the policy adopted in the mid-1970s, early in the history of the Museum's formal existence, to concentrate resources on the documentation of contemporary social life that would serve both to contextualise and inform our understanding of the earlier historical materials in the collections. This policy reinforced the Museum's focus on the collection of contemporary artworks and also reflected the principles driving the Berndts' long-established approach to their own collecting, so clearly articulated in their earlier writings. For, in focusing on the contemporary, it was possible for the Berndts to chart changing preoccupations of the day, and additionally provide a setting that enhanced an ongoing collaboration between anthropologists and the members of particular communities to document the meanings and significance of these cultural expressions. This has been something considered by Aboriginal people both at that earlier period and today to be a vital element of cultural maintenance and cultural integrity. Such long-term collaboration also provided communities with an opportunity to maintain their rights regarding the representation and use of cultural productions in environments sometimes very different from the ones in which they had been originally produced.

The contemporary art works that the Berndts collected since the mid-1940s are, of course, historic today, along with the additional layers of Indigenous interpretation and attribution that have accumulated with the passing of time. The same goes for their photographic collections, some of which are only now being registered, digitised and researched. These additions to the documentary records are, in themselves, vital elements in establishing and reaffirming the living significance of the Museum's object collections, both to those working within the institution and to those who live beyond it.

The second approach has been for the Berndt Museum to ignore what were considered by some non-Indigenous researchers to be established and conventional ideas about what is Aboriginal and what cultural productions are 'authentic' – or otherwise. Instead, the Museum has sought to focus its collecting on what Aboriginal people *themselves* regard as significant 'Aboriginal art', without interposing external (i.e. 'alien') evaluations or restrictions beyond those demanded by a lack of institutional resources – financial, curatorial, or archival storage.

It has been through the Museum's acquisition and research programmes, and the exhibitions and publications that have been the result of these, that the Berndt has sought to participate in the growth of new trends, of new ways of communicating culturally significant information. And we have not just participated: we have also promoted. It is, perhaps, the Museum's role as an advocate for contemporary Indigenous artists that our institution is best known, at least in Australia. Museums are not, in our eyes, about perpetuating the past: they are about confronting the future, the multiple futures, in fact. They are about using the present to inform the past, using the past to illuminate the present, all the time looking towards the future.

So by using these two approaches, which have long been embedded in the Museum's formal policies, we have sought to develop and maintain an original (though now hardly unique) engagement. As a result, the Museum has played a crucial role in changing non-Aboriginal ideas about 'things', of changing their attitudes to categories, and of changing their definitions of 'art'. In this context, the Museum has avoided perpetuating the distinction imposed by some collecting institutions between so-called 'art' and 'non-art', or of 'artefact', at all. Every material manifestation of culture is treated as a form of aesthetic expression, of 'art' as, indeed, it is so often labelled by Indigenous Australians themselves. Photographs and sound recordings associated with these art works are inherent components of these material manifestations of Indigenous cultures and are best treated, in Aboriginal terms, as a unity.

The Museum is currently focusing its curatorial activities on the digitisation of its photographic and sound collections. This prioritisation has provided an immediate response to a clearly identified requirement from Indigenous communities and individual families. While the preparation of documentation in support of claims under the Native Title Act has clearly heightened the level of interest in such materials, it certainly did not create it. Family records, including photographs, have long provided a key element for people seeking to know more about their own family origins, associations and affiliations. The impact of the so-called 'Stolen Generations' *Report of the National Inquiry into the Separation of Aboriginal and Torres Strait Islander Children from their Families* (1997) has further heightened such interest, enhancing collaboration and promoting engagement. We believe that objects and their histories, including their collected and accumulated histories (both within and without the institution), say as much about personal perceptions and individual pursuits as they do about a more collectively shared cultural placement.

In this environment, not only have individual institutional curators such as myself had an indelible influence, but so too have the artists, the creators ('creators' yes, but are they not also 'curators'?) of these material manifestations of cultures, the art works of which we speak. For some, at least, the Berndt has provided a place, an opportunity, a context, and even a home for their works of art, and for the documentation and photographs that in part inspired them.

As one Perth-based artist, Norma McDonald, said when she presented the Museum with several of what she regarded as her most important works:

> I'm glad that you've . . . got them. I decided to give them to you because I feel that, they'll always be here for my grandchildren. I'm trying . . . to do the right things so that . . . somewhere down the line in generations to come . . . they might know that they can come to a place like here and you've still got these works and they'll be able to look at their great-great-great grandma what she had done and, so that nothing's really lost. So our history of our people [is] not lost and that's the reason why you've got them. I feel it's security, for me that to sort of complete my journey that I've done by placing them here. That's what [it] means to me and for Mum so that I know that her Mum and Dad that lived the hardship that they did, and Mum, [it] hasn't been in vain; that we've picked up the pieces and we're proud of who they are and who we are.

> (Norma McDonald 2000)

140

These are strong words; strong imagery conveying how one local Indigenous artist feels about the role of the Berndt Museum and its place in a shared future. They are heartening words, indeed, for she is not alone. Other artists, from different places and at different times, have also sought to utilise the Museum – its name, its building and its reputation – to challenge and indeed attempt to change broader, non-Aboriginal Australian perceptions of Aboriginal art.

THE KIMBERLEY WEBSITE PROJECT

The Museum holds several large collections of materials relating to the Kimberley region in the very north of the state of Western Australia. Many of these were assembled by anthropologists working there from the mid-1960s to the mid-1970s. In the course of my own research, since the mid-1980s, I identified widespread interest in the Museum's holdings among communities. Ad hoc arrangements to return copies of materials required a rather more considered approach, in the light of increasing attention. The more the Museum collaborated in this process of restitution, the more other communities wanted to be similarly involved. The interest spread, via community newsletters and official reports, to other areas of the state, and beyond.

The website project was formulated to develop a culturally appropriate website to expedite the Museum's response to community demands for access to collections. It focused on the Kimberley materials as a prototype exercise. Employing Indigenous Kimberley staff, the project embarked on an ambitious programme of extensive consultation with artists, their families, and relevant community and regional cultural organisations, to establish just how, and which, materials should be made available on the Web. The project was developed with funding from the Federal Department of Education, Employment and Youth Affairs under the National Priority (Reserve) Fund for Improved Library Infrastructure administered by the AVCC Standing Committee on Information Resources. It was established to develop, in collaboration with the University, innovative protocols for the dissemination of research materials to scholars and others on the World Wide Web. Initiated in 1997, the original intention was to digitise, on a regional basis, the Museum's object and photographic collections, in order to provide a research tool of relevance to the international community of scholars, as well as to the broader public. These goals were subject to review, however, during the course of the project.

Of particular concern from the beginning, however, was the protection of Indigenous interests in these materials, given the significance of the Museum's collections to Aboriginal communities and families throughout Australia and, especially, in the western half of Australia, from where these objects primarily derive. These priorities shaped the scope of the project, and were ultimately to constrain its development – at least for the foreseeable future. Once adequate safeguards had been set in place to secure culturally sensitive information from public access, it was a relatively easy matter to automate the transfer of information on each item on the Museum's database to the website. Indeed, the project devised the means by which Filemaker Pro would drive the website itself, as well as operate the Museum's databases. These searchable, relational databases now require little in the way of ongoing maintenance, as any changes or additions are immediately mirrored on the website and the system is, therefore, highly efficient.

This was a significant and rapid learning environment, which I have detailed elsewhere (Stanton 1996). In embracing the new multimedia and network technologies, it rapidly became clear that museums such as our own were deliberately positioning themselves to increase their ability to communicate information about collections, research programmes, exhibitions and other activities. This approach, though, was founded on our own cultural presupposition that an increased rate of information flow was, of itself, a 'good thing'. It failed to identify contexts in which cultural sensitivities might require a diminution – rather than an expansion – of the rate of such information flow. The issue of community control was a key factor here, and the sheer scope of the World Wide Web threatened directly the viability of such curbs on the inappropriate dissemination of cultural material.

This was a serious issue, which the project had to address. Of chief concern were matters associated with maintaining control of intellectual property, including song and dance, as well as written recordings and visual art, particularly when these included information normally restricted to a limited range of appropriately qualified persons. Within this context, the benefits of the new technology can be viewed as a mixed blessing for the many Australian Aboriginal groups that are seeking to participate more actively both with and within the museum profession. Not only are new technologies improving Aboriginal access to culturally relevant information, but they are also addressing a much broader audience, perhaps worldwide.

Just how are Aboriginal people going to be able to restrict categories of secret information, as well as preventing others from copying their designs, their music, and their stories? How are museums, the present custodians of some of this information, going to respond to these concerns, and at what level? These and other issues, were addressed by a range of delegates at the recent UNESCO Seminar on New Technologies, Anthropology, Museology and Indigenous Knowledge (Stanton forthcoming).

Despite the enthusiasm and encouragement that the project received from many artists themselves, other interested parties expressed strong concern at the implications of providing images to such a wide, indeed potentially universal, audience. A recent Australian experience has been a case in point. The so-called 'carpet case' successfully demonstrated in the courts a serious and deliberate breach of copyright. Sacred clan designs and original artworks from other regions were reproduced on carpets woven in South-east Asia for sale in Australia. The distributors claimed that they had the Aboriginal artists' approval for these reproductions, and that they were receiving directly a share of the profits. The aggrieved artists were awarded subsequently a substantial financial settlement in compensation for this blatant infringement of copyright but the company went bankrupt before they received anything. It was, however, a moral victory which encouraged the federal government to introduce selected moral rights legislation as part of its revisions to the Copyright Act.

This experience developed a broader awareness of such issues among at least some Aboriginal artists and their representatives. This can only spread. Although it did not involve the internet itself, the 'carpet case' illustrated the ease with which published images could be reused. The potential for the misuse of images posted on the World Wide Web, even low-resolution ones is, however, of much greater magnitude. Following the so-called 'carpet case', members of at least one northern Aboriginal community contemplated the imposition of a 50-year moratorium on the publication of any art from their area. Had this move gone ahead, it would have had very serious implications for a wide range of curatorial and publication practices, as well as for the future of commercial art production in this region.

That the 'carpet case' engendered such fearful reactions by Aboriginal artists and their families represents a clear signal to the museum and publishing world that Aboriginal communities are seeking to control more directly the production, and re-production, of their cultural artefacts, and perhaps even the right to exclude them from the Web altogether. In general terms, then, museums have a crucial responsibility to ensure that they obtain informed consent from Indigenous intellectual and artistic creators before they place any elements of their collections on the so-called 'information superhighway'.

It was for this reason that any decision to proceed with the website project was postponed, beyond incorporating some generic images to convey something of the rich range of materials held by the Museum. Instead, new plans were made to expedite requests from Kimberley communities, by utilising the services provided by resource agencies such as the Kimberley Land Council and the Kimberley Aboriginal Law and Culture Centre (KALACC). In addition, this new approach could be extended to servicing other Aboriginal communities elsewhere in Australia, who were asking for the repatriation of copies of the materials held by the Museum, both in terms of objects and historical photographs.

BRINGING THE PHOTOGRAPHS HOME: ISSUES OF RESTITUTION AND REPATRIATION

The clearly expressed desire of Aboriginal communities to gain access to, and to share knowledge of, collections held by metropolitan museums throughout Australia encouraged the Museum to consider how it could assist in accomplishing these goals, within the restricted resources that were available. It was clear from the website project that the broader issues associated with mounting images on the Web remained, for the time, insuperable. At the same time, communities had a strong and very clear desire to obtain copies of the materials, and to collaborate in the safekeeping of the cultural knowledge associated with them. Historic photographs were of central concern in this respect, but other categories of collections were also relevant.

With these issues in mind, the Museum considered alternative strategies to achieve the same goals. During 1998, an Aboriginal Curatorial Assistant at the Museum, Ms Deborah Nordbruch, together with myself, identified a number of priorities and struc-tured responses to these requirements, and sought funding for personnel and equipment to digitise and 'restore' the photographs to their rightful owners. The National Inquiry into the Separation of Aboriginal and Torres Strait Islander Children from their Families (1997) published its report *Bringing Them Home*, detailing the long-term destructive and detrimental effects of government policies on Aboriginal families and individuals, the so-called 'Stolen Generations'. This greatly influenced the Museum's response to these issues, not least in part because the Report itself drew heavily on the Museum's historical photographic collections for its illustrations. It became clear to the Museum staff that these (and more recent) photographs could play a significant role in assisting grieving families to come to terms with both their individual and shared pasts, as well as to play a vital role in affirming contemporary values and future identities.

Ms Nordbruch and I identified the potentially therapeutic significance that the photographic collection had as a key element in the federal government's response to what became known as the Stolen Generations Report in our application for funds from ATSIC:

> This project will assist families of the Stolen Generations to cope better with their profound sense of loss and disorientation and, in turn, reduce the stress of everyday living.
>
> This project is urgent, as most of the Stolen Generations need to see these photographs now, as many are ageing and passing on. The Stolen Generations deserve the opportunity to reconnect to their families, even if it is only in the form of a photograph. Sometimes, a photograph is the only record of their forebears. Not only is it important for the older generations to identify their family history, but it is also crucial that this information be passed to the younger generations, which is imperative for reclaiming and forming identity:
>
> This project is targeted at the members of all Aboriginal families and their descendants who were subjected to the provisions of earlier discriminating Western Australian legislation that resulted in children being taken away from their families by State agencies – the Stolen Generations, subject of *Bringing them Home: Report of the National Inquiry into the Separation of Aboriginal and Torres Strait Islander Children from their Families* (Commonwealth of Australia, Human Rights and Equal Opportunity Commission, 1997).
>
> Planned outcomes from this project are to transfer the Museum's Western Australian photographic collection to the Photographic Database, have a print made of each photograph together with a slide, in preparation for the return of photographs of the Stolen Generations, and information about them, to relevant families and communities.
>
> (ATSIC Submission 1998)

With the successful outcome of the grant application came the commensurate responsibility of employing appropriately qualified and trained Indigenous personnel, as well as to manage the project and document the achievement of its principal goals. At this time, included in the Berndt Museum's photographic collection were approximately 15,000 historical photographs relating to Western Australia (it is envisaged that others, from the Northern Territory and South Australia, will be the subject of future funding applications through appropriate state/territory bodies). These archival photographs are from government and mission settlements and pastoral stations from the late nineteenth century to the mid-1970s. These photographic collections were only available as contact proofs on small file cards that were difficult to access. Only a fraction of the records were computerised and usable photographic prints were available only to order. The project was intended to change all this.

The initial ATSIC funding enabled the Museum to employ for a year Ms Lorraine Hunter, a Bardi woman from the Kimberley (herself a graduate in anthropology), to transfer information from the manual catalogue cards. She also entered additional documentation as it was obtained, into the photographic database, and sorted and located images for printing. A decision was made early in the project to continue the digitisation programme initiated for the website project, but not for transfer to the Web at this stage. Instead, digitisation provided an opportunity to build on the previous project by creating electronic copies of archival images and preparing these for printing. Not only did this programme safeguard the photographic originals from unnecessary handling, and subsequent deterioration; it also expedited the preparation of useable prints on-site, minimising potential loss, misfiling and physical damage.

Ms Hunter completed the transfer of the manual photographic collection records to the Museum's computerised database. The scanning and digitisation of a portion of the archival negatives were continued through 2000, during the second phase of the project, by Ms Dallas Wimar and Ms Dora Parfitt, both Nyungar women from the south-west of the state. It had originally been intended that the project should employ one female and one male Aboriginal person from each region in turn, but this did not eventuate for the south-west component of the project, due to the unavailability of a suitable male applicant and the constraints of the timeframe. Subsequent changes in staffing resulted in the appointment of Mr Brett Nannup (a Nyungar man) and Ms Donna Oxenham (a Yamatji woman), who are currently working on the project, now in its fourth year of funding from ATSIC.

Somewhat optimistically, we had originally envisaged that the digitisation programme would be completed within the first 12 months and that, during the second year, materials would be taken back to the communities around the state, as prints in albums for easy viewing and identification by community leaders. A key element of the project was documenting the process itself of returning the Stolen Generation's family photos. However, the regular process of review and the evaluation of feedback from project staff and participating community organisations assisted in the redefinition of goals, and the means by which these would be achieved.

Two key issues emerged, the first of which concerned the matter of just how the images would be repatriated. The prototype element, which once again had focused on the Kimberley region, further reinforced earlier suggestions made during the website project that families were particularly interested in receiving photo albums of prints. They did not want Web- or CD-based digital records, as they often lacked the technology to view them or else the older people did not have the relevant skills. Few felt comfortable with the new technologies. Many of the photographs in the Museum's collections are sensitive, and at times highly personal. These include images of kin now deceased, kin whom an individual may be prohibited from seeing, or ritual events or objects of a restricted, secret-sacred nature. Community leaders wanted to be able to control the process of dissemination themselves. They felt that they could do this only if they had photographic albums, where they could sit, in a relaxed and non-alienating environment, and inspect the materials that the Museum was sending back to them.

The second issue concerned problems in staffing the project, given the Museum's commitment to respect Aboriginal protocols on the involvement, on a purely regional basis, of both female and male staff as partners in the research programme. Given their experience of visiting Aboriginal communities throughout the south-west in 2000, field staff members Ms Dallas Winmar and Ms Dora Parfitt recommended that the project should, in future, focus on completing, region by region, the scanning and assembly of photographic albums, utilising trained staff working in Perth on the digitisation and organisational procedures. They felt that field trips to communities in the more densely settled areas of the state were an expensive, and at times, rather inefficient use of the project's limited resources. They recommended that future activities should focus more on informing Aboriginal communities of the existence of the photographic collection in particular, and the work of the Museum and the nature of its collections in general. Visits to key communities, particularly in remote areas, should be focused on places where local and regional cultural centres and museums could assist the Museum in the delivery of its services. They believed that the project should emphasise, at a community level, the need to improve the level of documentation associated with these photographs, since this would assist in meeting requests for assistance from Aboriginal community members elsewhere.

With these goals in mind, Ms Winmar and Ms Parfitt prepared a slide show to complement the prints in the albums:

> Interest in the slide display varied depending on where people grew up and their age. The value of having such a Photographic Display is that it can provide people with memories of family who have since passed on. This occurred for one of the older women who recognised a photograph of her grandmother. Several home visits were organised to visit some older people who could not attend due to the lack of transport or who were in poor health. It was also evident that the event was not well advertised locally given the Aboriginal population.
>
> The people who attended the display expressed [the view that] the project was worthwhile from an historical perspective. Further it was pleasing when people were able to identify and name a small number of people from the photographs in the display. On this trip, as with a previous field trip, people requested copies of photographs. Several attendees suggested this project could be utilised in schools to give an Aboriginal historical perspective about what really happened with Aboriginal people. Other attendees believed the project could be promoted to the wider community giving a perspective on Aboriginal history.
>
> (Winmar and Parfitt 2000)

In some communities there were difficulties organising the photographic display, for although there are many Aboriginal organisations in the region, it was occasionally difficult to pinpoint a particular organisation to act as an agent of the Museum. While they could not presume that any one organisation would have a commitment to assisting the Museum in carrying out its work, as this depended on the goodwill of various organisations, Indigenous staff had hoped that Aboriginal organisations would assist in advertising the display locally. However, in most instances this was not the case.

At all times they were aware, and conscious, of being inclusive of as many groups as possible by contacting as many government and Aboriginal organisations as they could as a means of overcoming any problems within the community. In some instances they conducted a separate presentation. Initial contact with various Aboriginal organisations varied between very good to fair, where a genuine interest was expressed but support was not forthcoming on the day.

Since Winmar and Parfitt made their report, its recommendations have been adopted by the Museum and, with the agreement of the ATSIC funding agency, a different strategy has been implemented. Two Aboriginal staff, one male and one female, have worked on a region-by-region basis to refine the database entries, checking for inconsistencies and errors. They have, at the same time, simultaneously digitised the region's historical photographs and created A4 prints, in colour as necessary, for the albums that are being sent back to the central community organisation in each region.

The identification of appropriate intermediaries in this process is complex, requiring experience and local knowledge, but it has helped the Museum conserve funds originally allocated to field trips for the preparation of additional materials. Regional cultural and heritage organisations, like the Goldfields Land Council, the Yamatji Land and Sea Council, the Ngaanyatjarra Cultural Centre (Warburton Ranges) and Wirimanu Cultural Centre (Balgo), have assisted in this process. They have arranged meetings with local groups, in order to identify particular interests and concerns (including the matter of controlling the distribution of sensitive images), as well as to organise how the materials are to be repatriated and where they are to be stored and handled. Materials have or are being returned formally to the Kimberley, the Murchison-Gascoyne and the Western Desert: in this context, as Director, I am visiting key regional organisations to make the official transfer of the materials, as well as to assist in assessing future needs and ongoing commitments. In this respect, for example, the above-mentioned community museums established recently at Warburton Range (Central Australia) and Balgo (southern Kimberley) will provide a focus for continuing collaborative activities, as well as potential future research projects, both museum and field-based.

The experience accumulated during the past four years of the *Bringing the Photographs Home* Project has greatly enriched the Museum's knowledge and appreciation of its collections. It has also demonstrated the Museum's commitment to the recruitment and training of curatorial staff to participate in this vital process, confirming its role in the recognition of Aboriginal interests in collections, and the formulation of strategies to achieve the outcomes sought by Indigenous individuals and communities.

PHOTOGRAPHS AND ADVOCACY

The Museum's photographic collections frequently form the stimulus for contemporary expressions of Indigenous historical and social interpretations. Travelling exhibitions toured by Art on the Move (the Western Australian component of the National Exhibition Touring Strategy) provide a means of addressing what are often particular and highly localised perspectives on Aboriginal experiences. Although the recent exhibition, *Aboriginal Artists of the South-West: Past and Present*, curated by local Perth Indigenous artist Sandra Hill, showcases contemporary artworks from the Museum's south-west collection, it also provides a focus for discussion of current political issues facing Indigenous artists and their families in this particular region. In developing it, Sandra (herself a lecturer at another of Perth's universities, Curtin University of Technology), had this to say:

> There was a strong philosophical reason for wanting to mount this exhibition. I was tired of hearing from visitors to galleries exhibiting contemporary South-West art saying, 'That's really nice, but it's not *real* Aboriginal art.'
>
> But this *is* the art of the South-West: it is how artists see their works in their environment, and how they tell their own stories, and express their own feelings about the experiences of their families in the past. These artists are putting something important together; they are making a vital statement about the processes of colonisation and their subsequent removal from their own lands. They are bringing

these experiences right into the present. The art unites the past with the present – and the future.

(S. Hill 2000: 5)

Reflecting on the feelings and emotions of being a practising artist herself, Sandra uses a collage of family documents and photographs, overlaid with terms of derision and shame, to address her own experience and that of her family:

For me, though, my painting here is in memory of my father, who has passed away. It depicts an exemption certificate, which is what people needed to become citizens of Australia. He didn't get this, though, even if he was in the Navy for 14 years. When he returned from overseas he couldn't be out at nights, he couldn't go into a pub, he wasn't a citizen. In the painting is a letter he wrote to his mother from New Guinea: it is a collage of suffering, of not having grown up with them, of being taken at seven years old until he was 21. I'm trying to get this story across to the wider community. It is the human face of the 1905 *Aborigines Act*.

In my work, *Stoker Hill*, this was a very difficult piece to complete, to confront. It is a page out of my own life, my own story: a letter from my father, who was a serviceman, and a newspaper article about him. It is very important to me, this painting, and I wanted it very much to be in the Berndt Museum collection.

It was constructed as a narrative to communicate the pain and emotion of the denial and discovery of family, identity and the past.

I have always drawn and painted. It has been the one true and real thing that has remained constant throughout my life.

(S. Hill 2000: 29–30)

Another local Nyungar artist, Valerie Takao Binder, was commissioned last year by the Perth International Arts Festival to create an art installation for the entry foyer of the Western Australian Museum. This work was subsequently purchased by our Museum. For Val, the world of the Nyungar experienced the full force of the disastrous impact of European settlement; because of this, the world of her ancestors was dramatically transformed. Today, as Sandra Hill has also noted, Nyungar people are still fighting to maintain, and sustain, their own unique culture. Elements of language, dance, song and, most importantly, art are being melded together to create what is, in effect, a new identity, a new place for Nyungar people in contemporary Western Australian society.

The historic written and photographic records of the Nyungar world are at the best, patchy. Nyungar families have their own stories, though – knowledge of their own associations with particular places, specific waters and other resources. It is these stories that provide the basis for what it feels like to be Nyungar today. And it is one of these stories, Val's story, which provides the context for her exhibition *Mia Mia/Dwelling Place*:

The paintings are just my way of telling the story, it doesn't mean to say that they are wonderful works in artistic terms, for me it's my way of telling my story, and for Aboriginal people this is the way we work.

It's more the story that's important here, than the paintings. This is what I would like to get across. This is really where Aboriginal people are coming from, and this is where a lot of people don't understand our work. You've got to look right into what's there.

(Takao Binder cited in Stanton 2001: 4)

The mia mia, the camping place, which Val recreated in the foyer of the Western Australian Museum (see Figure 8.1) reaffirms her background as a Swan Valley Nyungar:

> With the Camp, I did most of that from the old Native Welfare files, and when I found the file that spoke about the Camp the one that I constructed was almost exactly the same size. I was only a small child, and I remember it being only just large enough to sleep in, about 6ft × 8ft or something like that, and everything else was done outside, we lived outside, eating and all that as there was no room inside. There were four of us, myself and my sister, and my parents, four of us. We slept on a home-made bed made out of bushes, a bush bed . . . The reason I did all this is because it was my way of saying 'This happened to me, this happened to my family, this happened to my people'.

(Takao Binder cited in Stanton 2001: 6)

The Camp, Mia Mia, contains items that resonate with memories of childhood, of growing up in the Middle Swan Valley. The walls are lined with copies of 1950s newspaper advertisements. The oppressive policies of the state intruded on every aspect of people's lives, and Nyungar people, like Aboriginal people elsewhere, were forced to confront the effects of these policies. Valerie discusses these in a video recording accompanying the exhibition; an enlarged historical photograph of *wedjela* (White)

Figure 8.1 Val Takao Binder's sculpture 'Mia Mia Dwelling Place' installed in the foyer of the Western Australian Museum, with the cityscape in the background. (WU/P24489)

visitors to the Camp, referred to here, mirrors for the museum visitor their experience of the reconstruction. The Camp contains a trunk, which sits on the floor:

> The trunk was what kept all the good clothes. You had to have good clothes in case the Welfare came and we would put them on. In one of the photos of my grandmother's camp, which was at the back of Jane Creek . . . they've got an old tent with hessian bags thrown all over it and there are all these *wedjela* [White] ladies all dressed up in fur clothes and everything. It just looks so ridiculous. And in that photograph is A.O. Neville, the Chief Protector, who was visiting that day. My mother used to talk often about that all the time, about him visiting on one occasion, and she said that he was a 'lovely man' [Val laughs]. I think it was just something of the time.

(Takao Binder cited in Stanton 2001: 7)

Government policies of dispossession and relocation have had a devastating effect on Aboriginal families throughout the state, as elsewhere in Australia. The Museum's role in assisting these families to come to terms with their experiences, to reflect on the particularity of the colonial impact, and the responses of their own communities, is a critical ingredient in the elaboration of future relationships between Indigenous peoples and instrumentalities of the nation state.

Although the role of photographs in advocacy has focused here on its impact among south-west artists and their constituencies, its application is, in fact, much broader. Communities in remote areas, whose members are more frequently remaining in the occupation of their customary territories, rely nevertheless on photographs for the substantiation of what are sometimes inaccurate and misleading government records from the earlier era. Such images provide incontrovertible evidence of the residence of particular occupants at specific periods. Together with oral recordings, sometimes made decades earlier, photographs have assisted members of a number of communities to define and assert their own rights of membership to present-day corporate or residential associations, for varied purposes such as housing, schooling, or even hunting and foraging rights. Photographs have enabled communities to maintain and revive cultural practices, such as singing, dancing, and other art forms, as well as to reaffirm other social activities. Art works document contemporary experience, just as other visual records do: it remains for museums to harness these new opportunities for an enduring collaboration with Indigenous communities, rather than to discard these moments of insight and innovation.

Photographs may also have a role to play in the courts. They have, for example, played a highly significant part in the documentation of Applications for Native Title. They have amplified and validated oral records, to the satisfaction of the Native Title Tribunal, as well as providing applicants with recognisable images of past experiences, giving memories and passed-down accounts of cultural practices a yearned-for emotional valency.

Local community museums, keeping places and cultural centres, by whatever name they are known, represent a fundamental shift towards the restoration of Indigenous curatorship and, indeed, custodianship, into the hands of local community members and away from often remote metropolitan museums. This does not signal the end of the museum as we know it: merely its reformation, if not its revival.

Aboriginal families and their respective communities are, then, increasingly telling their own stories: historic and more recent photographs are a focus for community engagement and individual expression through both art and text. Together with objects collections and sound recordings, past imperatives inform present preoccupations; in the same way those contemporary perspectives help shape future understandings of these social processes.

EXPERIENCES AND PRACTICES

Projects such as these have assisted the University of Western Australia's Berndt Museum of Anthropology to achieve some of its longer-term goals, to assert its strategic plan to become one of Australia's leading heritage institutions, and to provide a benchmark for its future development. Above all, these projects have provided an experience, and a setting, for maintaining and enhancing a culturally appropriate and creative environment for advocating and supporting contemporary Indigenous artists in their engagement with the wider Australian society, and beyond.

Collections – such as photographs, sound recordings and, indeed, objects – are critical bridges to the future, as Malcolm Shaw's observation at the beginning of this chapter demonstrates. They provide an insight on past experiences, which is itself a matter for active engagement in the present, for the future. Just as objects incorporate the lives and knowledge of ancestral family members, and their respective communities; so too do photographs assist the interrogation of history, the history that informs the present and creates the future.

Museums are ideally situated within this paradigm, since working with their historic collections reinvigorates contemporary wisdom and understanding, prolonging internal discourses about the nature of history, culture and identity. Together, these bring new scholarship to museums, re-attaching data to collection items and confirming their contemporary relevance and significance. The reinvigorated objects in museum collections gain fresh meanings and a new element of engagement for visitors and scholars alike. The reassertion of Indigenous scholarship and the dynamics of its application impels museums to make a more critical apprehension of public (and, more specifically, Indigenous) engagement with their respective institutions. Nevertheless, they must not fall into the trap of assuming that communities that they engage with are necessarily homogeneous – nor that all reconnections with collections will be positive, resulting in collaboration. It is up to communities to define their own positions, and for museums actively to seek these alternatives; it is not enough to have these options simply thrust upon Indigenous communities.

This, then, is the end of museums seeking exclusive rights of custodianship and, indeed, curatorship: it is the beginning of a new process, which is open-ended. It will be part of a process that will redefine the role of museums in the twenty-first century, one that will end some of the patronising presumptions of the past, as well as encourage the debate of the future. It is, then, an end with a beginning, rather than a beginning with an end.

ACKNOWLEDGEMENT

I gratefully acknowledge the contribution of Ghislaine van Maanen for her comments on an earlier version of this paper.

Part 3

COMMUNITY COLLABORATION IN EXHIBITIONS

Toward a dialogic paradigm

INTRODUCTION

Ruth B. Phillips

There is no intelligibility that is not at the same time communication and intercommunication, and that is not grounded in dialogue.

(Freire 1998: 42)

Visual culture within the museum is a technology of power. This power can be used to further democratic possibilities, or it can be used to uphold exclusionary values. Once this is acknowledged, and the museum is understood as a form of cultural politics, the post-museum will develop its identity.

(Hooper-Greenhill 2002: 162)

Exhibits are the reason most people go to museums. They are the museum's premier product, designed to address the public directly through a unique language configured of visual, textual, and spatial elements. Through the creation of exhibits, museum professionals seek to render more intelligible and accessible knowledge that is specialized, esoteric, and complex. Through their selective sponsorship of exhibits, governments and private interest groups hope to educate and shape public opinion. The critical museological literature has identified exhibitions as a key area of cultural production with important agency in the inscription of constructs of nation, citizenship, race, and gender. It demonstrates how, historically, exhibits have contributed to the formation of the universalist ideologies and nationalist power structures that inform modern societies.[1] In collaboratively organized exhibits the intellectual, social, and political dynamics of these processes change in fundamental ways. On the one hand, the communities that choose to partner with museums have often been marginalized and/or exoticized by the museum's traditional state and private sponsors. On the other, by validating knowledge produced according to diverse cultural traditions, museums contribute to the erosion of the modernist universal values in which these sponsors have been invested. The paradigmatic shift being introduced through collaborative exhibit development thus raises fundamental questions not only about the ways that contemporary museums are repositioning themselves as they respond to the powerful currents of cultural pluralism, decolonization, and globalization, but also about the changing relationship between museums and the societies within which they operate.

THE OPENING

If the museum's messages are most concentrated in its public displays, its sponsoring social and political network is most clearly visible when a new exhibition is inaugurated. Museum openings are highly ritualized events. Typically, speeches are made by the director, the curator, the chairman of the board, artists, community representatives, and the officers of corporate sponsors and funding agencies. People dress a little more formally, wine is drunk from stemmed glasses, canapes are nibbled. The members, volunteers, 'friends', professional colleagues, critics and others in attendance make up the 'taste culture' (Gans 1974) or 'art world' (Becker 1982) specific to the particular museum or gallery. In Bourdieu's terms, the players on the 'field of cultural production' become, for an evening, visible within the museum's walls (1993: 37).

I open, therefore, with an opening, one that occurred on 23 April 2002 at my own institution, the University of British Columbia Museum of Anthropology, to mark the Vancouver showing of *Kaxlaya Gvilas: The Ones Who Uphold the Laws of Our Ancestors*. This exhibit was the first to display the historical and contemporary art of the Heiltsuk people of British Columbia's central coast,[2] and the opening ceremony was a particularly splendid example of the kinds of performances staged to mark the collaboratively organized exhibits discussed in this part. The contrast it presented to conventional museum openings is emblematic of the ways collaboratively organized exhibitions differ from those that preceded them.

Over 700 guests, many of them Heiltsuk, filled to overflowing the Museum's Great Hall. Sixteen hereditary chiefs, community members, artists, and dancers from both the urban and reserve Heiltsuk communities dressed in ceremonial button blankets, carved frontlets, and other regalia entered the Hall to begin the evening's ceremonies.[3] In accordance with First Nations protocol, they requested permission to enter Musqueam territory and to share their culture from the chief of the Musqueam First Nation on whose traditional lands the Museum and the University are located. The Heiltsuk guests then became the evening's hosts, and, for a night, the museum's foyer and major exhibition gallery (generically, as Carol Duncan has shown, already a ritual and ceremonial space) effectively became a Heiltsuk 'big house'.[4] The speaker formally announced the names and titles of the chiefs, displayed the inherited privileges of important families through song, dance, and masked performance, and publicly recognized the contributions made by different individuals through the presentation of gifts. The hosts then offered a feast of wild salmon and home baking to all the guests whose collective witnessing of the proceedings had conferred on them essential validation. The ritual performance translated the basic principles and components of the potlatch of the Northwest Coast First Nations into the language of a museum opening – or vice versa – and the brief speeches by museum, university, and sponsors' representatives which normally provide the substance of a museum opening were decentred and became enfolded within an indigenous Heiltsuk ceremonial event.

The bringing together of so many people, many of whom had made a long and expensive journey from the Heiltsuk community at Bella Bella, with all the ingredients of celebration, was the result of months of careful planning and a huge expenditure of time, energy, and money.[5] As Victor Turner has taught us, 'a celebratory performance rejoices in the key values and virtues of the society that produces it' (1982: 14). The communal values, unique traditions, and knowledge of the Heiltsuk people that were being affirmed that evening reflected the success of a collaborative process which had not only effected the transgenerational reunion of the historical objects with the descendants of their original makers and owners, but had also accurately expressed the community's contemporary understanding of itself. The contributions of the curator, Pam Brown, and the associate curator, Martha Black, model the collaboration that lay behind this success. Brown is a member of the Heiltsuk First Nation, while Black is an art historian whose doctoral research on the collection of objects made by a medical missionary at the height of the colonial era provided an essential research base for the project. To create the exhibit, Brown took that research back to the community, amplified it with further levels of community interpretation, added a substantial contemporary art component, and worked with community members to identify the themes and issues Heiltsuk people wanted to communicate to both the roughly half of their members who live in Vancouver and to broader southern Canadian publics.

THE EMERGENCE OF COLLABORATIVE EXHIBITIONS IN THE 1990s

The approach to exhibition development that informed the production of *Kaxlaya Gvilas* has established itself with remarkable rapidity during the past decade, initially in the settler societies of North America, Australia, and New Zealand and more recently in the former centres of European empire.[6] The five chapters in this part of the book present case studies of important collaborative exhibitions organized in Canada, Great Britain and Egypt.[7] As a group they offer a micro-history of the development of the new paradigm. Work on the earliest of the projects presented here – the two pioneering archaeological exhibits described by Michael Ames – began in the early 1990s. *Written in the Earth* and *From Under the Delta* were developed by Coast Salish communities and the University of British Columbia Museum of Anthropology in direct response to the challenge to develop new and equal forms of partnership that was issued to Canadian museums and indigenous peoples by the 1992 report of the national Task Force on Museums and First Peoples.[8] Anita Herle's chapter on the Cambridge University Museum of Archaeology and Anthropology's *Torres Strait Islanders: An Exhibition to Mark the Centenary of the 1898 Anthropological Expedition*, discusses a temporary exhibit opened in 1998 to commemorate a formative episode in the history of anthropology – and equally, as she shows us, in the history of the Torres Straits Islanders. Anthony Shelton's chapter documents the curatorial process adopted by the Horniman Museum for the new installation of its African collections designed to replace a typical mid-twentieth-century ethnographic exhibit. Entitled *African Worlds*, it opened in 1999. A second Canadian example, also a long-term installation, is discussed by Gerald Conaty. The Glenbow Museum's *Nitsitapiisinni: Our Way of Life*, was organized with Blackfoot community members and opened in 2000. The most recent of these collaborative exhibit projects is still in development. As described by Stephanie Moser and her colleagues, it brings together archaeologists from the University of Southampton with the Quseir Heritage Preservation Society to conduct archaeological research on the ancient Roman harbour of Myos Hormos and to co-develop exhibits based on this research for a new museum or heritage centre at Quseir al-Qadim, Egypt.

As all the examples make clear, the collaborative paradigm of exhibition production involves a new form of power sharing in which museum and community partners co-manage a broad range of the activities that lead to the final product. These usually include the initial identification of themes, the design of the research methodology, object selection, and the writing of text panels. It can also include the integration of training and capacity building for community members and community input into other activities, such as conservation, the design of the installation, and the selection of gift shop products and poster images.

Community consultants and advisory committees have long been features of exhibition development in anthropology museums, but collective decision-making in this broader array of activities, which are normally controlled by museum professionals with specialized training, requires a much more radical shift within the institution. It amounts to what Michael Ames calls in his article 'a realignment of power, achieved through a redistribution of authority'.

In the remainder of this introduction I shall discuss several key features of collaborative exhibitions which are revealed by the case studies as a group. These include the articulation of a post-colonial museum ethic, a shift in emphasis from product to process, and a renewed affirmation of the museum as a research site. I shall also seek to problematize two aspects of collaborative exhibits that seem to me to require deeper analysis at this stage in the develop-ment of the paradigm. First, I shall argue that this representative group of case studies reveals that there is no one single model of collaboration in exhibition development, as the literature to date seems to imply. Rather, a spectrum of models has emerged, bracketed by two distinct types which I shall term the community-based exhibit and the multivocal exhibit. Each of these models prescribes particular authorities, responsibilities, and forms of public recognition for the community and museum participants. I shall further argue that clarity in identifying the model to be used in a given collaborative exhibit project not only greatly enhances its chances of success, but also the long-term viability of the new paradigm. Finally, I shall raise the theoretical question of the role that museums play in processes of social change. Put simply, does the growing popularity of collaborative exhibits signal a new era of social agency for museums, or does it make the museum a space where symbolic restitution is made for the injustices of the colonial era in lieu of more concrete forms of social, economic, and political redress?

THE ETHICS OF COLLABORATIVE EXHIBITS: FROM POSTMODERNISM TO HUMAN RIGHTS

The case studies demonstrate that the move to collaborative curatorial practice in anthro-pology museums is rooted in two important intellectual and moral developments which have steadily grown in power during the past half century. First, the reflexivity in the humanities and social sciences associated with postmodernism has raised awareness among museum anthropologists of the ways in which earlier, objectifying traditions of material culture display have supported colonial and neo-colonial power relations. Second, the evolving discourse of human rights has, in the years since its first broad codification in the 1948 UN Universal Declaration of Human Rights, been vigorously argued to extend to cultural property and the protection of traditional indigenous knowledge (Bell and Patterson 1999).

Postmodern anthropology and rights-based arguments are reflected in the language used by the authors in this section. All begin by situating their projects in relation to the prior history of anthropological exhibits. Shelton, for example, refers to the 'old neo-colonial paradigm' in which people are represented 'through the voices of their foreign interpreters'. Similarly, the Quseir team affirms the legitimacy of community interest in the development of exhibits about their own histories and ways of life because these exhibits play an important role in the construction of the identities by which their members become 'known' to museum visitors. All the authors affirm either implicitly or explicitly the need to repair the psychological damage that has been done in the past to individuals forced to negotiate negative stereotypes by creating new exhibits that disseminate more accurate (and usually positive) images of contemporary ways of life.

The five exhibits described here adopt a number of specific strategies to counter the stereotypes and dehumanization that have been produced by the scientific objectification of earlier ethnographic exhibits. The 'African Voices' component of the Horniman's *African Worlds* foregrounds the photographic portraits and words of contemporary Africans and members of African diasporic communities in order to effect a 'conscious purge of some of the more familiar and perhaps comfortable illusions about Africa in the popular conscience'. Herle countered the historical legacy of objectification by meticulously attributing information, quotations, and objects to named individuals and by personalizing and considering as historical subjects not only the Islanders, but also the Western academic investigators.

A concept of knowledge as property also underlies these discussions. All of the authors point to past asymmetries of power in the treatment of intellectual property – justified, as Ames notes, by an uninterrogated notion of academic freedom – and all seek to rectify this imbalance through collaborative approaches. While the knowledge taken from communities has been used to create museum exhibits that advance the careers and status of anthropologists and curators, those who shared this knowledge and their descendants usually have not benefited. Rather, they have often suffered from the loss of cultural property and from the uses made of the knowledge taken away. A point of departure for Ames's discussion is, thus, the need to acknowledge indigenous people's right to own their own histories. Moser and her group state that 'it is no longer acceptable for archaeologists to reap the material and intellectual benefits of another society's heritage', and Conaty expresses similar principles through concepts of 'profit' and 'appropriation'.

A key ethical principle of collaborative exhibition projects is, then, that *both* sides should be able to define and gain the benefits they deem appropriate. Ames notes that his museum's innovative collaboration with Coast Salish communities illustrates the importance of the Canadian requirement, after 1992, for museums to provide letters of support from the First Nations communities being represented when applying for government grants. His insight that community partners thus assumed the rights of sponsors already defined in research ethics policies is crucial. As a result, he writes, the Salish communities had the power to insist that they 'should become the primary audience because their histories and cultures constitute the subject matter'. Similarly, Conaty points out that

> the Blackfoot made it clear that they were not participating just to help Glenbow create an exhibit. . . . They saw this project as an opportunity to develop an educational place where future generations of Blackfoot youth could learn the fundamentals of their own culture.

The multiple components of the Community Archaeology Project at Quseir are being designed to confer an array of economic and educational benefits even before there is an exhibit. While the Horniman and Cambridge projects could not so directly serve the educational needs of community partners thousands of miles away, Shelton and Herle found innovative ways to return research materials and information to them, and Herle was able to travel a version of the Cambridge exhibit to Australia where Islanders could more easily see it.

The flipside of the identification of benefits is the need to avoid harm. In addition to the damage caused by stereotyping, Conaty points out the harm that can be done to a cultural tradition when its system of knowledge management is not respected by outside scholars, and when information whose circulation is restricted because of its sacred or proprietary nature is made generally accessible through display or publication. In both Herle's and Conaty's projects decisions were made not to put on display certain kinds of objects or information. As Herle relates, while the changes and omissions that were requested by community members seemed relatively minor to the museum, from the Islanders' point of view they were critical to the exhibit's success.

Michael Ames points out the parallelism between the ethics that inform collaborative exhibition projects and the democratizing, activist research process known as Participatory Action Research (PAR) developed by social scientists, medical researchers, and others during the past few decades (Robinson 1996: 136, n. 1). As Joan Ryan and Michael Robinson have written,

> In essence, PAR addresses the perceived and felt needs in a community to reclaim knowledge, power, and decision making from the colonizers and/or oppressors, and the desire to have local knowledge accepted as equally valid and scientific as western knowledge.
>
> (1996: 8)

The overall purpose of Participatory Action Research projects, as they state, is change, and this is achieved through an involvement of the whole community 'in the definition of goals, in the research process, and in the verification of data'. Equally important, training for community members is built in at all stages of the project (ibid.). Collaborative museum exhibition projects are controlled by principles nearly identical to those of PAR, and they are proving to have similar impacts on community development in the areas of education, cultural preservation, and the tourist industry.

'TO-ING AND FRO-ING': THE PRIMACY OF PROCESS

Both Ames and Shelton refer to the characteristic movement of collaborative processes as 'to-ing and fro-ing', although they use this evocative phrase in different ways. For Ames it is 'the extended process of negotiation and consultation', while for Shelton it is the 'to-ing and fro-ing between a collection and a suitable discourse' that 'eventually gives rise to a coherent system which embraces both objects and narrative into a rationalised order'. All the authors stress the extended negotiations that collaborative museum projects require, and provide examples of the back-and-forth process. As Herle shows, the need for negotiation can be just as demanding within the partnering community as between it and the museum. As her examples illustrate, the historical legacy of colonialism is a Pandora's box, which, when opened, releases into the space of the museum unresolved conflicts or tensions among individuals, families, or communities. These need to be addressed by the communities before the project can proceed. In many collaborative exhibition projects the museum serves as a useful 'neutral space' where such conflicts can be provisionally or even permanently resolved.

Conaty emphasizes the need to give time to relationship building, pointing out that before the Glenbow exhibit project could be initiated, trust had to be built between the community and the museum. Not only are anthropology museums often categorically associated with the institutional machinery of state surveillance and oppression, but they also serve as repositories for human remains and cultural objects requested for repatriation. All the authors agree, however, that while collaborative projects take longer to develop than do conventional exhibitions, the added investment of time allows the project to become a much more effective site for research, education, and innovation. In collaborative exhibits the extended development process is, therefore, becoming as important as the physical exhibit itself. The emphasis on process is also a reflection of a fundamental insight of reflexive museology that the messages of an exhibit are carried not just by objects, texts, and design, but also by many other aspects of its realization (Phillips 1990). As Ames recounts, in collaborative projects all the phases of exhibit preparation and object handling need to be discussed and agreed upon, and a wide range of museum professionals must therefore become involved in the negotiation of their practices. Through the ensuing discussions both they and the community participants are called upon to articulate their reasons for procedures and requirements that may appear natural or unnatural, depending on the participant's subject position. The subject/object relationships constructed by collaborative exhibitions thus move away from the monologism of the past and toward a dialogic structure.

The emphasis on process in collaborative projects leads, then, to the redefinition of the scope of an exhibit, which is increasingly understood not just as a physical arrangement of objects and interpretive materials in a gallery, but as an interrelated set of activities that take place before, during, and after the show. These projects often encompass an array of educational initiatives that can include training opportunities and internships for community members, performances and public programs, the sharing of research and resources, and the building of an ongoing partnership that can lead to social and political advocacy. Eilean Hooper-Greenhill has discussed the museum's redefinition of its scope and mission in terms of a break with modernism.

> Where the modernist museum was (and is) imagined as a building, the museum in the future may be imagined as a process or an experience . . . it moves as a set of processes into the spaces, the concerns and the ambitions of communities.
>
> (2002: 152–3)

Her use of the term 'post-museum' for this enlarged and politicized scope and mission conveys the same sense of rupture with historical traditions of museology as my notion of paradigm shift. As this shift continues, the museum becomes a participant in the community as much as the community becomes a participant in the museum. Museums are just beginning to address the implications of their commitment to building long-term relationships with communities. As collaborative projects become normative and as museums engage serially with different communities, innovative solutions will have to be found to address the increased demands on staff and community members' time. It seems probable that new electronic media will play a major role in sustaining these relationships.

THE DEVELOPMENT OF NEW KNOWLEDGE AND THE MUTUALITY OF EDUCATION

The authors also argue that through collaborative exhibits, the museum is being renewed as a site for the production of new knowledge. Although anthropology museums were founded as active research sites during the late nineteenth and early twentieth centuries, this function has been in abeyance during much of the past century as the discipline of anthropology turned away from material culture study. As indigenous communities engage with museums, however, the power of museum objects to stimulate memories suppressed by the pressures of assimilationism and modernization becomes ever more apparent. The compelling examples of the new kinds of research questions that are being investigated in the course of collaborative exhibit development offered by Aldona Jonaitis and James Clifford were discussed in Laura Peer and Alison Brown's introductory essay to this volume. As Jonaitis writes, these questions go beyond relatively straightforward problems of ethnographic and art historical documentation to larger questions about colonialism and historical process. Her observation that the 'continuity, vividly disclosed as the full significance of the Siwidi material came to light, has served as an enlightening example of the enduring nature of many Kwakiutl traditions,' points to the value of such research for the understanding of our collective postcolonial condition (Jonaitis 1991: 251). Clifford also stresses the value of community/museum collaborations in illuminating, not standard ethnography, but rather the intercultural social relationships that have been constructed by colonial histories.

> In the contact zone of the Portland Museum's basement, the meanings addressed to white interlocutors were primarily relational: 'This is what the objects inspire us to say in response to our shared history, the goals of ongoing responsibility and reciprocity we differently embrace'.

(Clifford 1997b: 194)

The five case studies provide further examples of how collaborative research for museum exhibitions is yielding critical understandings about the workings of history and memory. The two archaeological exhibits are particularly interesting in this regard. Although contemporary people have traditionally been thought to have little if any 'hard' data to offer that can help to explicate materials dating back centuries or millennia, in both British Columbia and Egypt new data and new understandings resulted from collaboration between community members and archaeologists. The Quseir team not only learned of the location of new sites and the uses of unfamiliar objects, but also about 'how the past is experienced'. Similarly, Herle's work with Torres Straits Islanders produced not only new facts but also a more nuanced understanding of the capacity of anthropological research both to disrupt and to contribute to the preservation of traditional indigenous life. Shelton's African and Caribbean co-curators not only articulated African ways of categorizing cultural knowledge, but also their perspectives on such sensitive topics as the continued holding of confiscated Benin brasses in British museums (R. Phillips 2002).

The authors of these essays also reflect on the value of collaborative processes in terms of mutual learning and educating, sometimes as the result of initially difficult encounters. Conaty notes the surprise of Glenbow staff when some of their 'good ideas' could not be used because they breached cultural sensitivities. Yet, he says, as the partners continued to work together, not only did the museum staff come to understand the Blackfoot perspective, but the Blackfoot also developed a better understanding of the museum process. In this sense the process of collaborative exhibit development fosters a bilateral version of the radical pedagogy advocated by Paolo Freire. His anti-authoritarian, democratic practice insists on the recognition that both teachers and students have important knowledge and that, for education to occur, their different subject positions have to be respected and rendered mutually intelligible.

> Through dialogue, grassroots groups can be challenged to process their social-historical experience as the experience that is formative for them individually and collectively. And

through such dialogue the necessity of going beyond certain types of explanations of the 'facts' will become obvious.

(Freire 1998: 76–7)

The educational process invoked by collaborative exhibits is even more egalitarian and bi-directional. In it both community and museum partners are simultaneously 'teachers' and 'grassroots', experienced in their own worlds and inexperienced in each other's. When collaborative exhibit projects are successful, both museum and community partners come to new understandings through mutually respectful dialogue and exchange.

Members of the public regard museums, like the universities to which museums have historically been linked, as sources of authoritative knowledge. The new methods of knowledge production and dissemination fostered by collaborative exhibits thus have the potential to change radically the very definition of the educational mission which the museum shares with other institutions. Because the partners are aware that the narratives and formulations they present will be publicly accessible to and vetted by community, academic, and general audiences, collaborative exhibits come under particular pressure from these multiple sources of authority. When successful, they can convey the situated nature of knowledge even more effectively than can 'purer' formats of museum research. As the case studies show, these exhibits are serving as experimental sites where constructivist, pluralist, and multivocal theories of communication and representation are finding a practice.

A TYPOLOGY OF COLLABORATION: COMMUNITY-BASED EXHIBITS AND MULTIVOCAL EXHIBITS

Although we are accustomed to speak as if there were a single process for collaborative exhibition work, I should like to argue that these case studies reveal a tendency for individual projects to cluster around two distinct models, which I term the *community-based exhibit* and the *multivocal exhibit*. The identification of the specific model being used in a given exhibition project is not just an analytical exercise, but rather a practical necessity for both museum practitioners and viewers. Clarity about the approach chosen among museum and community participants will avoid unnecessary confusion, conflict, and frustration, while the disclosure to viewers of the model being used will provide the tools they need to assess the new pluralization of knowledge that collaborative exhibits foster. I shall now turn to a more detailed discussion of each of these two models and the characteristic problems each encounters.

In community-based exhibits the role of the professional museum curator or staff member is defined as that of a facilitator who puts his or her disciplinary and museological expertise at the service of community members so that their messages can be disseminated as clearly and as effectively as possible. The community is the final arbiter of content, text, and other key components, and the museum becomes an extension of its space, a place in which its own images of its members' lifestyles, values, and concerns are projected.[9] On one level, then, the community-based exhibit serves as a kind of semiotic repair kit which attaches new meanings to objects that museum visitors have become accustomed to see exclusively through the lenses of the Western disciplines (Redfield 1959; Phillips 1994, 2002). Furthermore, as Conaty's discussion shows, the decentring of objects in favour of narratives, stories, and performances is often a result of such processes.[10]

163

Kaxlaya Gvilas, the Heiltsuk exhibit whose opening I described at the beginning of this introduction, was a classic community-based exhibit. It resisted the standard presentation of ethnographic information about the functions, ceremonial uses, and meanings of the displayed objects. Rather, it focused on the lineage histories, names, and identities of the artists/ancestors who had made them and on contemporary issues of importance to the community. Although shown in southern Canadian cities, the exhibit was clearly intended to make sense in the first instance to Heiltsuk people and to serve their political ends. The privileging of community ways of knowing and the identification of community members as a primary audience – two hallmarks of the community-based exhibit – are also immediately recognizable in key decisions made in the Salish, Blackfoot, and Quseir exhibit projects. In *Written in the Earth* and *From Under the Delta*, 4,000-year-old archaeological objects were juxtaposed with images and narratives of contemporary Salish people. In *Nitsitapiisinni* visitor attention is focused on stories and on holistic environments, contexts of meaning of primary importance for Blackfoot, while the iconic Plains feather bonnets and painted shirts that fascinate museum visitors recede into the background. And at Quseir, the artefacts recovered from a Roman harbour city that can be assumed to interest Euro-American tourists will be presented against the context of the subsequent Arab and Egyptian history of the region.

Torres Straits Islanders and *African Worlds* differ from these three exhibits in important ways that typify the multivocal exhibit. In both, museum staff and community consultants worked to find a space of coexistence for multiple perspectives. Both were characterized by a reflexive historicization of the earlier traditions of museum anthropology against which the curators were working, and both sought to share this reflexive awareness with visitors. In the case of *African Worlds*, this was done in two ways. The first strategy was the development of an intentionally dissonant installation design that was intended, as Shelton writes, 'to convey a sense of alienation in the gallery: alienation in the sense that these objects were displaced, far removed from the conditions of their usage and original signification.' The second strategy was the use of four levels of text for each of the objects on display. These foreground the voice of a living community member, but also acknowledge Western ways of understanding the objects' identities, functions, and meanings. Herle, too, used strategies of juxtaposition rather than harmonization in *Torres Straits Islanders* in order to create an exhibit that displayed rather than elided the multiple meanings attributed to objects and events by anthropologists and Islanders, past and present. She exploited the ironic resonances that resulted from the fact that the commemorative exhibit was installed within the early twentieth-century architecture and cases contemporary with the anthropological project she was re-presenting. The goal of both exhibits was to encourage visitors to consider their own historical position in relation to colonial anthropology and the displacement of objects it achieved and to maintain an awareness of the dialogic tension between the European and community partners' points of view.

This typological distinction between the community-based and multivocal approaches is, of course, ideal rather than real, and neither model can be applied in a pure form. In the case of community-based exhibits, the ideal role of facilitator prescribed for the museum professional would, if taken literally, constitute a kind of museological ghost writing. Yet professional museum staff can never 'only' facilitate, because community-based exhibits, like multivocal exhibits, are always built on top of layers of information, interpretation, and museological conventions that have accumulated over time. This point can be most clearly illustrated by collaborative exhibit projects involving archaeologists, perhaps because of the harder scientific methods and tools they use to develop basic data. The two archaeological case studies demonstrate the ways in which a cognitive separation continues to be maintained within the model of the community-based exhibit project. In both examples, the communities decide which objects are displayed and what is said about them. At the same time, however, much of the 'what' is arrived at through the scientific methods of Western archaeology and is presented in specified registers of the exhibition text. And, through the publication of articles in professional journals, site reports, and academic conference presentations, professional archaeology continues to constitute the authoritative basis for representation.

The new interpretations and knowledge that are brought forward in collaborative exhibits do not, in fact, erase Western traditions of discourse and display, but rather intervene in them to a greater or lesser extent. The characteristic process of the collaborative exhibit, whether community-based or multivocal, is one of selection and supplementation. Discipline-based interpretation is always present, but certain elements are silenced, overlaid, or challenged in order to make room for new information and perspectives. The problem of acknowledging this – and of presenting adequately the grounds on which archivally or scientifically verifiable forms of knowledge are omitted – is particularly marked in community-based exhibits. As a result, they run the risk of producing only a partial intelligibility by ignoring the needs of one set of viewers in favour of those of another. During the initial showing of *Kaxlaya Gvilas* at Toronto's Royal Ontario Museum, for example, the non-Heiltsuk visitors who were in the vast majority were frustrated because the lack of standard ethnographic information made it difficult for them to learn what the objects were used for and what the imagery 'meant'.

In community-based exhibits there is a double danger, then, that legitimate modes of explanation will be dismissed along with oppressive constructs – that is, of trading one set of exclusionary practices for another. In their desire to atone for the historical legacy of colonialism museums as institutions and their staff members as individuals often seem to seek a degree of self-effacement that borders on the deceptive.[11] Curiously, for example, the names and photographs of the Glenbow staff who served over several years as full partners and collaborators in the development of *Nitsitapiissini* are not included in the credit panel which occupies a large wall as the visitor leaves the exhibition. This omission is in accordance with a general Glenbow policy not to name individual members of staff in exhibition credit panels. Unfortunately, however, the crediting of the Blackfoot consultants alone leaves the impression that the museum, having pulled off a superb, fully collaborative exhibit, wanted to silence its own role out of some misconceived belief that the inclusion of the non-Natives who contributed ethnographic and museological knowledge and skills throughout the duration of the project would have undercut the exhibit's authenticity as 'truly' Blackfoot.[12] The Glenbow example represents a more general tendency. At the Royal Ontario Museum, the text panel identifying the original collector of the objects displayed in *Kaxlaya Gvilas* and crediting the extensive research conducted by associate curator Martha Black was placed facing a wall at the far end of the gallery. It thus denied visitors an important point of orientation and also denied Black adequate credit for her work. As noted earlier, the collaborative paradigm is founded on a need to deconstruct the singular, distanced, and depersonalized authority of the modernist museum, but the deconstruction remains incomplete when museums fail to disclose their processes fully. Furthermore, if the contributions of both museum and community partners are not accurately and adequately credited, there is a real risk that either one or the other group will eventually turn to other forms of professional or community production in which their individual and collective voices can be heard clearly. I would urge, then, that the collaborative paradigm carries with it a particular need for museums to disclose the plural authorities behind the narratives they present, so that visitors are left free to evaluate new and possibly discrepant contents and interpretations for themselves. If the actual processes of research, exchange, and negotiation are not made clear, the exhibit will end up occluding its own constructive pluralism and will sabotage the public's ability to appreciate its dialogic achievement. Indeed, since collaborative exhibits model an ideal that the partners would usually like the public to take home and apply in other social interactions, such silences are, in the end, self-defeating.

Multivocal exhibits also carry their own characteristic dangers. Most viewers are conditioned to expect clarity, simplicity, inspiration, and/or pleasure in museums, yet these exhibits endeavour to make complexity and contradiction comprehensible and stimulating. If they are too successful in reconciling and aligning factual and perspectival differences contributed by community and museum partners, they can end up transmitting a falsely harmonious representation of conflicts not yet resolved in the world outside the museum. Successful efforts to even-handedly maintain multiple perspectives, however, can risk confusing and frustrating visitors. Exhibits that attempt to denaturalize the presence of foreign objects in Western museums can, furthermore, fail to provide for them adequately respectful contexts of display or, alternately, obscure the legitimate ways in which some were obtained. To use Stephen Greenblatt's terms (1991), while multivocal exhibits are more successful at conveying the historical and intercultural 'resonance' of museum objects, community-based exhibits are usually more successful in creating the sense of 'wonder' that most compellingly engages visitors and can most immediately instil in them the respect and admiration for the makers and their descendants that community partners usually want.

In the light of this analysis, the collaborative exhibit becomes recognizable as a typical hybrid product of the post-colonial era. It is made both possible and necessary by processes of mixing and mutual education that have been going on for centuries. Both the indigenous community member and the academically trained museum professional (the two, of course, are often found in one body) are hybrid beings, and the decision to engage in collaborative projects only intensifies this process of hybridization by promoting new dialogic exchanges. As Robert Young has noted, colonial hybridity was never a process of cultural fusion, but rather one that maintained a tension among discrepant elements – a tension out of which critical insights can be generated. His statement that, 'in its more radical guise of disarticulating authority, hybridity has also increasingly come to stand for the interrogative languages of minority cultures' (Young 1995: 23–4), can be taken as a gloss on collaborative exhibit projects. In these terms, the difference between the community-based and the multivocal exhibition resides in the degree to which each seeks to explore its own dialogic tensions by giving voice to coexistent and multiple points of view and by revealing its own hybridity to visitors.

It is also useful to think about collaborative museum processes as negotiations of the new languages through which the colonized have been forced to speak. Simon During has termed the two sides to contemporary negotiations of the colonial legacy as the 'post-colonized', who 'identify with the culture destroyed by imperialism', and the 'post-colonizers', who, 'if they do not identify with imperialism, at least cannot jettison the culture and tongues of the imperialist nations' (1995: 127).[13] The museum exhibit, like other European languages imposed by colonialism, is a Western expressive format which, while inevitably changing local meanings through processes of translation, also possesses a communicative power whose transnational reach is irresistible. What collaborative exhibits seek, in contrast to those they replace, are more accurate translations. In Shelton's words,

Representation of the 'other' is . . . a constant decolonisation and recolonisation of the imagination where truth is measurable only by the persuasive quality of the coherence and intelligibility of the discourse and its moral authority.

'SITTING WELL WITH EACH OTHER': THE MUSEUM IN THE COMMUNITY

We may logically ask, then, to what degree we can read the changes we have been examining as evidence of broader social and political shifts *outside* the museum, and to what degree they represent a new kind of agency *for* the museum. It has become a commonplace of the literature on museums to read earlier exhibits as expressions of a calculated and strategic program of enculturation to modernist notions of nation, empire, and colony. Yet today collaborative exhibits that directly challenge aspects of the status quo are being funded and even mandated by both liberal and conservative governments. They are being organized not only by smaller and more local museums, but also by large, national institutions like the Smithsonian, the Canadian Museum of Civilization, and New Zealand's Te Papa. Is the increasing acceptance of the collaborative paradigm by this last group, then, evidence that a pluralistic postcolonial ethos has established itself as ideology? Or do collaboratively produced exhibits present museum audiences with celebrations of diversity and dreams of social harmony that cannot be realized in the real world of legal rights, property, land, and money? Conaty's discussion of the difficulty in finding corporate sponsorship for *Nitsitapiisinni* and the disappointing initial visitor numbers suggests this last possibility.

Hooper-Greenhill has urged us to understand museum display as a technology generative of new forms of social interaction and as 'a form of cultural politics' (2002: 162). Her faith is justified by the demonstrable power of the lengthy dialogic interaction required by collaborative exhibits to effect permanent changes in both community and museum participants. Collaborative exhibits lead the participants to ask new questions and to identify new kinds of problems; they reorient professional and institutional activities and they change priorities; they stimulate the re-formulation of policies and procedures. I call these changes paradigmatic precisely because they are so pervasive, affecting and transforming a comprehensive range of museum practices. As of yet, however, we have less evidence of the impact of these exhibits on audiences. Museum exhibits do not do their work in a moment, and the creators of exhibits usually find out only years later, if ever, about the new perspectives that were suddenly glimpsed by a local visitor, a tourist, or a school child during a visit to an exhibit (and especially the school child), of the curiosity that was whetted, or of the small epiphanies that were sparked. Yet this accumulation of individual viewer experiences may well, over a long period of time, constitute the most lasting legacy of any exhibit project. Museums pursue collaborative exhibits in the hope of multiplying these small impacts and because of their faith that the directness of voice the exhibits privilege will remove distorting lenses and correct mistranslations, enabling rather than obstructing authentic communication across the boundaries of difference. The proponents of collaborative exhibits have, in the phrasing of Anthony Shelton and his African and British collaborators, 'embraced the vision of museums as places of dialogue where members of different cultures can "sit well with each other" '.

CONCLUSION: A CLOSING

A month after the opening of *Kaxlaya Givilas*, with which I began this essay, the University of British Columbia's Museum of Anthropology hosted another formal event. On that evening the monumental totem poles that ring its Great Hall witnessed not the singing of the First Nations, but the melodic chanting of verses of the Qu'ran. The evening's ceremonies marked not the opening but the closing of a collaboratively organized exhibition, *The Spirit of Islam: Experiencing Islam through Calligraphy*.[14] Closings, unlike openings, are not common museum rituals, and this ceremony had been improvised in response to a need, felt strongly by all the partners, for a communal, ceremonial marking of an extraordinary experience which had taken over their lives during the previous three years of development and public exhibition. The decision to begin the project had initially been made at the behest of Muslim communities in the Vancouver area who wanted to find ways to create a better understanding of Islam and to combat pervasive and inaccurate stereotypes of Muslims. It thus arose not from a desire to present and interpret an available collection of objects, but from a felt need to educate and to change public perceptions. The masterpieces of the Islamic art of calligraphy that were on display had been borrowed in order to provide an appropriate 'hook' for the educational project.

When the exhibit opened in October 2002, the terrorist attacks on New York and Washington of the previous September lent the project an even greater urgency. For the museum staff and the more than 70 community volunteers, however, the world had already changed during the more than two years of intensive collaborative work in positive ways that had prepared them to meet the unanticipated challenge. Museum staff had discovered in their city a geography of previously unknown Muslim schools, mosques, and cultural centres. They had attended numerous community functions, celebrated Muslim holidays with new friends, and begun to learn an unfamiliar history of calligraphy, art and belief. The community volunteers had raised hundreds of thousands of dollars through donations large and small. Perhaps most remarkably, the museum had proved to be an effective meeting place for the highly diverse Muslim communities that, although they had established themselves in the same metropolitan area, had not previously worked together on a common project. It provided a site from which a highly diverse assemblage of linguistic, diasporic, and religious groups could constructively articulate its own differences, identify a common ground of shared belief and experience, and find a unified voice with which to speak to non-Muslims.

The need for a 'closing' was also born of a collective desire to ensure that the end of the exhibition did not mean the end of the collaboration between the museum and the Muslim communities. It was an occasion both for self-assessment and for the affirmation of a joint commitment to continue to work together. Although the gallery space had to be cleared for a new project, and the loans of embroidered textiles, illuminated manuscripts, and inlaid furniture returned to their owners, a path of future collaboration was also being opened, not only between the museum and the communities, but amongst the communities themselves. The closing was a public testimonial of the transformative social power that can be generated by collaborative exhibit projects, when diverse communities with different intellectual, cultural, and social orientations come together in a museum, as equals, in determined and patient search of a language of common understanding.

ACKNOWLEDGEMENTS

I am grateful for the helpful readings of drafts of this paper by Michael Ames, Jill Baird, Sarah Casteel, Mark Phillips, and Judy Thompson. Responsibility for the final text is, of course, solely my own.

NOTES

1 Examples of key studies of museum exhibits and their socio-political functions are Duncan 1991, Bennett 1995, Haraway 1989, Butler 1999, Karp and Lavine 1991. For studies of museum practices as also inscribing Western values and of the development of new paradigms, see Clavir 2002 and Rosoff, this volume.

2 It displayed the most important extant collection made in the colonial period, assembled by medical missionary R.W. Large in the early twentieth century. The collection is now in the Royal Ontario Museum, which organized the exhibit (see Black 1997). The exhibit's Vancouver showing was made possible by support from the Audain Foundation and the Department of Canadian Heritage.

3 About 50 per cent of indigenous people in Canada now live in cities, and the Heiltsuk follow this pattern.

4 Duncan's analysis of the art museum as a ritual space applies equally to museums of anthropology and history (1991).

5 This was the second time such efforts had been expended, since a large group of Heiltsuk had made the even longer journey to Toronto for the opening of the exhibit at the Royal Ontario Museum two years earlier.

6 This statement describes a general pattern. There have been early experiments in community collaboration outside North America. For example, see early experiments in collaboration at a distance such as *A Time of Gathering* at the Burke Museum, University of Washington, curated by Robin Wright with tribal representatives from the state of Washington (1989); *The Living Arctic* at the Museum of Mankind in 1989 curated by J.C.H. King with Canadian First Nations partners; *Paradise*, also at the Museum of Mankind, curated by Michael O'Hanlon with partners from Papua New Guinea; and the reinstallation of North American exhibits curated by Peter Bolz at the Ethnographische Museum, Berlin. See also Jane Pierson Jones (1992) for a description of a 1990 project at the Birmingham Museum and Art Gallery.

7 I am fortunate to have been able to see all of these exhibitions and to have spoken with some of the collaborators. My remarks are therefore based not only on the essays, but also on several discussions and interviews and on my own observations. I did not, however, know I would be writing about all of the exhibits when I saw them, and therefore apologize to the authors for any unevenness in my text.

8 The Task Force was sponsored by the Canadian Museums Association and the Assembly of First Nations with funds from the federal Ministry of Communications (now the Ministry of Canadian Heritage). Its report, *Turning the Page: Forging New Partnerships between Museums and First Peoples*, was issued in Ottawa in 1992. On its recommendations, see Nicks (1992).

9 This response was recorded in comment cards filled out in the exhibition (pers. com., Kenneth Lister, Department of Anthropology, Royal Ontario Museum, 25 April 2002). It is too soon to assess whether visitor responses in Vancouver, where audiences are more familiar with the histories, cultures, and current concerns of Northwest Coast First Nations, will be different.

10 For example, Richard West, Jr, the Native American director of the Smithsonian's National Museum of the American Indian (an institution which is administered by indigenous people) has said repeatedly in public speeches that, unlike the mid-twentieth-century installations of the same collection at the old Museum of the American Indian, those in the new museum being built on the Mall in Washington DC will not be object-centred. (One such occasion was a lecture delivered at the symposium, 'Native Women and Art: Survival and Sovereignty', Cantor Arts Center, Stanford University, 9 May 2002.)

11 An exhibit is always a process of compromise and 'translation'. Even without community involvement, exhibits are always negotiations among collaborators with different and sometimes conflicting practices. Disparate logics must be reconciled (for example, the desire to preserve an object intact

versus the desire to risk alteration through display and handling), and information must be converted from textual and academic formats into a narrativized and spatialized language of objects, colours, forms, light, movement, and sound. The late Audrey Hawthorn, founding curator of the UBC Museum of Anthropology, for example, was fond of saying that an exhibition was 60 per cent curatorial content and 60 per cent design.

12 Conaty and other Glenbow staff are credited on another, smaller, and less prominent text panel. The Blackfoot members of the team, however, wanted the key Glenbow staff members' photos to be included in the large wall on the same basis as themselves, and acknowledged as full members of the team (Gerry Conaty, pers. com., 11 May 2002)

13 During uses the notion of the museum metaphorically to convey a concept of frozen reification in developing this argument: 'From the side of the post-colonizer, a return to difference is projected, but, from the side of post-modernity, English (multinational capitalism's tongue) will museumify those pre-colonial languages which have attached themselves to print and the image so belatedly' (During 1995: 128).

14 For further information and analysis see the exhibition website at *www.moa.ubc.ca/spiritofislam/ intro.html* and Hennessy (2003).

9

HOW TO DECORATE A HOUSE

The renegotiation of cultural representations
at the University of British Columbia Museum
of Anthropology

Michael M. Ames

The freedom to investigate and publish superior knowledge about serious things is the foundation of the scholarly professions (Shils 1978). In Western capitalist societies this principle of scholarly privilege has been coupled to the idea of private property. Researchers typically not only claim property rights over the knowledge they produce, but also proprietary rights over the subject matter – the field of raw data – from which they extracted their knowledge. This conceptual paradigm continues to be imposed upon the world – as a type of vestigial colonialism – long after the decline of those imperial regimes that gave rise to it in the first place. Contemporary examples are to be found in the ways museum and university scholars attempt to classify, represent, and control their fields of study in the name of 'science', 'academic freedom', and 'scholarship'. This chapter reviews how the assertion by Aboriginal peoples that they own their own histories served to interrupt and redefine that Western idea of scholarly privilege, at least as it applied to several public representations of indigenous languages and cultures at the University of British Columbia Museum of Anthropology.

Another way to describe the theme of this chapter would be: 'What happens to a museum when it is called upon to put its principles into practice?' Or it might be: 'How to decorate a house'. Let me explain.

The creation of an exhibit is a complex, multi-layered process that moves through all levels of a museum. The process typically includes articulating a theme or exhibition thesis, collecting research information, developing a storyline, establishing a budget, selecting objects to be included, reviewing and recording the condition of all the objects, preparing loan and insurance forms for any to be borrowed, drafting and editing labels, designing and fabricating object mounts and display furnishings, installing the exhibit, opening and marketing, and probably other steps I've missed. Each step involves one or more staff members specialized in that task. The question to be examined in this chapter is: What happens to that process and the people involved when it is changed to include as full partners representatives of those whose culture or history is to be represented, and who bring to the process their own skills and interests?

'Partnering' and 'collaboration' are popular terms with museums these days, though they are used to describe many different arrangements and usually from the perspective of a museum itself. That is, a museum typically asks outsiders to partner with the museum according to its own pre-arranged agenda. The customary museum model for managing the exhibition process does not easily lend itself to full collaboration with non-museum partners whose agendas or timetables might not be the same.

'Until museums do more than consult (often after the curatorial vision is firmly in place)', James Clifford states in his essay 'Museums as contact zones' (1997: 207–8), 'until they bring a wider range of historical experiences and political agendas into the actual planning of exhibits and the control of museum collections, they will be perceived as merely paternalistic by people whose contact history with museums has been one of exclusion and condescension.' There will be no easy solution, he warns.

The development of two archaeology exhibits at the University of British Columbia Museum of Anthropology (MOA) illustrate the process Clifford describes. Both projects began in the fashion that museums might consider collaborative and evolved into something rather different. Along the way questions were raised about institutional authority, museological procedures, the setting of agendas for collaboration, the rights to information and its use, and who constitutes a museum audience. I shall offer these two exhibit projects as a study case of negotiations in the 'contact zone'.

The first step is to outline in ideal-typical terms the customary model for managing the exhibition process, and then to describe how our experiences at the MOA, in developing the two exhibits in consultation with the First Nations communities whose heritage was to be displayed, fundamentally altered that model – all for the better, as it turned out, though not without some discomfort and uncertainty along the way.

The customary method of exhibition development could be summarized by saying it is governed by the 'curatorial prerogative'. By that I mean: (a) the final decision, authority, or prerogative for the exhibition usually lies with the curatorial team, subject to the approval of senior museum administration and budgetary constraints; and (b) the team is led or authorized by a content specialist or knowledge expert, designated as the curator or guest curator, rather than by a conservator, designer, educator, administrator, or specialist consultant.[1]

The process thus is hierarchical in structure: from the governing bodies of a museum, who set its mandate, to the director and/or senior management, to the curator, to the exhibition team composed of museological specialists. The assumption underlying the key role given to the curator is that specialized research knowledge is a primary consideration, subject to the exhibition and financial policies of the museum as monitored by the director or senior administrative official. Research or 'knowledge' is considered a primary good, therefore the person specializing in its production expects, and usually is accorded, privileged status in the decision-making process and in any public benefits that may accrue from the project. The appeal to 'scientific' expertise or use is treated as a powerful moral argument.

This system has worked well for museums, and for universities where the idea of scholarly privilege ('academic freedom') was established and where it continues to flourish. Some members of these 'knowledge industries' would even say that the pursuit of knowledge is a primary good in itself, wherever the pursuit might lead, across whatever social or intellectual boundaries, and whoever might benefit (or lose?).

The system may not work quite so well for those outside universities and museums who have less access to their inner workings. What happens to the exhibition process, for example, when the management model is expanded to include as full partners those outside the academy whose heritage is to be displayed? Obviously the customary model would then have to change, to open up, to be renegotiated. That in turn raises questions about the traditions of institutional authority, curatorial prerogatives, and the suitability of customary museum procedures: to be more precise, it raises concerns about the consequences of sharing power.

All the changes the MOA implemented as a result of the partnership described here, as it transpired, fell within the guidelines for working with First Nations which the museum had already accepted in principle, and were also in accord with the University's policy on research involving human subjects. Yet, especially during the early stages of each exhibit project, some museum staff expressed discomfort and uncertainty about the directions in which they appeared to be heading; and questions were asked by individuals both within and outside the museum, at home and abroad, about potential risks to research opportunities, academic freedom, and curatorial prerogatives.

What actually transpired, it is possible to say in retrospect, was an evolving relationship with the First Nations communities, and particularly with one group, which initially involved some anxiety and a learning curve for the museum but resulted in a positive outcome and two successful exhibits.

It was certainly a steep learning curve for me. I was director of the museum at the time, and it was my usual custom not to interfere in, or even pay much attention to, the workings of our exhibit projects (other than, as directors are wont to do, to express concern about keeping within the budget and ensuring labels are proofread). Furthermore, I am not an archaeologist and therefore have no relevant expertise or familiarity with the content of these two exhibits. Partway through the negotiations with local First Nations communities, however, it appeared (or at least I could no longer pretend not to notice) that matters were in danger of going off the rails, or at least were not progressing. I therefore suddenly became intimately and intensively involved. Obviously I should have been paying more attention and should have intervened earlier.

This chapter represents my own reflection upon the events that transpired between 1994 and 1996 while I was director of MOA. Others at the museum and among the communities involved may not agree with my interpretation; this would not be surprising considering the complexity of the projects.

It is time to introduce the two exhibits, which we might say became the heroes of this story. Both opened at the museum in 1996: *From under the Delta: Wet Site Archaeology from the Fraser Valley*, and *Written in the Earth*. Both dealt with 500- to 4,500-year-old materials, some rare and many extremely fragile, excavated from the greater Vancouver region. Their openings were one to two years later than the dates originally scheduled by the museum. *From under the Delta* is still on exhibit (December 1998), while *Written in the Earth* was transformed into several smaller travelling exhibits.

The First Nations communities whose heritage was to be exhibited were first approached officially by the exhibit teams when they sought support for grant applications. This is in keeping with the recommendations of the 1992 Canadian Task Force on Museums and First Peoples (Task Force 1992; Notzke 1996) and has since become a requirement of most funding agencies in Canada. The band[2] council representatives of each community offered support on the understanding that their representatives would be consulted on the selection and interpretation of materials. This also falls within the guidelines of the Task Force.

The council from whose traditional territories most of the objects came took a closer interest in the proceedings. 'We have reviewed the application for . . . funding prepared by the Museum of Anthropology,' the chief councilor wrote in December 1992 to a funding agency, 'and look forward to participating fully in the proposed research.' It took some time before the two curatorial teams, and subsequently the rest of us at the museum, realized that when the chief said his band wanted to participate 'fully', he really meant it. The two exhibits became vehicles for addressing larger issues relating to the museum's management and interpretation of First Nations heritage.

Approval or support from this principal band (henceforth to be referred to as 'the Band', with a capital 'B'), the two teams came to understand, was to be based on a process of continual consultation over each step of the exhibition process, from initial selection of objects to the final design, interpretation, installation, promotion, and maintenance of each exhibit, *and* extending to the subsequent restorage of those objects that would be returned to the care of the university. The Band council asked the museum to record these steps, and stated that it was reserving the right to withdraw approval for either exhibit at any point if the museum failed to meet the arrangements agreed upon. Withdrawal of approval would have effectively closed one or both exhibits because the museum already had requested the Band's approval to prepare the exhibits, most of the materials in both came from that Band's traditional territories (which extended beyond those recognized by the government), and some were on loan from the Band.

The concept of consultation thus quickly took on a more significant meaning for the two exhibit teams, and for the museum, practically reversing traditional roles. Museum staff became the resource people or knowledgeable museological informants, as it were, and the Band council became the client or sponsor with final authority over the projects. The development of the exhibition, including design, colours, graphic styles, every object to be included, every mount, every label, and every news release was to be a matter of consultation and mutual agreement. (See Holm and Pokotylo 1997 for a discussion of negotiations to develop *Written in the Earth*.)

Members of both exhibit teams expressed varying degrees of concern about possible challenges to their professional expertise and to their right to communicate their research in an unfettered manner. The museum, in fact, agreed not to publish anything connected to the second exhibit, *Written in the Earth*, without both the Band's and museum director's approval, at least for the duration of that project. From a university or museum perspective one might ask (as some did) whether the MOA was relinquishing its assumed right to free inquiry and/or jeopardizing the prerogatives of the curatorial teams or scholarly privileges of the curators.

The principle of free inquiry has long been taken as a natural right by scholars in the Western world, expressed in the university notion of academic freedom and the museum idea of the curatorial prerogative. It is still widely argued that the means of intellectual authority should rest with certain educational institutions and their controlling professions. James Nason (1981) warned the British Columbia Museum Association's annual meeting some 16 years ago to expect a growing number of challenges to these institutional privileges as aboriginal peoples increased their efforts to reclaim their own histories.

Challenging scholarly privilege is not necessarily a challenge to the value of scholarly research, however. When the Vancouver-area First Nations gave their support to the two exhibits, which they did willingly and out of natural interest in the subject matter, they were not attempting to deny the principle of free inquiry. They wanted to redefine for what purposes inquiry should be free. They are well aware of the value of systematic research and regularly draw upon it. The crucial difference lies in who should determine the direction and use of these empirical investigations (Robinson 1996: 129).

What occurred as a result of the project negotiations with the principal Band was a realignment of power, achieved through a redistribution of authority. First Nations communities acknowledged museum expertise in research, interpretation, and exhibition design, but asked MOA that this expertise better serve their own educational priorities, concerning which they are the experts. First Nations Communities, and not the academic professions or the anonymous 'general public', to which museums like MOA traditionally cater, should become the primary audience because their histories and cultures constitute the subject matter. Once the implications of this principle were clearly understood – and they took a while to sink in – the negotiating processes moved along more smoothly. As the designer for *Written in the Earth* remarked early in that project, he at first wondered what right the Band representatives had to challenge his notions of exhibition design since he was the design expert. Once he got it straight in his head that communities own their own histories, he said, he realized they had every right to say how their collections should be displayed and interpreted. (A parallel might be with those who write authorized biographies or histories and thus are granted access to privileged information.) The relationship that gradually evolved in the context of these two exhibits was similar in principle to what in applied anthropology is referred to as 'participatory community research' (Ryan and Robinson 1996), whereby research expertise is made available to a community which sets the agenda or topics to be studied.[3]

How did this redistribution of authority affect the exhibit planning process and resulting exhibition of archaeological 'evidence'? By becoming supporters required for MOA grant applications, local Band councils assumed the role of sponsors, and therefore the right of sponsorship to share in the determination of inquiry. Since the Museum of Anthropology accepts the principle that people own their own histories,[4] the museum was obliged to accept the corollary that people also own the right to determine how their histories are to be publicly represented. It was not an easy transition for museum staff to make in practice, even though we were committed to these ideas in principle.

Most of the changes resulting from negotiations – reduction of academic jargon, qualifications of generalizations, selection of particular design features – were individually minor in nature, though collectively they improved the overall clarity and visual appeal of the exhibits. A few changes had a greater impact on archaeological and museological sensibilities. The principal Band wanted reassurance that the museum and the Laboratory of Archaeology fully realized and accepted their responsibilities as university trustees of the materials in the museum's care, many of which are unique and extremely fragile. The Band also wanted to be assured that First Nations would be consulted about the potential transfer of their materials from the university's archaeology laboratory to museum collections, and that these transfers would be fully recorded. The Band, for example, asked the museum how it would arrange for the repair or replacement of any object that might be damaged during the exhibition project. The Band wanted archaeologists and museum staff to acknowledge and understand the magnitude of what they were asking First Nations to endorse: not only are many of the materials extremely fragile, but many are stored 'in trust' at the museum for First Nations. Prior to these negotiations there were no procedures in place for First Nations to be routinely consulted or advised when objects from their territories were being studied, treated, or exhibited.

MOA's traditional practice was to purchase special insurance for objects borrowed from other museums, but not for those in its care or for those 'borrowed' from the Laboratory of Archaeology (which is an administrative sub-unit of the nearby Department of Anthropology and Sociology but shares space in the museum building). The lab is a trustee for items, many of which belong to First Nations and/or are stored for First Nations. What was lacking prior to these negotiations was an explicit procedure for consulting with traditional owners before any transfer from one trustee to another. It is the policy of the Canadian Archaeological Association not to place dollar value on any archaeological material in the hope of discouraging pot hunters; thus, University of British Columbia archaeologists have not insured anything but their two trucks. All exhibited materials nevertheless were insured against loss or damage at the request of the Band.

Some museum staff wondered how the reduction of the archaeological perspective in *Written in the Earth* – in order to place an equal emphasis on the contemporary relevance of the materials for First Nations – would be judged by colleagues more familiar with the traditional way of exhibiting archaeology. Some archaeologists expressed disappointment that *Written in the Earth* did not look like a 'proper' archaeology exhibition.

At the Band's request, statements were included in both exhibits calling for better protection of historic sites, for the government to obtain First Nations' consent before issuing excavation permits, and for museums, archaeologists, and the government to fulfil their responsibilities to provide better protection of archaeological materials not only in the ground but also after excavation. One text read as follows:

> First Nations advocates assert that nothing should come out of the ground until all parties – developers, archaeologists, government, repositories, and First Nations – agree on a full management plan. Funds to cover all aspects of recovery must be committed prior to land alternation.

None of this is done at present, and in virtually no case do all the parties affected talk together. Typically, developers talk to government officials, who may consult with relevant band councils before issuing a permit to contract archaeologists, who may or may not talk to 'repositories' (i.e. museums) before they begin work; and said repositories may or may not consult with the relevant First Nations band councils regarding storage and display of these materials. Developers may be obliged to finance contract excavations, but funding is almost never provided the repositories.

The directors of the museum and the Laboratory of Archaeology were also asked to post a statement committing their institutions to providing improved storage facilities at the University:

> Governments that permit excavations, those carrying out excavations, as well as institutions responsible for the care of collections resulting from excavations, must address the need for adequate preservation of artefacts. At the request of the Band, we at the University of British Columbia are developing better procedures for

managing fragile wetsite materials in concert with First Nations recommendations and in consultation with them. We invite government agencies to assist in this endeavor.

The Band also asked the museum to list the names and titles of staff involved in both exhibits; describing their responsibilities for the care and handling of exhibited materials. The fact that some of those listed expressed concern that being so identified might make them personally liable for their actions perhaps was an indication of the level of anxiety they felt because of changes in their traditional procedures. They apparently had forgotten that the listing of names of responsible staff is routine when borrowing from other museums.

Collaboration at the level of detail involved in these two exhibits was a new experience for most of the museum staff, and it is the nature of such negotiations to lead inevitably into uncharted waters (even if they should have been charted much earlier). It is not surprising, therefore, that people experienced anxiety, frequently expressed in the form of good-natured grumbling along the lines of 'The ground is always shifting. What will we have to do next?' All the requests nevertheless were unhesitatingly implemented, the principal Band council issued permits granting permission to display its heritage, the exhibits were reviewed, and the exhibits approved by representatives of all the participating communities, and were then opened to the public.

How successful were the two projects? The single most difficult problem, and the only substantial one for the museum, was the amount of time required for the negotiations, including the 'learning time' for museum staff (and especially for me). In consequence, the exhibits were delayed one to two years beyond their original timetables, and this caused some staff discomfort because of disrupted personal and institutional schedules (though the museum was able to accommodate schedule changes without any serious problem).

On the other hand, both exhibits were expanded beyond original curatorial objectives by the inclusion of more, and more explicit, references than originally proposed to contemporary cultural meanings and cultural resource management issues. Negotiations led to stronger working relationships between the communities and the museum, both exhibits were favourably reviewed in the local press and by museum visitors who cared to record their opinions, and – perhaps most important of all – First Nations seemed pleased with the results.

One First Nations person, who had closely observed the entire process and carefully examined both exhibits, offered the analogy of decorating a home. Most museum exhibits of his heritage, he said, though dealing with familiar matters, never seemed to be quite right. It was like having a stranger decorate his house, he said. He would recognize all the furniture and the settings. Everything would be familiar. Yet somehow the resulting assemblage just wouldn't convey the right feeling. It would not be the way *he* would furnish his home. These two exhibits, on the other hand, did feel right to him, and to other band members he talked to. These exhibits conveyed the right ambiance, manifested familiar sentiments. Thus, the extended process of negotiation and consultation – the to-ing and fro-ing which at times made museum staff impatient and worried – taught the exhibit teams how to do a better job of decorating a home.

The question remains as to whether the museum unreasonably compromised the principle of free inquiry by granting participating bands what amounted to veto rights over the exhibits. Did the museum compromise the rights of the exhibit teams to determine the objectives of their exhibits, as some observers wondered? Did political correctness take precedence over intellectual integrity when the decision-making process was also subjected to negotiation? It might appear that way (and it did so appear to some), until one examines the University of British Columbia's policy on research (University of British Columbia 1996: 70–1). None of the changes resulting from negotiations would have been excluded by the University guidelines, though neither exhibit team thought of referring to those guidelines.

Two points in the University of British Columbia's policy on research have direct relevance. First, those proposing research involving human subjects must obtain informed consent. Research on what archaeologists like to call 'prehistoric artefacts' is not submitted for approval to the University of British Columbia's Committee on Research Involving Human Subjects, presumably because the subjects of prehistory are thought to be no longer around. Objects of the kind included in these two exhibits, however, have powerful resonance for the living descendants, and thus in a very real sense are contemporary as well as prehistoric. They might even be seen as 'post-historic' rather than 'prehistoric' because a First Nation's historical record is part of its assertion of continuing sovereignty over its territory, and thus over its future. The point here is that from the perspective of aboriginal peoples, archaeological research involves living human subjects in a very real way, people who experience a direct connection to the excavated materials. The excavation, storage, and interpretation of these materials therefore logically should be subject to the university's policy on informed consent.

The second point refers to the privilege of sponsors of research. According to the University of British Columbia's policy on research cited above, a sponsor – to protect its own interest – has the right to approve the publication of the results of research or to delay publication for a maximum of 12 months following the completion of the project. I presume this statement was written with financial sponsors in mind, since examples refer to commercial applications of research, though no such limitation is stated. In any case, by providing the required letters in support of the museum's grant applications, band councils in effect became 'sponsors' because such expressions of support are now a prerequisite to obtaining government exhibition grants. No band expressed interest in prohibiting or delaying either the exhibits or publications pertaining to them. As sponsors, and as the people whose heritage was to be represented, however, they requested the right to review materials before public dissemination.

My own principal area of research is South Asia, and my most recent field trip was to India in 1995. I was required to outline my study objectives in order to obtain a research visa from the Government of India, and once there to register with the local police. A graduate student under my supervision received a research visa to India in 1996 subject to the following conditions:

1 submission of a detailed travel itinerary 'well in advance' of beginning the research;
2 agreement not to engage in any activity that would be political, prejudicial to the interests of the host country, or embarrassing to the relations between the host country and any foreign country; and
3 agreement not to visit any restricted areas in the country for the purposes of research.

It has become customary in Canada to refer to Native or aboriginal communities as 'First Nations'. 'Nation' implies the concept of sovereignty. For the exhibit teams to respect First Nations' sovereign interests in their own heritage and its interpretation is no different in principle from what we must do when we apply for research visas to study in other lands.

How will these two exhibit experiences change the way MOA goes about its business? There obviously will be a redistribution of institutional authority, locating more of it in the process of project development itself. This means accepting the rights and interests of partners to participate from the beginning, and allowing projects to evolve naturally, even if awkwardly, in response to continuing participation. While there are unquestionably sound ethical and practical reasons for museums to continue to move in this direction, the financial implications are less clear. It takes time to build the trust a partnership requires, and joint projects require flexibility to develop successfully. However, most funding agencies will not support policy development or consultation processes and they typically impose reporting requirements that presuppose centralized, top-down institutional controls over projects. The Government of Canada's Museum Assistance Programme, for example, required in its 1997 programme assistance application the exact percentages of each staff member's time and salary that are to be devoted to each project, projected over a two-year period, *and* written approval from the Programme Office before deviating from this schedule. The only reasonable response to such guidelines is to report fictions while encouraging funding agencies to adopt more realistic, flexible procedures to allow for community participation.

The processes of collaboration never will be easy, Clifford warns:

> The solution is inevitably contingent and political: a matter of mobilized power, of negotiation, of representation constrained by specific audiences. To evade this reality – resisting 'outside' pressures in the name of aesthetic quality or scientific neutrality, raising the spectre of 'censorship' – is self-serving as well as historically uninformed. Community pressures have always been part of institutional, public life.
> (Clifford 1997: 208–9)

While agreeing with Clifford, it also needs to be said that museums do change, often ahead of other public agencies, that their lack of quick or unambiguous responses to obvious needs is often a condition of multiple and conflicting demands rather than a lack of good intentions, and that their shortcomings in cross-cultural encounters may be due less to ignorance or lack of integrity than to their taken-for-granted embeddedness in a different ('Enlightenment' or 'Eurocentric') paradigm of integrity – that is, in their own cultural tradition – which has, however, become somewhat out of step with the times.

ACKNOWLEDGEMENTS

The first version of this paper was presented in the session, 'The Quest for Honor and Authority in Anthropology', chaired by Nancy J. Parezo and John Troutman, University of Arizona, at the Annual Meeting of the American Ethnology Society, Seattle, Washington, 6 March 1997. Subsequent presentations were given upon kind invitation

179

to classes at the University of British Columbia, Vancouver, and Curtin University of Technology, Perth (during my tenure in 1997 as a visiting fellow); to the staff of the Rotorua Museum of Art and History, Rotorua, New Zealand, and to the Department of Anthropology, University of California at Berkeley. I am indebted to members of those audiences for helpful comments. The main points of the chapter also were discussed with various colleagues. Grateful acknowledgment is made especially to David Cunningham, Howard Grant, Margaret Holm, David Pokotylo, Leona Sparrow, Ann Stevenson, and Andrea Witcomb for helpful comments on earlier versions, though they are not responsible for, and may not agree with, opinions and observations recorded here. I am thankful to the Research Institute for Cultural Heritage, Curtin University of Technology, and its director Professor David Dolan, for the visiting appointment (August–November 1997), which provided the opportunity to revise this paper for publication.

NOTES

1   Larger museums may appoint a project administrator to 'lead' the team, but the curatorial expert would still claim priority over exhibition content.
2   'Band' is a legal entity with specified members and territories created by the Government of Canada for administrative purposes. The territories assigned to a particular band were inevitably less than those people traditionally used and for most of the country, with the exception of most of British Columbia, those territories were assigned through treaty processes. Treaty-making was not followed throughout in British Columbia, leaving a residue of land claims still to be resolved.
3   The term 'community participation research' has not been applied to the kind of collaborations in which museums are now engaging, though it is an appropriate designation at least in some cases. For a review of the procedures as practised in applied anthropology, see discussions by Ryan and Robinson (1996), who are Canadian leaders in this field.
4   This and other principles came with MOA's acceptance of the recommendations contained in the 1992 Task Force Report on the Relations between Museums and First Peoples (Task Force 1992).

10

CURATING *AFRICAN WORLDS*

Anthony Shelton

Exhibitions emerge from the conjunction of innumerable narrative, social, ethical, political, economic and technical circumstances and conditions. This is to say nothing of the effects of contingency, which today are as likely to be mediated by a museum or exhibitions manager, or an educationalist, as a curator. Distinct from other museum professionals, curators ideally bring to their practice historical circumspection, a self-conscious awareness of the theory of their practice, an understanding of how meaning and knowledge are negotiated and mediated, and a finely tuned and trained sensitivity towards the process of cultural translation, as well as scholarship based on cumulative and specialised knowledge. While all curators might reasonably be expected to curate, not everyone who curates is necessarily a curator. The relationship between curators and exhibitions is however complex and neither the analogy with authors nor with directors adequately describes this aspect of their work. Whatever the practice in the past, the tendency today is for curators to work as part of a wider team designed to fulfil the multiple agendas and increasing commitments with which museums have been charged, and which are necessary to achieve high and competitive standards of presentation, realisable only through the utilisation of new technologies, good design and adequate scientific support.

African Worlds was from its inception an idea-driven but object-centred exhibition which placed great emphasis on the curator as author. Nevertheless, the constant engagement and mediumship over the theory of the exhibition practice transformed this role early on into another which might better, but not adequately, be compared to that of a producer/director, who negotiates between different professional groups, assumes an advocacy role and cajoles research funding, while at the same time marshalling together variant interpretations into a coherent whole, sharing with designers the creation of a visual language, as well as transposing information between different mediums: texts and objects (Figure 10.1).

In this chapter I shall try to document the process through which this role evolved and in so doing describe the negotiations which gave form and content to the exhibition. I shall use six sets of themes through which to focus on some of the negotiations and resulting practices endemic to this specific exhibition-making process:

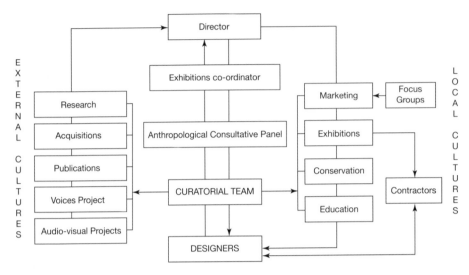

Figure 10.1 African Worlds exhibition development process.

1   general vs. specific exhibition;
2   local vs. paradigmatic knowledge;
3   object based vs. concept driven exhibitions;
4   aesthetic vs. ethnographic exhibition;
5   historical time vs. ethnographic present;
6   global vs. continental coverage.

GENERAL VS. SPECIFIC EXHIBITIONS: THE FORMULATION OF THE EXHIBITION CONCEPT

The Horniman's South Hall has always been dedicated to a general ethnographic exhibition which presented the diverse cultures of all five of the world's continents. However, the displays were removed in 1994 to allow remedial work on subsidence problems to take place. It was not until March 1999 that the gallery reopened with *African Worlds*.

When in 1995 we began to consider how best we might re-exhibit the ethnographic collections, three clear options emerged: (a) the Museum could organise a general ethnographic gallery based on geographical or cultural criteria, as had existed previously; or (b) it could arrange a display drawn from the rich Asian holdings, about 26,000 items which constitute about 45 per cent of the total collection; or (c) devote the gallery to African visual culture, the second largest collection, amounting to approximately 17,000 objects.

The first option, although originally considered, and some initial sketches made,[1] was subsequently discarded as a result of the space constraints imposed by a 380 sq m gallery and the limitations this would have imposed on the presentation of such a rich collection. After further discussion it was decided that Asia too would not be appropriate, given that London already possessed three institutions devoted partly or wholly to Asian art. Africa, however, despite the many collections scattered throughout the UK, the country's long and significant colonial engagement there, and the domestic presence of large immigrant populations, had no permanent museum gallery devoted to its visual and performative cultures. This was compelling reason enough to focus the new gallery on Africa. The decision was supported by Michael Houlihan, the then director, and Emmanuel Arinze, president of the Commonwealth Association of Museums, who saw the gallery as a means of reaffirming the achievements of Africans and people of African descent and providing a showcase through which part of their heritage could be kept alive for subsequent generations.

The African collections themselves have been accumulated through a rather peculiar and unique history, which like many other collection areas, sets the Horniman apart from some other UK institutions. Horniman himself, focusing on the preservation of items which, in his eyes, showed exemplary degrees of technical craftsmanship and artistic virtuosity, had limited his African interests mainly to Benin and Egypt. Even including the small numbers of objects that he, or his father John Horniman, had acquired from northern and southern Africa, his African acquisitions never amounted to more than 13 per cent of his total collection. Neither did the African collection grow significantly during the successive period, 1901–47, when the Museum was administered by the London County Council and developed under the aegis of Alfred Cort Haddon and his evolutionary followers. Not until well after the Scramble for Africa, with the appointment of Otto Samson in 1947, did the Museum enlarge its focus on African visual culture. Samson's German training led him to give greater emphasis to collecting figurative works and assisted his appreciation of stylistic traditions from countries that were outside the British zone of influence. It was, however, under the keeperships of Valerie Vowles (1976–82) and Keith Nicklin (1982–94) that the systematic collection of African material began.

Samson had established a tradition of conducting field work as a means of augmenting the collections, which was consolidated and expanded under future directors. David Boston, Samson's successor from 1965–93, enlisted outside fieldworkers to collect on the Museum's behalf. The Samson/Boston period resulted in outstanding collections of everyday material culture from the Sua pygmies (Colin Turnbull), the Hadza (James Woodburn), the Samburu (Jean Brown and Cordelia Rose), the Tuareg (Jeremy Keenan) and the Xhosa and neighbouring groups (Eric Bigalke). In addition, Jean Jenkins made collecting trips to Ethiopia (1960s–70s); Valerie Vowles to Botswana (1970–71); and Keith Nicklin collected in Nigeria (1980s, 1992, with Jill Salmons), Kenya (1987, with Jill Salmons), Republic of Benin (1998) and Brazil (1998, with Tania Tribe). In this way the Museum acquired important reference collections of the everyday material culture of specific African peoples.

Since 1995, the Museum has reasserted its commitment to the acquisition policy established by Samson, while continuing to support the fieldwork strategies developed under Boston. For Africa, our policies have been refocused on French-speaking countries where, in recent years, we have sponsored fieldwork in Mali, the Burkina Faso/Ghana border, Côte d'Ivoire and the Republic of Benin.

Another hallmark of the Museum's working practice has been the close and co-operative relations it has established to promote research and collecting with its sister institutions in Africa. Valerie Vowles' San collection was made with the co-operation of the National Museum and Art Gallery of Botswana; Eric Bigalke worked with the East London Museum in South Africa; Keith Nicklin routinely worked with the National

Commission on Museum and Monuments in Nigeria, and his 1998 season in the Republic of Benin was conducted with the help of the director of the Musée d'Histoire de Ouidah. Jennifer Oram's 1997 fieldwork in Sierra Leone was supported also by that country's museum. Collecting among the Lobi was assisted by the Ghana Museums and Monuments Board. Nigeria's National Commission for Museums and Monuments worked closely with the Museum on two field projects which resulted in outstanding commissions from the Igbo area and a close and innovative relationship with the National Museum in Benin, which has grown from a joint project to reinterpret the Benin plaques in our collection by the Bini themselves. The Museum's historical relationship with Africa has been and is anything but that of a colonial treasury or a passive and unquestioning recipient of fine art and material culture, which the new exhibition needed to reflect through innovative relationships and sensitive practices.

LOCAL vs. PARADIGMATIC KNOWLEDGE

I use 'paradigmatic knowledge' to refer to that body of formally codified and institu-tionalised information that Western societies privilege over and above 'local' knowledges, or what it has sometimes termed 'folk' knowledge. Paradigmatic knowledge presents itself as independent of human agency and reproduces a privileged and hierarchical relation between exhibition makers and the objectifications of their subject; a subject that takes in a long and tortuous history of direct and indirect capitalistic colonialism; ideological effacements occasioned by empiricist social sciences; and the contemporary political and economic alignments of dominant and subordinate polities (Wolf 1982). Exhibition managers, public services personnel, funding bodies, educationalists and curators themselves – those who select which objects should be used to represent another culture, the manner in which they should be represented, the show's narrative structure and content, and the modes of its public dissemination – are usually drawn from the established and vanguard sectors of the dominant class in Western neo-colonial states, as distinct from those who are represented, who are consigned to muteness and representation through the voices of their foreign interpreters. Cultural colonialism has persisted after the official death of the old-style European colonialism, which continues to police the categories of 'us' and 'them' (internally, between metropolitan values and those of minority groups through what Gonzalez Cassanova has called 'internal colonialism', and externally between polities embodying other cultural beliefs and values) to preserve an increasingly fragile mainstream moral and ethical hegemony. Exhibitions about Africa are noteworthy by their effacement of these conditions.

The trend towards the de-colonisation of museums has been most apparent in the Americas, where increasingly well-organised and influential First Nation peoples have questioned the right of museums not only to represent them unilaterally, but also to assume the mantle of being the legitimate heirs to their cultural patrimony (Ames 1992: 79; MacDonald and Alsford 1995: 20). The politicisation of anthropological and museological practice in the Americas, through the intervention of indigenous move-ments at various meetings of the International Congress of Americanists, and various indigenous declarations, particularly those of Barbados (1971, 1978), have forced Americanists to choose either to support or ignore the aspirations of indigenous peoples and work to develop democratic strategies to represent them. In Mexico, this led to a museological revolution headed by the Muséo Nacional de Culturas Populares, which worked together with indigenous peoples on various innovative exhibitions, beginning with *Nuestro Maíz* (Our Maize) (1981). This was the single greatest influence on our modest exhibition.

Nuestro Maíz first aimed to promote awareness and appreciation of the central role that the staple occupied during 3,000 years in most of the indigenous cultures of Mexico (Bonfil Batalla 1982: 7). The second guiding principle was to collect local knowledge about the significance and uses of maize from throughout the Republic. Crucial to the project was to ensure that this knowledge was drawn, in as unmediated a way as possible, directly from the voices and expressions of rural peoples themselves. The exhibition was based on living cultures, not separated from society nor seen as static or fossilised entities, but as changing creative tendencies and practices that were part of adaptive social and economic formations. The task of the curators was to collect together these diverse histories, instead of imposing the terms of an external ideology on them, which would have turned 'dynamic, interconnected phenomena into disconnected things' (Wolf 1982: 4). The curators strove to provide a forum where what was nothing less than a world-view could be expressed to the urbane citizenry of the Federal District. Attempts were made also to reverse the usual flow of information from subject communities to the metropolis by organising a text/photographic exhibition which travelled back to the villages that had contributed to it. Lastly, the Museum collected 130 monographs from different villages throughout the country, 30 of which were published to widen popular knowledge about maize and its common, unifying culture.

For *African Worlds*, the problem of the unidirectional flow of knowledge from the southern to northern hemisphere was partly addressed by providing a computer and internet facilities for visitor use at the National Museum of Benin, and ongoing work to put the exhibition on the World Wide Web. Publication of the large amount of original research done for the exhibition was edited by Karel Arnaut to be freely distributed to African museums and universities. This, it is hoped, will secure more egalitarian co-operative projects with African museums.

African Worlds attempted to grapple with representational problems (not unlike those encountered by *Nuestro Maíz*) in three ways. Shortly after the initial ideas for the exhibition had been formulated, the Museum established an international anthropology consultative panel (ACP) which met twice per annum, consisting of two curators from Africa, Joseph Eboreime and Emmanuel Arinze; one from Trinidad, Kathryn Chan; and two from the UK, Keith Nicklin and John Mack.

The ACP was established to serve several key functions in the planning and interpretation of *African Worlds*, but it also exerted a wider influence on the way the Anthropology Collections and Research Group worked:

1   It decided on the final selection of objects for the gallery.
2   It provided a forum to debate and resolve ideological issues involved in the representation of African art and culture.
3   It formulated interpretative strategies for the exhibition.
4   It advised on additional research programmes and provided a network of contact through which these could be expedited.
5   It provided an effective means through which the meaning and significance of certain categories of objects, about which there was little or contradictory published material,

could be clarified through dispatching field assistants with photographs to the communities or areas from which they had been collected.

6   It provided a network through which text could be written by African and Caribbean authors, and a means of peer review through which text could be written and approved.

An indication of the effectiveness of the Panel can be gauged by our joint decision at its first meeting to abandon the original plan for a geographic organisation of the objects in the display and in its place to adopt a thematic approach. The Panel then worked to establish the most appropriate themes: Patronage; Different Natures; Men/Women; Ancestors and Morality; Royalty and Power; Text, Image, History; Cycles of Life; Parody and Humour; and Creation and Recreation. It was, however, the responsibility of the curators and designers, albeit in consultation with the ACP, to develop an appropriate design specification for the gallery.

The themes were thoroughly debated in relation to the objects selected and were chosen in part to correct imbalances in the way African visual culture had been exhibited elsewhere in Western galleries. The theme of patronage, for example, was intended to introduce a very real sense of history and to chart changing relations of production and consumption as a result of European usurpation of traditional polities. The importance of the theme for the exhibition is highlighted by the inclusion of a case of Fon brass figures and a Shona stone sculpture, 'Chaminuka Spirit', sculptured by Albert Nathan Mamvura, inserted into the introductory panel to the gallery.

The theme Different Natures was intended to represent masquerade not as another form of exoticism or as the manifestation of an overt primitivism, but as embodying ideas of nature and different ontological perspectives. Text, Image, History was meant to give examples of how images can sometimes convey as much, or more, information than formal written systems, and Man/Woman was intended to readdress popular misconceptions about gender in Africa. Creation and Recreation was particularly concerned to look not only at creation myths and the origin of particular categories of objects, but also at the dynamics of recreating culture as a result of forced removal and exploitation under inhuman conditions in the newly formed communities of the New World. Parody and Humour introduced a cross-cultural perspective on satire, verbal punning and laughter, as important a part of our understanding of images as written texts, which is often missing from any Western appreciation of African and related cultures. Ancestors and Morality provided a link between figurative representations and the ethical ideas held by different societies. It is quite extraordinary, and unintentional, how these themes provide direct links between objects in the exhibition and specific aspects of the philosophical and religious heritage of Africa and African-related cultures worldwide.

A second strategy for breaking free from the usual object/subject dichotomy, was to instigate the Voices Project to incorporate the lived and experienced memories, feelings and opinions of local Black communities about objects within the exhibition. This was supplemented by recorded quotes from makers, musicians, elders and dancers from the different societies where the Horniman had sponsored fieldwork, and specially commissioned videos which showed objects either being made or used.

The third strategy was to reserve an area in which artists, guest curators and community groups could curate their own exhibitions and installations in response to the permanent displays. Earlier, we had envisaged exhibiting objects in individual cases, standing at different heights and arranged in groups clustered in the shape of an arc, to allow a large central area for temporary interventions. However, as the concept had changed radically after the first ACP meeting, and subsequent discussions on design between myself, designers and the director produced new strategies that impinged on this space, it was agreed to accommodate what Houlihan described as a 'living gallery' on the balcony area which encircles the gallery. This space opened with an exhibition of the works of the contemporary Nigerian artist Osi Audu, *The Moon is the Eye of the Sky*, which used a videoed interview to communicate the artist's own interpretations of his works.

OBJECT-BASED vs. CONCEPT-DRIVEN EXHIBITIONS

Although temporary exhibitions which freely draw on loan material can easily be predicated on independent concepts, institutions with permanent collections rely, by practical necessity, on a more dialectical approach to exhibition interpretation.[2] Shared awareness between senior management, curators and designers of the historical importance of the collection and a joint belief that the gallery should be object-centred pre-empted discussion on this subject. The object, in designer Michael Cameron's words, was to be 'the hero'. Our commitment to an object-centred exhibition was, however, an important criterion in the choice of designer. Moreover the museum was keen to find allegorical practitioners who had a demonstrable ability to manipulate objects to evoke different emotions and feelings and who shared a respect for artefacts as embodied texts. Lighting was crucial to this; in the final design Kongo power figures were uplit to enhance their commanding appearance; Pende mbuye masks were downlit with the light focused on their almost closed eyelids, spirits at the point of earthly death, to convey a sense of overwhelming melancholy. Shona headrests were juxtaposed against a dark, light-absorbent lapiz blue panel, broken up by gold inlays to allude to the story told in the accompanying pamphlet about how much older headrests had been the prey of nineteenth-century European grave robbers who had formed their own company to loot tombs systematically for the gold sometimes wrapped around them. This visual language was meant to reinforce the stories reproduced in the booklets and on the text panels, and was an important strategy within the process of cultural translation.

It was also considered essential to convey a sense of alienation in the gallery. Alienation in the sense that these objects were displaced, far removed from the conditions of their usage and original signification, and the subsequent gulf this engendered between viewers and objects; but also alienation, in as much as none of these objects could ever fulfil the public expectations encouraged by Western education, which has imputed them with an over-investiture of meaning. Museum objects are fragments; masks without costumes; figures without shrines; shrines without sacrifices; architectural pieces removed from their buildings, which can never provide the kind of general survey or re-totalise a particular aspect of history or culture that museums so treasure. The meaning of objects is hybrid, and it is this tension between their previous lives and the stories of their removal and reincorporation into foreign collections that denies us both the easy and comprehensive access we have been promised and the magic of a journey to an exotic land. Cameron has tried to express this alienation in the uncompromising modernism of the gallery design: red mud walls framed by steel; nextel, fibreglass and metal panels; underlit blocks of sandblasted perspex; large expanses of plate glass; and the use of non-parallel angles that configure some of the case displays according to expressionist aesthetics. Africa is here, but it is framed and transformed through Western institutions and Western technologies. Nothing again can ever be like the conditions under which these objects were once used, venerated, worn, bartered, treasured or reviled by those who collected them.

Exhibition-making is a dialectical process that can only emerge from as inclusive a knowledge as possible of the contents of a collection and the different narratives its constituent elements can tell. Rationalisation is the next stage, during which criteria are selected to choose and embrace a particular series or order of objects and subordinate them to a master discourse. The narrative thus chosen is then tested again more specifically against the object order and other objects previously discarded. This process of to-ing and fro-ing between a collection and a suitable discourse eventually gives rise to a coherent system which embraces both objects and narrative into a rationalised order that possesses a transparent coherency not unlike that found in literature. The move-ment away from the curator as author to facilitator and director was nowhere more determined than through the increasing responsibility the ACP undertook to assume this role. Though genres may differ (even those which most strongly deny or try to expiate order), exhibitions, no more than other narrative structures, escape Western or other rationalisation. Representation of the 'other' is therefore a constant de-colonisation and re-colonisation of the imagination, where truth is measurable only by the persuasive quality of the coherence and intelligibility of the discourse and its moral authority: both qualities based on historical circumspection and the theoretisation of practice.

AESTHETIC vs. ETHNOGRAPHIC EXHIBITION

Museum ethnography is littered with false oppositions and rhetorical debates that have precluded more serious discussion on the subject's historically compromised practices. The most pernicious of these juxtaposes aesthetic against ethnographic display techniques, which are then equated with cultural contextualisation and de-contextualisation respectively.

Early on in the project, members of the Anthropology Collections and Research Group, and later the designers and project co-ordinator, visited museums in Rotterdam, Leiden, Antwerp, Amsterdam, Brussels, Paris and Binche, to establish among themselves a common language and to examine concrete examples of different visual languages and their relationships to textual exegesis in specific genres of ethnographic exhibitions. This stimulated much discussion which continued throughout the project, with different members of the Group variously favouring the sociological model, used in the Tropenmuseum's African display and for some of its temporary displays; ethnographic contextualisation, represented for example by Binche's Musée International du Carnival et du Masque; and the cleaner, what was described as the more aesthetic, genre of display found at Antwerp or in the Tropenmuseum's permanent Indonesian exhibition. Disagreement eventually resolved itself through the simplified opposition between aesthetic and ethnographic displays.

The repeated reappearance of the debate caused some of us to deconstruct the categories from which it was made and ascertain a critical position. Aesthetic display models essentially equate a highly dispersed visual configuration of objects with minimal textual exegesis, whereas its ethnographic equivalent might juxtapose objects closely together using the criteria of complementary or similar use, mode of manufacture, or significance, with greater textual density. However, there could be no essentially natural or logical reason to support these two sets of relations between different modes of signification which, for much of the past 70 years, have circumscribed the limits of ethnographic displays. Beginning from this point, *African Worlds* constructed an alternative model which transposed the terms of the opposed equations to produce a formula that would match a low-density exhibition gallery to enhance the technical virtuosity or aesthetic form of the object, with a highly dense textual exegesis not unlike that previously realised in John Mack's *Emil Torday and the Art of the Congo*, nearly a decade ago (Mack 1990).

Ethnographic and aesthetic genres of exhibition both re-contextualise other societies and their modes of cultural expression, and it is this distance between 'us' and 'them' – a distance denied by the subterfuges of ethnographic naturalism pioneered by the Museum of Mankind and the Rijkmuseum voor Volkenkunde, Leiden, in the 1970s – that objectifies the subject, while rendering the process of its curation invisible. Furthermore, this empirical relation which insists on the radical break between object and subject, reinforces a monological narrative which, while purportedly scientifically describing other cultures 'out there', effaces their historical relations with our own societies. Emphasis on the objective presentation of other cultures usually ignores the stories about how the objects, which form the mode through which we view the 'other', finished up in European museums, and denies their epistemological hybridity. The implications of these effects on exhibition making has been explored in two previous papers (Shelton 1997; Levell and Shelton 1998) which summarise the area of debate on the importance of producing a paradoxical and ambiguous sense of presence and loss, meaning and its ellipses, physical nearness and distance, which must always characterise the alienated relations between ethnographic, as well as historical, objects and their viewers and interpreters. More recently, Nuno Porto's exhibition *Angola a Preto e Branco* at the University of Coimbra (Porto 1999) produced a radical sense of disjunction in its examination of the workings of the Dundo Museum in the context of Portuguese colonialism, by the use of distancing techniques such as photographic seriation and repetition, monochromatic design, steel exhibition furniture and strategies aimed to reveal the fabrication of photographic recording. Both roads from aesthetics or ethnography lead to alienation and it is its melancholy shadow that the designers were required to throw around the objects in *African Worlds*.

HISTORICAL TIME vs. THE ETHNOGRAPHIC PRESENT

While the ancient Greeks had fewer problems in perceiving the universal effects of time – Pliny opined 'out of Africa there is always something new' – the European Modern period has denigrated African cultures as bound by timeless traditions: as static, conservative and unchanging, locked into inescapable superstition and error which, it was decided retrospectively in the nineteenth century, could only be broken and redeemed by colonial tutorship. The more immediate problem was that British anthropology until very recently shared this view of the pervasive dead hand of tradition (Wolf 1982: 18–19), if not the ideological solution which had been proposed for its redemption. It is not the supposed opposition between aesthetics and ethnography that had been transposed into the choice between ideological absorption or intellectual enlightenment, but the even more pernicious opposition between an ahistorical ethnography and historical perspective which predicates the choice between colonialising ideology and critical narrative.

In the context of *African Worlds*, the ACP agreed on the incontrovertibility of a historical perspective. However, given that most museum ethnographic objects only bear the date when they were collected or, more usual still, when they were accessioned, precise dating is problematic. In the absence of historical documentation, a broad chronological schema was adopted by which objects were identified as being late nineteenth century or early, middle or late twentieth century. Such an approach at least allowed some sense of historical movement to be registered. This was further strengthened through purchasing contemporary or near-contemporary objects which were juxtaposed with older material to illustrate stylistic and technological changes as a result of global cultural encounters (a modern Gelede mask, painted in bright gloss colours, with a superstructure supported by four carved torches; a Dogon mask decorated with French writing; an oversized Kurumba antelope mask made for tourist consumption, but still having required a blessing before it could leave its place of manufacture).

Historical change was also introduced into written texts. The gallery guide contains a timeline that shows the succession of African civilisations, which is reiterated on the introductory panel. Two of the nine themes used to discuss objects – Patronage and Text, Image, History – were designed specifically to include a strong historical component, while changes in initiation rituals as a result of market forces or education and new political and symbolic meanings of objects have been highlighted under other themes.

Lastly, history has been reincorporated into the story of the continent by reappropriating ancient Egypt, Kemet, as an essential part of African history: a strategy also adopted by the Indianapolis Museum of Art in its recent exhibition *Egypt in Africa* (1996). The Egyptian case at one end of a rampway which cuts through a central avenue of cases, dominates the central vista, reminding visitors that Egypt has always been part of the continent's history. This is reaffirmed by the inclusion of an ancient Egyptian headrest alongside nineteenth- and twentieth-century Shona, Thonga and Somali versions, and by the inclusion of Egyptian votive figures in the section on metalwork. This latter area also includes Benin brass plaques and examples of Ethiopian metalwork, further emphasising the historical dimensions of the continent and the effect of external influences. That these influences were not one-way is strongly reiterated in another area which, through three reconstructed altars from the Republic of Benin, Brazil and Haiti, points to the influence of the continent's religious and spiritual thought on the wider world.

GLOBAL vs. CONTINENTAL PERSPECTIVES

'You are not a country Africa, you are a concept . . . You are a glimpse of the infinite.' Ali Mazrui's thoughtful and provocative statement welcomes visitors as they enter the gallery, preparing them for the realisation that *African Worlds* is not only about the many different cultural worlds of continental Africa, but about the worlds that Africans re-established for themselves elsewhere on the globe after the cruel and inhuman triangular trade forcefully captured them, sold and resettled them into slavery. It is also about the many voices of the Black community in or near London which have been transcribed on the text panels and which tell their own reactions to the objects around them.

Colonial ethnography differentiated ethnic groups, which their members had not themselves always acknowledged, on the basis of language (on a continent where bilingualism was common), and established a directly equitable classification of artistic styles. This allows museum displays still to distinguish stylistic categories, abstracted from historical considerations, and to present a picture of African peoples living in hermetically sealed and solitary isolation from each other, detached from trade, political and familial alliances, religious pilgrimage routes, and the vicissitudes of an inclement history responsible for massive forced resettlements. Such a view clearly stems from an ahistorical ethnography as well as a particular type of art history, and again eradicates the possibility of discussing hybridity, inter-culturality and the wider effects of globalised communication networks which link together and provide the possibility for the widespread dissemination of images among continents, nations and ethnicities (well illustrated by the three shrines in the exhibition).

Clearly it is difficult to appreciate how any exhibition about Africa, or any other part of the world for that matter, particularly when mounted in a multi-cultural city, can treat the continent as isolated or immune from global influences. To do so merely replicates the effects of ethnic/stylistic classifications of peoples and objects, on a much grander scale. Paradoxically, however, many museums possess only historical collections made prior, say, to the 1960s. Such collections do not represent Africa, but a period of European collecting, and are often insufficient to convey even very specific, meaningful aspects of African culture. At the Horniman, Keith Nicklin had instigated the collecting of contemporary African visual culture, particularly with the aim of documenting changes in the use of materials and stylistic borrowings (three Ekpo masks, collected in the 1980s, representing the idea of malevolence through the image of Darth Vader are particularly memorable). However, as with most other museums, collections that provided a testament to the African presence in Europe or the New World were conspicuously missing. The Horniman sought to correct this imbalance by sponsoring field research and collecting not only in Brazil and Haiti, as already mentioned, but also in Trinidad, where Kathryn Chan acquired extremely well-documented examples of Midnight Cowboy hats together with a sampling of the verbal duelling that occurs between them in the context of Carnival. Undoubtedly Carnival is something that needs to be incorporated much more fully into the gallery than it is at present, as are samples of printed textiles manufactured in Europe and sold throughout Africa, and the material culture of Black Europeans. These were much discussed projects, but were not realised at the time because of money, time and the already overstretched organisational capabilities of two curators co-ordinating nine field projects using outside personnel. Nevertheless, they remain important areas for future research and collecting.

The Voices Project, carried out by Patti Peach, was an attempt to render visible the presence of large numbers of people of African and Caribbean descent in the London area, and incorporate their views and immediate impressions of some of the objects that were going to be represented in the gallery. Out of a sample of about 30 interviews made with different people chosen at random, material from 12 of these were included on the text panels.[3] This material sometimes conveyed great pathos, such as Ayan Ayandosou's thoughts that: 'When I look back at all these masks in the Museum, I feel very sorry, they're not being used . . . To me a masquerader is like a musician. A musician cannot play on his own'. Sometimes they were critical of what museums do: 'Many people brought many things into this part of the world, without knowing what they are' (Oloye B.A. Adelakan), or Emmanuel Arinze and Joseph Eboreime talking about the looting of Nigerian antiquities: 'We . . . appeal to the conscience of the world for a meaningful dialogue for a peaceful resolution of this shame of history.' Some provided new information about objects: 'Imborivungu is believed to make people rich in terms of money, childbearing, good farming, etc. And, when using these things, you will make sacrifices with animals' (Amaa Bai). Other interviews uncovered lost recollections of lives in Africa: 'Now that I am working in a museum, I think back and wonder what happened to all those things of my childhood' (Victoria Lawson). The material was always powerful and poetically expressed and insightful, and attested to the great generosity of peoples to share what were often personal feelings with curators and the wider general public. 'The fact that you may not be from a particular culture doesn't mean you cannot understand and appreciate something as deeply as somebody who is from that culture' (Eki Gbinigie).

So rich was this material that we soon incorporated it not within the texts but alongside a photograph of the interviewee, as a preface that foregrounded each object label, to provide a kind of poetic hinge that brought together objects with the three text levels (descriptive case labels; inventory details; and thematic text presented in booklets). These voices, taken directly from our local communities, breathed new life into the exhibition, which more than counterbalanced our conscious purge of some of the more familiar and perhaps comfortable illusions about Africa in the popular conscience.

Taken together, these curatorial strategies not only represent a response to the philosophical problems of exhibition making, but also to their attendant political and ethical issues. They are the response of one museum which, deeply concerned about the divide between the countries of the northern and southern hemispheres, the one-way flow and concentration of information, the schism between interpretation and practice and issues of democratisation, has profoundly embraced the vision of museums as places of dialogue where members of different cultures can 'sit well with each other'. Finally, the academic debates to which these issues gave rise, the seminars and conferences which were a direct response to the problems with which we were grappling, and subsequent publications, clearly demonstrate the central and evolving role curators have in realising the very real and important principles of an institution's mission statement and the core values which give it its purpose and the style of its engagement with all the different societies that converge through its portal.

NOTES

1 Natalie Tobert had worked on a proposal for a cross-cultural display based on the natural elements, while I sketched a more conventional thematic approach.

2   Nevertheless *African Worlds* is only the first phase of the Ethnography Redisplay, and will itself be read as the fourth part of a wider, reflexive exhibition on the history of collecting and displaying the collections which will open in 2001 to mark the Museum's centenary.

3   The exhibition used original texts from 36 different people: 12 of these were drawn from interviews with local people; 12 originated from interviews with people in Africa, the Caribbean and Brazil; and 12 were written by professional authors.

11

OBJECTS, AGENCY AND MUSEUMS

Continuing dialogues between the Torres Strait and Cambridge

Anita Herle

I feel like I've met the people, the artists who created these magnificent artefacts.

(Alick Tipoti 2000)[1]

This exhibition includes artefacts which are in themselves visual expressions of belief, culture and traditions of profound social and spiritual values. The Haddon collection enables the modern Torres Strait Islander to re-discover and re-interpret the truth about himself in the light of the wisdom and strength of his ancestors throughout the ages. And enables him to revive, recreate and extend his culture in ways beneficial to our future generations to come.

(Bishop Passi 2001)[2]

Objects in museum collections have the potential of connecting people and events over time and space. Against the familiar criticism that museum objects have been ripped from their cultural context only to languish in mausoleums, objects may have entangled and transitive lives both before and after they enter a museum's collection. Nor does the museum context necessarily alienate material from the knowledge and interests of people in source communities. Through its role in preserving and documenting important cultural materials, the museum may provide opportunities for cross-cultural dialogue and innovative collaborations.

In the late twentieth century, much research on material culture has drawn attention to the biographies or social lives of objects as a means of illuminating complex social interactions and systems of value, meaning and exchange.[3] The underlying notion is that objects do not necessarily have fixed meanings but that meanings are attributed by the social contexts through which the objects pass. Yet, is the intrinsic or original meaning of particular objects so weak that it is lost by successive interpretive frameworks? What about the agency of the objects themselves?

The production and reception of *Torres Strait Islanders: An Exhibition to Mark the Centenary of the 1898 Cambridge Anthropological Expedition to the Torres Strait*[4] provides an opportunity to reflect on the role of the museum and the meanings associated with specific objects. I am particularly interested in the resonance that certain objects collected in the late nineteenth century by Alfred Haddon, the leader of the Expedition, have for Islanders and researchers today. Throughout my discussion the museum emerges as a particular kind of 'contact zone' (Clifford 1997: 188–219), a space charged by the agency of the objects emerging through the intersecting interests of producers and collectors, Islanders and curators. To clarify, my concept of the word agency here is not classificatory, it is relational and context dependent (Gell 1998). Whereas Gell uses abduction to analyse the agency of objects in a wide variety of historical and cross-cultural settings, here the process of re-interpreting material collected by Haddon enables both the observation of and participation in dynamic relationships between people and things. Turtle-shell masks, feather head-dresses, models, photographs, and texts make important intercultural links between past and present, and between Cambridge and the Islands.

The visual and textual material collected by the 1898 Expedition, and often generated by the encounter between the Islanders and the Expedition members, embodies successive layers of meaning. It contains ethnographic information about the people of the Torres Strait at the end of the nineteenth century. Some items are associated with named individuals and have specific biographies. Haddon recorded who made them, how they were used, and the circumstances of their collection. A close analysis of the production and collection of Islander material reveals the entangled and multilateral relationships between the Islanders, Expedition members, missionaries, colonial officials and academic communities. On another level the objects reveal trends in Western intellectual history. In Cambridge and elsewhere Torres Strait collections were placed within changing systems of classification and used for the dissemination of anthropological knowledge to specialist and popular audiences. More recently the collections have provided the opportunity to re-open a dialogue between Cambridge and the Torres Strait.

Over the last few decades, Islander interest in the Expedition's work has heightened. As noted by David Moore (1984: 7) in the preface to his comprehensive book, *The Torres Strait Collections of A.C. Haddon*, '[t]he catalogue will be of particular interest to the Torres Strait Islanders themselves, since they are now attempting a reconstruction of their own culture in order to clarify and consolidate their identity as a people.' The social and political implications of the Expedition's research has been reinforced by recent political events, notably the 1992 'Mabo Case', where information contained in the Expedition's *Reports* became crucial documents in contemporary struggles for Islander self-determination.[5] Images of Torres Strait objects and the designs they carry have become symbols of a strong resurgent Islander identity and sources of inspiration for contemporary artists. Some retain a powerful spiritual presence, directly connected to personal and family stories.[6]

THE EXPEDITION

The 1898 Cambridge Anthropological Expedition is a significant part of several distinct yet intersecting histories. In British academic and intellectual history the Expedition is noted for its comprehensive research agenda and its influence on the professionalisation of social anthropology in Cambridge and beyond.[7] Haddon, a natural scientist and ethnologist, had first been to the Torres Strait ten years earlier to study marine biology, but the focus of his attention soon shifted to the Islanders among whom he lived and worked. Concerned that Islander customs were fast disappearing as a result of the influence of colonialists, missionaries and the marine industry, Haddon determined to organise an anthropological expedition to return to the Torres Strait to collect ethnographic data 'before it was too late'. Within a paradigm of salvage ethnography, Haddon designed the Expedition as a multi-disciplinary project encompassing anthropology in its broadest sense.

The seven members of the Expedition included scholars in the fields of psychology, physiology, medicine, linguistics and natural sciences. Haddon recorded local customs, studied decorative art, oversaw the collection of artefacts and took anthropomorphic measurements. William Rivers, in charge of experimental psychology, investigated vision, and once in the field, developed a method of recording local genealogies. William McDougall studied tactile sensation while Charles Myers, a skilful musician, concentrated on hearing and music. The Expedition's linguist, Sidney Ray, compiled word lists, constructed grammars and assisted with translations. Charles Seligman researched native medicine and local pathology and also compiled comparative ethnographic data in Cape York and coastal Papua. Anthony Wilkin worked as the official photographer under Haddon's direction and investigated house construction and land tenure.

Driven by his concern for comprehensive and accurate recording, the work of the Expedition and their Islander assistants generated an enormous corpus of information: the six official volumes of the *Reports of the Cambridge Anthropological Expedition to Torres Straits* (1902–35) (hereafter *Reports*), numerous scholarly and popular publications, a collection of approximately 1,500 artefacts, over 400 photographs, several short sequences of moving film, sound recordings and extensive associated archival material. The majority of this material is now housed at the University of Cambridge, the main sponsor of the Expedition. The range of objects includes elaborate masks, ritual objects, body ornaments, musical instruments, clothing, baskets, household items, tools, weapons, commissioned models and samples of raw materials. Significant Torres Strait collections are held in numerous museums throughout Europe, Australia and the United States, but overall the material at Cambridge is acknowledged as the most comprehensive and well documented.[8]

The results of the Expedition have remained an important resource for subsequent researchers in the region as well as for Islander knowledge about the past. In contrast to the practices of many early ethnographers, Haddon took great care to acknowledge the sources of the Expedition's data. Islanders and other informants were referenced and often quoted verbatim, many of the people in the photographs were identified, and the names of an object's maker or previous owner were sometimes recorded. The attribution of knowledge to named individuals is of particular significance to people from Mer and Mabuiag, the islands where Expedition members spent the most time and home to the descendants of many of Haddon's assistants and friends. Haddon appears to have been unaware of the full implications of recording the names of the Islanders who provided the Expedition with information. Islander notions of ownership are directly related to kinship and include rights over land, sea resources and objects as well as knowledge of stories, songs, dances, etc. (Philp 1998a, 1998b). For contemporary Islanders, the *Reports* are also a record of the people who had the knowledge and authority to speak about particular things. An awareness of the source of information is a means by which some Islanders attempt to verify or challenge some of the details presented in the *Reports*. Access to particular types of knowledge is traced through kinship and used to ascertain whether an informant was in a position to have both the 'deep' knowledge and the right to tell a particular story.

Despite some inaccuracies, the details in the *Reports* and associated archival material allude to complex relationships that developed between researchers and local informants. The Expedition's work was greatly assisted by people such as Pasi, Jimmy Rice, Jimmy Day, Debi Wali, Gisu, Ulai, Enoch, and Wano on Mer and Nomoa, Gizu, Waria, Peter and Tom on Mabuiag and Maino on Tudu. These and other Islanders were actively involved in the work of the Expedition: demonstrating 'traditional' practices, sharing cultural stories, re-enacting rituals, participating in physiological and psychological tests, trading artefacts, producing commissioned objects and so forth.

Some Islanders were aware of the intended destination for the material collected by the Expedition. Although their knowledge of museums was limited, the exhibition of objects owned by named individuals was seen by some as an opportunity to display cultural status. Maino of Tudu was one of the first Islanders with whom Haddon established a lasting relationship, meeting with him several times in 1888, 1898 and finally in 1914. At their first meeting Maino organised a dance for him and later traded objects which had belonged to his famous father Kebisu.[9] Haddon recorded the transaction in his diary:

> I did not ask for them as I felt he valued them highly – he offered them to me and then I asked him what he wanted and I paid his price (a small oval looking glass, 2 pocket knives, a blue bead necklace, 2 clay pipes and 11 sticks of tobacco) . . . he wanted me to have them and he also wanted them to be exhibited in a big museum in England where plenty people could see his father's things.
>
> (Haddon 1888–9: 66)

It is worth noting that other objects owned by Kebisu are still owned and valued by his direct descendants.[10] Although local people appeared keen to trade some objects, they were reluctant to part with others and refused to give up items such as the sacred drum Wasikor, which remains on Mer today. Haddon was persistent in his efforts to record and collect as much as possible, often cajoling people to make models or replicas of sacred material that no longer existed or that was inappropriate to remove. He self-consciously recorded his intentions to trade fairly, but the negotiations reveal the political asymmetry and the discrepancies between different value systems. On Mer Haddon persuaded Gisu to trade a *doiom*, a stone charm used in rainmaking, and refused to return it when Gisu regretted the transaction the following day, 'the collecting instinct was stronger than pure sentiment, and I had to inform him that it was then too late' (Haddon 1901: 26).

In due course some Islanders became aware of the results of the Expedition's research and saw themselves and their work represented in print. Haddon sent copies of his publications back to the Torres Strait for comment, where they generated much interest and discussion.[11] Some Islanders soon recognised the potential of written texts and both Pasi of Mer and Waria of Mabuiag sent manuscripts to Haddon. Written in the Mabuiag language, Waria's 300-page account begins, 'I am Ned Waria. I wrote this book so that men coming afterwards might know' and his introduction finishes with the genealogies of the people with dugong and crocodile totems who lived at Panai village (*Reports*, Vol. III: 192). These and other stories were partially translated by Ray in the *Reports*. An awareness of the process of transforming oral stories into written text highlights the agency of specific Islanders in the production of anthropological knowledge.

THE EXHIBITION AS PROCESS

Nearly a hundred years after the Expedition, preparations for a centenary exhibition provided an opportunity to reflect on the Expedition and its legacies and to reactivate links between Cambridge and the Torres Strait. A brief account of the process of creating the exhibition will illuminate both its content and varied reception. As the curator responsible for the collections, I recognised that an adequate account of the complexity of this particular encounter and its multiple and diffuse legacies would necessarily have to include the insights of contemporary Islanders. To this end, I went to the Torres Strait in 1996 to discuss plans for the exhibition with members of the indigenous government, the Torres Strait Regional Authority (TSRA) established in 1994, and other political and cultural leaders both in the Strait and on the Australian mainland. From 1995–6 Jude Philp, then a research student in the Department of Social Anthropology at Cambridge, conducted fieldwork in the Torres Strait. Her insights and alliances were crucial to the preparations for the exhibition. In Australia I also made contact with Mary Bani, a Torres Strait Islander working at the National Museum of Australia, and invited her to come to Cambridge to research the collections (Bani and Herle 1998).[12] With the assistance of Philp and Bani, a short exhibition brief was prepared which was sent to over 60 people, mainly Islanders in the Strait and on the mainland and other specialists including anthropologists and curators. Although direct written responses were limited, the importance of the consultative process cannot be over-emphasised, both in terms of sharing information and generating support. Overall, the dialogue ultimately influenced both the content of the exhibition as well as various responses to it.

The overall aim of the exhibition was to review the Expedition and its legacies critically while presenting the strength and richness of *Ailan Kastom* (Island Custom), past and present.[13] The approach sought a nuanced understanding of historically and culturally specific encounters. A central concern in the preparations for the exhibition was the extent to which a presentation of contact history can be balanced, inclusive and consensual. Yet notions of inclusion and consensus may not be appropriate in relation to Islanders' understanding of authority and ownership, where knowledge is owned and selectively transmitted to descendants. Throughout the exhibition different types of knowledge were highlighted in order to illustrate some of the historical and cross-cultural complexities involved in the relationship between the Expedition members, Islanders, missionaries and colonial officers. The juxtaposition of narratives was intended to multiply the shifting and overlapping contexts of the objects on display. The Expedition *Reports* and associated archival material provided historical insights into the views of different individuals and groups while more recent 'voices' were drawn from contemporary field notes, publications, informal discussions and correspondence. Numerous comments, opinions and stories from named individuals were thus directly incorporated into the storyline of the exhibition, providing a forum for the transmission of anthropological and indigenous perspectives both past and present. The approach of interweaving historic and contemporary voices was also intended to highlight the dynamic strength and vitality of *Ailan Kastom*.

Throughout the exhibition preparations Philp and I were conscious of Islanders' notions of privacy and avoided topics that would be likely to cause offence. While reference was made to esoteric knowledge, we did not attempt to explain it. Some material, such as objects associated with sorcery or death, was rejected for display as these items may retain an inherent dangerous potency. Explicit permission was sought for the inclusion of some sacred material; in particular, the section on Malo-Bomai required careful consideration and negotiation. The name of Bomai continues to be a sacred name for the Meriam people. Bomai has such power that commonly even his name is not spoken, instead, people refer to this *agad* (god) as Malo. In 1898 Haddon commissioned Wano and Enoch to create two cardboard models of the sacred Malo-Bomai masks, originally made of turtle-shell and worn at the climax of a secret initiation ceremony.[14] The production of the masks provoked a strong emotive response in many of the senior men and eventually the Expedition members were privileged to witness parts of the performances relating to the Malo ceremonies. Detailed information about Malo-Bomai was recorded in the *Reports*, a re-enactment of the ceremony was photographed and filmed, related objects were purchased for the museum, and the stories and the associated songs were recorded on wax cylinders.

Given the centrality of Malo-Bomai to the Meriam and the complex interactions involved in the production of the masks and re-enactment of the ceremonies, we were keen to include this material in the exhibition. However, our concerns regarding cultural sensitivity and ownership of knowledge included not only the question of the public display of the masks but the stories associated with them. The movements of Malo (that is, Bomai) created the social structure of Mer, its laws, tenancy and instruction. Each of the eight tribes of Mer had quite specific duties and privileges associated with Malo which were restricted to initiates and passed on only to their descendants. As such, the story of Malo's arrival on Mer has very real socio-political implications for Meriam today. Over time, with the assistance of the Ron Day, the Chairman of Mer, and Meriam elders, the display text was discussed, modified and eventually approved. Although the changes to the text appear to be relatively small, concerning the sequence of Malo's movements and details of his encounters, the narrative alludes to a deeper knowledge regarding initiation and ownership which was not disclosed.

The exhibition intentionally and somewhat inevitably contained a number of tensions and ambiguities. Objects and information collected in 1898 with the intention of recording Torres Strait culture 'before it was too late', were displayed 100 years later to reinforce the ongoing vitality of *Ailan Kastom*. Even in Haddon's own writings there was a noticeable contrast between his laments for a dying culture and the lively vignettes of Islander life recorded in the journals, letters and more popular publications.[15] The contrast between the motivating goals of the Expedition members and the personal relationships that were developed in the field were highlighted in adjacent sections in the exhibition entitled 'Recording, Measurement and Collecting' and 'Fieldwork and Friendship'. The colonial infrastructure facilitated the movements of the Expedition members and nourished the desire to record, measure and collect data about distant peoples and places. But once in the Islands, the Expedition's fieldworkers had to improvise and Islander responses often challenged Eurocentric assumptions about cultural and racial differences.

In addition to nearly 300 Islander objects, the exhibition included the material culture of the Expedition: callipers, a microscope, a colour wheel, Lovibond's tintometer, cameras, a recording phonograph and a magic lantern projector. The technology used by the Expedition members along with its associated knowledge and skills played an important role in mediating between the Expedition members and the Islanders, often with unexpected results. For example, photography was initially a means of surveillance and scientific analysis, but photographs soon became objects of exchange, anthropometric photography shifted into portraiture, family photographs were made at Islander's request, and Haddon's magic lantern shows were popular local entertainment (Edwards 1998). The exhibition attempted to contextualise the anthropological practices that were developed during this period, not glorify the work of the Expedition members. It was crucial to acknowledge the active role of Islanders in the Expedition's research, as confirmed by both the historical records and Islander memory. However, a lingering curatorial concern was whether the assertion of indigenous agency in the production of anthropological knowledge inadvertently downplayed the devastating effects of colonisation and the Expedition's role in removing important cultural artefacts. As one reviewer commented,

> A cross-cultural exhibition that fails to display tensions, instead of coherence, exceptions as well as rules, and at least several stories rather than one is probably not doing justice to whatever, art, culture or history it is supposed to be representing.
>
> (Thomas 2000: 73)

RESPONSES

Over the last few years, the Museum has welcomed over 30 Islander visitors. Awareness of the exhibition was heightened through occasional updates in the *Torres Strait News* and radio broadcasts on Radio Torres Strait (Torres Strait Islander Media Association, *Voice Blo Ilanman*). Some individuals used the exhibition as an incentive to visit the UK. Other visits were more lengthy and formal. For example, an official delegation represented the TSRA at the opening of the exhibition on 1 July 1998. In attendance were Ron Day, Chairman of Mer, and Terrence Whap, Chairman of Mabuiag, both direct descendants of Haddon's close assistants and representatives of the two Islands where the Expedition members conducted most of their research. Shortly after the exhibition opened, John Abednego, then Chairman of the TSRA, came to Cambridge specifically to see it. The flag of the Torres Strait, presented to the museum when I first discussed the exhibition with the Regional Authority in 1996, hung over the final section of the exhibition that outlined the efforts of the TSRA and other Islander community groups.[16] In 1999 a delegation of five elders (David Passi, Goby Noah, Florence Kennedy, Ephraim Bani, Frances Tapim), and Leilani Bin-Juda, a representative of the National Museum of Australia, spent approximately two weeks in Cambridge. They came specifically to see the exhibition, to conduct their own research in the reserve collections and archives of the museum, and to recommend possible loan objects for the opening of the new National Museum in Australia in 2001 (Figure 11.1). Finally, artist Alick Tipoti, well known for his detailed and vibrant lino-cut prints, came to 'close' the exhibition in December 2000. Islanders have continued to be attracted to the Museum and there have been several visits in 2001–2, including a visitation by five members of the Mualgau Minarral Art Collective based on Moa Island.

Interactions with and between various Islanders and staff within the Museum have been extremely productive. The storyline of the exhibition and the varied objects on display roused strong and mixed emotive responses, animating conversations about the

Figure 11.1 Islanders in museum storeroom recording information about baskets in the 'Haddon' collection, (l-r) Frances Tapim, Florence Kennedy, Ephraim Bani, David Passi, 1999. (Photograph by Anita Herle)

past and its relevance to the present. Some of the objects remain connected to particular families and islands, highlighting the ongoing relationship between people and things as well as the distinction between members of various communities. They are often linked to stories that both convey and selectively encode important cultural knowledge. Other objects are re-appropriated as symbols of a resurgent Islander identity and are used as a source of inspiration for contemporary Islander artists.

Day, Whap and others were keen to see the exhibition and the material in the reserve collections but they also expected a detailed explanation of why and how the exhibition was arranged. Initially Islanders tended to be overwhelmed by the richness of the collections and the amount of material on display. Some of the objects sparked excited conversations, others less familiar provoked sadness – a reminder of the devastating impact of colonisation, the loss of knowledge, and the things that no longer exist on the Islands. Where possible the labels noted an object's maker or previous owner. The care with which we attempted to associate people and things, attributed quotes and identified individuals in the photographs had a powerful effect on Islander visitors. These were not simply 'multiple voices' but named ancestors – we heard stories about them and were reminded of their living descendants.

The importance of family connections was and continues to be central to people's interest in and understanding of the collections in Cambridge. People are identified through their relationships with others – as someone's child, sibling, cousin, auntie, uncle, wife, husband and so forth. The emphasis on family was particularly apparent when looking at the historic photographs in the exhibition and the archives.

Family relationships also animate specific objects, which in turn stimulate further discussions about how and to whom people are related. In the collection there is a group of six rather roughly carved and painted male figures, *ad giz*, each representing a Meriam ancestor figure associated with a particular district and lineage. It is uncertain whether these types of figures were ever made and used locally, the examples in Cambridge were specifically made for Haddon via Jack Bruce (the schoolteacher on Mer), their production encouraged by Haddon's investigations into the existence of ancestor cults. In Cambridge, the Meriam representatives, Passi, Noah and Tapim, were keen on seeing the *ad giz* models and the unpacking of these figures prompted a long and detailed discussion conducted both in English and Meriam Mir. The men looked closely at the carved figures as they recited genealogies, comparing details with each other and with Rivers' genealogical tables in *The Reports* (Vol. 6).[17] People frequently referred to the *Reports* while looking at the objects in the reserve collections. The volumes and their contents were treated with great respect and nearly everyone asked if it would be possible to get them reprinted.

Objects with totem marks were also of great interest. Totems such as crocodiles, turtles or hammerhead sharks were incised on personal items such as the characteristic hourglass shaped drums, *warup* or bamboo tobacco pipes. Viewing these objects often prompted long discussions about characteristics of various totems and some Islanders used it as an opportunity to reveal their own totems. The style and execution of totem designs were of particular interest to artists, as discussed below.

Some of the objects in Cambridge continue to be directly linked to stories and legends that illustrate characteristics distinctive to each Island and define the relationship between individuals, communities and the physical world. While much of the 'deep' knowledge contained within stories is restricted and only selectively revealed,[18] their overall importance as a means of transmitting knowledge is highly valued (Lawrie 1970). When Ephraim Bani, a noted cultural leader from Mabuiag, first came to the museum in 1995, he saw an elaborate composite turtle-shell mask on display in the main anthropology gallery. The mask, a human face with outstretched hands surmounted on top of a crocodile head, was made by Gizu of Nagir and collected in 1888. Significantly, the story of this mask was never recorded by Haddon. Upon seeing this mask, Bani spontaneously and with great emotion told the story of Uberi Kuberi, a man who was eaten by a crocodile kept as a pet by his daughter. His initial encounter and reaction to the mask were recorded on film.[19] In the exhibition, the sequence of Bani telling the story of Uberi Kuberi was positioned beside the object, a strong reminder of the link between contemporary Islander knowledge and the objects collected by the Expedition.

Stories are related to particular families and places, yet some stories link people and islands. A 'complete' story may be made up of numerous versions, each 'owned' by a different family. A group of dance staffs, which were collected by Haddon at Mer, an Eastern Island, refer to legendary figures believed to have originated from Mabuiag or Western Island stories.[20] Upon seeing these staffs, Bani (from Mabuiag) discussed the imagery with Passi, Noah and Tapim (all from Mer). These flattish wooden staffs, originally carried during dance ceremonies, are distinguished by a carved anthropomorphic head that protrudes above a sinuous painted line. The more elaborate staffs are further decorated with tufts of cassowary feathers with small white feather highlights. Bani explained that the imagery on the staffs alludes to *muri*, small spirits who employ waterspouts as spears for catching turtle and dugong and he told a story about them. Exceptionally, here it was appropriate for someone from the Western Islands to speak about a Meriam object. Generally, Islander visitors to the museum would only talk about objects that are either general to the Torres Strait or specifically associated with their own island community. The distinction between the Eastern and the Western islands is particularly marked, linguistically and ethnographically. When looking at photographs and objects in store, the delegation of elders divided themselves into groups based on family and community affiliations.[21]

For many contemporary Torres Strait artists, historic objects, particularly those collected by Haddon, are an important source of inspiration. Many have closely studied images of these objects reproduced in the *Reports* and Moore's (1984) *Torres Strait Collections of A.C. Haddon*. A more recent source that draws substantially from the collections made by Haddon is Lindsay Wilson's (1988) *Thathilgaw, Emeret Lu: A Handbook of Traditional Torres Strait Islands Material Culture*.[22] Wilson was a skilled artist and illustrator and his book contains detailed line drawings with clear and informative captions. Artists tend to prefer this format, which highlights the clarity of detail and facilitates a better understanding of the construction techniques.

Expressing his excitement at seeing the actual objects at the Cambridge Museum, artist Alick Tipoti said 'these are the designs that inspired me as an artist to produce my lino-cuts. These are the *exact* designs I've looked at in books so many times and thought, *wow*, my forefathers did that!' (pers. com. December 2000). When Tipoti left Horn Island to study art at the TAFE in Cairns,[23] he chose to focus on lino-cut printing, a skill that he further developed when awarded a place at the National Art School in Canberra. Although using different materials and techniques than his ancestors, Tipoti relates the process of print-making to carving and compares the cutting of intricate designs into the lino with the low relief carving found on 'traditional' objects such as bamboo pipes and drums. The patterns and totem marks carried by nineteenth-century objects are elaborated and form imaginative and complex designs, which fill the background and give a dynamic quality to the overall composition. But it is often difficult to discriminate between the apparent subject matter of the prints and the background. In Tipoti's more recent work, significant totemic images may be hidden in the background; they become visible only when the viewer is informed of their existence. As with other ways of encoding knowledge, such as stories expressed orally and through dance, 'deeper' meanings may be concealed and only made visible when deemed appropriate.

Tipoti and other artists such as Dennis Nona and Joseph Dorante also directly incorporate representations of historic materials, including objects and models collected by Haddon, into their work. Masks, drums, sardine scoops, coconut water containers and pearlshell ornaments, as well as characteristic creatures such as dugong, turtle, hammerhead shark and crocodile, are used as symbols of an enduring *Ailan Kastom*. Figures referencing a general heroic past or depicting the legendary exploits of fierce warriors, such as Kwoim, are common subjects.

The first Islander artist to study the Haddon collections directly was Victor McGrath, a noted carver and engraver of marine materials such as pearlshell, turtle-shell and ivory. In 1991 he conducted research at Cambridge and several other British museums in order to analyse the design and construction methods of selected objects. Describing his experience he wrote, 'I have vivid recollections of handling those rare and beautiful treasures, utmost respect for their [often] nameless and faceless creators and privilege in having had an experience denied to so many people back home' (McGrath 1998: 104).

203

McGrath's comments raise the issue of Islander access to historic collections and he notes the difficulty of reproducing 'traditional' objects without frequent reference to 'the outstanding quality of workmanship in the old artefacts' (ibid.). The potential of objects to embody and convey distinctive cultural knowledge is highlighted by a report on the arts environment in the Torres Strait conducted by Mosby on behalf of the Torres Shire Council.[24]

Despite the limitations on the production of 'traditional' art in the Torres Strait, feathered headdresses (*dharis*), dance objects, personal ornaments and domestic items such as mats and baskets are still being made. Dance is a central feature of *Ailan Kastom* and the movements, costumes and music are the principal forum for artistic creativity. Islanders are great connoisseurs of performances. Dance paraphernalia from Haddon's 1898 collections include hand-held ornaments and story-boards, many of which relate to a detailed knowledge of the movement of the stars, the currents of the sea and the changing seasons. These objects collected a hundred years ago are the precursors of the articulated dance machines, elaborate and distinctive objects held or worn during performances.[25] Ken Thaiday Senior's hammerhead shark masks, Patrick Thaiday and Ken Thaiday Junior's hand-held dance machines are outstanding examples of contemporary creations which intensify the dramatic nature of the choreography while advancing a multi-layered narrative sequence.

Islander artists, often based or trained on the mainland, are producing a wealth of material ranging from the lino-cuts mentioned above to the installations of Ellen José. For many of these artists, historic objects are seen to have the potential of providing a direct link to the past as well as being a source of inspiration for the future. An impressive range of contemporary material set against a smaller number of nineteenth-century pieces was recently brought together for the first major exhibition of Torres Strait art in Australia. Organised by two Islander curators, Tom Mosby and Brian Robinson, *Ilan Pasin (this is our way) Torres Strait Art*, opened at the Cairns Regional Gallery in November 1998 and travelled to numerous venues in Australia before closing in Canberra in February 2001. The ongoing dialogue with Cambridge is apparent – a *dhari* collected by Haddon is featured on the cover of the lavishly produced catalogue[26] and the then chairman of the Torres Strait, John Abednego, acknowledged the co-operation between Cambridge Museum and the Torres Strait in the preface.

CONCLUSION

Torres Strait Islanders: an exhibition to mark the centenary of the 1898 Anthropological Expedition attempted to emphasise the multiple and shifting contexts of the objects on display. The material collected by Haddon has been entangled in distinct but overlapping narratives for over a century. The objects embody information about Islanders in the late nineteenth century, but they were also agents in the relationships which developed between specific Islanders and the members of the Expedition. Once considered remnants of a 'traditional' past that had all but disappeared, specific objects have remained embedded in Islander knowledge and today are symbolic of a strong resurgent Islander identity.

The museum itself has become a fieldsite – a place for cross-cultural encounter and creative dialogue. A more inclusive and multi-perspectivist approach to material in museum collections is crucial in illuminating the multiple meanings of specific objects as well as the complex processes involved in their production, collection and interpretation. Working with members of source communities provides an opportunity for developing productive relationships and collecting contemporary material for future generations. Yet, one must also acknowledge practical limitations and political constraints. It would be impossible for Cambridge museum staff to work closely at any given time with people from the many Pacific (and other) communities represented by our collections. In this example, our approach was facilitated by numerous factors including: the historical and cultural specificity of the encounter between Expedition members and Islanders, the richness of the collections, the detailed information that was produced and recorded, the generous assistance of numerous Islanders, Philp's doctoral fieldwork, and sabbatical leave for the curator.

The renewed dialogue between Cambridge and the Torres Strait continues. The centenary of the 1898 Anthropological Expedition was just one more stage in the life histories of the objects made and used by Islanders and collected by Haddon. In collaboration with the National Museum of Australia and a Torres Strait Islander reference group, a special exhibition on loan from Cambridge, *Past Time: Torres Strait Islander Material from the Haddon Collection, 1888–1905*, is currently on display at the National Museum in Canberra (2001–2) and will then travel to the Cairns Regional Gallery (2002). Further meanings will be illuminated when these objects are made more accessible to Islanders and a broader Australian audience.

ACKNOWLEDGEMENTS

My main thanks go to the many Islanders who generously shared their time and knowledge with me, in particular Ephraim Bani, Mary Bani, Leilani Bin-Juda, Ron Day, Florence Kennedy, Victor McGrath, Goby Noah, David Passi, Frances Tapim, Alick Tipoti and Terrence Whap. I am also grateful to Jude Philp, who has been an invaluable collaborator. Support for background research and the production of the exhibition was provided by the British Academy, the Crowther-Beynon Fund and Smuts Memorial Fund (University of Cambridge). Support for Islanders to conduct research in Cambridge was provided by the National Museum of Australia, the Australian Arts Council, Winston Churchill Memorial Trust Fellowship grant, Crowther-Beynon Fund (University of Cambridge) and the Torres Strait Regional Authority.

NOTES

This paper is a slightly abbreviated and revised version of an article by the same name in A. Herle, N. Stanley, K. Stevenson, R. Welsch (eds) (2002) *Pacific Art: Persistence, Change and Meaning*. Hindmarsh: Crawford House Press (pp. 231–49).

1 Personal communication with Alick Tipoti, a Torres Strait Islander artist from Badu and Horn Island, Cambridge University Museum of Archaeology and Anthropology, December 2000.
2 Elder Bishop Passi from Mer commenting on the exhibition of material from the Haddon collection at the National Museum of Australia (Philp 2001: viii). Passi is the grandson of one of Haddon's main assistants and he came as part of a delegation to Cambridge in 1999 to help select Torres Strait material for the exhibition in Australia.

3 Numerous writers have looked at the social life of things following on from Appadurai (1986).

4 *Torres Strait Islanders: An Exhibition to Mark the Centenary of the 1898 Cambridge Anthropological Expedition to the Torres Strait* was at the University of Cambridge Museum of Archaeology and Anthropology from 1 July 1998 to 2 December 2000.

5 The Murray Island Land Case, commonly known as the 'Mabo Case' after one of the plaintiffs, overturned 200 years of *terra nullius* and marked the first time that the Australian Government recognised the prior ownership of land by an indigenous group. Information from the *Reports*, in particular Rivers' genealogies, provided crucial evidence.

6 My interest here in an object's agency is somewhat over-determined in that Islanders often refer to the animate power of particular things. For example, inappropriate contact with certain objects is potentially dangerous.

7 The significance of the Expedition's work has been discussed in disciplinary histories (Herle and Rouse 1998; Kuklick 1991; Stocking 1983, 1995; Urry 1993). The Expedition is primarily credited for its methodological innovations: the integration of field research with scholarly interpretation, Rivers' development of the 'genealogical method', and the use of film and photography.

8 See Cooper (1989) for an overview of the locations of Islander collections. The majority of the Torres Strait material collected by Haddon in 1888 is housed in the British Museum (Moore 1984).

9 Maino's father was described as 'Kabagi' in Haddon's unpublished journal (1888–9: xx).

10 Kebisu's great grandson, Mr Arther Kebisu, retains one of his clubs, gaba-gaba (Mosby and Robinson 1998: 33).

11 Cf. Letter from Bruce to Haddon, 26 December 1902, Haddon Papers Envelope 1004. Letter from Ned Waria to Haddon 21 July 1904, Haddon Papers, Envelope 3012.

12 Mary Bani came to Cambridge for three months and used the museum as a base to compile information about Torres Strait collections in Cambridge, in numerous museums throughout the UK, and in Dublin and Berlin.

13 *Kastom* is defined as 'the body of customs, traditions, observances and beliefs of some or all of the Torres Strait Islanders living in the Torres Strait area, and includes any such customs, traditions, observances and beliefs relating to particular persons, areas, objects or relationships' (Aboriginal and Torres Strait Islander Commission Act 1989).

14 Haddon states that the original masks had been burnt, presumably by zealous missionaries (Haddon 1898–99: 204). Local oral tradition asserts that Malo had been burnt but that Bomai was buried at the village of Las on Mer. For a more detailed discussion on the creation of the masks and the re-enactment of the Malo-Bomai ceremony, see Herle (1998: 77–105).

15 Despite Haddon's emphasis recording and preserving past practices, Philp (1998b) has convincingly argued that the *Reports* tell us more about what was happening in the present. See also Beckett (1998).

16 Abednego presented the museum with a framed photograph of the 20 recently elected representatives of the TSRA, and this was incorporated into the final section of the exhibition.

17 These men are well aware of the political significance of Rivers' genealogies; David Passi was one of the plaintiffs in the Murray Island land case.

18 Haddon's concern that the young men no longer know the old ways and hence his emphasis on salvage ethnography may have been exaggerated by his lack of awareness of how significant cultural knowledge was transmitted. Younger people often declined, as they continue to do today, to speak about things that are the domain of specific elders or inappropriate to reveal to outsiders. The suppression of 'traditional' beliefs and practices by missionaries and colonial officials would have reinforced Islanders' reluctance to speak about certain issues.

19 Ephraim Bani first came to the museum with Francis Calvert as the protagonist in her film *Cracks in the Mask*. The film focused on Ephraim's reactions to various museum collections in the UK and Europe, and thus Ephraim's activities in the museum were recorded.

20 Meriam legends and cults were noted for their tendency to borrow elements from elsewhere and reinterpret them (Beckett 1998: 40).

21 There are two main language groups in the Torres Strait: Meriam Mir, the language of the people of the Eastern islands and Kala Lagaw Ya, the language of the Western, Northern and Central islands (the later with mutually intelligible regional dialects). *The Reports* (Vol. 5)

Sociology, Magic and Religion of the Western Islanders (1904) and *The Reports* (Vol. 6) *Sociology, Magic and Religion of the Eastern Islanders* (1908) were based on research primarily conducted on Mabuiag and Mer respectively.

22 Published by the Department of Education in Queensland to coincide with the Australian bicentenary and the centenary of Haddon's first expedition to the Torres Strait.

23 A Visual Arts Course began in 1984 the Faculty of Aboriginal and Torres Strait Islander Studies at the TAFE in Cairns. A unique style of Torres Strait Islander art has developed within the Printmaking Department under the direction of Anna Eglitis. Islander printmakers have included Annie Gela, Dennis Nona, Brian Robinson and Alick Tipoti (Eglitis 1998: 135–41).

24 There is a growing interest, supported by the TSRA, in establishing a cultural centre with appropriate facilities to care for historic as well as contemporary material.

25 In the exhibition a large section on dance includes video sequences showing a variety of dances from the 1993 Cultural Festival on Thursday Island, which are intended to animate the objects on display and incorporate contemporary manifestations of a distinct cultural form.

26 There are several levels of symbolism at work here: the *dhari* has become symbol of the unity of the Torres Strait, but this particular *dhari* has also become the symbol of the Haddon collection, appearing on the cover of the comprehensive illustrated catalogue, *The Torres Strait Collections of A.C. Haddon* (Moore 1984). Its placement on the cover reinforces the continuity between past and present and acknowledges the links between the Torres Strait and Cambridge. On another level it may be interpreted as either an act of re-appropriation or a demonstration that some objects in museum collections may never be fully alienated from their original cultural owners.

12

TRANSFORMING ARCHAEOLOGY THROUGH PRACTICE

Strategies for collaborative archaeology and the
Community Archaeology Project at Quseir, Egypt

Stephanie Moser, Darren Glazier,
James E. Phillips, Lamya Nasr el Nemr,
Mohammed Saleh Mousa, Rascha Moatty Nasr Aiesh,
Susan Richardson, Andrew Conner and Michael Seymour

INTRODUCTION

Although there is an increasing amount of literature devoted to the development of 'community archaeology', the notion of collaborative practice in our discipline remains a vague concept, with many assuming that it refers simply to consultation with local communities. 'Community archaeology', however, goes far beyond that, incorporating a range of strategies designed to facilitate the involvement of local people in the investigation and interpretation of the past. In this chapter, we outline a methodology for ensuring effective community involvement in the study of the archaeological resource, the development of which has been the subject of a major research project in the city of Quseir, situated on the Red Sea coast of Egypt.

The Community Archaeology Project at Quseir began in 1999 as part of the large-scale excavation of the ancient harbour site known in Roman times as Myos Hormos and in the present as Quseir al-Qadim ('Old Quseir'). The aim of the project is to involve the local community in all aspects of the archaeological enterprise, culminating in the creation of a Heritage Centre that presents the findings from the excavations to the people of Quseir and tourists visiting the area. The project is the first of its kind in Egypt, seeking to bring about a change in the way archaeology is conducted in a country where local communities have been systematically excluded both from the process of discovering their past, and in the construction of knowledge concerning their heritage. Drawing on developments made in other countries with a colonial past such as Australia, Canada and the United States, the Community Archaeology Project at Quseir is inspired by the initiatives made in involving indigenous and local communities in the research process. The underlying premise of the project is that it is no longer acceptable for archaeologists to reap the material and intellectual benefits of another society's heritage without that society being involved and able to benefit equally from the endeavour. We endorse the general goal of 'community archaeology' to replace the traditional colonial model of archaeological practice with a socially and politically self-conscious mode of research, aiming ultimately to incorporate different cultural perspectives in the interpretation of the past.

There are two reasons why the community of Quseir should be involved in the archaeological investigations that are being conducted just outside the modern city. First, it has been suggested by many in Quseir that the findings from Quseir al-Qadim will play an important role in the formation of a sense of community heritage. Prior to the recent excavation of Quseir al-Qadim it was not widely known that this was the location of the port of Myos Hormos. It is thus only recently that many local people have discovered that they are living in an area of international archaeological significance, and this has already started to affect the way they perceive their city, their past and themselves.

It has also become apparent that the archaeological investigations will have an impact on the future economic status of the city, particularly as it seeks to reconstruct itself as the historical centre of the Red Sea. Following the demise of the local phosphate industry, Quseir has begun to occupy a unique niche in the Red Sea tourist trade as an upmarket resort combining marine and heritage tourism. The United States Agency for International Development (USAID), working in conjunction with the Egyptian government as part of their Environmentally Sustainable Tourism project, highlighted Quseir for special attention 'because its cultural and natural resources offer a potential for the development of tourism' (Salama 1997: 3), whilst the Swedish philanthropist Peder Wallenberg has already invested substantial efforts into the regeneration of heritage locations in the city.

Finally, and on a more general level, the residents of Quseir should be involved in the study of their own heritage simply because they, like most other Egyptians, have been excluded from Western scholarship in Egypt for so long. The historian Donald Reid (1985, 1997, 2002) has conducted detailed research into the hitherto neglected history of the efforts of Egyptian archaeologists to reclaim the past from Westerners, who appropriated it in the nineteenth century. Whilst Egyptians have successfully taken control of Egyptian Museums, the Antiquities Service and the export of antiquities from foreign powers, the majority of excavations are nevertheless still conducted by Western archaeologists who do not involve local communities in their interpretations. This is also true of the heritage industry in Egypt, where, as Mitchell highlights (2000), the interests of multinational corporations, tourists and archaeologists are considered paramount, to the detriment of local communities (see also Meskell 2001).

Second, we believe that community involvement in the investigations at Quseir will transform our approach to, and interpretation of, the archaeological evidence. Indeed, one of the primary aims of the Community Archaeology Project is to establish the extent to which community involvement in the archaeological investigations affects the research process itself. Over the past four years we have learned that collaboration constitutes far more than simply showing respect for the values of another culture. Indeed, the involvement of local communities in archaeological investigations from the outset results in better archaeology. Not only have we gained specific information about the site and the types of remains recovered, but also we have also been given access to different perspectives and interpretations of Quseir al-Qadim. These more diverse and culturally sensitive interpretations of the archaeological data provide a more comprehensive understanding of the site than would have been possible through traditional archaeological analysis alone.

It is important to stress that Quseir is not a homogeneous community. An influx of economic migrants in the nineteenth and early twentieth centuries is reflected in the diverse make-up of the modern city, where a number of different groups including Nubians, migrants from the Hajjaz, the Nile Valley and Suez, and the Ababda Bedouin, comprise a significant proportion of the population of some 45,000 people. This does not, however, negate the possibility of undertaking a community archaeology project in Quseir, as many members of the community have stressed their interest in both the project and the history of Quseir itself.

COLLABORATIVE PRACTICE IN ARCHAEOLOGY

It is possible to identify several developments that relate directly to the adoption of a community-oriented approach within the discipline, including the growing literature devoted to the socio-political analysis of archaeological research, increased involvement of descendant groups in the creation of museum exhibitions, and political pressures placed upon researchers by communities directly affected by their findings. Increasing indigenous involvement has perhaps had the greatest impact upon the practice of archaeology, and consultation with parties who may have an interest or stake in archaeological investigations is gradually becoming more integrated into the discipline.

The concept of working with communities whose heritage is under investigation has been addressed on three levels in archaeology: the ethics of working abroad; the preservation of sites; and the necessity of consultation with indigenous and descendant communities. With regard to the ethics of working abroad, Healy (1984: 128–9) emphasises our professional responsibility to convey the results of research to both the host government and the community within which the project is based. Numerous archaeologists have also outlined the benefits of public involvement in the excavation/ investigation process, primarily to ensure site preservation (e.g. Jameson 1997; McManamon 2000). Often referred to as 'public' or 'outreach' archaeology, the participation of non-professionals is deemed beneficial as it fosters respect for the value of the archaeological resource, and thus discourages vandalism and the looting of sites. McManamon (2000), for example, highlights the need to present the results of archaeological investigations to local communities in a clear and concise manner; a necessary and important step if the discipline is to avoid social isolation. The concept of outreach nevertheless appears to be one-way, with archaeologists assuming the role of educators and community members playing no part in the interpretative process. Although a principle of the Society for American Archaeology – 'Public education and outreach' (Principle Number Four), which is outlined in their 'Principles of Archaeological Ethics', states that 'Archaeologists should reach out to, and participate in co-operative efforts with, others interested in the archaeological record with the aim of improving the preservation, protection, and interpretation of the record' (cited in McManamon 2000: 14), the majority of researchers continue to neglect the contribution that 'others' can make to the intellectual dimensions of archaeological practice. As Franklin (1997: 44) suggests, 'as academics we often think about how our scholarship can enrich the lives of others. Seldom do we consider how our own lives, including our research, could benefit from knowledge and experiences of non archaeologists'. It is essential that we redefine this notion of community or public archaeology to ensure that it is not simply dismissed as a methodological or ethical issue, of secondary importance to research questions.

The third level on which community archaeology is discussed is in relation to consultation with indigenous and descendant communities. Here researchers have begun to develop the concept of collaborative practice in archaeology, where a number of professional organisations have revised their principles to emphasise the importance of consultation with communities directly affected by archaeological practice (Lynott and Wylie 1995; Lilley 2000). Two recent examples serve to demonstrate the potential of collaborative work in archaeology: the research conducted in Australia by Field *et al.* (2000), and in North America by McDavid (1997, 1999, 2000). The case study from New South Wales, Australia, is one of many examples where the interests of both Aboriginal people and archaeologists were equally met, but more importantly where the project itself evolved beyond its scientific aims to incorporate and address the concerns of the local community (Field *et al.* 2000: 35). Drawing on the pioneering work conducted in Australia in the 1980s and 1990s by researchers such as Colin Pardoe (1985, 1990, 1991, 1992) and Annie Clarke (1994), Field and her colleagues recorded the views of local people on archaeology, the excavations and consultation (see also Lewis and Rose 1985). They make several suggestions for conducting community-based research of this nature, emphasising the importance of

1   fostering social relationships between the community and the archaeological team,
2   maintaining a presence in the area between field seasons,
3   seeking funding for the employment of local people,
4   members of the local community relaying archaeological information to the wider community, and
5   the retention of some kind of archaeological collection in the area.

They conclude that working with local communities not only enriches the project, but 'provides a broader continuity from prehistory past to present' (Field *et al.* 2000: 46).

McDavid's (1997, 1999, 2000) work with local citizens on the Levi Jordan Plantation project in Brazoria highlights how the inclusion of African American perspectives has resulted in the production of more contextualised histories of the area. By involving individuals in every stage of the project, from planning, design, content development and delivery, and with a focus on creating an interactive internet site, McDavid has achieved a democratic sense of archaeological practice. Other researchers working in African American and plantation archaeology have adopted similar positions. Franklin (1997: 46), for example, suggests that the involvement of descendant communities constitutes the difference between 'histories viewed through a single lens, and bolder, fuller histories viewed through multiple lenses' (see also McDavid and Babson 1997; Logan 1998).

Despite promising work by the individuals mentioned above, very few researchers have acknowledged the intellectual contributions that local groups can make to research, nor how collaborative practice can transform the understanding of sites under investigation. Over ten years ago in his introduction to *Who Needs the Past? Indigenous*

Values and Archaeology, Layton (1989: 12) rightly emphasised the extent to which archaeologists' research interests failed to coincide with the concerns of indigenous communities, and that taking into account the values and knowledge of indigenous peoples would 'benefit both archaeological theory and practice'. What was missing, however, was an explanation of *how* the incorporation of such values could prove beneficial. In *Making Alternative Histories*, edited by Schmidt and Patterson (1995), this question was more specifically addressed. Here it was argued that the texture of narratives we write about other cultures could only be enhanced by the incorporation of local histories. Readers are encouraged to challenge the false distinctions between scientific, mythic and historical domains of knowledge and to appreciate the interplay between archaeological remains, written accounts and oral traditions, rather than perceiving them as distinct domains of knowledge (ibid.: 14).

Detailed analyses of the impact of indigenous involvement on research have been pioneered in Australia. Almost 20 years ago Ucko (1983) introduced the notion that indigenous involvement was transforming the very nature of the discipline, whilst in the early 1990s one of us demonstrated that Australian Aboriginal people transformed the research agenda in archaeology through their participation in the affairs of the Australian Institute of Aboriginal Studies (Moser 1995). Studies on the benefits gained from a collaborative relationship between archaeologists and local people have also been published in relation to work with Native American communities. Contributions to Swidler *et al.* (1997), for example, demonstrate the possibility of producing more holistic interpretations of the past through the integration of Western scientific methods and non-Western perspectives. The volume redefines consultation as a dialogue that involves listening as much as speaking; no longer do the contributors deem it acceptable for archaeologists simply to inform Native Americans of their discoveries. The use of oral history to enhance archaeological interpretations is advocated, challenging the assumption that oral traditions are somehow less valid than 'science'. More recently, Watkins has highlighted the methodological changes within the discipline that have facilitated the development of indigenous archaeology. The importance of mutual education is emphasised, where archaeologists not only educate affected cultural groups about a project, but also *become* educated about the concerns and interests of the cultural groups within which they work (Watkins 2000: 171).

Doing community archaeology demands making fundamental changes to our research practice. As Wylie (1995: 267) argued in *Making Alternative Histories*, it is not enough to 'make a commitment to write up 'plain language' reports on the results of scholarly research'. She rightly advocates that these measures will be effective 'only if those whose lives are affected are directly involved in the research enterprise from the outset, as partners, not merely as subjects, as sources of insight, and as progenitors of new lines of evidence' (ibid.: 267). She concludes that the challenge for archaeologists is to find ways of creating these partnerships. Before directly addressing this challenge, we present a brief history of the excavations and the Community Archaeology Project at Quseir.

HISTORY OF THE EXCAVATIONS AND THE COMMUNITY ARCHAEOLOGY PROJECT

Some 6km north of the modern city of Quseir lies Quseir al-Qadim, an ancient settlement of major international significance. The site was initially believed to be the relatively minor Roman port of Leucos Limen (Whitcomb and Johnson 1979; 1982a, 1982b), however, the suggestion that it was Myos Hormos, a Ptolemaic and Roman port founded in the third century BC (Huntingford 1980; Reddé and Golvin 1987), was supported by Peacock (1993). Large-scale excavations of the area begun in 1999 have confirmed the status of the site in antiquity, with a papyrus contract dated 25 March AD 93 giving the full name of the site as 'Myos Hormos on the Erythraean Sea'.

One of the great trading centres of the ancient world, the port of Myos Hormos, together with its sister port Berenike (300km to the south), articulated Rome's commerce with the orient as an integral part of a trade axis that linked Rome and the Mediterranean with the East. Situated at one end of a caravan route linking the Nile port of Coptos to the Red Sea, pearls, precious stones, silks, textiles, medicines and exotic spices from India and the Far East were exchanged for gold and silver, coins, glass, textiles, wine, fine pottery and human cargoes. The site appears to have been abandoned in the second century AD, but rose again to prominence in the thirteenth and fourteenth centuries, flourishing as a Mamluk port devoted to pilgrims travelling to the holy cities of Mecca and Medina, as well as the revitalised trade with India and the Arabian peninsula. Archaeological investigations suggest that the Islamic port was abandoned some time prior to the foundation of modern Quseir in the early sixteenth century. Four seasons of excavations at Quseir al-Qadim have yielded a vast amount of materials that attest to the extensive occupation of the site in both the Roman and Mamluk periods (Peacock *et al.* 1999, 2000, 2001, forthcoming), including the discovery of a large number of amphorae, located upon what may have been the shore's edge.

The Community Archaeology Project at Quseir was initiated at the invitation of the director of the excavations, David Peacock. In 1998, one of us (Stephanie Moser) visited Quseir with Peacock to evaluate the potential for community involvement in the creation of a museum or heritage centre based upon the findings from the archaeological investigations. During this first visit to Quseir it became clear that many local people had a strong interest in their heritage and in the idea of creating a museum. Furthermore, meetings with representatives from the Quseir Heritage Preservation Society and the mayor, Mr Mohammed Amin, demonstrated that there was widespread concern about the potential impact of tourism on the city. The chairman of Quseir Heritage, Mr Farid Mansour, and its manager Mr Adel Aiesh, were particularly interested in fostering projects that ensured the preservation of the city's heritage, and had already collaborated in a programme of purchasing old houses in the city with the intention of restoring them for commercial purposes. This programme of restoration was initially funded by the Carpe Vitam Trust of Peder Wallenberg and is now supported by the Egyptian Social Fund (a government organisation). Associated with this programme was the restoration of the Ottoman fort in Quseir by the American Research Center in Egypt in 1998. These developments, together with the recent establishment of the Quseir Heritage Preservation Society in 1998, suggested that there was a great deal of potential for community involvement in the archaeological investigations.

When work began in February 1999, the principal aims of the Community Archaeology Project were to discuss the nature of our proposed project with community representatives; to acquire feedback from as many people as possible concerning the creation of a community museum; to produce educational resources based on the site; to obtain people's views on their heritage; and to compile a video record of the excavation as it progressed. While the excavations were being conducted, we worked with the manager of Quseir Heritage, Adel Aiesh. In addition to liaising with community members, we organised the employment of local people to work with us and interview members of the local community.

A STRATEGY FOR COLLABORATIVE PRACTICE

One of the key research objectives of the Community Archaeology Project at Quseir is to develop a methodology for conducting community archaeology. To this end we have identified seven components, which we suggest form the basis of this kind of work:

1   communication and collaboration;
2   employment and training;
3   public presentation;
4   interviews and oral history;
5   educational resources;
6   photographic and video archive;
7   community controlled merchandising.

While not intended as a 'recipe' for doing community archaeology, this methodology may offer some useful ideas for others seeking to undertake work of this nature. It is important to stress that this project is ongoing. The latest updates on the progress of the project can be found the website *www.arch.soton.ac.uk/Research/Quseir.*

1 Communication and collaboration

Of central importance to the success of any community archaeology project is an emphasis on communication and collaboration between team members and representatives of the local community at every stage of research. As opposed to simply 'bringing in' local people to seek their approval, every effort has to be made to involve them from the outset of the project. Indeed, communication and collaboration for the project was initiated before work commenced and remains a key priority. As Derry (1997: 24) has suggested, 'if the community does not help define the questions, the answers probably will not interest them.' It is therefore necessary to surrender some authority and control over the direction the project will take, as successful collaboration will be limited if archaeologists seek to 'own' every aspect of the project. Collaboration does not simply refer to a one-way process of communication, where members of the team inform the people of Quseir about the project's progress and objectives. Rather, the aim is to achieve a continuous dialogue or two-way communication that enables us to interpret and present the heritage of Quseir in a fully collaborative way.

Partnerships with local organisations

Collaboration with local councils and heritage organisations is essential because it provides a framework for integrating the results of the archaeological investigations into community plans for the future. In this, we were fortunate to have the recently formed Quseir Heritage Preservation Society with whom to establish a partnership. Recognising the potential of the excavation to have significant implications for future heritage related developments in city, Quseir Heritage have been extremely supportive of the project. The manager, Adel Aiesh, has taken a very active role in introducing us to various interest groups within the community and in keeping the mayor informed of our progress. Our close relationship with Quseir Heritage not only provides a valuable source of feedback on all aspects of the project, but is also the vehicle through which future developments based on the excavations will be carried out.

Work updates and strategies

The production of regular reports on the project and proposals outlining each year's strategy for fieldwork is a fundamental part of the collaboration objective. Each year the team has produced a report summarising the results of the project, with images of activities undertaken during the course of fieldwork. This is separate from the main excavation report submitted annually to the Supreme Council of Antiquities in Cairo, and is distributed to local organisations, individuals and published on the internet. These materials give people a sense of how the project is evolving and serve to encourage feedback. We also produce annual outlines of our fieldwork objectives, which are submitted to Quseir Heritage for comment and revision.

Plain language reports

It is fundamental that the results of the archaeological investigations are communicated to the local community. The production of 'plain language reports' in archaeology has been adopted over the last decade, particularly in Australia and North America. In his suggested method for this kind of public writing, Gibb (1997: 56) rejects the passive voice and contrived style of the third person, advocating the use of a narrative, rather than an analytical format, and the peopling of the 'story' with site occupants, professional archaeologists and site visitors.

To communicate the findings from Quseir al-Qadim in this manner, we produce an annual bilingual (Arabic–English) report that covers all aspects of the project, including the excavations and the community archaeology work (Glazier 1999; J.E. Phillips 2000, 2001a, forthcoming). Prior to its distribution to schools, local authorities, hotels, coffee shops and other interested members of the community, a draft version of the report is presented to various members of the community to ensure that we get feedback on how it might be improved. The mayor, for example, provided suggestions regarding the types of information he felt should be included, whilst Lamya Nasr el Nemr selected the images she deemed would be of most interest to the community. The distribution of the report to members of the local community employed as excavators on the site has also proved extremely positive. Not only has it provided them with an insight into the significance of the work taking place, but it has also served to foster a sense of pride in their city. After consultation with members of the local community, it was felt that the initial versions of the report were still too detailed and did not adequately explain archaeological research. To remedy this, the latest version includes a more detailed introduction to the project and a description of archaeological methodology.

Openness

Informing local residents about all the aspects of community archaeology work is imperative because local people should not feel that the members of the team are being selective in the information they divulge. In Quseir, we have sought to achieve this by employing local people to work as part of the Community Archaeology team (see below) and by involving them in all the day-to-day activities of our work, both in Egypt and the UK. We have also adopted a policy of open communication, where we hide nothing about the work we are doing from the people we work with. On one level this includes conversations about the stresses of trying to negotiate the many levels of local politics that have implications for our work, while on another it includes frank discussions about aspects of our behaviour that may be considered inappropriate to particular groups in the community.

In addition to talking openly, we have also placed great emphasis on doing jobs together, ensuring that the Egyptian members of the team are involved in every task, no matter how big or small. When the UK-based members of the team are not in Egypt, regular contact is kept and developments relating to the project are communicated. This has resulted in far less suspicion about the presence of our team in the city; this is of particular importance at a time when increasing numbers of tourists in the region are offending sections of the local community with inappropriate dress and disrespectful behaviour. Furthermore, many individuals now feel comfortable about expressing their opinions of the project as we pass them in the street, or stand next to them in a queue at the bank. Spontaneous feedback of this kind is essential to the success of the project, as people have begun to recognise that we are interested in the views of *all* sections of the community, not just those in authority or with a direct connection to the project.

Authorship and ownership

A major concern in collaborative projects that culminate in some kind of public presentation is that the local community should work closely with the curators or archaeologists to determine what is exhibited. If local people are not involved in the presentation of their heritage, their sense of ownership and concern for maintaining a site or museum will not be as great. We thus envisage our role as facilitators, presenting as much of the 'raw data' from the excavations as possible to the local community and enabling them to decide what should be displayed and what stories should be told.

One of the key problems in achieving this aim is that access to artefacts recovered from sites in Egypt is restricted. Once unearthed, artefacts are recorded by archaeologists, registered with the Antiquities Service and sent to storehouses where they cannot be viewed by the public (in the case of Quseir, some 200km away in Quft). Understandably, the Egyptian government cannot provide funding to establish local museums to display the vast amount of antiquities recovered by excavations throughout the country. Furthermore, physical access to the finds for those who cannot visit the dig and see artefacts *in situ* is extremely difficult as we are not permitted to take finds off site or out of our desert camp into the city to show people.

Despite this, and prior to the application for permission to recover artefacts for display in a future museum, we have attempted to develop methods that ensure that people are aware of the types of material recovered. While viewing images of the finds does not constitute an ideal solution, we have created a digital artefact database that is accessible to the community before the final analyses are published. It is hoped that this will assist the community in making decisions about what kinds of artefacts they would like to learn more about and to see displayed.

Social interaction

Successful collaboration demands that contact between the team and the people of Quseir is not simply perceived as a business relationship. During our visits, it has become increasingly clear that for many in the community it is desirable for us to make a personal investment in our work, developing friendships that involve regular and long-lasting contact. In other words, they want to know that we are coming back because we care about the place and the people, and not just about our research. This is also noted by the Australian team working at Brewarrina, who suggest that the 'establishment and continual renewal of social communication provides the foundation of successful collaboration' (Field *et al*. 2000: 35; see also Watkins *et al*. 2000: 73 for similar conclusions in North America). Furthermore, researchers working in the archaeology of slavery in the United States have emphasised how successful collaboration depends upon long-term commitment and a 'willingness to work through difficult issues *with* the community' (Derry 1997: 24). Related to this is the importance of making regular visits to the community, not just when excavations are taking place but in the intervening period. Although it is very expensive to get the team to Quseir outside the excavation season because hotel accommodation, rather than camping, becomes necessary, it has been a priority to visit our Quseir colleagues at least twice every year.

Acknowledging difficulties

It is important to recognise that difficulties will arise as a result of working so closely with community groups; to suggest that things progress smoothly with little disagreement would be misleading. As we highlighted earlier, there is no such thing as a homogeneous 'local community', and it is naturally difficult to engage every different interest group with the aspirations of the project 100 per cent of the time. However, by accepting from the beginning that tensions are inevitable, the team is more prepared for conflicts when they do arise.

2 Employment and training

A major priority in conducting a community archaeology project should be the employment and training of local people to work on all aspects of the project. The passing on of skills related to archaeological study, heritage management and museum display is fundamental because it ensures that local people will be qualified to co-ordinate the presentation of the site or the running of a visitors' centre or museum once established. Employing local people on the Quseir Community Archaeology team ensures that there is continuity in project work when the European members of the team are absent; it also enables members of the community to play a critical role in making decisions about what will be displayed. Unfortunately, as Field *et al.* (2000: 43) have observed, securing funding for the employment of local people is one of the major problems that archaeologists face when engaging in community projects of this kind. Indeed, it is only because salaries are comparatively low in Egypt that our grants have enabled us to 'indulge' in the luxury of employing individuals in this manner. By demonstrating the benefits of providing full-time employment to members of the local community, we hope to convince funding organisations that such expenditure is necessary.

Field *et al.* (2000: 43) have emphasised the positive aspects of employing local people on the site itself during the excavations, where individuals are able to acquire skills that will enhance future employment prospects, learn something about archaeology, have input into the process of investigating their own history, and become active in relaying information from the project to the wider community. This is already evident at Quseir, where many of the local people employed as excavators have expressed a genuine interest in the process and results of the investigation. However, while the employment of local people as excavators at Quseir al-Qadim has been crucial in involving the community and disseminating information, the employment of individuals to work with the Community Archaeology team has proved even more successful and is an ongoing priority. The importance of full-time employment to the integrity of the project became apparent in the second year of work, when the team returned to Quseir and found that we were unable to re-employ the two people who were initially involved in the project (Eman Mohammed Attia and Diaa Abdul Aziz Gad) as they had secured full-time employment elsewhere. We determined that when four new Quseir graduates began working with us (Lamya Nasr el Nemr, Hanaan Shazly, Mohammed Saleh Mousa and Rascha Moatty Nasr Aeish), we would have to provide a full-time salary for at least one person – Lamya Nasr el Nemr.

Training

Training the Quseir members of the community archaeology team operates on two levels. On one level we are sharing knowledge and skills associated with archaeology, heritage presentation, museum display and computing and IT, while on another level we are assisting with the acquisition of more formal qualifications. The aim is to provide access to professional qualifications in the UK, thus enhancing the archaeological knowledge of the Quseir team members and providing them with the requisite skills in heritage presentation. To this end we have submitted scholarship applications for Lamya

Nasr el Nemr to study in the UK, have funded her enrolment in English courses in Cairo, and financed a visit for her to the UK to participate in an undergraduate unit on museum display in the Department of Archaeology at Southampton University.

3 Public presentation

The exhibition strategy

One of the fundamental objectives of community archaeology is the public presentation of archaeological findings, thus ensuring that the wider community is informed of the results and significance of work undertaken in their region. The primary objective of the Community Archaeology Project at Quseir is to create a Heritage Centre in the city that will bring the results of the excavation to the community (Moser 2001). Equally important, however, is that the Heritage Centre will function as a place where historical and cultural information about the community will be presented. The Centre is therefore founded upon community involvement from the outset, with extensive 'front-end' evaluation that will result in local people playing a key role in decisions regarding the themes and forms of presentation in the Centre. Prior to the Centre's construction, reports outlining preliminary suggestions for displays have been presented to the community for feedback and have generated a great deal of discussion and interest in the concept of a local museum (Moser 1999, 2001). The more recent exhibition plan incorporates many of the suggestions made by local residents, most notably that the Heritage Centre should engage with the past and the present, bringing the findings from the excavation to light, whilst also presenting the more recent history of the city and other subjects of community interest. Thus, while a key focus will be the story of the Roman trading port of Myos Hormos and the Islamic port of Quseir al-Qadim, it will also present the development of the city in the nineteenth century under the patronage of Mohammed Ali and the pivotal role it played in the pilgrim trade and the exportation of grain.

The exhibition strategy for the Heritage Centre draws on the latest research in museology, where concepts such as multiple narratives, constructive learning, artefact life histories, audience knowledge, and the exposition of the interpretative nature of exhibits have been promoted (e.g. Roberts 1997; Hein 1998; Moore 1997; McLoughlin 1999; Falk and Dierking 2000; Hooper-Greenhill 2000). To this end, a research project examining how to display the 'life histories' of objects from Quseir has already been undertaken (Phillips 2001b). When the excavations at Quseir al-Qadim have been completed, the team will also begin to prepare the site for presentation, incorporating it into the overall display strategy and thus ensuring a more holistic museum visitor experience. In undertaking this part of the project, we will seek guidance from successful 'archaeological parks' such as Empúries in Spain (Pardo 2000: 16–17). The exhibition plans have also provided residents with the opportunity to comment on the display environment, which we suggest should have an artistic and handcrafted 'feel', as opposed to being high-tech and full of multimedia gadgetry.

Temporary exhibits

Rather than waiting until the excavations have finished, we have begun to prepare temporary displays designed to generate interest in the public presentation of Quseir al-Qadim amongst the wider community. These exhibits will ensure that residents are kept informed of the excavation's progress, whilst providing yet another forum for feedback. Discussions with Quseir Heritage resulted in a joint proposal for a temporary exhibit and we applied for funding to rent a building that would house such displays for the next five or so years, until a larger, more permanent Heritage Centre is established. When Quseir Heritage informed us that they had found a suitable location (a house in the centre of the city), the UK team members returned to Quseir to begin the production of preliminary displays. As the building was not ready to be occupied, we spent much of our time discussing the renovations required to effectively display the results from Quseir al-Qadim whilst producing posters and other material with our Quseir colleagues. In 2001 funds for the restoration of this building fell through, however the mayor has now offered a new site for the establishment of the Heritage Centre.

International connections

Recently a link has been established between the Quseir Heritage Centre and the Petrie Museum of Egyptology, London, who are seeking to make their collections accessible to Egyptians, especially those of Egyptian and African descent who reside in London (Macdonald 2000: 79). The partnership will enable Quseir graduates to gain some experience at the Petrie whilst contributing to displays on their heritage presented in the United Kingdom. Such connections will thus prove beneficial to both institutions.

4 Interviews and oral history

Interviews with local people about their heritage should be a central component of any 'community archaeology' project. Not only do they provide us with insights into how people respond to the archaeological discoveries and how they experience and negotiate archaeology in the present, they also provide valuable opportunities to analyse how this information relates to established ideas about the heritage of the site being investigated.

By focusing upon oral history and local perceptions of the past, interviews conducted in Quseir by Darren Glazier and Mohammed Saleh Mousa have enhanced our knowledge of Quseir al-Qadim, providing us with more diverse cultural interpretations of the evidence and facilitating the construction of a total life history of the site. Interviews with the community are also a vital means of communicating the aims of the project and thus engendering further community involvement. The oral history component of our project is founded upon research undertaken in fields such as the socio-politics of archaeology, anthropology and the construction of identities (e.g. Gero 1989; Said 1989; Anderson 1991; Ahmed and Shore 1995; Meehan 1995; Shankland 1996, 1999; Gazin-Schwartz and Holtorf 1999; Glazier 2001). In addition to Darren Glazier's interviews about heritage, Lamya Nasr el Nemr has been recording the views of workers employed on the site, which will form a vital part of James Phillips' future displays on object life histories.

Interview questions

An outline of general questions provides a starting point for the interview programme. These should then be discussed with appropriate heritage organisations, which may have suggestions regarding the appropriate points of focus for the interviews. In the first year of fieldwork, discussions were held with a number of people prior to the production of a list of interview themes. The list, when produced, was intentionally informal and unstructured, allowing the interviewee to cover the areas of most importance to them, as well as those deemed to be of most interest to the project. Since then over 100 interviews have been conducted with a range of people in the city, both in groups and on a one-to-one basis. All were taped and transcribed, and as such form the core data for Glazier's PhD thesis (Glazier 2001). The interviews themselves focus upon four main themes: national, local and regional perceptions of the past; knowledge of Quseir al-Qadim (including history, folklore and recent activities at the site); the excavations and the archaeologists (encompassing social, economic, political and religious issues); and the role of archaeology and the past in the future development of Quseir.

Analysis

The interviews have uncovered new information on the recent history of Quseir al-Qadim and its relationship to the modern city of Quseir, whilst providing significant insights into how archaeological practice impacts upon people in terms of the construction of self-identity. They also gave the community archaeology team a chance to keep people in the city informed of the progress of the excavation, increasing contact with the community beyond the education programme by providing a forum for people to express their opinions on what they wished to see in the Heritage Centre. Interviewees have already emphasised the need to construct a Heritage Centre that encompasses the whole history of the region, from the ancient ports at Quseir al-Qadim to the modern, industrial history of the city.

Preliminary analysis of the data gathered suggests that the past does indeed play an active role in the construction of local identity in Quseir, primarily through a number of distinctive folktales related to both the site and the modern city itself. This natural identification of a society with its past is amplified by the continued archaeological investigations at Quseir al-Qadim. Indeed, one of the major issues raised during the interviews was the desire of many interviewees to know more about the excavation and to be kept informed of its progress.

5 Educational resources

An important component of the Community Archaeology Project is the creation of educational materials that introduce younger members of the community to findings about ancient Quseir. Initially this involved a series of school visits to the site, which was organised and carried out by Quseir Heritage and Susan Ballard, a graduate from the department of Archaeology at the University of Southampton. Currently, we are collaborating with teachers at the recently established Learning Development Centre of Quseir, which offers courses in English, Computing and Special Needs, and is funded by the Carpe Vitam Trust. An office in this Centre has been generously made available for the Community Archaeology Project, and Lamya Nasr el Nemr is now working closely with the 20 local teachers employed here to determine what kinds of archaeology-related teaching materials she can produce for use in their classes.

Site visits

Access to excavations provides a memorable educational experience for children, and Quseir Heritage have facilitated the organisation of visits to the site for children undertaking courses at the Learning Development Centre. Visits to the site are incorporated into the English and Special Needs classes, where children and adults engage in activities designed to promote their understanding of the ancient port. These activities have been designed by the teachers from the Centre, working in collaboration with Lamya Nasr el Nemr.

Children's books

The production of children's books based upon the site have been the resource most valued by the teachers at the Learning Centre (Conner *et al.* 2002a, 2002b). Based upon research in archaeological education (e.g. Cracknell and Corbishley 1986), and consultation with teachers and writers (both Egyptian and British), two books aimed at children of primary school age have been completed by Andrew Conner, Lamya Nasr el Nemr and Michael Seymour. A research project on the concept and design of these books was also produced by Conner (2001), who demonstrated the complexities of writing about antiquity for children. These books are currently used in classes at the Learning Centre, where they foster pride in Quseir and imaginative thinking about life in the past.

Artefact database

Community access to the digital database of all artefacts from the excavations is an educational priority. However, the size of the database (approximately 4,000 images) has made this unworkable in practical terms. In order to create a more accessible educational resource, our finds supervisor (Jill Phillips) has worked with Lamya Nasr el Nemr to produce a smaller database of the major finds, which will be used in the courses offered by the Learning Development Centre.

6 Photographic and video archive

As part of the Community Archaeology Project at Quseir, we have begun to create a photographic and video archive for exhibition in the Heritage Centre. The creation of a visual archive of the excavation ensures that the community has a record of both the event and the experience of the archaeological project. Furthermore, for those in Quseir who have not been able to visit the excavations – both in the present and in the future – there will be a permanent historical record of this key event in the history of city.

Photographic record

Photography of all aspects of the excavations at Quseir has been carried out, primarily focusing upon the people involved in the investigation and the activities in which they are engaged. This archive is intended to complement the 'scientific' photographic records produced as part of the excavations. While photos of local people are often taken during excavations, they have a tendency to get 'lost' in personal collections and are rarely sent to the community on completion of the project. During the most recent field season, James Phillips photographed all members of the local community working on the site, with the intention of creating a display in the Heritage Centre. The workers themselves will take an active role in selecting the images they wish to see presented.

Video record

Video footage of the day-to-day activities on the excavation and of the finds specialists working in camp has been taken, both as a record of the archaeological project and with the production of a display in mind. Lamya Nasr el Nemr and James Phillips have also conducted video interviews with site employees, where they discuss the significance of their work and the excavation itself.

7 Community-controlled merchandising

For communities like Quseir, where archaeological investigations have the potential to impact significantly on tourist development, it is important to consider the role of heritage-related merchandising in the local economy. One of the greatest concerns of the Community Archaeology Project is the manner in which the archaeological investigation at Quseir al-Qadim will be used in the context of tourism. As Silberman (1995: 259) has argued, modern mass tourism can have the effect of forcing a nation to become a parody of itself. This is particularly evident in Egypt, where the manufacturing of souvenirs is focused on reproducing age-old stereotypes of the Pharaonic period. For instance, the hotels in Quseir are adorned with Pharaonic representations of the past and the shops and bazaars brim with quasi-Pharaonic trinkets, yet the city itself is at least four and-a-half hours from any major Pharaonic monument. The Community Archaeology team has therefore initiated a programme for the production of merchandise inspired by finds from the site. Quseir Heritage will be involved in managing this programme, which aims to produce quality products that provide an alternative to the majority of souvenirs currently available. A set of pottery has been produced by a historic ceramic specialist, which we have placed on display in the Learning Development Centre to encourage feedback. The production of children's books (see above) also forms part of the merchandising strategy. Copies in English, German and Italian will be made available for sale to tourists in the Heritage Centre. The local community will not only be active in selecting the kinds of souvenirs that will be produced, but will play a key role in designing and marketing these products. The merchandising scheme will also contribute to the Heritage Centre becoming a self-sustaining resource.

Project logo and t-shirts

For both merchandising and communicative purposes, the team have produced a logo that represents and visually signifies the nature of the project (Figure 12.1). The project logo aims to convey something about the relationship between the past and the present in Quseir, highlighting features of the city such as the community, the buildings, the sea and the ancient heritage of the area; its design being the result of a joint effort between the team members and Quseir residents. More recently Lamya Nasr el Nemr

Figure 12.1 The logo for the Community Archaeology Project at Quseir.

has redesigned this logo so that it is suitable for reproduction on t-shirts and other merchandise. All profits from the sale of these items will go to Quseir Heritage.

SUMMARY

The Community Archaeology Project at Quseir is ongoing and at this stage it is difficult to present any firm conclusions. Throughout this chapter, we have highlighted the need for collaborative practice in archaeology, suggesting that it is no longer acceptable for archaeologists to reap the intellectual benefits of another society's heritage without providing that society with the opportunity to benefit equally from the endeavour. This is exaggerated in Egypt, a country in which local communities have been excluded from the process of discovering their past. The project has already served to foster an interest in the past amongst the local community, evident in the increasingly active role played by residents in making decisions concerning the direction of the Heritage Centre. Of more importance, however, is the extent to which the project has engendered a sense of ownership of the past and of pride in the history of the city: as one member of the local community remarked, 'History gives Quseir value; archaeology gives us substance.'

Community archaeology is not simply an ethical issue. As we suggested earlier, community involvement in the investigation of Quseir al-Qadim has the potential to transform our approach to, and understanding of, the archaeological evidence. Though interpretation is limited at this stage of the excavations, this is already apparent, particularly amongst those involved in the investigation of Mamluk levels. For instance, two members of the excavation team were taken by local excavators on a tour of a local mosque to examine the spatial layout of Islamic buildings; a trip that led them to question their initial interpretation of a trench. It is unlikely that this would have proved possible without community interaction in the investigation process. Similarly, excavators and finds specialists have been assisted in the identification of artefacts (particularly items of religious significance or charms), by members of the local community employed on site and by individuals visiting the camp. We believe that such assistance will prove immensely beneficial throughout the interpretation of the evidence.

Community involvement in an archaeological investigation also gives access to the considerable amount of local knowledge concerning archaeological sites; without discussion with the local community we would be unaware of the more recent activities conducted at Quseir al-Qadim. Interviews with elderly residents of Quseir, for example, have revealed the presence of a small fishing village at the northern extent of the site, abandoned some 50 years ago and now buried beneath an international hotel. Local knowledge is therefore of immense importance if we wish to create a total life history of Quseir al-Qadim.

The benefits of increased community involvement in archaeological practice do not end here. Interviews and discussions with members of the community have highlighted alternative perceptions of the past in Quseir, and through the incorporation of these perspectives a more comprehensive understanding of the site is attained. Quseir al-Qadim is not simply a Roman or Mamluk harbour, it is a place with much wider cultural meaning. The wealth of folklore that relates to the site provides us with further insights into how the past is experienced, and how it is negotiated and understood in the present. This is essential not simply because the modern climate of archaeology tells us that it is so, but because as archaeologists we benefit from a more diverse understanding of the past. As Shankland (1999) suggests, it is foolish to fix any one single meaning onto a monument, whether it is archaeological, historical, mythic or folkloric.

Community archaeology demands that we make fundamental changes to our disciplinary practice. While there are many strategies that can be adopted to initiate a community archaeology project, we have outlined a set of seven components that we believe are central to undertaking work of this nature. The Community Archaeology Project at Quseir has made a promising start – the start of something that will probably occupy many of us on the team for the rest of our lives.

ACKNOWLEDGEMENTS

Very special thanks go to Farid Mansour and Adel Aiesh of the Quseir Heritage Preservation Society, without whose support and advice it would not have been possible to undertake a project of this kind. We would also like to thank the mayor of Quseir, Mr Mohammed Amin, for his invaluable assistance during fieldwork. This research project is funded by the Peder Sager Wallenberg Charitable Trust, the British Academy, the Arts and Humanities Research Board (UK), and the Southampton University Research Grants Scheme. We are particularly grateful to Mr Peder Wallenberg for his substantial financial input into the project, and to Marie Johansen for organising office space for us in the Learning Development Centre. We are grateful for the advice and support provided by Dr Ali Soliman and the contributions of Eman Mohammed Attia, Diaa Abdul Aziz Gad and Mairin Ni Cheallaigh to fieldwork. Thanks also to Graeme Earl and Jill Phillips for work on the digital artefact database, and to the whole archaeological team who have been so supportive of our work. Finally, we would like to express our deepest thanks to David Peacock for providing the opportunity to initiate this project. Darren would like to dedicate this article to the memory of Ray Hewett, a man whose encouragement knew no bounds and whose support was never less than unstinting.

13

GLENBOW'S BLACKFOOT GALLERY

Working towards co-existence

Gerald T. Conaty

Over the past two decades considerable debate has arisen in anthropology juxtaposing the rights and obligations of the anthropologist with those of the people who constitute the subject matter of anthropological discourse. This intersection of anthropology and indigenous (and other marginalised) people is especially magnified within museums. These institutions have long served as repositories for the exotica collected from Native cultures and museum exhibits have been windows into these Other cultures. With rare exceptions these windows have been constructed and illuminated by Western curators and, therefore, present refracted views of their subjects. And yet, these exhibits are tremendously powerful vehicles for informing public knowledge and shaping public attitudes toward Other cultures.

As anthropologists have become increasingly aware that their ethnographies often say more about the authors than they do about the subject matter (Clifford 1988; Marcus and Fisher 1986), at the same time, indigenous people are resisting objectification and the exclusion from meaningful participation in the anthropological discourse (Said 1978). In Canada, this has led to a number of important collaborations between First Nations and museums (e.g. Conaty 1989).

The Glenbow Museum in Calgary, Alberta, Canada, working with a team of Blackfoot people and museum staff, has developed an extensive exhibit about the Blackfoot entitled *Nitsitapiisinni: Our Way of Life*. In this chapter I examine this exhibit in light of the issues of representation and explanation in the museum world. First, Glenbow will be situated within the general development of museums. This will let me assess if what we are doing is truly unique. Then an overview of Blackfoot culture and history will illustrate how the historical background of the Blackfoot affects the way they interact with museums. Finally, I shall discuss some of the public's reaction to the gallery and evaluate if, by doing what we know to be right and important with our Blackfoot partners, we are distancing ourselves from the mainstream of society's values and norms.

MUSEUM HISTORY

Museums are the product of the society that supports them. Although the concept of a museum can be traced back to ancient Greece, the philosophy and purpose of contemporary museums were shaped in eighteenth-century Europe. It is important to understand these developments if we are to ascertain the value of our current endeavours.

As the Age of Discovery made Europeans aware of the vastness and diversity of the world which lay beyond the continental boundaries, the explorers of these new worlds brought back samples of natural and human phenomena for those who had financed the expeditions. These collections were often housed in rooms filled with 'cabinets of curiosities' where the gentry could reflect upon the strange wonders of the world. This structure began to change near the end of the eighteenth century. With the French Revolution, collections that had belonged to the Crown, the Church, and the aristocracy became the property of the State (Grasset 1996: 190) and were put on exhibit for all the people of France. The Decree of 27 July 1793 opened the Louvre and guaranteed that the people of France would have the right of access to the collections. Later, as Napoleon I (1804–15) conquered most of Europe and North Africa, his plunder was brought back to France and housed in museums throughout the country. Collections that initially served as mementoes of the past and evidence of present wealth soon became objects of study, sources of patriotism, and a medium for post-revolutionary propaganda.

In Britain, the creation of a national collection began earlier with the founding of the British Museum in 1753. But real democratising of museums in Britain lagged behind as conservative opinion reacted to the revolutionary attitudes of the continent and access to the national collection continued to be restricted to those who were regarded as acceptable (i.e. aristocratic males). However, by the 1850s a new role of civic responsibility was emerging for museums in Britain (Bennett 1996). The gentry believed that if museums were opened for public access, labourers would eschew the local tavern for a chance to ponder the art and artefacts of Western civilizations. Time spent in such contemplation would lead to character reformation and a general improvement in the nature of the working class.

This civic responsibility continues to be important to museums, although it is now globally extended. The underlying message has come to reflect the value of progress. Often this message is conveyed most effectively through the use of the ethnological collections, where the inevitability of progress emerges from cross-cultural comparisons.

As both Cameron (1971) and Ames (1992) observe, the creation of these public collections had a profound effect on the meaning embedded within them:

> the public . . . came to believe that they had the right to expect that the collections would present and interpret the world in some way consistent with the values they held to be good, with the collective representations they held to be appropriate, and with the view of social reality they held to be true.
>
> (Ames 1992: 21)

Museums thus became temples for society (Cameron 1971: 17), reifying principles and beliefs. They became places where the individual could compare his/her private view of reality with the view held by society in general. However, it is important to remember that this reality had been constructed by the educated classes of society and that the perceptions of more marginal groups were often excluded from this reality.

The Glenbow is firmly rooted in this tradition. The collection was amassed during the mid-twentieth century by Eric Harvie, a wealthy Albertan with eclectic interests and a passion for collecting (Dempsey 1991). As his collections grew, he established the Glenbow as a venue through which he could share his treasures with other Albertans. Staff were hired to actively collect in various disciplines and to develop exhibits and public programmes. In 1967, Harvie gifted much of his collection to the Province of Alberta in commemoration of Canada's centennial. The collection has helped Albertans to define who they are by showing them the wealth of their collective heritage. Those parts of the collection that were not from Alberta, such as the medieval armour or the West African material, affirm Alberta as a unique place which attracts treasures from around the world.

THE BLACKFOOT

The Blackfoot people are a cultural and linguistic entity who, according to their own traditions, occupied an area on the northwestern plains which extended southward from the North Saskatchewan River to the Yellowstone River and eastward from the Rocky Mountains to the Cypress Hills and Great Sand Hills of present-day western Saskatchewan.[1] They refer to themselves as Nitsitapi – the Real People – and believe that they were created within this territory.

Prior to contact with European fur traders and explorers, the Blackfoot were nomadic hunter-gatherers who relied largely upon dogs for transportation. Bison provided a substantial portion of their diet and a preponderance of large, complex bison kill sites within their territory attests to the importance of this species. Other animals were also important and plant resources were regularly harvested. While it is difficult to reconstruct the social system of long ago, oral tradition indicates that the people regarded themselves as a single cohesive cultural group; they had not separated into the present tribal divisions.

After the beginning of the eighteenth century the history of the Blackfoot people began to reflect world history (Arima 1995; Cocking 1908; Dempsey 1965, 1972, 1980; Ewers 1980, 1982; Hanks and Hanks 1950; McClintock 1910; Raczka 1979; Schultz and Donaldson 1930; Thompson 1962). The acquisition of the horse and gun, together with increasing incursions of Euro-Canadian and American traders, changed the social and political structures of people throughout the northwestern plains (Conaty 1995; Ewers 1980, 1982; Lewis 1942; Nugent 1993). Ultimately, the contact with Euro-Canadian/American traders brought disease and alcoholism. The winter counts of Bad Head (Dempsey 1965) and Bull Plume (Raczka 1979) record that epidemics of smallpox and other diseases devastated the Blackfoot people at least every 20 years between about 1765 and 1879. Often, as many as two-thirds of the population died during each of these catastrophes. In addition, by the 1870s the bison were becoming scarce and the influx of Europeans was increasing.

Trans-Mississippian immigration swelled in the American West by the mid-nineteenth century. Gold discoveries in California and mineral strikes in Montana lured fortune-seekers westward, stressing the ecology and intensifying conflicts among the First Nations of the Plains. As the United States government searched for a feasible rail route to the Pacific, they also attempted to end the disputes among the First Nations and enable safer passage for the immigrants. The Lame Bull Treaty (1855) acknowledged Blackfoot priority to an area which included most of modern-day Montana. Continued pressure from miners and ranchers led the federal government to reduce this area several times over the next 50 years. Most of these reductions were done unilaterally through executive orders of the President of the United States.

In Canada, the Peigan, Kainai, and Siksika entered into Treaty Seven (1877) with the federal government. Oral tradition (Treaty Seven Elders *et al.* 1996) demonstrates that this peace treaty enabled Euro-Canadians to settle in and use the resources of traditional Blackfoot territory in exchange for helping the Blackfoot meet the challenges of their changing world. The federal government regarded these negotiations as a land transaction and, soon after the signing, confined the Blackfoot to reserves as wards of the state. Over the next few decades, large portions of the reserves were sold as a means of paying for the expense of maintaining the Blackfoot people, or were given away by the government to politically influential neighbours. The concerted effort to destroy traditional culture and force assimilation, which was detailed in the Indian Act (1876),[2] promoted education by religious denominations and a directed loss of language. At the same time, political leaders were appointed by the government, thereby denying the people responsible and representative government.

Although it was argued that assimilation was the goal, contact with the broader society was severely limited. No goods could be sold outside of the reserve without written consent of the Indian Agent, a clause that has never been officially repealed from the Indian Act. From the late 1880s until the early 1900s, people could not leave the reserve without a pass issued by the Indian Agent. Food rations were distributed by the Indian Agent. Voting in federal elections was prohibited in the United States until 1924 and in Canada until 1962. These restrictions could be revoked for individuals who were willing to renounce their Native affiliation and thereby abandon the services that were their right through the Treaty.

As a result, the Blackfoot people find themselves marginalised within Canadian and American societies. They feel that as signatories to peace treaties, they have not abrogated their aboriginal rights or their status as a nation. They believe sacred objects, many of which are held by museums, are of central importance to their own cultural and physical survival. But the Blackfoot find that their perspective and their requests for repatriation have not always been heard within the museum community. They do not necessarily agree with the idea of a museum as repository of a national identity, especially when the national identity often has no room for their own cultural identity.

GLENBOW'S CHANGING PERSPECTIVE

Glenbow began to develop a new kind of relationship with First Nations[3] in 1990 (Conaty 1999, 2000, 2001, nd; Conaty and Janes 1997; Janes and Conaty 1992, 1998). Sacred objects were returned on loan to First Nations communities for use in traditional ceremonies that are vital for the survival of their cultures. We also established a First Nations Advisory Council to offer insights and advice on First Nations-related issues at the museum. To facilitate our growing commitment to First Nations concerns, a Treaty Seven liaison position was created and a Siksika person was recruited to fill it. As well, First Nations people were hired to develop and deliver school and public programmes about First Nations cultures.

By the mid-1990s we had expanded our community-based programmes and were working with the Plains Indians Cultural Survival School in Calgary. This project brought students to the museum one day each week throughout the school year. In each of the four years of the project, the students conceived and developed an exhibit which opened to the public in May, near the end of the school year. The public response to these exhibits was very positive. As a museum, we saw the power of personal statements and exhibits which were developed from a first-person perspective.

In 1998 Glenbow signed a formal Memorandum of Understanding with the Mookaakin Foundation of the Blood Tribe (or Kainai).[4] The Mookaakin Foundation had been established as an entity to negotiate the repatriation of Kainai sacred material. They felt that a formal agreement with Glenbow would enhance their stature in the view of many museums. Glenbow has subsequently assisted in the return of several sacred bundles from other institutions in Canada and the United States as well as from our own collection. In return, members of the Mookaakin Foundation have provided advice and assistance in the care and interpretation of items of their material culture in the collections of Glenbow and other museums.

These developments created an atmosphere of openness and experimentation at Glenbow. They also contributed to a foundation of mutual trust and respect between Glenbow and First Nations. As our relationships with First Nations unfolded, it became increasingly clear that our permanent exhibits no longer reflected the spirit of our partnerships. In 1998 we invited 17 Blackfoot people to work with us in developing an exhibit that would reflect their culture and history as they know it. These individuals are ceremonial leaders and teachers and, according to Blackfoot practices, have the right to speak about their traditional ways. They carefully considered our invitation and then accepted it. However, the Blackfoot made it clear that they were not participating just to help Glenbow create an exhibit. They saw this project as an opportunity to develop an educational place where future generations of Blackfoot youth can learn the fundamentals of their own culture. This perception of Glenbow as a site of Blackfoot education is an incredible demonstration of the interconnectedness that has developed between us. We are no longer an imperialistic institution which misrepresents their culture. We have become partners in presenting their story, in their words, so that it can be explained and preserved. This is a considerable shift from the more traditional nature and purpose of museums.

CONCEPTUALIZING AND DEVELOPING THE GALLERY

The exhibit development process was lengthy, but not arduous. We brought people together at bi-weekly or monthly intervals and listened to open and sometimes wide-ranging discussions. These meetings took place alternately at the Glenbow and in the Blackfoot communities. As the Blackfoot became more frequent visitors at Glenbow, their sense of ownership in the project and in the museum grew. Meetings in the community took the museum staff outside the institutional walls and introduced new ways of thinking.

At meetings the staff needed to be involved in the discussions while, at the same time, creating a record of those discussions for future reference and reflection. Our team was hesitant to discuss issues openly in the presence of mechanical recording devices. At the same time, we found that note-taking kept us focused on recording the conversation without necessarily listening to what was being said. Our solution was to designate two people as recorders who would try to capture the discussions verbatim. These recorders could later cross-check their notes, enhancing the content. Other staff participated more fully in the discussions, listening especially from the perspective of their various roles in the project. The designers, for example, focused on issues that might shape the form and look of the exhibit, while the curators looked for content material.

The discussions were generally informal and wide-ranging, guided only by the most skeletal of agendas. At this early stage we were trying to discover the essential elements of Blackfoot culture, elements that are intuitive to the Blackfoot but may not be at all obvious to a non Blackfoot person. At times we focused the discussion on particular topics or clarification of specific issues. Often, however, attempts at an agenda-driven, Eurocentric meeting led to frustration on everyone's part. In keeping with Blackfoot protocol we ended each topical discussion by having each person speak, in turn, thereby ensuring that everyone's voice was heard. Blackfoot team members were adamant that Glenbow staff contribute to this discussion.

Many of the concepts and issues that were raised could not be expressed well in English. At these times the Blackfoot team members engaged in discussions that were entirely in Blackfoot. Staff understood very little of the language and waited patiently for issues to be resolved and the discussion to be translated. However, because the two languages are so different, these translations seldom reflected the range and depth of the Blackfoot discussion. Our development process was also prolonged by an inability to easily communicate complex ideology. Blackfoot world-view is vastly different from Euro-Canadian understanding and cannot easily be discussed in English. The appropriate words just do not exist. At times we all became frustrated as we struggled to find a common understanding. Yet it was crucial to find this common ground, for if the Glenbow staff could not grasp the meaning of issues, then we would never be able to convey this knowledge to the larger public. In the end, the language and designs we finally agreed upon are accurate reflections of the Blackfoot reality. Yet, they are conveyed in terms which all members of the team – both Blackfoot and Glenbow staff – understand. Communication is the underlying principle of any exhibit and our cross-cultural exchanges within the team enhanced our presentation to the public.

Many smaller ad hoc meetings took place between the larger gatherings. Often staff were invited to attended sacred ceremonies in the communities. These occasions kept the discussions going and enabled staff and Blackfoot to become better acquainted. They were also opportunities for people to elaborate on any discussion which had taken place in Blackfoot. As people reflected on the meetings, some issues stood out as important. These issues were explored in the small-group meetings. As we came to know each other better as individuals, we found that our discussions became more fruitful. We were becoming aware of each other's underlying assumptions about the world and the project. We were beginning to develop a common world-view.

After two years of discussion we had amassed a copious compendium of notes without having a firm theme or storyline emerge. One attempt at forging a single-sentence gallery vision statement was a disaster – this was not a Blackfoot methodology. At this stage, museum expertise became important. The three ethnology staff members met for two days to review all of the notes. Each separate idea was written on a piece of paper. These were then sorted into piles of similar ideas which became the storyline framework for the exhibit. This framework was to shift as artefacts and visual components were selected, but it was a first step. We took this framework back to the entire team for approval and revision. Several meetings were necessary as people reflected on our presentation and offered their careful critique.

The gallery layout, selection of artefacts, images, two- and three-dimensional designs, and the creation of text then proceeded together. Repeated visits by Blackfoot team members to our collection storage taught us how to understand the meaning behind beadwork and quillwork designs. Similarly, we began to understand how the Blackfoot felt about the photographs, paintings and sculptures. With this background, museum staff made a preliminary selection of images and artefacts. The entire team reviewed these selections, suggested some changes, and eventually approved the material to be exhibited.

The text was also subjected to close scrutiny. The Blackfoot story is very complex and it was tempting to create long, detailed narratives. However, museum experience has shown that it is very difficult to create text that the visitor will read (Carter 1999; Ekvar 1999; Gilmore and Sabine 1999). Words needed to be chosen extremely carefully. At the same time, the Blackfoot were ever-mindful of ensuring that the text was accurate and that the language conveyed a positive image rather than reinforcing negative stereotypes. Moreover, as we had found at earlier meetings, it can be very difficult to translate or interpret Blackfoot concepts. We all struggled together to find clear, concise ways of expressing these cultural foundations. Each version of the text was read to small groups (four or five individuals at the most) and careful notes were made of changes. These changes were then compiled and another draft was read to the small groups. All of the text was written in the first person, and needed to be constructed as though the Blackfoot were speaking. This can be a perilous undertaking for a non-Blackfoot curator as it raises issues of cultural appropriation and can even be interpreted as creating a work of fiction. How could I, as a Euro-Canadian, presume to understand how the Blackfoot would write about their history and culture?

After many close readings, text was approved which captured the essential elements of Blackfoot culture without providing an encyclopaedic description of the culture. As the Blackfoot indicated at the start of the project, the intent is to provide an introduction and overview. More detailed information should be sought from the traditionalists, who can teach properly in an oral context.

We also wanted to include Blackfoot words in the text as a constant reminder that this is not an exhibit about Glenbow's collection of Blackfoot artefacts; it is an exhibit about Blackfoot culture. People, places and objects are all referred to by using Blackfoot words with English translations. Unfortunately, there is no standardized Blackfoot spelling and many variations exist among all four communities. We resolved these differences by having a small sub-committee work out spellings we could use. This has provided us with a rationale for using particular variations whenever our spelling has been criticized.

The graphic designs were also carefully reviewed to ensure accuracy and appropriateness. For example, the circular 'drums' which are suspended from the ceiling to help hide the open duct-work, are painted with traditional Blackfoot design elements. At first the designs we proposed were copies of drums which are currently used in ceremonies. It soon became clear that these designs are very special and that it is inappropriate to use them out of context. The elements of the design could be used separately, as long as they are not combined in certain ways. This type of culture-specific knowledge was not always immediately apparent to the non-Blackfoot team members. These discussions helped us identify topics that needed clarification for the public and informed our presentations in the gallery.

This process required incredible patience on the part of everyone. Museum staff, who had developed skills and expertise in creating interesting, dynamic exhibits, were taken aback when 'good' ideas could not be operationalized because they contravened a cultural protocol. Often, a more detailed explanation from the Blackfoot could not be articulated because this would have revealed sacred information which should be conveyed only by way of a formal ceremony.

Over the course of the exhibit development many of the Blackfoot team members expressed frustration at the length of time the project was taking. It can take a long time to conceptualize, develop and produce an exhibit. *Nitsitapiisinni* is an especially complex exhibit, transforming a rectangular cement box into a similitude of the Blackfoot environment. Text overlaid with audio and video created a multi-layered information system. All of this required time to compile, edit, design, install and co-ordinate. Team members were kept aware of the progress of the physical development, and special arrangements were made for the team to view and assist in the production and installation. During the course of the project the Blackfoot gained a new appreciation for the culture of museums. In the end, they were well satisfied at how their ideas had been given form. It was a process that was new to all of us and, in the end, the Blackfoot were able to say that the museum had 'got it right'.

NITSITAPIISINNI: OUR WAY OF LIFE

We begin the gallery by introducing the visitor to the Blackfoot world-view. Blackfoot understand themselves to be a part of Creation in which almost everything is animate. Stars, planets, animals, plants, rocks and the earth itself are the Other Beings with whom the Blackfoot share their world. In order to survive and prosper, it is important that all beings understand how they are related to one another and to strive to maintain balance and equilibrium. The Blackfoot contribute to this balance through ceremonies and songs given to them by other living beings and by the Creator. Songs that accompany the ceremonies invoke the spirit of the Other Beings and are aural expressions of the linkages between humans and all Other Beings. This introductory area relates some of the ancient stories which explain how human beings were helped by Other Beings. We also use this area to discuss the spiritual significance of tipi designs and the importance of proper Blackfoot protocol in the transfer of sacred objects. Above the tipi, a fibre-optic skyscape changes in time with an audio explanation of star stories which tie the Blackfoot to the beings in the heavens.

Throughout our discussions it was reiterated that Blackfoot traditions are taught through storytelling. We created a space for storytelling by designing a circular mini-amphitheatre, where visitors can sit on wooden benches and select one of five videos. Artefacts related to the stories are clearly visible from the seats and a canvas curtain, painted to resemble a tipi liner, creates a pathway behind the viewer and helps confine sound. When school groups or public programme audiences convene here, the video is turned off and the space becomes an intimate, relaxing classroom.

When visitors leave the stories they enter a clan camp (Figure 13.1). An open platform has: a bison hide staked out, ready for processing; berries and dry meat, which are being combined into pemmican; a pit where bones are being boiled for their fat; and a variety of tools. Another case contains children's umbilical cord amulets, clothes and toys. Photographs and clothing lead to discussions of leadership and the meaning behind eagle feather headdresses, face painting and hairstyles. We have also re-created part of an arbour from a pow-wow. These displays put Blackfoot people within their social context. We discuss gender roles and the responsibilities and authority of everyone toward each other. The setting is idealized, not tied to a specific time or place. While the values discussed are ancient, they continue to be relevant.

Figure 13.1 In the clan camp area there is a sense of the outdoors while topics are discussed such as traditional leadership, pow-wows, and the *ookaan*, or sundance. (Photograph courtesy of Glenbow Museum)

235

Although the clans usually camped separately, each year they gathered for an *ookaan* (often called a sundance). This is a very sacred occasion and it required a great deal of consideration before we could determine how to portray it. We created a circular space and used enlarged archival photographs to create a mural impression of a circle camp. Each tribe is represented by one photograph. Rather than use artefacts or text, we produced a video in which people speak of the importance of the *ookaan* and of their own experiences. This presents an accessible, human perspective for the non-Blackfoot visitor.

It is impossible to understand the Blackfoot world without experiencing the immensity of the northwestern Plains. Leaving the circle camp, the visitor walks onto the prairie. A mounted bison stands on an fibreglass cliff, the base of which contains both articles made from the bison and those that were used to hunt them. *Iniskim* (stones used in a buffalo calling ceremony) and a split-horn headdress relate the sacred aspects of the animal. To one side, two large (8ft × 10ft) rear-projection screens take the visitor on a visual trip across traditional Blackfoot territory in each season. To the other side, maps and photographs help explain the economic and the sacred geography and their interconnection. Finally, an exhibit of horse tack underscores the continuing importance of the equestrian culture.

Up to this point, the gallery has been very open and curvilinear with long sight lines. As the visitor enters the section concerned with the arrival of Euro-Canadian/American traders, the circles break apart into hemispheres and the space becomes confined. The visitor learns that trade, which was initially between equals, became weighted in favour of the newcomers. In each generation alcoholism, smallpox and other diseases reduced the population by up to three-quarters. As well, the bison began to disappear and people from other cultures encroached on traditional Blackfoot land. The governments of Canada and the United States signed treaties with the Blackfoot but the intent of these agreements and the extent to which they have been honoured remain matters of serious contention.

The Reservation Era of the gallery is constructed with walls at right angles, creating small spaces with relatively low ceilings. The feeling is one of confinement. The imposition of a foreign culture is portrayed by examining housing, residential schools, loss of land, and stereotyping at tourist resorts and rodeos. Photographs of ranching, farming, residential schools, and the Calgary Stampede as well as paintings by Winhold Reiss and Nicholas de Grandmaison document the perseverance of these people. Regardless of the circumstances of the images, the people who are portrayed are strong and proud.

The gallery ends by re-entering an open circle where people speak on video of the important issues of today. Young and old explain their current challenges and reveal the pride they feel for their culture and traditions. Education will prepare people for the modern world and will also instil traditional values in the youth. Health care is the responsibility of everyone in the community. Repatriation is bringing sacred items back home, making communities strong again. We also invite young artists to create works to be exhibited where they can tell of the challenges of youth. The message is positive.

The gallery is a very rich aural experience. Sounds from the video and audio carry throughout and create a living ambience without distracting or interrupting the visitor experience. We have also created listening stations where the visitor can lift a telephone receiver and hear one of the Blackfoot team members discussing some element of the displays. This is available in both English and Blackfoot. All of this creates a living atmosphere and visitors seem to react by being more animated and by interacting with one another. There is a sense of exploration and discovery.

GALLERY ASSESSMENT

In 1989 the Canadian Museums Association and the Assembly of First Nations convened the Task Force on First Peoples and Museums.[5] The final report (Task Force 1992) called for Canadian museums to become more inclusive of First Nations at all levels of their operations. Changes were called for in museum governance, employment opportunities, collections care, exhibits and interpretation. *Nitsitapiisinni* embodies the spirit of those recommendations. Blackfoot people worked with Glenbow staff as full partners, not as consultants or advisors. The gallery reflects the co-existence of two peoples and their co-operation in achieving a common goal.

Reaction from the public during the first three months of the exhibit confirms the success of this collaborative approach. Over 1,300 people (Native and non-Native) attended the opening on 3 November 2002, and expressed overwhelmingly positive reactions. The gallery has already become a destination for school groups from the Blackfoot reserves in Canada and the United States and teachers are using the book which was developed in conjunction with the gallery as a learning aid. It will take several years to assess the gallery's impact on programmes for both reserve and non-reserve schools. Comment forms are given to teachers at the end of each programme, but considerable time must elapse before identifiable trends emerge from these responses.

Within Glenbow the success of exhibits is measured more directly by comparing actual with projected attendance. Three times each year the museum completely revamps its temporary exhibit space and focuses promotion of a particular theme. Projected audience growth has been made for a five-year period and the success of these themes is measured, in part, by how close actual attendance is to the estimate. These projections are based on a steady linear growth in attendance with an expected increase in visitor-generated revenue. Continued growth in attendance-based revenues is necessary for Glenbow's survival as a not-for-profit organization.

Nitsitapiisinni was the themed attraction from November 2001 to the end of January 2002. The projected attendance for the first six weeks of the exhibit was 29,700, while actual attendance was 11,598, creating a shortfall of 59.74 per cent. Visits by schools are not included in these numbers, but the period does include the Christmas holiday season. For managers and Board members who are concerned with an institution's appeal to the public, these numbers may indicate a lack of success.

Another indicator of an exhibit's acceptability is the response of funding bodies. A project which strikes a sympathetic chord should find a host of sponsors. One that presents controversial issues or is critical of normative values may be less readily supported. As Glenbow staff and management began to conceive of the Blackfoot Gallery Project we considered hiring a consultant to undertake an environmental scan to assess funding potential. However, we were convinced that this project was both necessary and appropriate and assumed that funding would be relatively easy to acquire.

In fact, fund-raising was one of the most difficult aspects of the project. We thought that the private sector would be very supportive of this initiative. As Table 13.1 shows,

Table 13.1 Financial support for the development of Nitsitapiisinni: Our Way of Life

Source	Amount $ Can.	% of total
Government of Alberta		
Government of Alberta 2005 Centennial Initiative	1,000,000	52.2
Calgary Community Lottery Board	400,000	20.8
Community Facility Enhancement Program	125,000	6.5
Calgary Region Arts Foundation	2,000	0.1
Subotal	1,527,000	79.4
Government of Canada		
Canada Council for the Arts	2,000	0.1
Museum Assistance Program	51,000	3.6
Subotal	53,000	3.7
Corporate		
Shell Canada Ltd.	250,000	13.0
(For admission of First Nations people for two years; Blackfoot Gallery programmer for three months)		
Subotal	250,000	13.0
Private Donations		
Calgary Foundation New Sun Fund	50,000	2.6
(Private donation for Blackfoot School Programmer)		
Other donations	35,000	1.8
Subtotal	85,000	4.4
Total	1,915,000	

our funding came primarily from the more traditional government sources. Why did we misjudge the project's appeal?

In part, our experience reflects changes in gifting philosophies and the priorities of Calgary's corporations. Rather than donating very large sums to projects situated in a single metropolitan area, these companies now tend to spread their money throughout entire regions or the whole country. Smaller amounts of money donated over a broader geography bring greater exposure to the largess of the sponsor.

Calgary is still largely a resource-based city and the companies we targeted for funding were the major oil companies. Most of their holdings in southern Alberta (i.e. Blackfoot territory) are old fields. Relationships with the people of southern Alberta are well established. Most of the new developments are occurring in the oil sands of northeastern Alberta and there is a priority to support initiatives that show the sponsors to be good corporate citizens in that region. Our focus was not aligned with the focus of Calgary corporations.

A second approach to fund-raising involved soliciting members of Calgary's wealthy to spearhead a fund-raising campaign among their peers. The response was surprising and disheartening. Older members of this establishment contributed cash but felt that it is now time for a younger generation to show their community commitment. Yet, we could not find a younger person (50 years old or younger) to lead this initiative. This reflects a growing trend in Canada where potential donors, who are faced with a growing number of requests for help, are showing signs of donor fatigue and are reacting by being more selective in their placement of resources. The arts and culture communities in Canada are finding that it is increasingly difficult to recruit support as they vie with health care and education for funding.

Important exceptions to this pattern were the individual contributions of several anonymous donors and the generous support of Shell Canada Ltd. One donor has directed money toward Glenbow's First Nation programmes for several years and is now specifically supporting the development of new school programmes to be conducted in the new gallery. Shell's funding has enabled Glenbow to hire a Blackfoot person as a full-time gallery interpreter and is paying the admission of all First Nations people from 2001 to 2003. The senior management of Shell Canada Ltd. saw the importance of the gallery's message in strengthening understanding among all segments of Canadian society.

Glenbow is a non-governmental institution which prides itself on an ability to work with the support of corporate Alberta. Alberta, perhaps more than most provinces in Canada, espouses an ethic of free enterprise where the marketplace determines the value of goods and services. We need to think carefully about these funding and attendance issues and consider what they say about the public's response to our initiative to work so closely with the Blackfoot and to enable them to speak for themselves.

DRAWING CONCLUSIONS

What are we to make of this assessment? The concept of the project and the process by which it was developed lie at the very forefront of museological practice. If the postmodern arguments for inclusion and full participation of First Nations (and other marginalised groups) reflect a societal shift of values, then this project should have attracted more funding more easily and should have higher visitation rates.

The issue of funding is, of course, very complex and this project is not the only museum exhibit that has had a difficult time finding sponsors. As I mentioned earlier in this chapter, corporate sponsors are more receptive to projects that have close links to their own images and self-interests. Moreover, the arts sector is a phenomenally underfunded segment of the Canadian economy. While programming receives some federal money, there is very little available for infrastructure, including the construction of new permanent exhibits. All of the major Canadian museum and art gallery facilities are approaching middle age and are in great need of overhaul.

Layered on the politics of the arts is the subject matter of *Nitsitapiisinni*. The gallery singles out a particular First Nation and considers its distinctiveness from the rest of Canadian society. It is tempting to draw the conclusion that Canadian society (or at least the Calgarian element of it) is disinterested in learning about a marginalised segment of our society. A much more pessimistic view would see this as intolerance toward First Nations cultures and perspectives.

These responses to the gallery also reflect the structure of Canadian society and the historical relationship between First Nations and the majority. First Nations and the newcomers were equal at the time of contact. This equality was reflected in the nature of the interactions. By the late nineteenth century First Nations had become dependent and the settlers were no longer compelled to honour or respect aboriginal rights. In writing about the current relationship between First Nations and Canadian society, Michael Ignatieff cogently argues:

> the meaning they [First Nations] draw from the failure to assimilate them is clear: they must reacquire their rights of self-government and take responsibility, at the individual and collective level, for their destiny.
>
> This fundamental lesson, however, is still not accepted by the majority community in Canada. You could blame this on simple racism, but that would be to ignore the real problem. Assimilationist policies would never have been pursued . . . had settlers not believed that a political community must be composed of people who share the same values, culture, and assumptions, and that political equality can be accorded only to those who are recognizably the same. Shedding this belief is hard, for it is an ideal and not just a prejudice.
>
> (Ignatieff 2000: 61–2)

The Blackfoot people who participated in the development of *Nitisitapiisinni* understand this project in these ideological terms. It is their chance to tell their story in their own words. This is a firm resistance to assimilation. They also see the gallery as a statement of their right to exist as a unique cultural and political entity within the larger Canadian society.

At the same time, the Blackfoot strongly believe in the principle of co-existence. That is, they believe in the necessity of living side by side, with respect for one another in spite of significant differences. They have co-existed with the plants and animals of their world since the time the Creator brought them together in this part of the world. Their ancestors believed that their treaties with the Crown and with the government of the United States were agreements to co-exist with new immigrants. The Blackfoot would share their territory and knowledge and the newcomers would provide assistance through a most traumatic time. Neither party, the Blackfoot thought, would dominate the other. For the many reasons discussed here, this has not been the case.

Those of us who have worked on this gallery believe that it is an example of what can be achieved when people believe in co-existence. The issues I have raised regarding funding and attendance suggest that an ideological gap remains between the assimilationist and the co-existence model of Canadian society. Perhaps this gallery can become a forum for the open debate of these models and the ideals which underlie them. We can only hope that ultimately this will help us understand ourselves as a community in a world of ever-increasing complexity.

ACKNOWLEDGEMENTS

An earlier version of this paper was presented at the 28th Chacmool Conference, University of Calgary, 11–14 November 1999. I want to thank Mike Robinson, Irene Kerr, Bob Janes, Frank Weasel Head, Gwyn Langemann, Beth Carter, Margaret Hanna, Alison Brown and Laura Peers for their thoughtful comments on various drafts of this paper. Members of the *Nitsitapiisinni* Gallery team are: Frank Weasel Head (Kainai),

Andy Black Water (Kainai), Charlie Crow Chief (Kainai), Pete Standing Alone (Kainai), Rosie Day Rider (Kainai), Louise Crop Eared Wolf (Kainai), Jenny Bruised Head (Kainai), Pat Provost (Apatohsipikani), Allan Pard (Apatohsipikani), Jerry Potts (Apatohsipikani), Jim Swag (Apatohsipikani), Earl Old Person (Amsskaapipikani), Tom Blackweasel (Amsskaapipikani), Doreen Blackweasel (Amsskaapipikani), Donna Weaselchild (Siksika), Herman Yellow Old Woman (Siksika), Clarence Wolfleg (Siksika), Cliff Crane Bear (Siksika/Glenbow), Beth Carter (Glenbow), Terry Gunvordahl (Glenbow), Irene Kerr (Glenbow), Lynette Walton (Glenbow), Cindy Maurice (Glenbow), Gwyneth Claughton (Glenbow), Anita Dammer (Glenbow), Gerry Conaty (Glenbow).

NOTES

1 'Blackfoot' is an Euro-American term which encompasses the Kainai (Blood), Siksika, Apatohsipikani (North Peigan) and Amsskaapipikani (South Peigan) people who share a common language (with significant dialect differences) and other cultural practices. Each group has a unique identity and there is no word in their language for the general term 'Blackfoot'.
2 The Indian Act (1876) was federal legislation which defined who Indians were and limited their rights. Although this act predates the 1877 treaty negotiations, there is no historical record indicating that the Blackfoot were informed of this act or the restrictions that it placed on them.
3 In Canada the term 'First Nations' refers to people of aboriginal descent who, in the past, would have been called Indians. It does not include either the Métis or the Inuit.
4 The Mookaakin Foundation was established by members of the Kainai as a not-for-profit organization which could raise funds to facilitate the repatriation of sacred material from museums and private collectors. The Foundation has also acted on behalf of the Kainai in repatriation negotiations with various museums. The Mookaakin board includes Francis First Charger, Pete Standing Alone, Frank Weasel Head, Narcisse Blood, Martin Heavy Head, Dorothy First Rider, Eugene Creighton and Gerry Conaty.
5 The Assembly of First Nations (AFN) is a political organization which represents the majority of Status Indians (that is, people whom the Government of Canada recognizes as of 'Indian' descent) in Canada. The Canadian Museums Association is the professional association of museums and museum workers in Canada. Membership is voluntary and the CMA has no means of enforcing standards or practices.

AFTERWORD

Beyond the frame

Paul Tapsell

'I was born here, and I die here. It is not what it was, yet – it is my home, my *kainga tuturu*. I am 80 years old and more, and I have looked upon many strange sights in my time . . . Work, work every day, every day – What does the *pakeha* [white man] work for anyway? He makes a terrible lot of trouble for himself, and he has got such expensive *wahines* [women] to keep, with their hats as big as the wheels of a bicycle, and their shoes so soft and fine and pretty that they are not fit to walk on the common earth in. Yet the *pakeha* seems to like it all! He is a strange being the *pakeha*. My thought is this: He is *porangi* – he is mad! You're a *pakeha* too, friend, but I'm glad you're not a *turihi* [tourist], one of those people who come round with little picture-machines hung over their shoulders by yellow straps, and who want to make pictures with them of every single thing they see, and who go sniffing around our *whares* (homes) and poking our beds with their umbrellas and saying "How dirty!" They're a particularly *porangi* tribe of *pakehas*, I think.'[1]

We navigate through life from one experience to the next, framing our perceptions of the world and sending them into the future as formalised memories from which we hope the next generation will benefit. One hundred years ago my ancestor spoke his thoughts about tourists – their cameras and intrusions, the results of which now rest, disconnected, in hundreds of museums worldwide. His musings of yesterday allow us a special opportunity to reflect on our discipline in the present, especially concerning those memories that still frame ancestral portraits, and gently remind us that defining any culture continues to be more than a one-way conversation exclusive to the living.

YESTERDAY

From birth to death, our everyday thoughts and perceptions are shaped by what we believe are important and we deal with such judgements accordingly. Measuring and prioritising the importance of any particular event, action or thing remains as critical to our social, economic and political survival today as it did for our ancestors. The context and associated challenges may have changed over millennia, but the finality of misreading importance has not. An error in judgement can still be fatal both individually (for example, the thousands of people who die on roads around the world daily) and

242

Figure 14.1 Tauwhitu, Ohinemutu Village, Rotorua, c.1900. (Photograph courtesy June
    Northcroft Grant)

collectively (as was the case with Chernobyl). It was the same for our ancestors, but
with one critical difference: genealogical accountability. Error in judgement could amount
to extinction of not just individuals, but also a whole kin group and associated identity
to estates. That we exist today is testament to the fact that we descend from survivors;
from ancestors who, when faced with crises requiring decisions of consequence,
upholding of principles or shifts in belief, made appropriate choices ensuring the
perpetuation of us, their kin, who carried down the generations their treasured memories
of identity – acts of belonging – to estates and resources for future benefit.

Today, we fondly remember our ancestors who made difficult decisions – sometimes
at the cost of their own lives – to ensure wider kin-community survival. Throughout
all cultures such acts of selflessness continue to be immortalised via song, dance, poetry,
art, literature and imagery (for example, ancestors depicted through carving, weaving
or photography). These memories provide us with valued glimpses of our forebears'
community-orientated morality (see Mordell *et al.* 2002 for discussion on moral
communities in the Pacific) and are all the more interesting given today's confusing
reality of urban-dominated, commercially driven, electronically broadcasted values of
individualism. Nevertheless, such ancestral portraits remain powerful symbolic representations of the past, and in the right context can become authoritative guides, providing
descendant communities with direction on matters of principle, from which decisions
particular to the occasion can be made. Many of these ancestral portraits now rest in
museums, and their originating contexts (for example *marae*[2] throughout the Pacific)
have long since been dismantled by invading imperial powers or made legislatively
impotent. In spite of this, museums and the ever-permeating colonial ethos out of which
they arose continue to throw up new and interesting challenges for today's indigenous
communities.

243

AGENCY

Responsible indigenous community leaders carry the weight of past, present and future generations on their shoulders. Every decision, be it regarding a perceived opportunity or imposed constraint, continues to be measured in terms of kin group accountability that falls beyond the frame of Western individualised contexts. This is not unlike an ancestral portrait representing a moment in time: what falls beyond one's immediate attention invisibly defines, shapes and empowers or limits what is being seen or not seen. In kin settings elders ritually bring to life ancestral portraits by collapsing the genealogical boundary (time/frame) between image (the past) and descendant (the future) so they may meet in the ceremonial present (transformative space/place: plaza, court-yard, marae). By 'performing' the ancestor, elders expertly manipulate boundaries between living and dead to affirm genealogical identity to surrounding land/seascapes in terms of inclusiveness or exclusiveness, dependent on audience and reason for assembly (see Tapsell 1997 for Maori examples and discussion).

What elders allow museums to see is also no accident. The future well-being of kin groups hinges on identity being transferred across generations. From the time elders began comprehending the role of museums in the colonisation process – the capture and representation of indigenous knowledge – many have sought to engage with them in a manner that might provide yet-to-be-born descendants with an opportunity to access ancestral values in future non-customary contexts. Since the nineteenth century the conscious *agency* (Thomas 1991) by elders of planting object-associated knowledge within museums – eagerly accepted by curators for their own ethnocentrically driven reasons – is now providing an invaluable bridge over which today's urban-raised kin are beginning to reconnect with their ancestral past if they so choose.

Until recently, it appears neither museums nor urban-raised kin have understood the foresight of agency that elders have quietly carried when engaging, or not engaging with museums. Each group has been too absorbed in their own mirror worlds of colonial action/reaction to take notice of the subtle leadership that has been at play for generations. Curators busied themselves exhibiting (performing) ancestral portraits according to mutually exclusive Western values of ownership, capture and otherness. Genealogically specific knowledge presented by elders was recast to fit depersonalised narratives of colonial domination and Western expansion, recasting codified patterns of social relationships into ethnographically curious images of primitive art for non-kin consumption and articulated to a non-indigenous audience. Meanwhile descendants of the 'native other', who have since come to live in the vicinity of museums, found cause to react to such genealogically alienating exhibitions. 'Rediscovery' of museum-held ancestral portraits triggered feelings of cultural dislocation and guilt having themselves eagerly exited their home kin communities to participate in the post Second World War years of rapid global economic expansion. Massive unemployment associated with the 1980s recession brought these descendants back to reality, especially the responsibility of maintaining families far from home kin support. Not unexpectedly, the perceived museum capture of ancestral portraits three or more generations prior to their own departure from home, came to mirror perceptions of themselves as also being victims of a colonial agenda of indigenous exploitation (see Tapsell 1998: sec. III; Tapsell 2002b for discussion surrounding post-Second World War migration of Maori to urban centres). Thereafter, actualities behind any particular museum-held ancestral portrait's separation were obscured by emotive feelings of loss, guilt and foul play. In this context, demands for return are not unexpected initial reactions despite not really knowing what to do if successful. After all, ancestral portraits are but reflections of our genealogical past, and how we view them is dependent on our capacity to interpret the context that continues to exist beyond their frame.

Today's curators welcome opportunities to engage with community elders who, for reasons not immediately apparent, are far more willing to meaningfully interpret patterns embedded in ancestral portraits than are urban-raised descendants (on elders' accompaniment of the *Te Maori* international exhibition 1984–87, see Mead 1984, 1986; Tapsell 1998: sec. IV; Neich 2001). This shift has been recent, but subtle. In the past, curators went out into the field to access kin knowledge and then repackaged it for a non-indigenous audience. Today that knowledge continues to flow, but more as a result of elders coming to 'town' to visit grandchildren than as the result of fieldwork. Some of these same grandchildren are now beginning to visit museums, interacting with their ancestral portraits as taught by elders. Some appear to be less inclined than their urbanised parents' generation to see themselves or their portraits as victims of colonisation. Consequently, having endured the reactive 1980–90s years of repatriation demands, museums in New Zealand, Australia, Canada and elsewhere have begun to shift toward re-presenting ancestral portraits according to elder narratives, especially now that the audience is more likely to contain third-generation descendants who are becoming qualified to assist making collections more meaningful and vital to viewers.

The ritual transference of important identity-associated knowledge in museum contexts does not occur often. When it does, however, it provides curators with a rare opportunity to better understand particular museum-held ancestral portraits as maintained by source community elders. Due to geographical separation, however, perceptions of such ancestral exchanges are prone to erroneous interpretation if appropriate contact with the elders is not maintained by museums. Knowledge-transfer vacuums can contribute to institutional discomfort if inappropriate communication occurs in its place with less informed, non-mandated descendants who may lead curators to believe that all ancestral portraits are trapped victims of colonisation. However, sustained contact with knowledgeable elders usually dispels any institutional fear. Accepting elders' narratives and the future kin obligations they represent will have its economic downside – for example, maintaining direct contact with knowledgeable elders worlds apart – but it will prevent undue concern, rebuild trust, make for exciting exhibits (performances) and facilitate wider co-operation between kin-source communities and those museums holding their ancestral portraits.

HORIZONS

According to my own research experiences within Maori society, when source community elders visit museums they generally experience a sense of wonder, privilege and awe at having been afforded the opportunity to engage with their ancestors mid-flight on a journey beyond customary community horizons. Thereafter thoughts often turn to keeping the portraits 'warm', cloaking them in knowledge and prayers, thereby allowing local elders and curators to better protect and maintain them on behalf of the wider kin group. Elders almost always express gratitude towards the local kin group for spiritually protecting their ancestral portraits, while thanking the museum for its physical custodianship. If issues of repatriation are raised, I have heard elders express their deeply held belief that in time ancestors do find their way home, but not before home kin have resolved outstanding colonially fuelled issues concerning genealogical accountability and reconnection to alienated estates and resources. No one wants their grandparents – ancestral portraits – to come home to find their place now in a mess, the children fighting or even worse run away, and those left behind unwilling to provide them with long-term care.

In the mid-1980s more meaningful conversations between elders and museums evolved out of the *Te Maori* exhibition experience. Past misunderstandings have been approached sensitively allowing new relationships between museums and their indigenous source communities to emerge. However, until such time indigenous leadership resecures kin identity to customary estates and resources – ensuring survival, benefit, sustainability and perpetuation of communities' descendants living at home and away – museums will need to be patient and supportive of the wider issues occurring beyond their museological frames of reference. In the interim they can assist indigenous source communities by providing access to valuable research knowledge and also begin identifying upon which of the four pathways (prestation, sale, loan or inappropriate acquisition) every ancestral portrait resting in their collections arrived. Each pathway requires a different manage-ment strategy, ensuring that the relationship between community and museum continues to strengthen and grow, and each portrait can continue along its destined pathway in a customarily and morally appropriate manner. In time successful resource outcomes back home provide the economic, social and political power base on which communities can rebuild wider kin identity. It is at that stage of redevelopment that the ancestral portraits resting in museums, especially those pivotal to genealogical identity, become integral to source communities' re-establishment of their ancestral links to lands, waterways and resources, thus rebuilding sustainable well-being.

To take a Maori case in point: the issue of power and authority over our museum-held ancestral portraits, or *taonga*[3] is not the number one priority for my people, *Ngati Whakaue* of *Te Arawa*. Top of our list are education, housing, health, employment, capital development, *Treaty of Waitangi* claims,[4] local government taxes, access to geothermal waters and *marae* sustainability. Nevertheless, my elders remain very aware of the historical actualities behind sometimes dubious acquisition of museum-held *taonga*, but they are also cognisant that museums provide valuable sites of preservation, which are not in the habit of changing rapidly. Not unlike *whare koiwi* of old,[5] museums are seen as appropriately restricted repositories into which ancestral treasures are today still being kept safe. In modern contexts the ongoing protection of *taonga*-associated values of *mana* (customary authority, prestige), *tapu* (restricted, set apart, associated with ancestors) and *korero* (narrative, story) remains just as important, be it in an elder's closet or on display in an international museum. If these three values have been main-tained and protected, it is understood the ancestral presence of the *taonga* is intact and its journey ongoing. And when younger descendants, especially those who have grown up away from the home-*marae* context, become over-eager in requesting museum-held *taonga* home, elders gently remind them that as descendants we 'belong to', rather than 'own', our ancestors. Museums may have legal evidence to support they own such items, but from a *Te Arawa* perspective this matters little because ancestors are ordered within a genealogical matrix of belonging or *whakapapa*,[6] which transcends legal parameters

(Tapsell 1997). Although our museum-held 'ancestral portraits' remain important to us, they are generally not expected to reappear across the horizon until such time that the initial reasons behind their separation from land and descendants have been resolved. Thereafter the ancestors (*taonga*) decide when they are ready to travel and will conspire to journey home once the intentions of all parties, living and dead, are in alignment. In that way *taonga* fulfil their destiny as unifying ancestral figures that are capable of providing a genealogical focal point to a grounded celebration of identity.

OBLIGATIONS

Tidying up Treaty of Waitangi relationships is an important part of realigning Maori well-being today. Rectifying relationships launches *taonga* on new trajectories: as some return, others are prestated away. My tribe remain prolific weavers and carvers, thereby keeping the knowledge behind creating *taonga* alive so this too can travel down the generations. Since arriving over 20 generations ago, the wealth of my people has been measured not so much by keeping, but in giving; our ability to *manaaki*[7] all visitors and make them feel at home. It is therefore not surprising that many of our most significant *taonga* can be found not on our *marae*, but rather in museums and private collections throughout the world. Such *taonga* were kept apart for occasions where their prestation would signify the importance of the receiver and the genealogical significance of the occasion. These occasions were conducted in *marae* contexts and usually involved rights of access to lands and resources, especially with the advent of the Crown's Native Land Court.[8] Some of these most valued *taonga* were prestated beyond the *Rotorua* horizon as the result of land sales to Crown agents in the 1880s. In most cases the non-*Maori* receivers did not value our *taonga* in the same way as we still do and recast them as ethnographic objects of curiosity that were launched into foreign orbits of museums, auction houses and private collections.

After the 1993 official renewal of *Ngati Whakaue's* Treaty relationship with the Crown, our *taonga* have begun returning home, often unannounced and seemingly on their own volition. The *taonga* named *Pukaki* who resided in the Auckland Museum for 120 years is a good example of an ancestor returning home when ready. In 1877 he was prestated to the Crown on *Te Papa-i-Ouru marae* as a symbol of trust regarding the Crown's promise to protect *Ngati Whakaue's* land interests in the proposed township of *Rotorua*. Rather than being delivered to Wellington, *Pukaki* was taken away to the Auckland Museum and his Crown relationship to the *Rotorua* lands obscured. In 1881 the Crown kept true to its word and confirmed the township agreement in legislation (Stafford 1967). By the 1890s, however, the Crown reneged and the township lands and wider estates were compulsorily purchased and on-sold. Not until 1993 did the Crown accept responsibility and began rectifying its less than honourable actions. A new agreement was signed, reconfirming the primacy of *Ngati Whakaue's* association with *Rotorua* and we were compensated with the return of prime lands, resources to manage them, and shared responsibility over our geothermal parks and reserves (Tapsell 2000). It was at this stage, after 100 years (four generations) of depression, that my people began to proudly lift their heads again and look beyond the horizon of one-day-at-a-time living. *Taonga* particular to *Ngati Whakaue* and the township came to the fore, and leading the way was *Pukaki*. His unsolicited return home by the Auckland Museum in 1997 is without precedent, allowing an old relationship to be renewed. The return was all the more remarkable given that it enabled my elders to complete finally what *Ngati Whakaue* began in 1877: the prestation of *Pukaki* to his intended recipients, the Crown (Tapsell 2002a).

A decade ago my tribal community was talking about building its own museum in reaction to the Crown's failings. Today, however, especially since the formation of the Pukaki Trust[9] (Tapsell 2002a), there are new conversations exploring development of meaningful partnerships, not only with the Crown and the city of *Rotorua*, but also with the Auckland Museum in which the majority of our most important *taonga* still rest. Dominating the discussions is not so much the exercising of any particular individual's rights, but now rather the emergence of joint-responsibility issues regarding care, insurance, conservation and accountability to all descendants who may claim to belong to any particular *taonga*, and how best this can be maintained. Ten years ago conversations of this nature were unheard of in museum contexts. Today, with the increase in Crown settlements bringing more and more tribes back onto the front foot, proactive discussions regarding *taonga* and human remains are providing new direction and purpose to Aotearoa New Zealand's museum profession who wish to remain important to source communities.

RECIPROCITY

We must remain mindful that such an event as *Pukaki's* return – a celebration of identity by way of prestating home an 'ancestral portrait' – only became conceivable after the underlying core issues of control over associated peoples, lands and resources had been resolved with the State (Crown). Involvement in such resolutions falls well beyond the mandate of museums, but at the same time our industry needs to remain cognisant of its own historical duplicity and how indigenous source communities – not least urban-based descendants – may continue to perceive museums as part of a wider colonising deceit.

One way of overcoming such perceptions is for museums to maintain meaningful communication with kin leaders, facilitating source community access to valuable archival print and photographic documentation and assisting grievance research and repatriation of valuable, identity-rich knowledge. Over time trust will develop and set the platform on which future partnership initiatives can proceed if or when the underlying core issues of the wider political grievance with the state are resolved. As *Pukaki* demonstrates, land, waterways and resource resolution clears the way for ancestral portraits to find their way home and become unifying or healing agents for the communities involved. Conversely, if return home is proposed when the originating context of alienation remains unresolved, the museum must weigh up the political, social and economic risks of prestating a key ancestral portrait back to a community that is neither prepared nor ready to receive it. Rather than increasing the prestige of the ancestor, mistimed returns carry the potential to create wider controversy, divide communities further rather than heal them, and ultimately diminish the importance of the occasion and especially the ancestor itself. Furthermore, because community energy has often been focused directly on addressing land/resource grievances, sometimes for generations, the premature return of ancestral portraits risks becoming a mere secondary distraction and their subsequent well-being may suffer until such time resolution of the wider grievance is achieved.

As much as museums in Aotearoa New Zealand have become conscious of the value of engaging with wider indigenous source communities, realising the primary importance and authority of the local community on whose customary land their institution stands – *mana whenua*[10] – is proving to be the new challenge (Tapsell 2000). Although Maori tribes have ritually acknowledged this home–visitor relationship boundary for countless generations, most museums today are struggling to comprehend the impact on their indigenous collections and have not yet recognised this fundamental differentiation. This is occurring mainly because the two intersecting value systems represented by museum-held ancestral portraits – law and lore – have yet to be understood and institutionally integrated as one seamless policy structure. In the past it has been too easy for museums to consult with any Maori and claim to have done nothing inappropriate.

Fortunately, beliefs and attitudes are shifting, not least at the Auckland Museum, where successful integration of Maori principles and policies has occurred throughout its governing board and operations (Auckland War Memorial Museum 2003). In colonial contexts, successful integration requires relationship building from the ground up, literally. Local source communities (*tangata whenua*[11]) and the museums built upon their ancestral estates (*mana whenua*) – irregardless of legal title – must first agree on a shared set of principles before there is any chance of successful engagement with wider indigenous source communities. Agreed principles should highlight each party's lines of accountability, wider responsibilities, obligations, duties, expectations and boundaries. Out of such principles can then flow governance policies and operational procedures that align with both the legal and customary requirements of the museum and its local indigenous community. Thereafter sustainable relationships with wider kin source communities can be jointly negotiated by museums alongside their local indigenous community partners who will actively protect and interpret ancestrally defined values (lore – custom) so they may be accurately understood and maintained in museum contexts (law – policies).

Once the partnership with the local indigenous community has been firmly established (both in law and lore), treating with wider indigenous source communities who have already resecured their identity to estates and resources provides museums in colonial contexts (for example North America, South Africa, Australia, New Zealand and the South Pacific) with far more exciting opportunities to develop sustainable relationships. As new partnerships begin flourishing in (post) colonial contexts, they will provide opportunities for international museums (Europe and Asia) to partner with metropolitan institutions of colonised nations, assisted by their local indigenous communities to negotiate – in aligned kinship terms of guardianship and hospitality – with any wider related indigenous source community in that vicinity. Stronger international museum relationships will facilitate beneficial indigenous partnership development and knowledge exchange for those institutions committed to rebalancing the colonial past, gaining access to the deeper narratives of identity their indigenous collections represent, and reviving out-of-context exhibitions. Thereafter it is for every museum and its associated source communities to negotiate a shared vision of mutual benefit so each can remain vital, important and accountable to future generations.

TOMORROW

Today's leading museums are shifting from colonial upholders of the world captured and made miniature for all to behold, to institutions seeking to share responsibility and become meaningful to tomorrow's generation of globally connected descendants. Failure to recognise the importance of making this shift is likely to result in some institutions taking their place beside the empires they once championed: historical curiosities representative of a time and place since made extinct.

The key to museums successfully shifting contexts lies not simply in what they hold, but in the relationships such holdings represent to indigenous source communities, who have defied colonial expectations of dying out and continue to wrestle for kin survival. Whereas 'native others' were once safely contained in reservations beyond the horizon of civilised society, today they are on the doorsteps of all the major museums of the world. Museums and indigenous source communities not only have a shared past, but now need to find new ways to share the future if both are to move out of survival mode and into domains of sustainability. Tolerance of differing viewpoints, understanding one another's expectations and beliefs, and learning to recognise and negotiate boundaries, are critical factors both parties will need to accept if there is any hope of developing relationships for future benefit.

It is in this shifting relational context that indigenous source community elders continue quietly to engage with museums as part and parcel of fulfilling their genealogical responsibility to all kin – past and present, not least those born and living beyond the home horizon, and especially those still to be born, on whose shoulders the future identity of the community ultimately rests. By actively sharing this responsibility, museums are becoming reinvigorated as dynamic contact zones; sites of comparative learning, innovation and reciprocity; status quo challengers; collaborative research partners; and champions of knowledge repatriation to source communities. Rather than only reflecting colonial viewpoints, museums can also choose to tell it as it is from affected indigenous communities' perspectives, exploring multiple voices and beliefs, allowing audiences to reflect on the entangled histories all cultures of the world share so they may begin grasping the traumas inflicted and their consequences.

The relatively recent migration of kin to urban settings is an ongoing part of these traumas, having resulted in massive community depopulation and descendants being raised in non-indigenous contexts of individualism. The long-term economic consequences of state dependency – poor health, crime, poverty and lack of education or skills – is the price for this, which all society is now paying. Museums are well positioned to assist elders and their communities in ameliorating this shared crisis because they are the custodians of the symbols of identity – ancestral portraits and associated knowledge – that can reunite and empower the most important resource of all: people. The return home of skills like law, commerce, economics, politics, anthropology, science, medicine, resource management and museology, now rests with a new generation of urban-raised descendants and their sense of obligation toward home kin communities. By providing elders with kin-originating resources, museums can facilitate urban bridging of identity, becoming active on-the-ground partners with indigenous source communities beyond their four walls and reignite young minds with the passion to explore and create, like their ancestors once did.

For now, today's new generation of urbanised kin are becoming accustomed to walking past each other in our crowded city streets, neither recognising one another nor pausing to celebrate their ancestral relationships. The few elders familiar with this crisis are investing time with urban grandchildren in the presence of ancestral portraits, passing on values and principles of identity that are as vital to today's descendants as they were for their ancestors. These portraits provide the common genealogical link by which kin can also meaningfully reconnect with each other and with their kin community, bringing home professional skills capable of rebalancing a shared past of division and colonial rule. In time, more and more associated museum-held ancestral portraits like *Pukaki* will also flow along this pathway, reconnecting urban and home kin in celebrations of identity to ancestral estates and resources. Perhaps then, a future of specialist research centres – community repositories for ancestral portraits and archives; virtual access sites to worldwide collections and knowledge; research bases for international and returning kin academics; sources of mentors and role models for a new generation of descendants – aligned with major global institutions, but located within source communities, will become tomorrow's pathway to resecuring robust kin identity. As old portraits return, new ones will continue to be launched back over the horizon to partnering museums, accompanying new generations of grandchildren who may be eager to explore their world beyond the frame, but remain connected to their community, both the living and the dead.

It is for my generation to ensure their pathway home never again becomes overgrown.

NOTES

1 Excerpt from a conversation between Ngati Whakaue elder, Kiharoa Akuhata, and James Cowan, historian and correspondent, while the two were sitting on Pukeroa hill overlooking the Rotorua village of Ohinemutu, c. 1900. (Author's personal notes.)

2 *Marae*: the quintessential focus of Eastern Polynesian land tenure in pre-contact times.

3 *Taonga*: dynamic ancestral representations of genealogical relationships to our customary lands.

4 Treaty of Waitangi: a solemn pact signed between the Crown and tribes of New Zealand in 1840 by which British sovereignty was established; see Kawharu 1989 for full explanation of the Treaty of Waitangi and its consequences from both Maori and Pakeha (British descent) perspectives.

5 *Whare koiwi*: carved house in which *urumoko* (ancestral heads) and *taonga* were stored when not being used during life crises.

6 *Whakapapa*: to layer, genealogical accounting of the universe; to order relationships according to kinship and descent from common ancestors.

7 *Manaaki*: the provision of hospitality to visitors by *tangata whenua*.

8 Native Land Court: judicial process legislatively set in place in 1865 (Native Land Act) initially designed to facilitate individualising title of commonly held Maori land in preparation for Crown (New Zealand Government) purchase, on-selling or development.

9 Constituted as the result of the 2 October 1997 return home and prestation of *Pukaki* to the Crown, the Trust comprises of one representative each from the Crown (Minister for Arts and Heritage on behalf of the nation); Ngati Whakaue (paramount elder of Te Papa-i-Ouru Marae on behalf of all descendants); Rotorua District Council (mayor on behalf of the City of Rotorua); and Auckland War Memorial Museum (chair of the Auckland Museum Trust Board).

10 *Mana whenua/mana o te whenua*: customary authority of and over any particular ancestral landscape (whenua), associated waterways and resources as exclusively exercised by the local kin group or *tangata whenua*.

11 *Tangata whenua*: recognised descendants – local kin group – of particular ancestral estates; 'descendants of the land'.

BIBLIOGRAPHY

Agthe, J. (1994) 'Interpretation historischer Fotos durch Africkaner heute' in E.C. Raaba and H. Wagner (eds), *Kulturen in Bild: Bestände und projeckte des Bildarchives*, Frankfurt/Main: Museum für Völkerkunde.

Ahmed, A. and Shore, C. (eds) (1995) *The Future of Anthropology: its relevance to the contemporary world*, London: Athlone.

AIRFA Task Force (1980) 'American Indian Religious Freedom Act: Task Force report', *Council for Museum Anthropology Newsletter*, 4 (3): 3–23.

Akbar, S. (1999) *Shamiana – The Mughal Tent: V&A education project developed and co-ordinated by Shireen Akbar*, London: V&A Publications.

Alfredsson, G. (1989) 'International discussion of the concerns of indigenous peoples. The United Nations and the rights of indigenous peoples', *Current Anthropology*, 30 (2): 255–65.

Alger, A. and Welsh, P.H. (2000) 'Creating hybrid space: the Native American high school student guide program at the Heard Museum', *Journal of Museum Education*, 25 (3): 14–19.

Ames, M.M. (1991) 'Biculturalism in exhibitions', *Museum Anthropology*, 15 (2): 7–15.

—— (1992) *Cannibal Tours and Glass Boxes: the anthropology of museums*, Vancouver: University of British Columbia Press.

Anderson, B. (1991) *Imagined Communities*, London: Verso.

Anon (nd) 'Cliff dwellers of the far north', handbill for lecture presented by Father Bernard Hubbard, SJ, Constitution Hall, Washington, DC, 15 March, year unknown, but probably 1939.

Appadurai, A. (ed.) (1986) *The Social Life of Things: commodities in cultural perspective*, Cambridge: Cambridge University Press.

—— (1996) *Modernity at Large: cultural dimensions of globalization*, Minneapolis: University of Minnesota Press.

Archer, W.G. (1966) *Paintings of the Sikhs*, London: HMSO.

—— (1970) *Paintings of the Punjab Hills*, London: HMSO.

Arima, E.Y. (1995) *Blackfeet and Palefaces: the Pikani and Rocky Mountain House*, Ottawa: The Golden Dog Press.

Asad, T. (1991) 'Afterword. From the history of colonial anthropology to the anthropology of Western hegemony', in George W. Stocking (ed.), *Colonial Situations. Essays on the Contextualization of Ethnographic Knowledge*, Madison: University of Wisconsin Press.

Askari, N. and Crill, R. (1997) *Colours of the Indus: costume and textiles of Pakistan*, London: Merrell Holberton in conjunction with the Victoria & Albert Museum.

Auckland War Memorial Museum, *Te Papa Whakahiku* (2003) *Annual Plan* 2002–3, Auckland: Auckland War Memorial Museum.

Bani, M. and Herle, A. (1998) 'Collaborative projects on Torres Strait collections', *Journal of Museum Ethnography*, 10: 115–20.

252

Banks, M. (1996) 'Constructing the audience through ethnography', in P.I. Crawford and S. Baldur Hafsteinsson (eds), *The Construction of the Viewer: media ethnography and the anthropology of audiences*, Højbjerg: Intervention Press in association with the Nordic Anthropological Film Association.

Barringer, T. and Flyn, T. (1998) *Colonialism and the Object*, London: Routledge.

Barthes, R. (1977) *Image, Music, Text*, trans. S. Heath, London: Fontana Communication Series.

—— (1984) [1980] *Camera Lucida: reflections on photography*, trans. Richard Howard, London: Fontana.

Bayly, C.A. (ed.) (1990) *The Raj: India and the British 1600–1947*, London: National Portrait Gallery Publications.

Bean, S. (1999) 'Museum anthropology into a new millennium', *Museum Anthropology* 23(3): 3.

Becker, H. (1982) *Art Worlds*, Berkeley, CA: University of California Press.

Beckett, J. (1987) *Torres Strait Islanders: custom and colonialism*, Cambridge: Cambridge University Press.

—— (1998) 'Haddon attends a funeral: fieldwork in Torres Strait, 1888, 1898', in A. Herle and S. Rouse (eds), *Cambridge and the Torres Strait: centenary essays on the 1898 anthropological expedition*, Cambridge: Cambridge University Press.

Beier, U. and Kiki, A.M. (1970) *Hohao: the uneasy survival of an art form in the Papuan Gulf*, Melbourne: Nelson Limited.

Bell, C.E. and Patterson, R.E. (1999) 'Aboriginal rights to cultural property in Canada', *International Journal of Cultural Property*, 8 (1): 17–211.

Bell, J. (2001) ' "If the Purari was like a kina shell, on whose neck would it hang?": The dilemma of resource ownership and ancestral objects in the wake of industrial logging in the Purari Delta, Gulf Province', paper presented at Australian National University Melanesian Seminar, 29 November.

Bennett, T. (1995) *The Birth of the Museum: history, theory, politics*, London: Routledge.

—— (1996) 'The museum and the citizen', in T. Bennett, R. Trotter and D. McAlear (eds) *Museums and Citizenship: a resource book*, Brisbane: Memoirs of the Queensland Museum, 39 (1).

Berger, J. (1980) *Uses of Photography*, London: Writers Cooperative.

Bernstein, B. (1991) 'Repatriation and collaboration: the Museum of New Mexico', *Museum Anthropology*, 15 (3): 19–21.

—— (1992a) 'Collaborative strategies for the preservation of North American Indian material culture', *Journal of the American Institute of Conservation*, 31 (1): 23–9.

—— (1992b) 'Repatriation and collaboration: the Museum of New Mexico', *Museum Anthropology*, 15 (3): 19–21.

—— (1992c) 'Communities in collaboration: strategies for cultural negotiation', paper presented at the 90th Annual Meeting of the America Anthropological Association, Chicago.

Binney, J. and Chaplin, G. (1986; 3rd edn 1990) *Ngā Mōrehu: the survivors*, Auckland: Oxford University Press.

—— (1991) 'Taking the photographs home: the recovery of a Maori history', *Visual Anthropology*, 4: 431–42.

Binney, J., Chaplin, G., and Wallace, C. (1979; 2nd edn 1987) *Mihaia: the prophet Rua Kenana and his community at Maungapohatu*, Wellington: Oxford University Press.

Black, M. (1997) *Bella Bella: a season of Heiltsuk art*, Toronto: Royal Ontario Museum.

Blair, B. (1979) 'American Indians vs. American museums: a matter of religious freedom, parts one and two', *American Indian Journal*, 5 (5): 13–21 and 5 (6): 2–6.

Bodenhorn, B. (2000) 'He used to be my relative: exploring the bases of relatedness among Iñupiat of northern Alaska', in J. Carsten (ed.), *Cultures of Relatedness: new approaches to the study of kinship*, Cambridge: Cambridge University Press.

Bogojavlensky, S. and Fuller, R.W. (1973) 'Polar bears, walrus hides and social solidarity', *Alaska Journal*, 3 (2): 66–76.

Bolton, L. (1996) 'Tahigogona's sisters: women, mats and landscape on Ambae' in J. Bonnemaison, C. Kaufmann, K. Huffman and D. Tryon (eds), *Arts of Vanuatu*, Bathurst: Crawford House Publishing.

—— (ed.) (1999) *Fieldwork and Fieldworkers: developments in Vanuatu research*, special issue of *Oceania*, 70 (1).

Bonfil Batalla, G. (1982) 'Prólogo', *Nuestra Maíz: treinta monografías populares*, Mexico: Museo Nacional de Culturas Populares.

Bourdieu, P. (1993) 'The field of cultural production', in P. Bourdieu, *The Field of Cultural Production: essays on literature and art*, trans. R. Nice, New York: Columbia University Press.

Boyd, T.H. and Haas, J. (1992) 'The Native American Graves Protection and Repatriation Act: prospects for new partnerships', *Arizona State Law Journal*, 24 (1): 253–82.

Bradford Art Galleries and Museums (1983) *Petals from a Lotus: an introduction to the arts and history of the Indian sub-continent*, Bradford: Bradford Art Galleries and Museums.

Brown, A.K. (2000) 'Object encounters: perspectives on collecting expeditions to Canada', unpublished DPhil thesis, University of Oxford.

—— (2001) 'Artefacts as "alliances": perspectives on First Nations collectors and collecting', *Journal of Museum Ethnography*, 13: 79–89.

Brown, A.K. and Peers, L. (in prep.) *'Pictures Bring us Messages': Photographs, Histories, Reconnections* (working title).

Brown, H.A. (1973) 'The Eleman language family', in K. Franklin (ed.), *The Linguistic Situation in the Gulf District and Adjacent Areas, Papua New Guinea*. Pacific Linguistics, C-26. Canberra: Linguistic Circle of Canberra.

Brown, K. (ed.) (1999) *Sikh Art and Literature*, London and New York: Routledge in collaboration with the Sikh Foundation.

Bruner, E. (1996) 'Tourism in Ghana. The Representation of Slavery and the Return of the Black Diaspora', *American Anthropologist* 98 (2): 290–304.

Butler, S.R. (1999a) *Contested Representations: revisiting* Into the Heart of Africa, London: Gordon & Breach.

—— (1999b) 'The politics of exhibiting culture: legacies and possibilities', *Museum Anthropology*, 23 (3): 74–92.

Byrne, A. (1995) 'Responsibilities and response: Aboriginal and Torres Strait Islander protocols for libraries', Archives and Information Services. First Roundtable on Library and Archives Collections and Services of Relevance to Aboriginal and Torres Strait Islander People. Online. Available HTTP: *http://www.ntu.edu.au/library/protocol.html* (accessed 3 May 2002).

Cameron, D. (1971) 'The museum: a temple or the forum?', *Curator*, 14 (1): 11–24.

Canclini, N.G. (2000) 'Cultural policy options in the context of globalization', in G. Bradford, M. Gary and G. Wallach (eds), *The Politics of Culture: policy perspectives for individuals, institutions, and communities*, New York: The New Press.

Carsten, J. (ed.) (2000) *Cultures of Relatedness: new approaches to the study of kinship*, Cambridge: Cambridge University Press.

Carter, J. (1999) 'How old is this text?', in E. Hooper-Greenhill (ed.), *The Educational Role of the Museum*, London: Routledge.

Castaneda, A. (1992) 'Women of color and the rewriting of Western history: the discourse, politics, and decolonization of history', *Pacific Historical Review*, LXI (4): 501–33.

Chaat Smith, P. (1995) 'The ghost in the machine', in *Strong Hearts: Native American visions and voices*, New York: Aperture.

Christal, M., Roy, L., Resta, P. and Cherian, A. 'Virtual museum collaborations for cultural revitalization: the Four Directions model', paper presented at the Museums and the Web 2001, Seattle, March 2001. Online. Available HTTP: *http://www.archimuse.com/mw2001/papers/christal/christal.html* (accessed 23 March 2002).

Clarke, A. (1994) 'Winds of change: an archaeology of contact in the Groote Eylandt archipelago, Northern Australia', unpublished PhD thesis, Australian National University.

Clavir, M. (2002) *Preserving What Is Valued: museums, conservation and First Nations*, Vancouver: University of British Columbia Press.

Clifford, J. (1988) 'Histories of the tribal and the modern', in *The Predicament of Culture: twentieth century ethnography, literature, and art*, Cambridge, Mass.: Harvard University Press.

—— (1991) 'Four Northwest Coast museums: travel reflections', in I. Karp and S.D. Lavine (eds) *Exhibiting Cultures: the poetics and politics of museum display*, Washington, DC: Smithsonian Institution Press.

—— (1997a) 'Paradise' in J. Clifford, *Routes: travel and translation in the late twentieth century*, Cambridge, Mass.: Harvard University Press.

—— (1997b) 'Museums as contact zones', in J. Clifford, *Routes: travel and translation in the late twentieth century*, Cambridge, Mass.: Harvard University Press.

Clifford, J. and Marcus, G.E. (1986) *Writing culture: the poetics and politics of ethnography*, Berkeley, Ca.: University of California Press.

Cocking, M. (1908) *An Adventure from Hudson Bay. Journal of Matthew Cocking, from York Factory to the Blackfeet Country, 1772–73*, in L.J. Burpee (ed.), *Proceedings and Transactions of the Royal Society of Canada*, 3rd series, 2 (2): 89–121.

Cole, D. (1985) *Captured Heritage: the scramble for Northwest Coast artefacts*, Norman: University of Oklahoma Press.

Collier, J. (1967) *Visual Anthropology: photography as a research method*, New York: Holt Rinehart & Winston.

Collier, Jr., J. and Collier, M. (1986) *Visual Anthropology: photography as a research method*, revised edition, Albuquerque: University of New Mexico Press.

Conaty, G.T. (1989) 'Canada's First Nations and museums: a Saskatchewan experience', *The International Journal of Museum Management and Curatorship*, 8 (4): 407–13.

—— (1995) 'Economic models and Blackfoot ideology', *American Ethnologist*, 22 (2): 404–13.

—— (1996) 'Working with Native advisory groups', *Alberta Museums Review*, 22 (2): 52–3.

—— (1999) 'Interpreting Blackfoot culture and history at the Glenbow', paper presented at the 28th Chacmool Conference, Department of Archaeology, University of Calgary, Calgary, November.

—— (2000) 'Change and innovation at Glenbow', paper presented at the Parks Canada Aboriginal Heritage Presentation Workshop, Calgary, March.

—— (2001) 'First Nations education at Glenbow', paper presented at the Plains Indian Seminar, Plains Indian Museum, Buffalo Bill Historical Center, Cody, WY, September.

—— (nd) 'Two approaches to the repatriation of Blackfoot sacred material', unpublished paper.

Conaty, G.T. and Janes, R.R. (1997) 'Issues of repatriation: a Canadian view', *European Review of Native American Studies*, 11 (2): 31–7.

Conner, A. (2001) 'Sharing stories, drawing on the past: strategies for producing educational resources for the Community Archaeology Project at Quseir, Egypt', unpublished MA dissertation, University of Southampton.

Conner, A., el Nemr, L. and Seymour, M. (2002a) *Salma and Samir in Roman Quseir*, Southampton: Quseir Heritage and Department of Archaeology, University of Southampton.

—— (2002b) *Salma and Samir in Islamic Quseir*, Southampton: Quseir Heritage and Department of Archaeology, University of Southampton.

Connerton, Paul (1989) *How Societies Remember*, Cambridge: Cambridge University Press.

Coombes, A.E. (1994) *Reinventing Africa: museums, material culture, and popular imagination in late Victorian and Edwardian England*, New Haven and London: Yale University Press.

Cooper, C. (1989) *Aboriginal and Torres Strait Islander Collections in Overseas Museums*, Canberra: Aboriginal Studies Press.

Council of Australian Museum Associations (1993) *Previous Possessions, New Obligations: policies for museums in Australia and Aboriginal and Torres Strait Islander people*, Melbourne: Council of Australian Museum Associations.

Cracknell, S. and Corbishley, M. (eds) (1986) *Presenting Archaeology to Young People*. London: Council for British Archaeology.

Crawford, P.I. and Baldur Hafsteinsson, S. (eds) (1996) *The Construction of the Viewer: media ethnography and the anthropology of audiences*, Højbjerg: Intervention Press in association with the Nordic Anthropological Film Association.

Cruikshank, J. (1995) 'Imperfect Translations: rethinking objects of ethnographic collections', *Museum Anthropology*, 19 1): 25–38.

Dark, P.J.C. (1990) 'Tomorrow's heritage is today's art, and yesteryear's identity', in A. Hanson and L. Hanson (eds), *Art and Identity in Oceania*, Bathurst: Crawford House Publishing.

—— (1999) 'Old models and new in Pacific art: real or spurious?', in B. Craig, B. Kernot and C. Anderson (eds), *Art and Performance in Oceania*, Bathurst: Crawford House Publishing.

Dempsey, H.A. (1965) *A Blackfoot Winter Count*, Occasional Paper 1, Calgary: Glenbow Museum.

—— (1972) *Crowfoot, Chief of the Blackfoot*, Edmonton: Hurtig Publishers.

—— (1980) *Red Crow, Warrior Chief*, Saskatoon: Western Prairie Producer Press.

—— (1991) *Treasures of the Glenbow Museum*, Calgary: Glenbow-Alberta Institute.

Dening, G. (2001) 'Reading to write', in M. Halligan (ed.), *Storykeepers*, Sydney: Duffy & Snellgrove.

Derry, L. (1997) 'Pre-emancipation archaeology: does it play a role in Selma, Alabama?' in C. McDavid and D.W. Babson (eds), *In the Realm of Politics: prospects for public participation in African-American and plantation archaeology. Historical Archaeology*, 31 (3): 18–26.

Desai, G. (2001) *Subject to Colonialism*, Durham, NC: Duke University Press.

Dissellhoff, H.D. (1935) 'Bemerkungen zu einigan Eskimo-masken der Sammlung Jacobsen des Berliner Museum für Völkerkunde' [Observations on a Eskimo shaman mask in the Berlin Museum für Völkerkunde], *Baessler-Archiv*, 18: 130–7.

—— (1936) 'Bemerkungen zu Fingermasken der Beringmeer-Eskimo' [Observations on finger masks of Bering Sea Eskimos], *Baessler-Archiv*, 19: 181–7.

Douglas, B. (1999) *Across the Great Divide: journeys in history and anthropology*, Amsterdam: Harwood Academic Press.

Doxtator, D. (1985) 'The idea of the Indian and the development of Iroquoian museums', *Museum Quarterly*, 14 (2): 20–6.

—— (1988) 'The home of Indian culture and other stories in the museum', *Muse*, 4 (3): 26–8.

Driscoll, B. (1995) 'Silent echoes: the displacement and reappearance of Copper Inuit clothing', paper presented at the 94th Annual Meeting of the American Anthropological Association, Washington DC.

Drumheller, A. and Kaminitz, M. (1994) 'Traditional care and conservation: the merging of two disciplines at the National Museum of the American Indian', *Preprints of the Contributions to the Ottawa Congress, 12–16 September 1994*, London: International Institute for Conservation.

Duncan, C. (1991) 'Art museums and the ritual of citizenship', in I. Karp and S.D. Lavine (eds), *Exhibiting Cultures: the politics and poetics of museum display*, Washington, DC: Smithsonian Institution Press.

Dunstan, C. (1999) 'Fostering symbiosis: a collaborative exhibit at the California State University Sacramento Museum of Anthropology', *Museum Anthropology*, 22 (3): 52–8.

During, S. (1995) 'Postmodernism or post-colonialism today', in B. Ashcroft, G. Griffiths, and H. Tiffin (eds), *The Post-colonial Studies Reader*, New York: Routledge.

Dutton, T. (1985) *Police Motu: iena sivarai (its story)*, Port Moresby: University of Papua New Guinea Press.

Edwards, E. (1994) 'Visualizing history: Diamond Jenness's photographs of D'Entrecasteaux Islands, Massim, 1911–1912 – a case study in re-engagement', *Canberra Anthropology*, 17 (2): 1–26.

—— (1998) 'Performing science: still photography and the Torres Strait Expedition', in A. Herle and S. Rouse (eds), *Cambridge and the Torres Strait: centenary essays on the 1898 anthropological expedition*, Cambridge: Cambridge University Press.

—— (1999a) 'Photographs as objects of memory', in M. Kwint, C. Breward and J. Aynsley (eds), *Material Memories: design and evocation*, Oxford: Berg Press.

—— (1999b) 'Torres Strait Islanders', *Anthropology Today*, 15 (1): 17–19.

—— (2000) 'Surveying culture: photography, collecting and material culture in British New Guinea, 1898', in M. O'Hanlon and R. Welsch (eds), *Hunting the Gatherers: artefact collecting in Melanesia*, Oxford: Berghann Press.

—— (2001) *Raw Histories: photographs, anthropology and museums*, Oxford: Berg.

Edwards, R. and Stewart, J. (eds) (1980) *Preserving Indigenous Cultures: a new role for museums*, Canberra: Australian National Commission for UNESCO.

Eglitis, A. (1998) 'A new art from the Torres Strait', in T. Mosby and B. Robinson (eds), *Ilan Pasin (this is our way) Torres Strait art*, Cairns: Cairns Regional Gallery.

Ekvar, M. (1999) 'Combating redundancy: writing texts for exhibitions', in E. Hooper-Greenhill (ed.), *The Educational Role of the Museum*, London: Routledge.

Eldridge, D. (1996) 'Aboriginal people need to control their own heritage', *Curatorship: indigenous perspectives in post-colonial societies*, Proceedings, Mercury Series 8, Hull: Canadian Museum of Civilization with the Commonwealth Association of Museums and the University of Victoria.

Eoe, S.M. (1991) 'The role of museums in the Pacific: change or die', in S.M. Eoe and P. Swadling (eds), *Museums and Cultural Centres in the Pacific*, Port Moresby: Papua New Guinea National Museum.

Eoe, S.M. and Swadling, P. (eds) (1991) *Museums and Cultural Centres in the Pacific*, Port Moresby: Papua New Guinea National Museum.

Erickson, P. and Murphy, L.D. (2001) 'Conclusion: making anthropological histories', *Readings for a History of Anthropological Theory*, Peterborough, Canada: Broadview Press.

Ewers, J.C. (1980) *The Horse in Blackfoot Culture, with Comparative Material from other Western Tribes*, Washington, DC: Smithsonian Institution Press.

—— (1982) *The Blackfeet: raiders of the northwestern plains*, Norman: University of Oklahoma Press.

Fabian, J. (1983) *Time and the Other: how anthropology makes its object*, New York: Columbia University Press.

—— (1998) 'Curios and curiosity: notes on reading Torday and Frobenius', in E. Schildkrout and C. A. Keim (eds), *The Scramble for Art in Central Africa*, Cambridge: Cambridge University Press.

Falk, J.H. and Dierking, L.D. (2000) *Learning from Museums: visitor experiences and the making of meaning*, Walnut Creek: Altamira Press.

Faris, J. (1996) *Navajo and Photography: a critical history of the representation of American peoples*, Albuquerque: University of New Mexico Press.

Field, J., Barker, J., Barker, R., Coffey, E., Coffey, L., Crawford, E., Darcy, L., Fields, T., Lord, G., Steadman, B. and Colley, S. (2000) ' "Coming back". Aborigines and archaeologists at Cuddie Springs', *Public Archaeology*, 1: 35–48.

Fienup-Riordan, A. (1990) 'Eskimo iconography and symbolism: an introduction', *Études/Inuit/Studies*, 14 (1–2): 7–12.

—— (1994) *Boundaries and Passages: rule and ritual in Yup'ik Eskimo oral tradition*, Norman: University of Oklahoma Press.

—— (1996) *The Living Tradition of Yup'ik Masks: Agayuliyararput (our way of making prayer)*, Seattle: University of Washington Press.

257

—— (1998) 'Yup'ik elders in museums: fieldwork turned on its head', *Arctic Anthropology*, 35 (2): 49–58.

—— (1999) 'Collaboration on display: A Yup'ik Eskimo exhibit at three national museums', *American Anthropologist*, 101 (2): 339–58.

—— (2002) 'Inuguat, iinrut, uyat-llu: Yup'ik dolls, amulets and human figures', *American Indian Art Magazine*, 27 (2): 40–7.

Filer, C. (ed.) (1997) *The Political Economy of Forest Management in Papua New Guinea*, Boroko, Papua New Guinea: National Research Institute [and] International Institute for Environment and Development.

Fitzhugh, W. and Kaplan, S.A. (1982) *Inua: spirit world of the Bering Sea Eskimo*, Washington, DC: Smithsonian Institution Press.

Flynn, G. and Hull-Walski, D. (2001) 'Merging traditional indigenous curation methods with modern museum standards of care', *Museum Anthropology*, 25 (1): 31–40.

Foana'ota, L.A. (1994) 'Solomon Islands national museum and cultural centre policy', in L. Lindstrom and G.M. White (eds), *Culture, Kastom, Tradition: developing cultural policy in Melanesia*, Suva, Fiji: Institute of Pacific Studies, University of the South Pacific.

Fourmile, H. (1990) 'Possession is nine tenths of the law – and don't Aboriginal people know it', *COMA*, 23: 57–67.

—— (1991) 'The case for independent but complementary Aboriginal cultural institutions', *Extending Parameters*: 35–40.

Fox, L. (2001) *Kipaitapiiwahsinnooni. Alcohol and Drug Abuse Education Program*, Edmonton: Duval House Publishing and Kainai Board of Education.

Frank, G. (2000) ' "That's my dinner on display": a First Nations reflection on museum culture', *B.C. Studies*, 125/6: 163–78.

Freire, P. (1998) *Pedagogy of Freedom: ethics, democracy, and civic courage*, trans. P. Clarke, New York: Rowman & Littlefield.

Friedman, J. (1998) 'Knowing Oceania or Oceanian knowing: identifying actors and activating identities in turbulent times', in J. Wassman (ed.), *Pacific Answers to Western Hegemony*, Oxford: Berg.

Franklin, M. (1997) ' "Power to the people": sociopolitics and the archaeology of black Americans', *Historical Archaeology*, 31: 36–50.

Galla, A. (1996) 'Promoting equity: museums and indigenous peoples', in *Curatorship: indigenous perspectives in post-colonial societies*, Proceedings, Mercury Series 8, Hull: Canadian Museum of Civilization with the Commonwealth Association of Museums and the University of Victoria.

Gans, H. (1974) *Popular Culture and High Culture: an analysis and evaluation of taste*, New York: Basic Books.

Gazin-Schwartz, A. and Holtorf, C. (eds) (1999) *Archaeology and Folklore*, London: Routledge.

Gell, A. (1998) *Art and Agency: an anthropological theory*, Oxford: Clarendon Press.

Gero, J.M. (1989) 'Producing prehistory, controlling the past: the case of the New England beehives', in V. Pinsky and A. Wylie (eds), *Critical Traditions in Contemporary Archaeology*, Cambridge: Cambridge University Press.

Gibb, J.G. (1997) 'Necessary but insufficient: plantation archaeology reports and community action', in C. McDavid and D.W. Babson (eds), *In the Realm of Politics: prospects for public participation in African-American and plantation archaeology. Historical Archaeology*, 31 (3): 51–64.

Giesen, M. (1999) 'Introduction: the management of federal archaeological collections', *Museum Anthropology*, 23 (2): 3–5.

Giles, S. (2001) 'The great circuit: making the connection between Bristol's slaving history and the African-Caribbean community', *Journal of Museum Ethnography*, 13: 15–21.

Gilmore, E. and Sabine, J. (1999) 'Writing readable text: evaluation of the Ekvar method', in E. Hooper-Greenhill (ed.), *The Educational Role of the Museum*, London: Routledge.

Glazier, D. (1999) *The Ancient Port of Myos Hormos at Quseir al-Qadim*. Plain language report of the 1999 field season, Southampton: Department of Archaeology, University of Southampton and Quseir Heritage Preservation Society.

—— (2001) 'Archaeological communities? A socio-political analysis of archaeological investigation at Quseir al-Qadim', unpublished PhD upgrade document, University of Southampton.

Goforth, L. (1993) 'First Nations and museums – a Native perspective, *Muse*, 11 (1): 14–16.

Gonyea, R. (1994a) 'Repatriation project plan', presented to NMAI Senior Management, January 31.

—— (1994b) Interview with Nancy Rosoff, November 18.

—— (1994c) Interview with Nancy Rosoff, November 25.

Gonzalez Cassanova, P. (1986) *Sociologia de la Explotación*, Mexico DF: Siglo Veinteuno.

Grasset, C.D. (1996) 'Museum fever in France', *Curator*, 39 (3): 188–207.

Greenblatt, S. (1991) 'Resonance and wonder' in Ivan Karp and Steven D. Lavine (eds), *Exhibiting Cultures: the Poetics and Politics of Museum Representation*, Washington, DC: Smithsonian Institution Press, pp. 42–56.

Greenfield, J. (1989) *The Return of Cultural Treasures*, Cambridge: Cambridge University Press.

Griffin, D. (1996) 'Previous Possessions, New Obligations: A Commitment by Australian Museums', *Curator*, 39 (1): 45–62.

Griffiths, D.J.F. (1977) 'The career of F.E. Williams, government anthropologist of Papua, 1922–1943', unpublished MA thesis, Australian National University.

Griffiths, T. (1996) *Hunters and Collectors: the antiquarian imagination in Australia*, Cambridge: Cambridge University Press.

Gross, L., Katz, J.S. and Ruby, J. (eds) (1988) *Image Ethic: the moral rights of subjects in photography, film and television*, New York: Oxford University Press.

Gupta, A. and J. Ferguson (1997) *Anthropological Locations: boundaries and grounds of a field science*, Berkeley and Los Angeles: University of California Press.

Haddon, A.C. (1894) *The Decorative Art of British New Guinea*, Cunningham Memoirs 10, Dublin: Royal Irish Academy.

—— (1895) *Evolution in Art: as illustrated by the life-histories of designs*, London: Walter Scott Ltd.

—— (1901) *Head-Hunters: black, white and brown*, London: Methuen.

—— (1919) 'The Kopiravi cult of the Namau, Papua', *Man*, 19 (12): 177–9.

—— (1920) 'Migrations of cultures in British New Guinea', *JAI*, 50: 237–80.

—— (1924a) 'Introduction', in J.H. Holmes *In Primitive New Guinea*, London: Service and Co. Ltd.

—— (1924b) 'New Guinea cannibals and other Papuans', *Country Life*, 55 (1417): 311–15.

—— (1946) 'Smoking tobacco pipes in New Guinea', *Philosophical Transactions of the Royal Society of London*, 232 (586): 1–278.

—— (ed.) (1901–35) *Reports of the Cambridge Anthropological Expedition to Torres Straits*, Cambridge: Cambridge University Press.

—— (1901) *Physiology and Psychology*, vol. II, Part I.

—— (1902) *Physiology and Psychology*, vol. II, Part II.

—— (1904) *Sociology, Magic and Religion of the Western Islanders*, vol. V.

—— (1907) *Linguistics*, vol. III.

—— (1908) *Sociology, Magic and Religion of the Eastern Islanders*, vol. VI.

—— (1912) *Arts and Crafts*, vol. IV.

—— (1935) *General Ethnography*, vol. I.

Haddon, A.C. and Hornell, J. (1936–38) *Canoes of Oceania*, Bernice P. Bishop Museum Special Publication 27–29. Honolulu: Bernice P. Bishop Museum.

Haddon, K. (1929) 'In the Gulf of New Guinea', *Country Life*, 66 (1701): 268–70.

Hall, B. (1979) 'Knowledge as a commodity and participatory research', *Prospects*, 9 (4): 393–408.

Hall, C.M. (1989) 'Problems with the exhibition of sacred objects', in G. Horse Capture (ed.), *The Concept of Sacred Materials and Their Place in the World*, Wyoming: Buffalo Bill Historical Center.

Handler, R. (1993) 'An anthropological definition of the museum and its purpose', *Museum Anthropology*, 17 (1): 33–6.

Handler, R. and Gable, E. (1997) *The New History in an Old Museum: creating the past at Colonial Williamsburg*, Durham, NJ: Duke University Press.

Hanks, L.M. and Hanks, J.R. (1950) *Tribe under Trust: a study of the Blackfoot Reserve in Alberta*, Toronto: University of Toronto Press.

Hanna, M.G. (1999) 'A time to choose: "us" versus "them" or "all of us together"', *Plains Anthropologist*, 44 (170): 43–52.

Haraway, D. (1989) *Primate Visions: gender, race, and nature in the world of modern science*, New York: Routledge.

Harlan, T. (1995) 'Creating a visual history: a question of ownership', in *Strong Hearts: Native American visions and voices*, New York: Aperture.

Harrison, J.D. (1993) 'Completing a circle: *The Spirit Sings*', in N. Dyck and J.B. Waldram (eds), *Anthropology, Public Policy and Native People in Canada*, Montreal and Kingston: McGill-Queen's University Press.

Hartman, W., Silvester, J. and Hayes, P. (eds.) (1998) *The Colonialising Camera: photographs in the making of Namibian history*, Cape Town: University of Cape Town Press.

Heald, S. (1996) 'Siletz dance house dedication loan, June 20–24', unpublished fieldnotes.

Healy, P. (1984) 'Archaeology abroad: ethical considerations of fieldwork in foreign countries', in E.L. Green (ed.), *Ethics and Values in Archaeology*, New York: Free Press.

Hein, G. (1998) *Learning in the Museum*, London: Routledge.

Hennessy, G. (2003) 'The spirit of collaboration: exploring critical pedagogical principles in transforming the museum through space and time', MA thesis, Department of Anthropology and Sociology, University of British Columbia.

Herle, A. (1998) 'The life-histories of objects: collections of the Cambridge Anthropological Expedition to the Torres Strait', in A. Herle and S. Rouse (eds), *Cambridge and the Torres Strait: centenary essays on the 1898 anthropological expedition*, Cambridge: Cambridge University Press.

—— (2000) '*Torres Strait Islanders:* stories from an exhibition', *Ethnos*, 65 (2): 253–74.

Herle, A. and Rouse, S. (eds) (1998) *Cambridge and the Torres Strait: centenary essays on the 1898 anthropological expedition*, Cambridge: Cambridge University Press.

Herzfeld, M. (2001) *Anthropology. Theoretical Practice in Culture and Society*, Oxford: Blackwell.

Hill, Sr., R.W. (2000) 'The museum Indian: still frozen in time and mind', *Museum News*, 79 (3): 40–74.

Hill, S. (2000) 'Introduction', in J.E. Stanton, *Aboriginal Artists of the South-West: past and present*, Occasional Paper 5, Perth: The University of Western Australia Berndt Museum of Anthropology.

Hipszer, H. (1971) 'Les masques de chamans du Musée Ethnographique de Berlin' [Shaman masks in the Berlin Museum of Ethnography], *Baessler-Archiv*, NF 19: 421–50.

Hirsch, E. and O'Hanlon, M. (eds) (1995) *The Anthropology of Landscape: perspectives on place and space*. Oxford: Clarendon Press.

Holm, M. and Pokotylo, D. (1997) 'From policy to practice: a case study in collaborative exhibits with First Nations', *Canadian Journal of Archaeology*, 21: 1–11.

Holman, N. (1996) 'Curating and controlling Zuni photographic images', *Curator*, 39 (2): 108–22.

Holmes, J.H. (1924) *In Primitive New Guinea*, London: Seeley, Service & Co.

Hooper-Greenhill, E. (2002) [2000] *Museums and the Interpretation of Visual Culture*, London: Routledge.

Hopfner, G. (1995) 'Die Rückfuhrung der "Leningrad-Sammlung" des Museums für Völkerkunde' [Return of the "Leningrad Collection" of the Museum for Folklore], *Jahrbuch Preubischer Kulturbesitz*, Band XXIX, Gebr. Mann Verlag, Berlin.

Horse Capture, G. (ed.) (1989) *The Concept of Sacred Materials and Their Place in the World*, Wyoming: Buffalo Bill Historical Center.

—— (1994) Interview with Nancy Rosoff, January 11.

Huntingford, G.W.B. (1980) *The Periplus of the Erythraean Sea*, London: Hakluyt Society.

Hurley, Frank (1924) *Pearls and Savages: adventures in the air, on land and sea in New Guinea*, New York: Putnam's Sons.

Ignatieff, M. (2000) *The Rights Revolution*, Toronto: House of Anansi Press Ltd.

Isaac, G. (2002) 'Museums as mediators', unpublished DPhil thesis, University of Oxford.

Issenman, B. (1985) 'Inuit clothing: construction and motifs', *Études/Inuit/Studies*, 9 (2): 101–19.

—— (1990) 'Inuit and museums: allied to preserve Arctic patrimony', paper presented at the Eighth Inuit Studies Conference, Quebec, Canada, 1990.

—— (1991) 'Inuit power and museums', *Information North: the Arctic Institute of North America*, 17 (3): 1–7.

Jacobsen, J.A. (1884) *Capitain Jacobsen's Reise an der Nordwest-küste Amerikas, 1881–1883*, A. Woldt (ed.), Leipzig.

—— (1977) *Alaskan Voyage 1881–1883: an expedition to the Northwest Coast of America*, abridged trans. E. Gunther, from the German text of A. Woldt, Chicago: University of Chicago Press.

Jameson, J.H, Jr. (ed.) (1997) *Presenting Archaeology to the Public: digging for truths*, Walnut Creek CA: Altamira Press.

Janes, R.R. and Conaty, G.T. (1992) 'Museums and Aboriginal peoples: the contact continues', plenary paper presented at the twenty-fifth Chacmool Conference, Department of Archaeology, University of Calgary, Calgary, November 1992.

—— (1998) 'To be or to have: museums and repatriation', paper presented at the 1998 Conference of the Museums Trustee Association, San Antonio, Texas, November 1998.

Jessup, L. with S. Bagg (2002) *On Aboriginal Representation in the Gallery*, Mercury Series Canadian Ethnology Service Paper 135, Ottawa: Canadian Museum of Civilization.

Jonaitis, A. (1991) 'Chiefly feasts: the creation of an exhibition', in A. Jonaitis (ed.) *Chiefly Feasts: the Enduring Kwakiutl Potlatch*, New York: American Museum of Natural History.

Jones, A.L. (1993) 'Exploding canons: the anthropology of museums', *Annual Review of Anthropology*, 22: 201–20.

Jones, J.P. (1992) 'The colonial legacy and the community: the Gallery 33 project', in I. Karp, C.M. Kreamer and S.D. Lavine (eds), *Museums and Communities: the politics of public culture*, Washington, DC: Smithsonian Institution Press.

Kahnapace, G. and Carter, B. (1998) '*Circle of Honour*: a unique partnership between Glenbow and the Plains Indians Cultural Survival School', *Alberta Museums Review*, 24 (1): 39–42.

Kaminitz, M. (1994) Interview with Nancy Rosoff, January 13.

Kaplan, F. (1994) 'Introduction', in F. Kaplan (ed.) *Museums and the 'Making of Ourselves': the role of objects in national identity*, London and New York: Leicester University Press.

Karp, I. and Lavine, S.D. (1991) *Exhibiting Cultures: the poetics and politics of museum display*, Washington DC: Smithsonian Institution Press.

Karp, I., Kreamer, C.M. and Lavine, S.D. (eds) (1992) *Museums and Communities: the politics of public culture*, Washington, DC and London: Smithsonian Institution Press.

Kasaherou, E. (1995) 'The role of the museum in culturally diverse New Caledonia', in A. Galla, B. Murphy and D. McMichael (eds), *Museums and Cross-Cultural Understandings: papers from the fifth regional assembly of the Asia Pacific organisation of the International Council of Museums, 24–27 September 1993*, [s.l.]: Australian National Committee of International Council of Museums.

Kawharu, I.H. (ed.) (1989) *Waitangi: Maori and Pakeha perspectives of the Treaty of Waitangi*, Auckland: Oxford University Press.

Kawharu, M. (2002) 'Indigenous governance in museums: a case study, the Auckland War Memorial Museum', in C. Fforde, J. Hubert and P. Turnbull (eds), *The Dead and Their Possessions: repatriation in principle, policy, and practice*, One World Archaeology, 43, London: Routledge.

Kelly, L. and Gordon, P. (2002) 'Museums and reconciliation in Australia', in R. Sandell (ed.), *Museums, Society, Inequality*, London: Routledge.

Khushwant Singh, Poovaya-Smith, N. and K. Ponnapa, K. (1991) *Warm, Rich and Fearless: a brief survey of Sikh culture*, Bradford: Bradford Art Galleries and Museums.

King, J.C.H. (2001) 'Native museums. A response to Laura Peers', *Anthropology Today*, 17 (1): 22–3.

King, M. (1985) 'Maori images: to the Maori, photographs are both sacred and profane', *Natural History*, 94 (7): 37–43.

Kingston, D. (1996) 'Illuweet (Teasing Cousin): songs as an expression of King Island Inupiaq identity', *Anthropology Northwest* 9. Corvallis: Oregon State University.

—— (1999) 'Returning: twentieth century performances of the King Island Wolf Dance', unpublished PhD dissertation, University of Alaska Fairbanks.

—— (forthcoming) 'Remembering our namesakes', in H. Norris Nicholson (ed.), *Screening Culture: constructing image and identity*, Lanham, MD: Lexington Books.

Kirsch, S. (1996) 'Myth and history along the New Guinea border', unpublished paper.

Knauft, B. (1993) *South Coast New Guinea Cultures: history, comparison, dialectic*, Cambridge: Cambridge University Press.

Kopytoff, I. (1986) 'The cultural biography of things', in A. Appadurai (ed.), *The Social Life of Things*, Cambridge: Cambridge University Press.

Kratz, C. (2002) *The Ones that are Wanted: communication and the politics of representation in photographic exhibition*, Berkeley: University of California Press.

Krause, A. (1956) *The Tlinget Indians: results of a trip to the Northwest Coast of America and Bering Straits*, trans. E. Gunther, American Ethnological Society Monograph 26, Seattle: University of Washington Press. Originally published in German in 1885.

Krech, III, S. and Hail, B.A. (eds) (1999) *Collecting Native America, 1870–1960*, Washington DC: Smithsonian Institution Press.

Kreps, C. (1998) 'Museum-making and indigenous curation in Central Kalimantan, Indonesia', *Museum Anthropology*, 22 (1): 5–17.

Kuklick, H. (1991) *The Savage Within: the social history of British social anthropology 1885–1945*, Cambridge: Cambridge University Press.

Kwa'ioloa, M. and Burt, B. (1997) *Living Tradition. A Changing Life in Solomon Islands*, London: British Museum.

Ladd, E.J. (1993) 'Repatriation. Zuni sensitive material: a case study', in A. Tabah (ed.), *Native American Collections and Repatriation*. Washington DC: American Association of Museums.

Lavine, S.D. (1992) 'Audience, ownership, and authority: designing relations between museums and communities', in I. Karp, C.M. Kreamer and S.D. Lavine (eds), *Museums and Communities: the politics of public culture*, Washington DC and London: Smithsonian Institution Press.

Lawrie, M. (1970) *Myths and Legends of the Torres Strait*, Brisbane: Queensland University Press.

Layton, R. (1989) 'Introduction: conflict in the archaeology of living traditions', in R. Layton (ed.), *Who Needs the Past? Indigenous values and archaeology*, London: Unwin Hyman.

Leicht, R.C. (1989) 'The reburial of skeletal remains found on BLM lands', in G. Horse Capture (ed.), *The Concept of Sacred Materials and Their Place in the World*, Wyoming: Buffalo Bill Historical Center.

Levell, N. and Shelton, A. (1998) 'Text, illustration and reverie: some thoughts on museums, education and new technologies', *Journal of Museum Ethnography*, 10: 15–34.

Lewis, D. and Rose, D.B. (1985) 'Some ethical issues in archaeology: a methodology of consultation in northern Australia', *Australian Aboriginal Studies*, 1: 37–44.

Lewis, O. (1942) *The Effects of White Contact upon Blackfoot Culture: with special reference to the role of the fur trade*, American Ethnological Society Monograph 6. Seattle: University of Washington Press.

Lilley, I. (ed.) (2000) *Native Title and the Transformation of Archaeology in the Postcolonial World*, Oceania Monographs 50, Sydney: University of Sydney.

Lippard, L.R. (ed.) (1992) *Partial Recall: photographs of Native North Americans*, New York: The New Press.

Logan, G.C. (1998) 'Archaeologists, residents, and visitors: creating a community based program in African American archaeology', in P.A. Shackel, P.R. Mullins and M.S. Warner (eds), *Annapolis Pasts: historical archaeology in Annapolis, Maryland*, Knoxville: University of Tennessee Press.

Lost Identities (1999) '*Lost Identities: a journey of rediscovery*': historical photographs of Aboriginal people from Southern Alberta. Online. Available: *http://www.head-smashed-in.com/frimidentity.html* (accessed 22 February 2002).

Lowenthal, D. (1985) *The Past Is a Foreign Country*, New York: Cambridge University Press.

Lutkehaus, N. (1995) *Zaria's Fire: engendered moments in Manam ethnography*, Durham, NC: Carolina Academic Press.

Lyman, C. (1982) *The Vanishing Race and Other Illusions: Photographs of Indians by Edward S. Curtis*, Washington, DC: Smithsonian Institution Press.

Lynott, M.J. and Wylie, A. (eds) (2000) [1995] *Ethics in American Archaeology: challenges for the 1990s*, Washington, DC: Society for American Archaeology.

Lyon, L. (1988) 'History of prohibition of photography of Southwestern Indian ceremonies', Reflections: papers on Southwestern culture history in honor of Charles H. Lange, *Papers of the Archaeological Society of New Mexico*, 14: 238–72.

Macaulay, S.P. (1999) '"Keeping Taonga warm": museum practice and Maori guardianship', *Journal of Museum Education*, 24 (3): 14–17.

McClintock, W. (1910) *The Old North Trail: or the life, legends, and religion of the Blackfeet Indians*, London: Macmillan.

McDavid, C. (1997) 'Descendants, decisions, and power: the public interpretation of the archaeology of the Levi Jordan Plantation', in C. McDavid and D.W. Babson (eds), *In the Realm of Politics: prospects for public participation in African-American and plantation archaeology*, Historical Archaeology, 31 (3): 114–31.

—— (1999) 'From real space to cyberspace: contemporary conversations about the archaeology of slavery and tenancy', *Internet archaeology* 6. Online. Available http:*http://intarch.ac.uk/journal/issue6/mcdavid_toc.html* (accessed 15 May 2002).

—— (2000) 'Archaeology as cultural critique: pragmatism and the archaeology of a southern United States plantation', in C. Holtorf and H. Karlsson (eds), *Philosophy and Archaeological Practice: perspectives for the 21st century*, Gothenburg: Bricoleur Press.

McDavid, C. and Babson, D.W. (eds) (1997) *In the Realm of Politics: prospects for public participation in African-American and plantation archaeology*, Historical Archaeology, Vol. 31 (3).

MacDonald, G. and Alsford, S. (1995) 'Canadian museums and the representation of culture in a multicultural nation', *Cultural Dynamics*, 7: 15–36.

Macdonald, S. (2000) 'University museums and the public: the case of the Petrie Museum', in P.M. McManus (ed.), *Archaeological Displays and the Public*, 2nd edn, London: University College London.

McGrath, V. (1998) 'Contemporary Torres Strait Arts', in T. Mosby and B. Robinson (eds), *Ilan Pasin (this is our way) Torres Strait Art*, Cairns: Cairns Regional Gallery.

Mack, J. (1990) *Emil Torday and the Art of the Congo*, London: British Museum Press.

McKevitt, Gerald, (1979) *The University of Santa Clara: a history 1851–1977*, Palo Alto, Ca.: Stanford University Press.

McLoughlin, M. (1999) *Museums and Representation of Native Canadians: negotiating the borders of culture*, New York: Garland Publishers.

McManamon, F.P. (2000) 'Archaeological messages and messengers', *Public Archaeology*, 1: 5–20.

McMaster, G. (1992) 'Colonial Alchemy: reading the boarding school experience', in L.R. Lippard (ed.), *Partial Recall: photographs of Native North Americans*, New York: The New Press.

—— (1993) 'Object (to) sanctity: the politics of the object', *Muse*, 11 (3): 24–5.

McMaster, G. and Martin, L. (eds) (1992) *Indigena: contemporary native perspectives in Canadian art*, Vancouver and Hull, Quebec: Douglas & McIntyre in association with the Canadian Museum of Civilization.

Madra, A.S. and Singh, P. (1999) *Warrior Saints: three centuries of the Sikh military tradition*, London and New York: I.B. Tauris in association with the Sikh Foundation.

Magnarella, P. (2000) 'Human rights of indigenous peoples in international law', *Anthropology News*, April: 35–6.

Maher, R.F. (1961) *New Men of Papua: a study in culture change*, Madison, WI: University of Wisconsin Press.

—— (1967) 'From cannibal raid to copra kompani: changing patterns of Koriki politics', *Ethnology*, 6 (1): 309–31.

—— (1974) 'Koriki chieftainship: hereditary status and mana in Papua', *Ethnology*, 13 (3): 239–46.

—— (1984) 'The Purari River Delta societies. Papua New Guinea, after the Tom Kabu movement', *Ethnology*, 23 (3): 217–27.

Manihera, I. (1978) Dialogue with Judith Binney and Gillian Chaplin, Whakatane, December 10.

Marcus, G.E. and Fisher, M.M.J. (1986) *Anthropology as Cultural Critique: an experimental moment in the human sciences*, Chicago: University of Chicago Press.

Martinez, W. (1996) 'Deconstructing the "viewer": from ethnography of the visual to critique of the occult', in P.I. Crawford and S. Baldur Hafsteinsson (eds), *The Construction of the Viewer: media ethnography and the anthropology of audiences*, Højbjerg: Intervention Press in association with the Nordic Anthropological Film Association.

Mauger, J.E. and Bowechop, J. (1995) 'Tribal collections management at the Makah Cultural and Research Center', *Perspectives: a resource for tribal museums*, 2: Washington, DC: American Indian Studies Program, Smithsonian Institution.

Mead, S.M. (ed.) (1984) *Te Maori: Maori Art from New Zealand Collections*, New York: Abrams.

—— (1986) *Magnificent Te Maori: Te Maori Whakahirahira*, Auckland: Heinemann.

Meehan, B. (1995) 'Aboriginal views on the management of rock art sites in Australia', in K. Helskog and B. Olsen (eds), *Perceiving Rock Art: social and political perspectives*, Oslo: Instituttet for Sammenlignende Kulturforskning.

Meskell, L. (2001) 'The practice and politics of archaeology in Egypt', in A.M. Cantwell, E. Friedlander and M.L. Tram (eds), *Ethics and Anthropology: facing future issues in human biology, globalism and cultural property*, New York: Annals of the New York Academy of Sciences.

Mibach, L. and Wolf Green, S. (1989) 'Sacred objects and museum conservation: kill or cure?' in G. Horse Capture (ed.), *The Concept of Sacred Materials and Their Place in the World*, Wyoming: Buffalo Bill Historical Center.

Michaels, E. (1991) 'A primer of restrictions on picture-taking in traditional areas of Aboriginal Australia', *Visual Anthropology*, 4: 259–75.

Mitchell, T. (2000) 'Making the nation: the politics of heritage in Egypt', in N. Al Sayyad (ed.), *Consuming Tradition, Manufacturing Heritage: global norms and urban forms in the age of tourism*, London: Routledge.

Moore, D. (1984) *The Torres Strait Collections of A.C. Haddon: a descriptive catalogue*, London: British Museum Press.

Moore, K. (1997) *Museums and Popular Culture*, London: Cassell.

Morauta, L. and Ryan, D. (1983) 'From temporary to permanent townsmen: migrants from the Malalaua District, Papua New Guinea', *Oceania*, 53 (1): 39–55.

Mordell, J. *et al.* (2002) *Moral Communities*. Special Issue of *Pacific Studies*, 25 (1/2), Hawaii: Brigham Young University.

Morphy, H. (1991) *Ancestral Connections: art and an Aboriginal system of knowledge*, Chicago: Chicago University Press.

Morphy, H. and Banks, M. (1997) 'Introduction: rethinking visual anthropology', in M. Banks and H. Morphy (eds), *Re-thinking Visual Anthropology*, New Haven: Yale University Press.

Morris, K. (1994) 'Consultation: an ongoing process. An interview with George Horse Capture', *News and Notes of the American Indian Ritual Object Repatriation Foundation*, 1 (2): 1–3.

Morris, R. (1994) *New Worlds from Fragments: film, ethnography and the representation of Northwest Coast cultures*, Boulder, CO: Westview Press.

Mosby, T. and Robinson, B. (eds) (1998) *Ilan Pasin (this is our way) Torres Strait Art*, Cairns: Cairns Regional Gallery.

Moser, S. (1995) 'The "Aboriginalisation" of Australian archaeology: the contribution of the Australian Institute of Aboriginal Studies to the indigenous transformation of the discipline', in P.J. Ucko (ed.), *Theory in Archaeology: a world perspective*, London: Routledge.

—— (1999) *The Quseir Museum Project*, Report for the Quseir Heritage Preservation Society, May 1999.

—— (2001) *The Quseir Heritage Centre – an Exhibition Plan*, Report for Quseir Heritage Preservation Society.

Muktoyuk, A. (1986a) 'Home to King Island', *Alaska Magazine*, 52 (2): 26–9.

—— (1986b) 'Home to King Island', *Alaska Magazine*, 52 (3): 36–7, 85–7.

Murray Scarborough, C. (1993) 'The mind and the vision of "the Glacier Priest" ', unpublished BA thesis, Santa Clara University.

Museum News (2000) 'NAGPRA at 10. Examining a decade of the Native American Graves Protection and Repatriation Act', *Museum News* 79 (5): 42–9, 67–75.

Museums Australia (1996) *Previous Possessions, New Obligations: a plain English summary of policies for museums in Australia and Aboriginal and Torres Strait Islander peoples*, Melbourne: Museums Australia.

Nason, J.D. (1981) 'A question of patrimony: ethical issues in the collecting of cultural objects', *Museum Round-Up*, 83: 13–20.

—— (2002) ' "Our" Indians: the unidimensional Indian in the disembodied local past', in A. Kawasaki (ed.), *The Changing Presentation of the American Indian: museums and Native cultures*, Washington DC, New York, Seattle and London: National Museum of the American Indian, Smithsonian Institution in association with the University of Washington Press.

National Inquiry into the Separation of Aboriginal and Torres Strait Islander children from their families (1997) *Bringing Them Home*, Sydney: Human Rights and Equal Opportunity Commission.

National Museum of the American Indian (NMAI) (1991) 'National Museum of the American Indian policy statement on Native American human remains and cultural materials', *Museum Anthropology*, 15 (2): 25–8.

—— (1993) 'National Museum of the American Indian, Smithsonian Institution Collections Policy', in A. Tabah (ed.), *Native American Collections and Repatriation*, Washington, DC: American Association of Museums.

—— (2000) *The Changing Presentation of the American Indian. Museums and Native Cultures*, National Museum of the American Indian Smithsonian Institution in association with University of Washington Press.

Neich, R. (2001) *Carved Histories*, Auckland: Auckland University Press.

Nelson, E.W. (1899; reprinted 1983) *The Eskimo about Bering Strait*. Bureau of American Ethnology Annual Report for 1896–1897, Vol. 18, Pt. 1, Washington, DC: Smithsonian Institution Press.

Neumann, K. (1992) 'Finding an appropriate beginning for a history of the Tolai colonial past: or, starting from trash', *Canberra Anthropology*, 15 (1): 49–68.

Newton, D. (1961) *Art Styles of the Papua Gulf*, New York: The Museum of Primitive Art.

Nicks, T. (1992) 'Partnerships in developing cultural resources: lessons from the Task Force on Museums and First Peoples', *Culture*, 12 (1): 87–93.

—— (2002) 'Expanded visions. Collaborative approaches to exhibiting First Nations histories and artistic traditions', in L. Jessup with S. Bagg (eds), *On Aboriginal Representation in the Gallery*, Mercury Series, Canadian Ethnology Service Paper 135, Ottawa: Canadian Museum of Civilization.

Niessen, S.A. (1991) 'More to it than meets the eye: photo-elicitation amongst the Batak of Sumatra', *Visual Anthropology*, 4: 415–30.

Notzke, C. (1996) 'Co-managing Aboriginal cultural resources', *Muse*, 14 (3): 53–6.

Nugent, D. (1993) 'Property relations, production relations and inequality: anthropology, political economy, and the Blackfeet', *American Ethnologist*, 20: 336–62.

Oberholtzer, C. (2001) *Our Grandmothers' Voices: East Cree material culture in museums*, CD-ROM. Copyright Cree Regional Authority.

O'Hanlon, M. and Welsch, R.L. (eds) (2000) *Hunting the Gatherers: ethnographic collectors, agents and agency in Melanesia, 1870s–1930s*, Methodology and History in Anthropology 6, Oxford and New York: Berghahn Press.

Onekawa, P. (1978) Dialogue with Judith Binney and Gillian Chaplin, Maungapohatu, January 21.

Oswalt, W.H. (1983) 'The anthropological significance of the Bernard R. Hubbard photographic collection', memo to Santa Clara University Archives, 10 December 1983, in possession of D. Kingston.

Pardo, J. (2000) 'The development of Empuries, Spain, as a visitor-friendly archaeological site', in P.M. McManus (ed.), *Archaeological Displays and the Public*, 2nd edn, London: University College.

Pardoe, C. (1985) 'Cross-cultural attitudes to skeletal research in the Murray-Darling region', *Australian Aboriginal Studies*, 2: 63–78.

—— (1990) 'Sharing the past: Aboriginal influence on archaeological practice, a case study from New South Wales', *Aboriginal History*, 14 (2): 208–23.

—— (1991) 'The eye of the storm. The study of Aboriginal human remains in Australia', *Journal of Indigenous Studies*, 2: 16–23.

—— (1992) 'Arches of Radii, corridors of power: reflections on current archaeological practice', in B. Attwood and J. Arnold (eds), *Power, Knowledge and Aborigines. Journal of Australian Studies*, Melbourne: La Trobe University Press in association with the National Centre for Australian Studies, Monash University.

Parker, P. (1990) *Keepers of the Treasures: protecting historic properties and cultural traditions on Indian lands. A report on tribal preservation funding needs submitted to Congress by the National Park Service*, Washington, DC: The Branch.

Partos, L. (1996) 'The Victorian Aboriginal photograph collection in the Museum of Victoria', *COMA*, 28: 63–5.

Paulius, N.E. (1991) 'The cultural heritage of the Pacific: preservation, development and promotion', in S.M. Eoe and P. Swadling (eds), *Museums and Cultural Centres in the Pacific*, Port Moresby: Papua New Guinea National Museum.

Peacock, D.P.S. (1993) 'The site of Myos Hormos: a view from space', *Journal of Roman Archaeology*, 6: 226–32.

Peacock, D.P.S., Blue, L., Bradford, N. and Moser, S. (1999) *Myos Hormos, Quseir al-Qadim. A Roman and Islamic port/trade site on the Red Sea coast of Egypt.* Interim report for Supreme Council of Antiquities, Cairo, Egypt. Southampton: Department of Archaeology, University of Southampton.

—— (2000) *Myos Hormos, Quseir al-Qadim. A Roman and Islamic port on the Red Sea coast of Egypt.* Interim report for Supreme Council of Antiquities, Cairo, Egypt. Southampton: Department of Archaeology, University of Southampton.

—— (2001) *Myos Hormos Quseir al-Qadim. A Roman and Islamic port on the Red Sea coast of Egypt.* Interim report for Supreme Council of Antiquities, Cairo, Egypt. Southampton: Department of Archaeology, University of Southampton.

Peacock, D.P.S., Blue, L. and Moser, S. (forthcoming) *Myos Hormos Quseir al-Qadim. A Roman and Islamic port on the Red Sea coast of Egypt.* Interim report for Supreme Council of Antiquities, Cairo, Egypt. Southampton: Department of Archaeology, University of Southampton.

Peers, L. (2000) 'A review of the Chase Manhattan Gallery of North America', *Anthropology Today*, 16 (6): 8–13.

—— (2001) 'Author's response', *Anthropology Today*, 17 (1): 23.

—— (2003) 'Strands which refuse to be braided: Beatrice Blackwood's Ojibwe collection at the Pitt Rivers Museum', *Journal of Material Culture*, 8 (1): 75–96.

Peers, L. and Brown, A.K. (2002) 'Sharing knowledge', *Museums Journal*, 102 (5): 24–7.

Peterson, N. and Pinney, C. (eds) (forthcoming) *Photography's Other Histories*, Durham, NC: Duke University Press.

Petr, T. (ed.) (1983) *The Purari: tropical environment of a high rainfall river basin*, The Hague: Dr. W. Junk.

Phillips, J.E. (2000) *Myos Hormos, Quseir al-Qadim: a plain language report of the 2000 field season*, Southampton: Department of Archaeology, University of Southampton and Quseir Heritage Preservation Society.

—— (2001a) *Quseir al-Qadim: a short introduction to the ancient trading port of the Red Sea*, Southampton: Department of Archaeology, University of Southampton and Quseir Heritage Preservation Society.

—— (2001b) 'Object lifeways: "archaeological" objects, collaborative field methods and strategies for presenting the past at Quseir, Egypt', unpublished MA dissertation, University of Southampton.

—— (forthcoming) *Quseir al-Qadim: a guide*, Southampton: Department of Archaeology, University of Southampton and Quseir Heritage Preservation Society.

Phillips, R.B. (1990) 'The public relations w(rap): what we can learn from *The Spirit Sings*', *Inuit Art Quarterly*, 5 (2): 13–21.

—— (1994) 'Fielding culture: dialogues between Art History and Anthropology', *Museum Anthropology*, 18 (1): 39–46.

—— (1998) *Trading Identities. The Souvenir in Native North American art from the Northeast, 1700–1900*, Seattle and Montreal: University of Washington Press and McGill-Queen's University Press.

—— (2002) 'Where is Africa? Re-viewing art and artifact in the age of globalization and diaspora', *American Anthropologist*, 104 (3): 11–16.

Phillips, R.B. and Steiner, C.B. (eds) (1999) *Unpacking Culture: art and commodity in colonial and post-colonial worlds*, Berkeley: University of California Press.

Philp, J. (1998a) 'Owning artefacts and owning knowledge: Torres Straits Island material culture, *Cambridge Anthropology*, 20 (1–2): 7–15.

—— (1998b) 'Resonance: Torres Strait Islander material culture and history', unpublished PhD thesis, University of Cambridge.

—— (2001) *Past Time: Torres Strait Islander Material from the Haddon Collection, 1888–1905: a National Museum of Australia exhibition from the University of Cambridge*, Canberra: National Museum of Australia.

Poignant, R. (1992) 'Wurdayak/Baman (Life History) photo collection: report on the setting up of a life history photo collection at the Djomi Museum, Maningrida', *Australian Aboriginal Studies*, 2: 71–7.

—— (1994–5) 'About friendship; about trade: about photographs', *Voices: Quarterly Journal of the National Library of Australia*, 4 (4): 55–70.

Poignant, R. with Poignant, A. (1996) *Encounter at Nagalarramba*, Canberra: National Library of Australia.

Poole, D. (1997) *Vision, Race, and Modernity: A visual economy of the Andean image world*, Princeton, NJ: Princeton University Press.

Poovaya Smith, N. (1991) 'Exhibitions and audiences: catering for a pluralistic public', in G. Kavanagh (ed.), *Museum Languages: objects and texts*, Leicester: Leicester University Press.

Porter, G. (1989) 'Economy of truth: photography in the museum', *Ten-8*, 34: 20–33.

Porto, N. (1999) *Angola a Preto e Branco. Fotografia e ciência os Museo do Dundo 1940–1970*, Coimbra: Museu Antropológico da Universidade de Coimbra.

Powell, Father P.J. (1989) 'Sacred material', in G. Horse Capture (ed.) *The Concept of Sacred Materials and Their Place in the World*, Wyoming: Buffalo Bill Historical Center.

Powers, W. (1996) 'Images across boundaries: history, use, and ethics of photographs of American Indians', *American Indian Culture and Research Journal*, 20 (3): 129–36.

Pratt, M.L. (1992) *Imperial Eyes: travel writing and transculturation*, London: Routledge.

Raczka, P.M. (1979) *Winter Count: a history of the Blackfoot people*, Brocket: Old Man River Cultural Center.

Rankin, E. and Hamilton, C. (1999) 'Revision; reaction; re-vision. The role of museums in (a) transforming South Africa', *Museum Anthropology*, 22 (3): 3–13.

Ray, D.J. (1984) 'Report on the Bernard R. Hubbard collection of photographs, Santa Clara University', 9 January 1984, in possession of D. Kingston.

Reddé, M. and Golvin, J.C. (1987) 'Du Nil à la Mer Rouge: documents anciens et nouveaux sur les routes du désert oriental d'Egypte', *Karthago*, 21: 5–64.

Redfield, R. (1959) 'Art and icon', *Aspects of Primitive Art*, New York: Museum of Primitive Art.

Regenvanu, R. (1997) 'Preface' to C. Kaufmann, *Vanuatu Kunst aus der Südsee: Eine Einführung*, Basel: Museum der Kulturen and Cristoph Merian Verlag.

Reid, D.M. (1985) 'Indigenous Egyptology: the decolonisation of a profession?', *Journal of the American Oriental Society*, 105 (2): 233–46.

—— (1997) 'Nationalizing the Pharaonic past. Egyptology, imperialism, and Egyptian nationalism 1922–1952', in I. Gershoni and J. Jankowski (eds), *Rethinking Nationalism in the Arab Middle East*, New York: Columbia University Press.

—— (2002) *Whose Pharaohs? Museums, archaeology and Egyptian national identity from Napolean to World War I*, Berkeley, Ca.: University of California Press.

Renner, S.J., L.L. (1979) *Pioneer Missionary to the Bering Strait Eskimos: Bellarmine Lafortune, S.J.*, Portland: Binford & Mort.

—— (1987) 'Father Bernard Hubbard, S.J., 1888–1962', *The Alaskan Shepherd* 25 (3): 1–4.

Repatriation Office (1996) 'The Repatriation Office Annual Report', The National Museum of the American Indian, Smithsonian Institution, Repatriation Office.

Rishbeth, H. (1999) 'Kathleen Haddon (1888–1961)', *Bulletin of the International String Figure Association*, 6: 1–16.

Roberts, H. (1978) Dialogue with Judith Binney and Gillian Chaplin, Tataiahape, May 17.

Roberts, L. (1997) *From Knowledge to Narrative: educators and the changing museum*, Washington, DC: Smithsonian Institution Press.

Robinson, M.P. (1996) 'Shampoo archaeology: towards a participatory action research approach in civil society', *The Canadian Journal of Native Studies*, 16 (1): 125–38.

Rodman, M.C. (1998) 'Creating historic sites in Vanuatu', *Social Analysis*, 42 (3): 117–34.

Rosoff, N. (1992) 'We are not "Jivaros": the misrepresentation of cultural materials in museums', paper presented at the American Anthropological Association Meeting, San Francisco, December 1992.

Ruby, J. (1996) 'The viewer viewed: the reception of ethnographic films', in P.I. Crawford and S. Baldur Hafsteinsson (eds), *The Construction of the Viewer: media ethnography and the anthropology of audiences*, Højbjerg: Intervention Press in association with the Nordic Anthropological Film Association.

Rumsey, A. and Weiner, J. (eds) (2001) *Emplaced Myth: the spatial and narrative dimensions of knowledge in Australia and Papua New Guinea*, Honolulu: University of Hawai'i Press.

Ryan, D. (1985) 'Bilocality and movement between village and town: Toaripi, Papua New Guinea', in M. Chapman and R. Mansell Prothero (eds), *Circulation in Population Movement: substance and concepts from the Melanesian case*, London: Routledge & Kegan Paul.

—— (1989) 'Home ties in town: Toaripi in Port Moresby', *Canberra Anthropology*, 12 (1–2): 19–27.

Ryan, J. and Robinson, M. (1990) 'Implementing participatory action research in the Canadian North: a case study of the Gwich'in language and culture project', *Culture*, 10 (2): 57–71.

—— (1996) 'Community participatory research: two views from Arctic Institute practitioners', *Practicing Anthropology*, 18 (4): 7–11.

Sackler, E., Sullivan, M., and Hill, R. (1992) 'Three voices for repatriation', *Museum News*, 71 (5): 58–61.

Said, E.W. (1978) *Orientalism*, New York: Pantheon Books.

—— (1989) 'Representing the colonised: anthropology's interlocutors', *Critical Inquiry*, 15: 205–25.

Salama, A.M. (1997) 'Proposed action plan for Quseir. Final draft', The Promotion of Environmentally Sustainable Tourism Project and the United States Agency for International Development.

Sam, J. (1996) 'Audiovisual documentation of living cultures as a major task for the Vanuatu Cultural Centre', in J. Bonnemaison, C. Kaufmann, K. Huffman and D. Tryon (eds), *Arts of Vanuatu*, Bathurst: Crawford House Publishing.

Sandell, R. (2002) 'Museums and the combating of social inequality', in R. Sandell (ed.), *Museums, Society, Inequality*, London: Routledge.

Sarris, G. (1993) *Keeping Slugwoman Alive: a holistic approach to American Indian texts*, Berkeley, Los Angeles and Oxford: University of California Press.

Schildkrout, E. and Keim, C.A. (eds) (1998) *The Scramble for Art in Central Africa*, Cambridge: University of Cambridge Press.

Schmidt, P.R. and Patterson, T.C. (eds) (1995) *Making Alternative Histories*, Santa Fe: School of American Research Press.

Schultz, J.W. and Donaldson, J.L. (1930) *The Sun God's Children*, Boston: Houghton-Mifflin Company.

—— (1993) 'Interpreting Aboriginal history in a museum context', *Museums Australia Journal*, 2–3: 49–55.

Seremetakis, C.N. (ed.) (1994) *The Senses Still: perception and memory as material culture in modernity*, Boulder, CO: Westview Press.

Shankland, D. (1996) 'Çatalhöyük: the anthropology of an archaeological presence', in I. Hodder (ed.), *On the surface: Çatalhöyük 1993–1995*, Cambridge: McDonald Institute for Archaeological Research and the British Institute of Archaeology at Ankara.

—— (1999) 'Integrating the past: folklore, mounds and people at Çatalhöyük', in A. Gazin-Schwartz and C. Holtorf (eds), *Archaeology and Folklore*, London: Routledge.

Sharp, N. (1993) *Stars of Tagai*, Canberra: Aboriginal Studies Press.

Shelton, A. (1997) 'The future of museum ethnography', *Journal of Museum Ethnography*, 9: 33–48.

Shils, E. (1978) 'The academic ethos', *American Scholar*, 47 (2): 165–90.

Silberman, N.A. (1995) 'Promised lands and chosen peoples: the politics and poetics of archaeological narrative', in P.L. Kohl and C. Fawcett (eds), *Nationalism, Politics and the Practice of Archaeology*, Cambridge: Cambridge University Press.

Simpson, M. (1992) 'Celebration, commemoration or condemnation?', *Museums Journal*, March: 29–31.

—— (1996) *Making Representations: museums in the post-colonial era*, London: Routledge.

Singh, K. (1999) 'The Sikh religion', in S. Stronge (ed.), *The Arts of the Sikh Kingdoms*, London: V&A Publications.

Singh, Khaur N. (1995) *The Name of My Beloved: verses of the Sikh Gurus, devotional poetry from the Guru Granth Sahib and the Dasam Granth*, San Francisco: Harper San Francisco (The Sacred Literature Series of the International Sacred Literature Trust in association with HarperCollins) supported by the Sikh Foundation.

Singleton, J. (2002) *Investigation of Missing Artifacts at the Anthropology Museum of the University of Winnipeg*, Manitoba: Office of the Auditor General.

Smallacombe, S. (1999) 'Indigenous peoples' access rights to archival records', Australian Society of Archivists Conference. Online. Available HTTP: *http://www.archivists.org.au/events/con99/smallacombe.html* (accessed 22 February 2002).

Smith, L.T. (1999) *Decolonizing Methodologies: research and indigenous communities*, London: Zed Books.

Sontag, S. (1978) *On Photography*, London: Allen Lane.

Specht, J.R. (1979) 'Anthropology', in R. Strahan (ed.), *Rare and Curious Specimens: an illustrated history of the Australian Museum 1827–1979*, Sydney: Trustees of the Australian Museum.

Specht, J and MacLulich, C. (1996) 'Changes and challenges: the Australian Museum and indigenous communities', in P.M. McManus (ed.), *Archaeological Displays and the Public*, London: University College London.

Stafford, D.M. (1967) *Te Arawa*, Wellington: A.H. & A.W. Reed.

Stanton, J.E. (1996) 'Opening the highway or tying the Net? A conundrum for Australian Aborigines and museums', in Museums Australia Conference Proceedings, *Communicating Cultures*, Brisbane, November 1995, Melbourne: Museums Australia.

—— (2001) 'A Nyungar world' in V. Takao Binder (ed.), *Mia Mia/Dwelling Place*, Perth: Perth International Arts Festival.

—— (forthcoming) 'Sustaining futures: museums, anthropology and indigenous peoples', introduction to the *UNESCO Conference on New Technologies, Anthropology, Museology and Indigenous Knowledge*, Paris: UNESCO (CD-Rom).

Steiner, C. (1994) *African Art in Transit*, Cambridge: Cambridge University Press.

Stewart, Susan (1984) *On Longing: narratives of the miniature, the gigantic, the souvenir, the collection*, Baltimore: Johns Hopkins University Press.

Stocking, G.W., Jr. (1983) *The Ethnographer's Magic: fieldwork in British anthropology from Tylor to Malinowski*, Madison: University of Wisconsin Press.

—— (ed.) (1983) *Observers Observed: essays on ethnographic fieldwork*, History of Anthropology 1, Madison: University of Wisconsin Press.

—— (ed.) (1985) *Objects and Others: essays in museums and material culture*, History of Anthropology 3, Madison: University of Wisconsin Press.

—— (1995) *After Tylor: British social anthropology, 1888–1951*, Madison: University of Wisconsin Press.

Strathern, M. (1988) *The Gender of the Gift*, Berkeley: University of California Press.

Stronge, S. (ed.) (1999) *The Arts of the Sikh Kingdoms*, London: V&A Publications.

Swidler, N., Dongoske, K.E., Anyon, R., and Downer, A.S. (eds) (1997) *Native Americans and Archaeologists: stepping stones to common ground*, Walnut Creek: Altamira Press.

Tabah, A. (ed.) (1993) *Native American Collections and Repatriation*: Technical Information Service's Forum. Occasional Papers on Museum Issues and Standards Washington, DC: American Association of Museums.

Taipo [George Bourne] (1908) 'A dusky dowie. A Maori prophet at home', *Life*, 1 December: 495–500.

Tamarapa, A. (1996) 'Museum *Kaitiaki*: Maori perspectives on the presentation and management of Maori treasures and relationships with museums', *Curatorship: indigenous perspectives in post-colonial societies*, Proceedings, Mercury Series 8, Hull: Canadian Museum of Civilization with the Commonwealth Association of Museums and the University of Victoria.

Tapsell, P. (1997) 'The flight of Pareraututu: an investigation of *Taonga* from a tribal perspective', *Journal of the Polynesian Society*, 106 (4): 323–74.

—— (1998) *Taonga: A tribal response to museums*, Unpublished DPhil thesis, School of Museum Ethnography, University of Oxford.

—— (2000) *Pukaki : a comet returns*, Auckland: Reed.

—— (2002a) 'Partnerships in Museums: A Tribal Response to Repatriation', in C. Fforde, J. Herbert and P. Turnbull (eds), *The Dead and their Possessions: Repatriation in Principle, Policy and Practice*, London: Routledge.

—— (2002b) 'Marae and Tribal Identity in Aotearoa New Zealand', in *Moral Communities*, Special Issue of Pacific Studies, 25 (1, 2): 141–71.

Task Force on Museums and First Peoples (1992) *Turning the Page: forging new partnerships between museums and First Peoples*, Ottawa: Assembly of First Nations and the Canadian Museums Association.

Taylor, B. (1999) *Art for the Nation: exhibitions and the London public 1747–2001*, New Brunswick and New Jersey: Rutgers University Press.

Thode-Arora, H. (1989) 'Für fünfzig Pfennig um die Welt', Frankfurt/Main: Campus Verlag, 52.

Thomas, N. (1991) *Entangled Objects: exchange, material culture, and colonialism in the Pacific*, Cambridge, Mass.: Harvard University Press.

—— (1997) 'Partial texts: representation, colonialism and agency in Pacific history', in N. Thomas, *In Oceania: visions, artifacts, histories*, Durham, NC: Duke University Press.

—— (2000) 'Islands of history: reflections on two exhibitions of Torres Strait Islander culture', *ART Asia Pacific* 28: 70–7.

Thompson, D. (1962) *David Thompson's Narrative 1784–1812*, Richard Glover (ed.), Toronto: Publications of the Champlain Society 40.

Thompson, R. (1991) 'Dealing with the past, and looking to the future', *Museum News*, 70 (1): 36–40.

Treaty Seven Elders, Hildebrandt, W., Carter, S., and First Rider, D. (1996) *The True Spirit and Original Intent of Treaty Seven*, Montreal: McGill-Queens University Press.

Tsinhnahjinnie, H. (1998) 'When is a photograph worth a thousand words?', in J. Alison (ed.), *Native Nations: journeys in American photography*, London: Barbican Art Gallery.

Turner, V. (1982) 'Introduction', in *Celebration: studies in festivity and ritual*, Washington, DC: Smithsonian Institution Press.

Tuzin, D. (1997) *The Cassowary's Revenge: the life and death of masculinity in a New Guinea society*, Chicago: University of Chicago Press.

Ucko, P.J. (1983) 'Australian academic archaeology: Aboriginal transformation of its aims and practices', *Australian Archaeology*, 16: 11–26.

University Museums Review Committee (1996) *Cinderella Collections: university museums and collections in Australia*, Canberra: Australian Vice-Chancellor's Committee.

University of British Columbia (1996) *1996–1997 University of British Columbia Policy Handbook*, Vancouver: The University of British Columbia.

271

Urry, J. (1993) *Before Social Anthropology: essays on the history of British anthropology*, Chur: Harwood Academic Publishers

US Government (1990) *Native American Graves Protection and Repatriation Act*, Public Law 101–601, 25 USC 3001 et seq., 16 November.

Venturi, Scott Brown & Associates, Inc. (1993) *The Way of the People: National Museum of the American Indian.* Vol. 2, A Detailed Architectural Program for the Cultural Resources Center, Suitland, Maryland. Master Facilities Programming, Phase 2, Preliminary Final Report.

Wagner, R. (1981) *The Invention of Culture*, Chicago: University of Chicago Press.

Warry, W. (1990) 'Doing unto others: applied anthropology and Native self-determination', *Culture*, 10: 61–73.

—— (1998) *Unfinished Dreams: community healing and the reality of Aboriginal self-government*, Toronto: University of Toronto Press.

Watkins, J. (2000) *Indigenous Archaeology. American Indian values and scientific practice*, Walnut Creek: Altamira Press.

Watkins, J., Pyburn, K.A. and Cressey, P. (2000) 'Community relations: what the practicing archaeologist needs to know to work effectively with local and/or descendant communities', in S.J. Bender and G. Smith (eds), *Teaching Archaeology in the Twenty-first Century*, Washington, DC: Society for American Archaeology.

Wendy Jessup & Associates (1993) 'National Museum of the American Indian collections storage requirements for the Cultural Resources Center to be constructed in Suitland, Maryland', draft report, vols 1 and 3.

West, R. (1994) 'The National Museum of the American Indian. Perspectives on museums in the 21st century', *Museum Anthropology*, 18 (3): 53–56.

Westphal-Hellbusch, S., Koch, G. and Hartmann, H. (1973) '100 Jahre Museum für Völkerkunde', *Baessler-Archiv* 20, Beitrage zur Völkerkunde, Dietrich Reimer Verlag.

Whitcomb, D.S. and Johnson, J.H. (1979) *Quseir al-Qadim, 1978. Preliminary report*, Cairo: American Research Center in Egypt.

—— (1982a) *Quseir al-Qadim, 1980. Preliminary report*, American Research Center in Egypt Reports 7. Malibu: Undena Publications.

—— (1982b) 'Season of excavations at Quseir al-Qadim', *Newsletter of the American Research Center in Egypt*, 120: 24–30.

White, R. (1997) 'Representing Indians. Art, history, and the new museums', *The New Republic*, April 21: 28–34.

Williams, F.E. (1923) *The Collection of Curios and the Preservation of Native Culture*, Territory of Papua Anthropological Reports No. 3. Port Moresby: Government Printer.

—— (1924) *The Natives of Purari Delta*, Territory of Papua Anthropological Reports No. 5. Port Moresby: Government Printer.

Wilson, L. (1988) *Thathilgaw, Emeret Lu: a handbook of traditional Torres Strait Islands material culture*, Brisbane: Queensland Department of Education.

Winmar, D. and Parfitt, D. (2000) 'Report on the South-West Photographic Project: Bringing the Photographs Home', Perth: Bemdt Museum of Anthropology. Unpublished manuscript.

Wolf, E. (1982) *Europe and the People without History*, London and Berkeley: University of California Press.

Wood, M. (1998) 'Logging, women and submarines: some changes in Kamula men's access to transformative power', *Oceania*, 68 (4): 228–48.

Wylie, A. (1995) 'Alternative histories: epistemic disunity and political integrity', in P.R. Schmidt and T.C. Patterson (eds), *Making Alternative Histories*, Santa Fe: School of American Research Press.

Yellowhorn, E. (2000) 'Out of the mist, but still in a haze!' *Muse*, XVIII (2): 16–17.

Young, L. (2002) 'Cultural policy and inclusion', in R. Sandell (ed.), *Museums, Society, Inequality*, London: Routledge.

Young, M. and Clark, J. (eds) (2001) *An Anthropologist in Papua: the photography of F. E. Williams 1922–1939*, Hindmarsh and Canberra: Crawford House Publishing in association with the National Archives of Australia.

Young, R. (1995) *Colonial Desire: hybridity in theory, culture, and race*, New York: Routledge.

Zelenietz, M. (1981) 'Sorcery and social change: an introduction', *Social Analysis*, 8: 3–14.

INDEX